W0410429

EUROPA-FACHBUCHREIHE
für metalltechnische Berufe

Dr. Eckhard Ignatowitz, Christina Murphy, Falko Wieneke

TECHNISCHES ENGLISCH
zur
FACHKUNDE METALL

2. Auflage

VERLAG EUROPA-LEHRMITTEL · Nourney, Vollmer GmbH & Co. KG
Düsselberger Straße 23 · 42781 Haan-Gruiten

Europa-Nr.: 12357

Autoren:

Dr. Eckhard Ignatowitz	Dr.-Ing., Dipl.-Ing.	StR. a. D.	Waldbronn
Christina Murphy	Dipl.-Berufspäd. (Univ.)	OStRin	Wolfratshausen
Falko Wieneke	Dipl.-Ing.	StD	Essen

Bei der Übersetzung war behilflich:

Heinz Berhard	OStR	Waldbronn

Leitung des Arbeitskreises und Lektorat:

Dr. Eckhard Ignatowitz

Bilder und Bildentwürfe:

Ein Teil der Bilder stammen aus dem Buch Fachkunde Metall oder sind auf der Basis dieser Bilder erstellt. Weitere Bilder wurden von Unternehmen zur Verfügung gestellt, entstammen dem Bilderarchiv des Verlags oder wurden von den Autoren entworfen.

Die Autoren danken den Autoren der Fachkunde Metall, den Unternehmen sowie dem Verlag Europa-Lehrmittel für die Bereitstellung der Bilder.

Bildbearbeitung:

Zeichenbüro des Verlags Europa-Lehrmittel, Ostfildern

2. Auflage 2018

Druck 5 4 3 2 1

ISBN 978-3-8085-1555-6

© 2018 by Verlag Europa-Lehrmittel, Nourney, Vollmer GmbH & Co. KG, 42781 Haan-Gruiten
http://www.europa-lehrmittel.de

Satz: Satz+Layout Werkstatt Kluth GmbH, 50374 Erftstadt
Umschlag: Grafische Produktionen Jürgen Neumann, 97222 Rimpar
Umschlagfotos: Sauter Feinmechanik GmbH, 72555 Metzingen, © md3d und © somartin – Fotolia.com
Druck: Kessler Druck + Medien GmbH & Co. KG, 86399 Bobingen

Vorwort

Das Buch **TECHNISCHES ENGLISCH zur FACHKUNDE METALL** dient zum systematischen Erlernen des technischen Englisch für die metalltechnischen Berufe.

Es erfüllt damit die Forderung der Rahmenlehrpläne zur Erlangung der sprachlichen Kompetenz in technischem Englisch im Berufsfeld der metalltechnischen Berufe: Werkzeug- und Industriemechaniker, Feinwerk-, Fertigungs- und Zerspanungsmechaniker sowie der entsprechenden Meister und Techniker des Berufsfeldes.

Auch für Schüler technischer Gymnasien, für Praktikanten und Studierende der Fachrichtung Maschinenbau sowie für Praktiker in der metallverarbeitenden Industrie und im Metallhandwerk ist es geeignet.

Voraussetzung des Lernens und Arbeitens mit dem Buch **TECHNISCHES ENGLISCH zur FACHKUNDE METALL** sind Grundkenntnisse des Englischen, die einem mittlerem Schulabschluss (Sekundarstufe 1) entsprechen und im Europäischen Fremdsprachen-Referenzrahmen in A2/B1 eingeordnet werden können.

Das Buch basiert auf den Inhalten wesentlicher Kapitel der FACHKUNDE METALL.

Es kann begleitend zum Unterricht mit der FACHKUNDE METALL oder anderen Lehrwerken des Berufsbereichs eingesetzt werden. Zu empfehlen ist z. B. nach der Einführung der Fachinhalte im deutschen Fachkundeunterricht der Einsatz des Buches **TECHNISCHES ENGLISCH zur FACHKUNDE METALL** zur Vertiefung und Festigung der Fachinhalte in englischer Sprache.

Eine weitere Vertiefung der Englisch-Kompetenz ist durch ein paralleles Arbeiten mit einem englisch-sprachigen Tabellenbuch, wie z. B. MECHANICAL AND METAL TRADES HANDBOOK des Verlags Europa-Lehrmittel, möglich.

Die Lerneinheiten im Buch **TECHNISCHES ENGLISCH zur FACHKUNDE METALL** werden in derselben Reihenfolge wie im Buch FACHKUNDE METALL dargeboten.

Es handelt sich beim Buch TECHNISCHES ENGLISCH zur FACHKUNDE METALL jedoch nicht um eine Übersetzung der entsprechenden Kapitel und Inhalte aus dem Buch FACHKUNDE METALL.

Im Buch **TECHNISCHES ENGLISCH zur FACHKUNDE METALL** ist der Inhalt der jeweiligen Kapitel in Englisch in einem Konzentrat zusammengefasst. Darin werden die Fachausdrücke des Sachgebiets, wichtige Redewendungen und die erforderlichen englischen Sachwörter eingeführt und vertieft.

Durch die erworbene Sprachkompetenz beim Arbeiten mit dem Buch ist auch das Lesen und Verstehen anderer Texte zu diesem Sachgebiet möglich.

Das Buch **TECHNISCHES ENGLISCH zur FACHKUNDE METALL** ist in Lerneinheiten gegliedert, die einem technischen Sachgebiet entsprechen. Die im Text der Lerneinheit neu verwendeten englischen Fachausdrücke werden am rechten Rand der Seite in einem Kurzwörterbuch (Words) mit deutscher Übersetzung genannt. Dadurch ist ein zügiges Erarbeiten des Textes und der Inhalte ohne Umblättern oder zeitraubendes Suchen in einem Wörterbuch oder einem Übersetzungsprogramm des Internets möglich. Der Lernende kann sich voll auf das Verstehen des Textes konzentrieren.

Jede Lerneinheit des Buches enthält vielfältige Übungen (Exercises) mit unterschiedlichem Schwierigkeitsgrad zu den technischen Inhalten der Lerneinheit. Mit ihrer Hilfe kann die Englischkompetenz zum Sachthema vertieft und/oder geprüft werden. Die Aufgabentypen decken auch Teilkompetenzen (Comprehension, Writing, Mediation) ab, die zur Vorbereitung der KMK-Zertifikatsprüfung Englisch dienen können.

Am Ende des Buches befindet sich ein **Dictionary Englisch – Deutsch** sowie ein **Wörterbuch Deutsch – Englisch** mit sämtlichen im Buch verwendeten Fachwörtern. Dies ermöglicht auch die Bearbeitung fremder Texte zu den im Buch behandelten Sachgebieten.

Die Englischschreibung entspricht dem **britischen Englisch.**

In der vorliegenden 2. Auflage wurde ein Anhang eingefügt (Seite 102). Er enthält die englischen Zahlwörter, Ordnungs-, Dezimal- und Bruchzahlen sowie die mathematischen Operatoren.

Die Autoren und der Verlag sind allen Nutzern des Buches für kritisch-konstruktive Hinweise und Verbesserungsvorschläge dankbar. Bitte senden Sie Ihre Hinweise per E-Mail an: Lektorat@europa-lehrmittel.de.

Sommer 2018 Die Autoren, der Verlag

Table of Contents

Inhaltsverzeichnis

1 Measuring technique

1.1 Physical quantities and units

The properties, states and processes of an object, which can be measured, are called physical quantities **(figure)**.

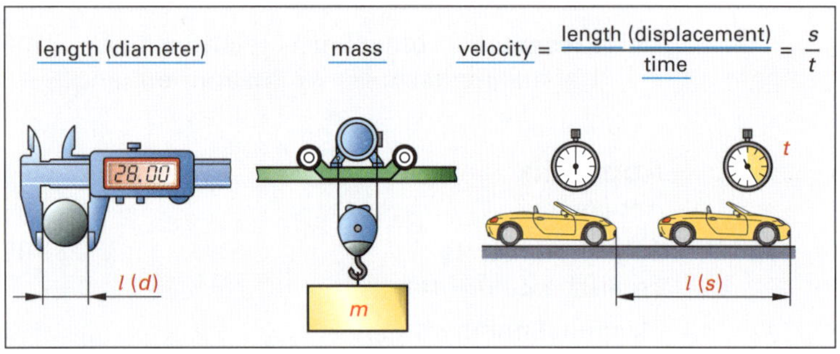

Base quantities

The base quantities are described in accordance to DIN 1304 by a defined symbol (quantity symbol), for example *l* for length, *s* for displacement, *m* for mass, *t* for time, *I* for electric current, *T* for temperature and so on.

The value of a physical quantity is written in abbreviated form by a letter and equals the product of a numerical value and a unit.

Example:

A workpiece has a diameter *d* of 28.00 mm **(figure):** ⇒ ***d* = 28.00 mm**

The expression consists of:

d physical quantity (*d* stands for diameter)

28.00 numerical value

mm unit for length (mm stands for millimeter)

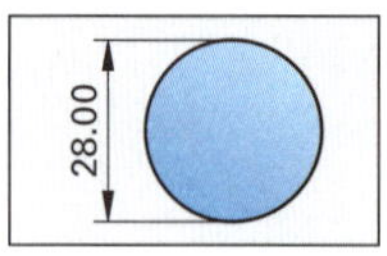

Units

Every physical quantity has a certain unit. The International System of Units SI is based on seven basic quantities **(table).** These basic quantities cannot be transferred into another quantity.

They form the basis for other derived quantities.

Table: Base quantities and base units in accordance to SI

Base quantity	Quantity symbol	Base unit	
		Name	Symbol
Length	*l, d, s*	meter	m
Mass	*m*	kilogram	kg
Time	*t*	second	s
Electric current	*I*	Ampere	A
Temperature	*T*	Kelvin	K
Amount of substance	*n*	mole	mol
Luminous intensity	I_v	Candela	cd

Words

English	German
measuring technique	Messtechnik
physical quantity(-ies)	physikalische Größe(n)
unit	Einheit
property (-ies)	Eigenschaft(en)
state	Zustand
process	Vorgang
length	Länge
diameter	Durchmesser
mass	Masse
velocity	Geschwindigkeit
time	Zeit
displacement	Weg, Strecke
base quantity	Basiseinheit
to describe	bezeichnen
in accordance	gemäß
defined	festgelegt
electric current	Elektrischer Strom
value	Wert
abbreviated form	Kurzform
letter	Buchstabe
to equal	gleichen
product	Produkt
numerical value	Zahlenwert
example	Beispiel
workpiece	Werkstück
diameter	Durchmesser
expression	Ausdruck
System of Units SI	SI-Einheitensystem
to base on	basieren auf
table	Tabelle
to transfer	umrechnen
derived quantity	abgeleitete Größe
quantity symbol	Formelzeichen
amount of substance	Stoffmenge
luminous intensity	Lichtstärke
second	Sekunde
speed	Geschwindigkeit
to define	definieren
to answer	beantworten
following	folgende
questions	Fragen

Exercises

1. Working with words. Which words from the text are described here?
   a) Every material has certain ________________ for example it can be very hard.
   b) In order to find out the correct diameter of a workpiece, you need to ______________ it with an instrument.
   c) The speed of a car is also called ______________________.
2. Define physical quantities in German by using the information from the text above.
3. Answer the following questions in English.
   a) Which two elements does a physical quantity have? Find an example to explain it.
   b) Which 7 base quantities does the International System of Units IS define?
   c) What is the difference between base quantities and derived quantities?

Prefixes

It is easier to use decimal multiples or factors in front of units to avoid very high or low values **(table)**.

Example: The length of a shaft is 0.030 m.

The prefix milli (m) is added: $l = 30.00$ mm

Table: Prefixes for decimal multiples and factors of units		
Prefix	**Meaning**	**Factor**
M mega	millionfold	10^6 = 1 000 000
k kilo	thousandfold	10^3 = 1 000
h hecto	hundredfold	10^2 = 100
da deca	tenfold	10^1 = 10
d deci	tenth	10^{-1} = 0.1
c centi	hundredth	10^{-2} = 0.01
m milli	thousandth	10^{-3} = 0.001
µ micro	millionth	10^{-6} = 0.000 001

Derived quantities and units

Derived quantities are needed to describe physical properties of materials or processes in machines and production. The derived units are determined by a formula and consist of two or more base units **(table)**.

Table: Examples for derived quantities and units				
Derived quantity	**Derived unit**	**Unit symbol**	**Relationship (formula)**	**Definition of the derived unit**
Volumen V	Cubic meter	m^3	$V = l \cdot b \cdot h$ $[V] = 1\ m \cdot 1\ m \cdot 1\ m = 1\ m^3$	One cubic meter
Force F	Newton	N	$F = m \cdot a$ $[F] = 1\ N = 1\ \frac{kg \cdot m}{s^2}$	One kilogram times meter **per (over)** square second
Work W	Joule	J	$W = F \cdot s$ $[W] = 1\ N \cdot m$	One Newton times one meter

Example: The volume is calculated by the formula $V = l \cdot b \cdot h$

The volume equals the length times the width, times the height (e.g. $V = 2\ m \cdot 3\ m \cdot 4\ m = 24\ m^3$)

The unit of the volume V results from inserting the base units into the formula:

$[V] = [l] \cdot [b] \cdot [h] = m \cdot m \cdot m = m^3$ (cubic meter)

Imperial Units

Imperial units (Non SI-Units) are used in Great Britain and in the USA. This is a traditional measuring system, in which short distance units are based on standardised dimensions of the human body, e.g. one inch represents the width of a thumb. The foot (= 12 inches) is the length of a human foot. These countries have also different units for weight, mass and temperature.

The imperial units can be converted into the SI-Units.

Example:

1 inch (*in*/″)	= 25.4 mm	1 pound (*pd*)	= 453.6 g
1 foot (*ft*)	= 0.3048 m	1 barrel (*bl*)	= 158.8 dm^3
1 mile (*mi*)	= 1.609 km	1° Fahrenheit (*F*)	= –17.77 °C

Words	
prefix	Vorsatz
decimal multiples	dezimale Vielfache
in front of	vor
to avoid	vermeiden
high	groß, hoch
low	niedrig
millionfold	Millionenfaches
tenth	Zehntel
shaft	Welle
to add	hinzufügen
to need	benötigen
process	Prozess
to determine	bestimmen
formula	Formel
to consist of	bestehen aus
relationship	Beziehung
times	multipliziert mit (mal)
per (over)	dividiert durch
force	Kraft
square second	Quadrat Sekunde
times	mal
work	Arbeit
to calculate	berechnen
equals	entspricht, ist gleich
width	Breite
height	Höhe
to result	(sich) ergeben
to insert	einsetzen
imperial unit	britisch-amerikanische Maßeinheit
bar	Stange
Great Britain	Großbritannien
standardised dimension	festgelegtes Maß
human body	menschlicher Körper
e.g. (for example)	z.B. (zum Beispiel)
thumb	Daumen
foot	Fuß
weight	Gewicht
to convert	umrechnen
tension	Spannung
pressure	Druck
rod	Stab
density	Dichte
turning tool	Drehmeißel
feed velocity	Vorschub-geschwindigkeit

Exercises

1. Write down the formula and explain the correct derived units. (Use your **Metal Trades Handbook**)
   a) pressure p b) velocity v c) density ϱ
   d) tension σ e) electrical energy W f) frequency f
2. Convert the measurements from imperial units into metric units. (Use your **Handbook**)
   a) 120 miles in km b) 3.300 ft in meters c) $1^1/_2$ pints in litres
   d) 4.5 ounces in kilogram e) $^1/_8$ inch in mm f) 22.5 pounds in kg
3. Calculate the physical quantities by using SI-Units.
   a) A compact disc (CD) has a diameter of 120 mm. Calculate the area in mm^2.
   b) The volume of a steel rod is 0.5 dm^3 and has a density of 7.85 kg/dm^3. Calculate the mass in kg.
   c) A turning tool moves 9.3 cm in a time of 3 seconds. Calculate the feed velocity in mm/s.

1.2 Fundamentals of measuring technique

If components are produced in a workshop, e.g. a slide rail **(figure)**, the dimensions of the workpiece must be given precisely. Important dimensions of the slide rail are the length of 22 mm, the height of 24.5 mm, the angle of 90° and the internal diameters of 6.6 mm and 11 mm.

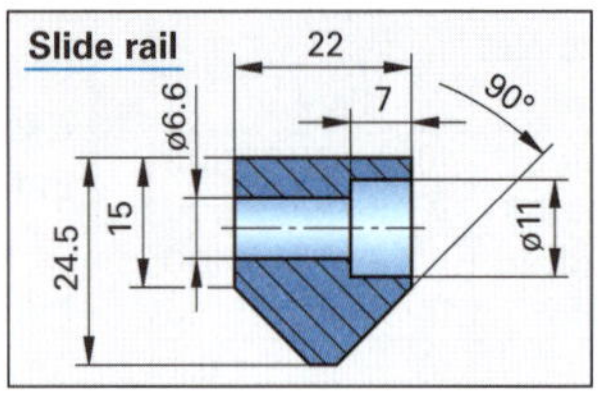

In order to measure these features, different inspection aids are needed **(figure)**. They can be divided into three main categories: measuring devices, gauges and auxiliary aids.

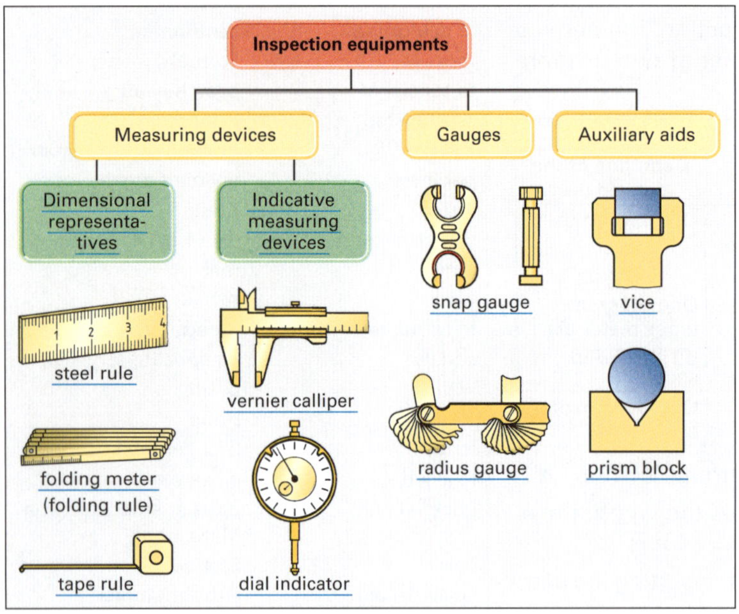

With some measuring devices you compare a certain dimension, such as the height of 24.5 mm with a scale of a measuring device. These instruments are called dimensional representations, e.g. steel rules or folding meter.

If you read the dimension from a scale of the measuring device you use an indicative measuring device, such as a vernier calliper, a protractor, or a micrometer.

With gauges you can test e.g. the diameter of a ∅ 6.6 mm hole (bore) with a plug limit gauge, or you can check the radius of R9 by a radius gauge.

Words

English	German
fundamentals	Grundlagen
measuring technique	Messtechnik
component	Bauteil
workshop	Werkstatt
slide rail	Führungsschiene
precise	präzise, genau
important	wichtig
angle	Winkel
internal diameter	Innendurchmesser
feature	Größe
different	unterschiedlich
inspection aid	Messmittel
to divide	unterscheiden
category (-ies)	Bereich, Kategorie
measuring device	Messgerät
gauge	Lehre
auxiliary aid	Hilfsmittel
dimensional repre-sentative	Maßverkörperung
indicative measuring devices	anzeigende Messgeräte
steel rule	Stahlmaßstab
folding meter (folding rule)	Gliedermaßstab
tape rule	Bandmaßstab
vernier calliper	Messschieber
dial indicator	Messuhr
snap gauge	Rachenlehre
radius gauge	Radienlehre
vice	Schraubstock
prism block	Prisma, V-Block
to compare	vergleichen
scale	Skala
protractor	Universalwinkelmesser
micrometer	Bügelmessschraube
to test	prüfen
hole (bore)	Loch/Bohrung
plug limit gauge	Grenzlehrdorn
groove	Nut
result	Ergebnis

Exercises

1. Translate the following inspection aids and name the main group of these devices.
   a) plug limit gauge b) prism block c) folding rule
   d) micrometer e) snap gauge f) vernier calliper

2. Name the correct inspection aid to find out these measurements.
   a) the diameter of a shaft of 22 mm b) the length of a rail of 1.80 m c) the angle of 120°
   d) the hole of ∅ 20 mm e) the depth of 10 mm of a groove f) the radius R5

3. Answer the questions in English.
   a) What are dimensional representatives?
   b) Which result do you get when you use a gauge? Give an example.
   c) Which result do you get when you use an indicative measuring device? Give an example.
   d) When do you need an auxiliary help? Give an example.

Measuring errors

The indicated values of a measuring instrument are afflicted with different measuring errors. The errors can be caused by:
- Deviation of the standard temperature of 20 °C

Operator variations:
- thin workpieces could be deformed by a high measuring force
- parallax error is due to the incorrect eye position when reading the scale

Measuring errors can be divided into two categories:
Systematic errors: They are caused by constant variations, such as the temperature in the workshop, the measuring force or an inaccurate scale or wear of the measuring instrument. Systematic errors can be avoided by eliminating the cause of the error, such as a proper calibration of the measuring instrument.

Random errors are caused by unknown variations, such as an unintended change in temperature or measuring force or parallax error. They can be reduced by repeating the measurement for a few times and using a calculated mean value.

Measuring capability

If you need to measure a workpiece, it is difficult to know which measuring instrument should be used. The correct choice of measuring device saves time, money and can provide you with an accurate result.

The choice of a suitable measuring instrument for a certain measuring task depends on the required accuracy and the dimension of the workpiece.

By using your Metal Trade Handbook **(extract in the table)** you can find out the uncertainty and the range of the instrument.

Example:
The uncertainty of mechanical measuring instruments is one scale interval. Digital measuring instruments have an uncertainty of three numerical intervals.

Table: Range of measuring and uncertainty of measuring instruments

Measuring instrument	Measuring range	Measuring uncertainty
Calliper 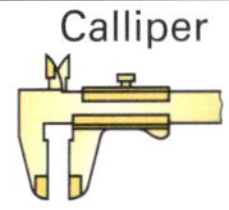 Scale interval 0.05 mm	0...150 mm	$U \geq 50$ µm = 0.05 mm
Micrometer 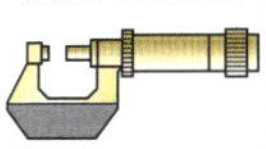 Scale interval 0.01 mm	50...75 mm	$U = 10$ µm = 0.01 mm

Words

measuring error	Messfehler
indicated value	angezeigter Wert
to be afflicted with	mit etwas behaftet sein
deviation	Abweichung
operator variation	Ableserabweichung
thin	dünn
to be deformed	verformt sein
measuring force	Messkraft
parallax error	Parallaxefehler
to be due to	bedingt werden durch
reading	Ablesung
systematic error	systematischer Messfehler
to be caused by	verursacht werden von
inaccurate	ungenau
wear	Abnutzung/Verschleiß
to avoid	vermeiden
to eliminate	beseitigen
calibration	Kalibrierung, Einstellung
random error	zufälliger Messfehler
unknown	unbekannt
unintended	unbeabsichtigt
repeating	wiederholen
mean value	Mittelwert
measuring capability	Messfähigkeit
choice	Auswahl
measuring device	Messgerät
to save	sparen
to provide	liefern
accurate result	genaues Ergebnis
the choice	die Auswahl
suitable	geeignet
measuring task	Messaufgabe
uncertainty	Unsicherheit
required	gefordert
range	Messbereich
scale interval	Skalenteilungswert
numerical interval	Ziffernschrittwert
to match	zuordnen
common	üblich

Exercises

1. Match the pictures a) – d) to the type of measuring error (1) – (4). Explain if it is a systematic or a random error.

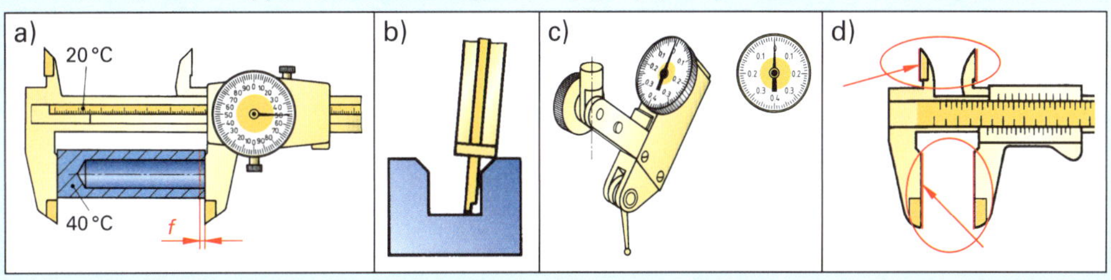

Type of measuring error: (1) parallax error (2) wear of measuring surfaces
(3) bad positioning of device (4) high temperature

2. Make a list of six common measuring devices (e.g. steel rule, vernier calliper, gauge block, dial gauge protractor, etc) and find out their type of inspection aid/range/accuracy.
(Use a webpage of a company for measuring devices e.g. www.mitutoyo.com; www.mahr.de; www.hoffmann.de).

Measuring device	Type of inspection aid	Range	Accuracy
steel rule	dimensional representative	150 – 1000 mm	0.5/1 mm
...	...	...	...

1.3 Length Measuring Instruments

For measuring the length of a workpiece, there is a variety of test instruments with different degrees of accuracy. You can measure the length with a rule or a tape rule and check the size with a gauge or a gauge block.

Rules (figure) represent the length measurement by the distance of little lines on a scale. There are different types of rules available: flexible steel rules, tape rules or folding meters.

Steel rule

Scales (figure) for the position measurement systems are made of glass or steel and are operated by the photoelectronic scanning principle. When parallel light passes through a scale, light and dark surfaces are projected at a certain distance and signals are generated.

Impulse scale

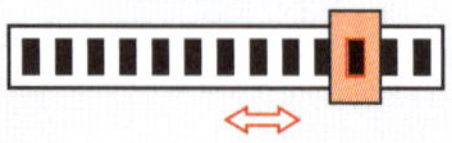

Straight edges (figure) are used to check the straightness and flatness. They have lapped test blades with a high flatness. These accurate test blades enable the naked eye to realize different tiny light gaps. The light gap between the test blade and the workpiece could be as small as 2 µm.

Straight edges

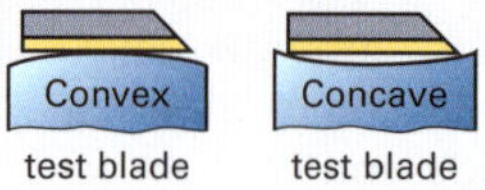

Engineer's squares (figure) are form gauges and represent mostly an angle of 90°. They are used to check the perpendicularity and flatness of surfaces. Besides, cylindrical or flat surfaces can be adjusted.

Engineer's square

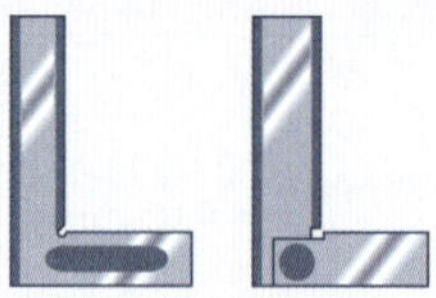

The measuring tubes can have dimensions up to 100 × 70 mm with a class of accuracy of 00. The limit of perpendicularity deviation is only 3 µm.

Gauges represent certain dimensions or geometric forms **(figure).**

Measurement gauges come in sets, e.g. gauge blocks or test pins.

Form gauges can check angles, radii and threads using the light gap method.

Plug gauges and **snap gauges** represent the admissible maximum and minimum limit dimension. Some gauges represent also the form, e.g. to test the cylindrical form of a bore as well as the dimension of the hole.

Gauges

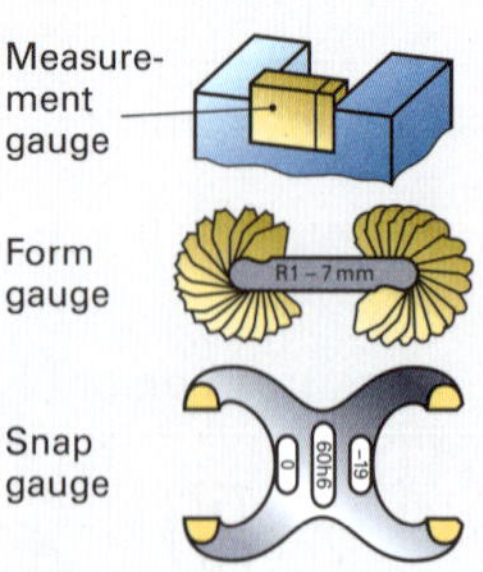

Words	
degree of accuracy	Genauigkeitsgrad
rule	Lineal
tape rule	Maßband
size	Größe
gauge	Lehre
gauge block	Endmaß
to represent	darstellen
distance	Entfernung
folding meter	Meterstab
scale	Maßstab
position measurement system	Wegmesssystem
to operate	bedienen, arbeiten
scanning principle	Abtast-Prinzip
impulse scale	Impulsmaßstab
light	hell
dark	dunkel
surface	Fläche/Feld
to project	projizieren
to generate	erzeugen
straight edge	Haarlineal
straightness	Geradheit
flatness	Ebenheit
lapped	geläppt
test blade	Messfläche
naked eye	mit bloßem Auge
tiny	winzig
light gap	Lichtspalt
engineer's square	Haarwinkel
perpendicularity	Rechtwinkligkeit
to adjust	einstellen
measuring tube	Messschenkel
class of accuracy	Genauigkeitsklasse
test pin	Prüfstift
thread	Gewinde
plug gauge	Lehrdorn
snap gauge	Rachenlehre
admissible	zulässig
absolute scale	Absolutmaßstab
to mention	nennen

Exercises

1. Match the correct expression of the following measuring devices to the pictures at the right.
   a) absolute scale b) flexible steel rule c) tape rule
   d) folding rule e) impulse scale

	1	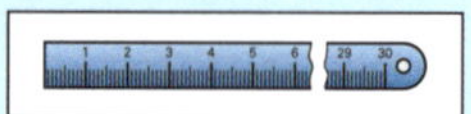
	2	
	3	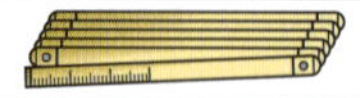
	4	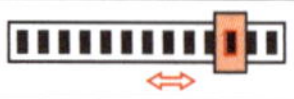
	5	

2. Answer the questions below in English.
   a) What is the difference between measuring instruments and gauges?
   b) Why do straight edges and engineer's squares have lapped test blades?
   c) What can you check with straight edges?
   d) What is the light gap method?
   e) Mention 3 different types of gauges and choose a certain measurement of a workpiece which can be checked by them.

Working with plug gauges, snap gauges and gauge blocks

The specified limits of bores of toleranced workpieces can be checked by plug gauges. Snap gauges or ring gauges are used to test the specified limits of shafts.

Plug gauges (figure)
When using a cylindrical plug gauge, the diameter of one side, the Go should enter while the No Go should fail to enter the hole. As a result, it is stated to be within the specified limits.

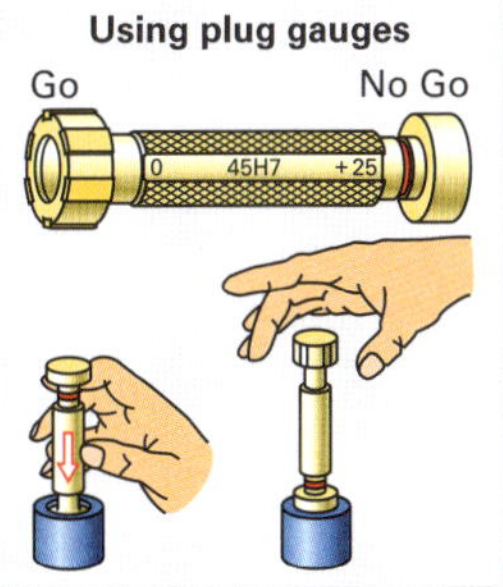

Cylindrical plug gauges are made from alloyed steel or tungsten carbide. They are ground and lapped. They can be produced to any size up to 250 mm diameter.

The Go side should slide into the bore by its own weight. A minimal insertion of the No Go gauge may be tolerated at the entry fit. The Go side is longer and often has carbide inserts to reduce the wear of the surface. The No Go side is shorter, marked with a red ring and shows the maximum limit size.

Snap gauges (figure)
The Go side represents the maximum limit size. It must slide over the measured surface by its own weight. The No Go member is smaller and should fail to slide over the surface. It has slightly angled measuring surfaces, which are red and show the minimum limit size.

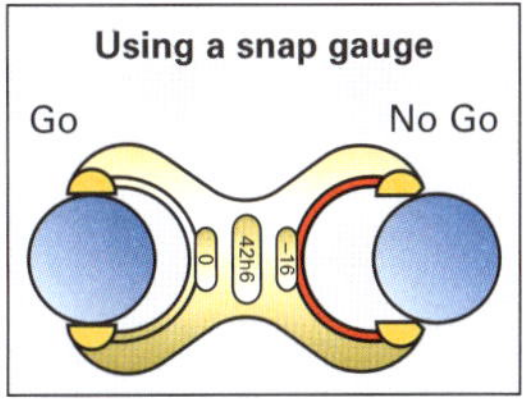

Gauge blocks
Gauge blocks are the most important and precise dimensional representations. They are usually made in sets of rectangular, square or angular steel blocks or ceramic blocks **(figure)**. Each block has two opposite faces lapped flat and parallel to a definite size within an extremely tight tolerance. In order to assemble a gauge block stack of a certain size, you first write down the correct combination of gauge blocks for these dimensions. Tip: start with the smallest available gauge block.

Example: Assemble a gauge block stack for the dimension: 57.005 mm.

Careful: There is no gauge block of 0.005 mm. It would break!

Gauge block combination	
1. Gauge block	1.005 mm
2. Gauge block	6.000 mm
3. Gauge block	50.000 mm
Total dimension	57.005 mm

Words	
plug gauge	Grenzlehrdorn
snap gauge	Grenzrachenlehre
gauge block	Endmaß
specified limit	Grenzmaße
ring gauge	Lehrring
shaft	Welle
diameter	Durchmesser
Go side	Gutseite
to enter	eindringen
No Go side	Ausschussseite
to fail	scheitern
result	Ergebnis
to state	feststellen
alloyed steel	legierter Stahl
tungsten carbide	Wolframkarbid, Hartmetall
to grind, ground	schleifen, geschliffen
to lap	läppen
to slide	gleiten
own weight	Eigengewicht
minimal insertion	Anschnäbelung
to tolerate	tolerieren
entry fit	Ansatz-Passung
carbide insert	Hartmetalleinsatz
wear	Abnutzung, Verschleiß
surface	Oberfläche
to designate	beschriften
maximum limit size	Höchst-Grenzmaß
slightly angled	leicht angeschrägt
rectangular	viereckig
square	quadratisch
angular	winkelig
opposite	gegenüberliegend
definite size	bestimmte Größe
tight	eng
to assemble	zusammenstellen
gauge block stack	Endmaßstapel
available	verfügbar
to tick	ankreuzen
mating	passend
to create	herstellen

Exercises

1. Find the correct answer of the questions and tick it in the table below ✓

a) A tolerance is a ...	clearance between a shaft/mating bore	measurement error	variation in manufacturing
b) Which of the following statement of plug gauges is true (only 1)?	The Go side is smaller than the No Go side of the plug gauge.	Only slight pressure is needed to slide the Go member into the bore.	The No Go member is designated with the minimum limit size.
c) Which of the following statement of snap gauges is true (only 1)?	The Go member should fail to slide into the bore.	The Go member is marked in red.	The Go member doesn't represent the minimum limit size.

2. Create a stack of gauge blocks and write down the combination of blocks.
a) 42.123 mm   b) 74.357 mm   c) 81.685 mm

1.4 Vernier calliper

The vernier calliper, also called sliding calliper or shortly calliper, is the most common precision measuring instrument used in mechanical engineering. It can be used to measure internal and external distances as well as the depth of e.g. holes or grooves of parts. There are mechanical and digital callipers. The mechanical calliper is more difficult to read. A digital calliper has a display to show the measurement.

The mechanical calliper, used in Germany and in other countries of the EU, has a metric scale with $^1/_{10}$, $^1/_{20}$ or $^1/_{50}$ mm nonius. In the United Kingdom and USA, it has an imperial scale with an inch nonius.

A mechanical calliper consists of a bar which shows the amount of millimetres **(figure)**. It has two jaws; a movable jaw and a fixed measuring jaw. The workpiece is placed between the fixed and movable jaw.

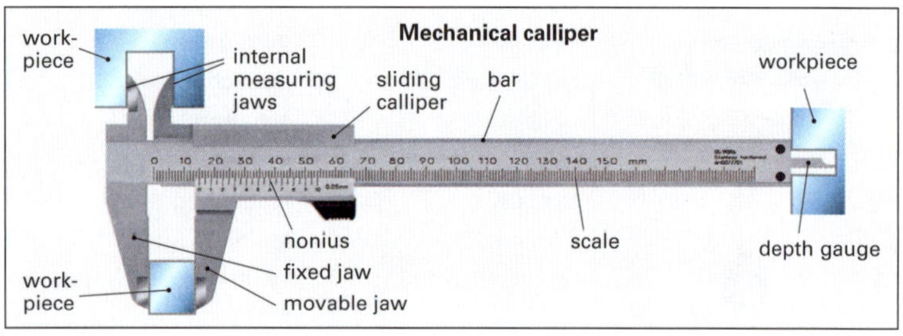

The depth of a workpiece can be checked by the depth gauge. The width of a groove can be measured by the internal measuring jaws.

The reading of a mechanical calliper is a little difficult. When you want to find out the exact value, shown on a mechanical calliper, first read the millimeter mark on the scale of the fixed jaw: 81 mm **(figure)**. Then look along the ten marks on the scale of the movable jaw and the millimeter marks on the adjacent fixed scale, until you find the two marks that line up: 0.55 mm. To get the correct reading, add the two values: 81 mm + 0.55 mm = 81.55 mm.

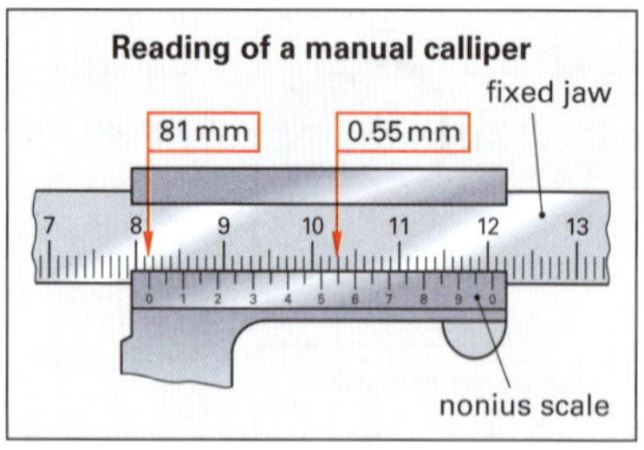

Most common today is using a **digital calliper**. It shows the reading directly on the display **(figure)**. It is much easier and faster to read. There are no errors in reading precise measuring values. The accuracy is between 0.01 mm to 0.02 mm.

Additionally, a digital calliper has certain functions:

- Choosing the reading in mm or inch.
- Reset the zero-point at any position.
- Presetting tolerances.
- Setting for absolute and comparison measurements.
- Possibility for a serial data output to be interfaced with a PC.

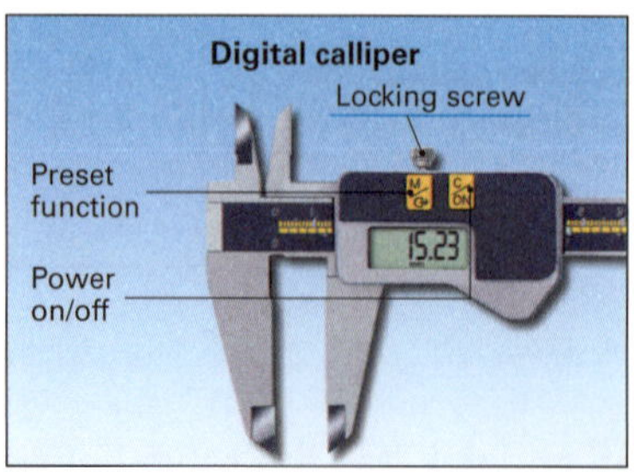

Words	
vernier calliper	Messschieber
shortly	kurz
most common	gebräuchlichste(r)
mechanical engineering	Maschinenbau
internal	Innen-
external	Außen-
depth	Tiefe
groove	Nut
mechanical calliper	mechanischer Messschieber
display	Anzeige
nonius	Nonius
bar	Schiene
amount	Betrag, Anzahl
jaw	Schenkel
movable	beweglich
fixed	fest, fixiert
to place	platzieren
depth gauge	Tiefenmaß
reading	Ablesen, Ablesewert
mark	Markierung
adjacent	anschließend
to line up	übereinstimmen
digital calliper	digitaler Messschieber
accuracy	Genauigkeit
to choose	auswählen
to reset	zurücksetzen
presetting	Voreinstellung
locking screw	Feststellschraube
comparison measurement	Unterschiedsmessung
to interface	verbinden
least	wenigsten(s)
thickness	Dicke
possible	möglich(e)
nowadays	heutzutage

Exercises

1. Five of the following six statements are wrong. Find these statements and correct them.
   a) A vernier calliper is the least frequently used measuring device in the workshop.
   b) A calliper can measure diameters of bores and shafts, the width and thickness of a part.
   c) There are three different types of callipers: manual, digital and CNC callipers.
   d) With the aid of a $^1/_{20}$ nonius a measuring of 0.02 mm is possible.
   e) Measurements of 0.001 inch, 0.01, 0.02 and 0.05 mm are also possible.
   f) Digital callipers are easier to read, cheaper and more often used nowadays.
2. Translate the example of reading a mechanical calliper into German.

1.5 Micrometer (screw gauge)

The micrometer can be used to measure even smaller dimensions than the vernier callipers. There are mechanical and digital micrometers.

The **mechanical micrometer (figure below the page)** has a main scale for reading the millimeters and an auxiliary scale for measuring hundredths of a millimeter. The auxiliary scale is on a rotary thimble. The main scale is on the sleeve of the micrometer. The basic structure of a micrometer is a screw with an accurately constant pitch. It is the amount by which the thimble moves forward or backward for one complete revolution.

In order to measure a workpiece, the part is placed between the two measuring faces, the anvil and the spindle. These parts are connected by the frame, which is covered by an insulation plate. The thimble is rotated using the ratchet until the workpiece is secured. It is locked by three clicks of the ratchet before reading the measurement. The clicking noise comes from a little spring which is inside the ratchet. The lock may be used to ensure that the thimble does not rotate while you read the value.

Example of reading an imperial micrometer (figure):

First read the whole inch marking (1) and the 25 thousandth-markings (2) on the scale ⇒ **1 inch + 0.75 inch**
Then read the value (3) on the thimble.
⇒ **0.000 inch**

Finally add the three values:
1 inch + 0.75 inch + 0.000 inch
⇒ **1.750 inch**

Reading an imperial micrometer

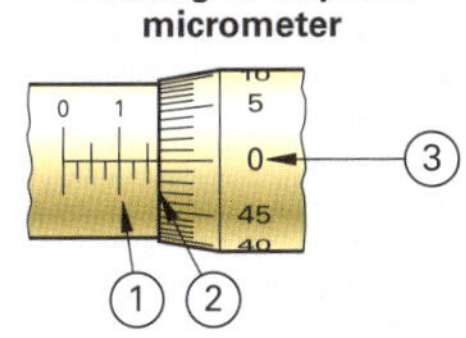

The **digital micrometer** has a similar construction and mode of operation as the mechanical micrometer **(figure)**. The measuring is quicker. Errors don't appear as often because of the reading of the value on the display. It has an accuracy of 0.01 mm.

Digital micrometer

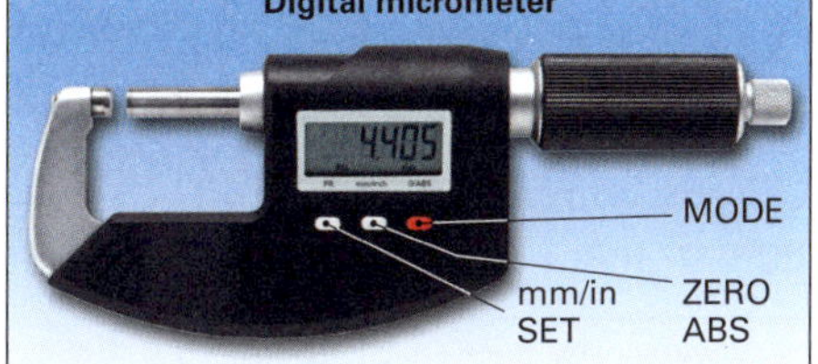

The digital micrometer has the same **additional functions** as the digital calliper:
- Readings can be displayed in mm and inches.
- Absolute and comparison measurements can be set.
- Tolerances can be preset, zero-point can be reset.

Words (English)	Words (German)
micrometer/ screw gauge	Bügelmessschraube
auxiliary scale	Hilfsskala
rotary	drehbar
thimble	Skalentrommel
main scale	Hauptskale
sleeve	Skalenhülse
basic structure	grundsätzlicher Aufbau
screw	Schraube
pitch	(Gewinde-) Steigung
to move	bewegen
forward	vorwärts
backward	rückwärts
complete	ganz, vollständig
revolution	Umdrehung
measuring face	Messfläche
anvil	Amboss
spindle	Spindel
to connect	verbinden
frame	Bügel
insulation plate	Isolierplatte
ratchet	hier: Kupplung
to secure	fixieren
to lock	klemmen
noise	Geräusch
spring	Feder
lock	Spindelfeststellung
to ensure	sicherstellen
marking	Markierung
thousandth	Tausendstel
to add	addieren
similar	ähnlichen
construction	Aufbau
mode of operation	Betriebsweise
to appear	vorkommen
accuracy	Genauigkeit
to label	beschriften
sketch	Skizze, Zeichnung

Exercises

1. Label the sketch of the mechanical micrometer a) to l) by reading the text above.

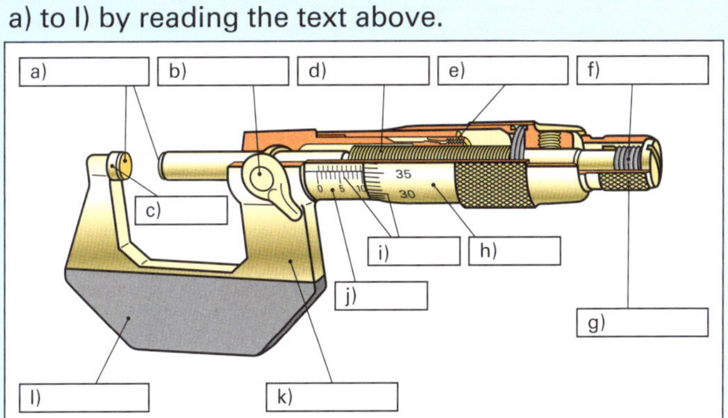

2. Read the correct measurements of the micrometers shown below.

a) in inch

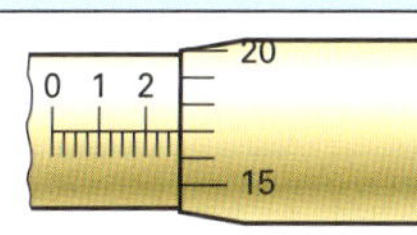

b) in mm

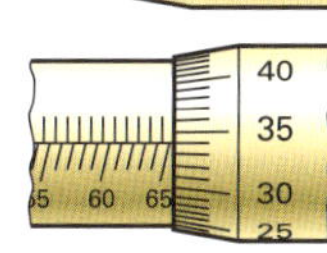

c) in inch

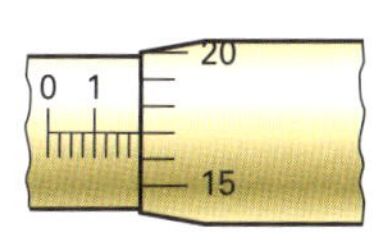

1.6 Surface testing

In industrial manufacturing the machined surface has a major influence on the quality and performance of the end product.

The surface texture of a workpiece is the deviation of a surface from its ideal shape e.g. perfect flat, cylindrical or spherical form. The measure of the surface texture indicates the form, the waviness and the roughness **(figure)**.

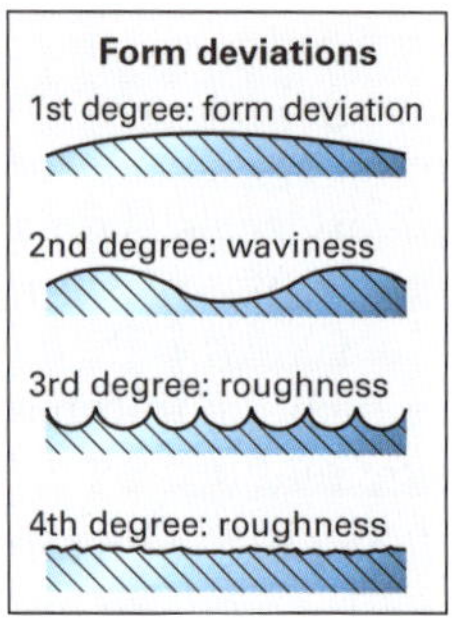

The **form deviation** (1st degree of deviation describes the straightness or roundness of the part. Deviations from the required form can result from clamping marks or wear in the guides of the machine tool.

Waviness (2nd degree deviation) usually relates to the characteristics of an individual machine or to external environmental factors. It may result from the machine itself, e.g. its vibrations.

The **roughness** (3rd/4th degree deviation), e.g. grooves or bumps result from the production process. It is influenced by the geometry or the material structure of the cutting tool and the feed or the depth of the tool.

The irregularities of a surface can be checked by different measuring instruments. The output of these devices are certain profiles. The base of a roughness (R) and waviness (W) profile is the primary (P) profile.

Types of surface testing

Surface roughness comparators are used for touch and sight comparison. In order to get an accurate measuring result you need to use the same material of the test specimen and workpiece and the correct manufacturing technology, e.g. turning, milling, grinding etc.

You need to scrape the comparator specimen with your fingernail or use a small copper coin. Then you can compare the surface of the workpiece with the comparator specimen. If you compare it visually, you need an optimum light source angle or use a magnifying glass.

Stylus instruments are surface roughness testers, which record the peaks and valleys by a diamond stylus **(figure)**. The stylus is drawn at a constant speed across the workpiece. The amount to which the stylus is raised or lowered is printed in a diagram. It shows the increased surface profile.

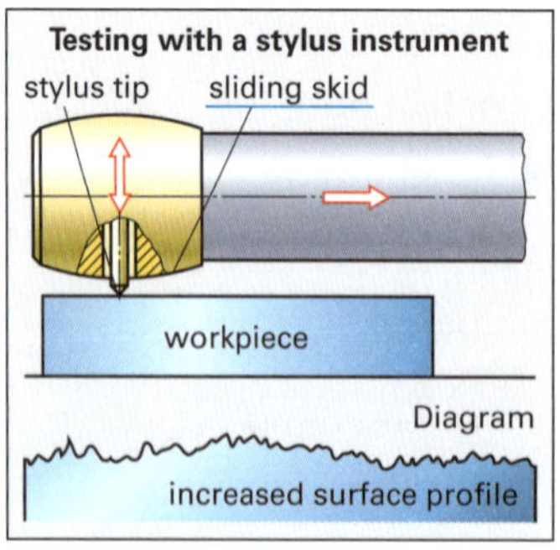

Words (English)	Words (German)
machined surface	bearbeitete Oberfläche
major	bedeutend
influence	Einfluss
performance	Leistung
texture	Struktur
deviation	Abweichung
shape	Form
spherical	kugelförmig
to indicate	kennzeichnen
waviness	Welligkeit
roughness	Rauheit
degree	Grad
clamping mark	Einspannkratzer
wear	Abnutzung
guide	Führung
to relate to	zusammenhängen
characteristic	Kennzeichen
environmental	umgebungsbedingt
groove	Rille
bump	Erhebung
feed	Vorschub
depth	Tiefe (hier: Zustellung)
irregularity	Unregelmäßigkeit
output	Ausgabe
roughness comparator	Oberflächenvergleichsmuster
touch sight comparison	Tast-/Sichtvergleich
turning	Drehen
milling	Fräsen
grinding	Schleifen
to scrape	kratzen
fingernail	Fingernagel
copper coin	Kupfermünze
light source angle	Lichteinfallwinkel
magnifying glass	Lupe
stylus instrument	Tastschnittgerät
to record	aufzeichnen
peak	Spitze
valley	Tal
stylus	Tastnadel
to be drawn	gezogen werden
to raise	anheben
to lower	senken
sliding skid	Gleitkufe

Exercises

1. Complete the missing information about form deviations in the table.

Degrees of form deviation	Examples	Possible cause
1st degree: form deviation	...	...
...	waves	...
3rd degree: roughness	...	...
...	...	Sequence of chip formation surface deformation during fabrication

2. Answer the questions in English.
   a) Which surface testing instrument is very quick and easy to use? Why?
   b) Explain why you can compare the surface roughness visually and by touching.
   c) Describe how a stylus instrument works.

Surface texture parameters

The scanned primary profile **(figure)** shows the total heights of a surface.

Filtering the primary profile (P-profile) leads to the roughness profile (R-profile) and the waviness profile (W-profile).

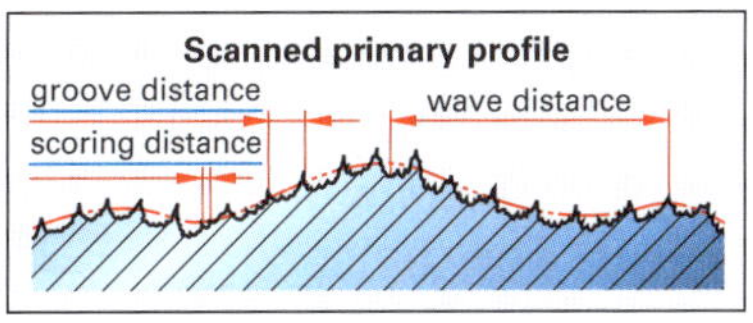

The R-profile **(figure)** shows the peaks, the valleys around a centre line.

The surface texture parameters are mostly calculated by the R-profile. There are several surface parameters:

R_z is widely used in Europe, R_a is the most specified U.S. parameter. Another parameter is R_{max} (maximum peak to valley height).

R_a (arithmetic average roughness) considers all peaks and valleys of the roughness profile **(figure)**. One deep scratch in material is neutralised and has no significant influence on the final result.

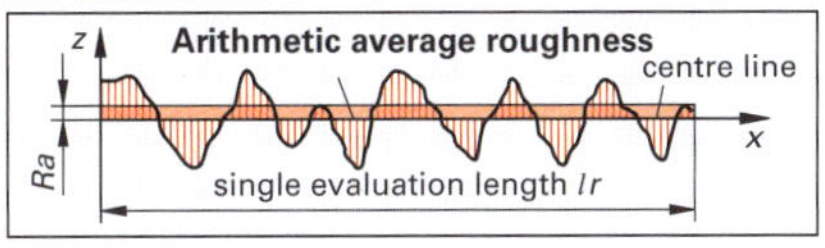

R_z (average peak to valley height) considers only the five highest peaks and the five deepest valleys **(figure)**. Extremes have a much greater influence on the final result. The complete evaluation length is divided into 5 cut-offs. In each cut-off the highest distance between peak and valley is a value (R_{z1}–R_{z5}).

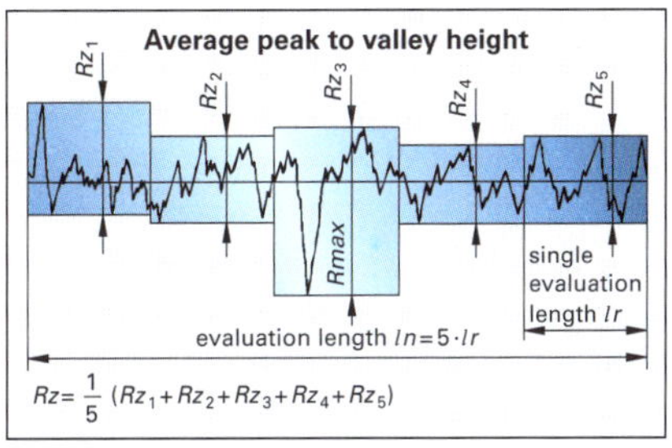

R_{max} (maximum peak to valley height) is the maximum height of the five values in the sampling length.

The surface parameters are shown in technical drawings by symbols **(table)**. To achieve a very high surface texture you need to choose the correct type of manufacturing. In your *Metal Trades Handbook* are tables to choose the correct manufacturing technology.

Table: Surface finish symbols

Symbol	Meaning
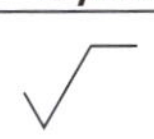	All manufacturing processes are allowed
	Material removal not allowed or surface remains in delivered condition
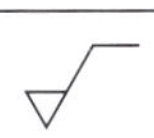	Material removal specified, e. g. turning, milling
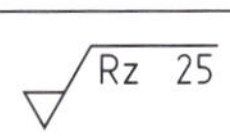	Material removal machining R_z = 25 µm

Achievable R_z-values:

Grinding: R_z = 1.6–4 µm
Milling: R_z = 10–63 µm
Drilling: R_z = 40–160 µm

Words

English	German
surface texture parameter	Oberflächenkenngröße
to scan	abtasten
primary profile	Primärprofil
total height	Gesamthöhe
groove distance	Rillenabstand
wave distance	Wellenabstand
scoring distance	Riefenabstand
roughness profile	Rauheitsprofil
waviness profile	Welligkeitsprofil
peak	Spitze
valley	Tal
centre line	Mittellinie
specified	vorgeschriebene
arithmetic average roughness R_a	Mittelrauwert R_a
to consider	berücksichtigen
scratch	Kratzer
to neutralise	ausgleichen
significant	bedeutend
final result	Endergebnis
average peak to valley height R_z	Mittlere Rautiefe R_z
extreme	Grenzwert
evaluation length	Messstrecke
cut-off	Einzelmessstrecke
maximum peak to valley height R_{max}	Maximale Rautiefe R_{max}
technical drawing	technische Zeichnung
to achieve	erreichen
to choose	wählen
type of manufacturing	Fertigungsverfahren
grinding	Schleifen
milling	Fräsen
drilling	Bohren
material removal	Materialabtrag
to allow	erlauben
to remain	verbleiben
delivered	angeliefert
reliable	zuverlässig

Exercises

1. Answer the questions in English.
   a) Which surface texture parameters are often used in USA and which in Germany?
   b) Explain the difference between the surface parameter R_{max} and R_z.
   c) Why is the surface texture parameter R_{max} not a very reliable value?
   d) Explain the surface texture parameter R_a.
2. Name the type of surface parameters and its value of the positions (1) to (4) shown in the right figure.
3. Draw a roughness profile and add the three parameters: R_{max}, R_{z1-z5} and R_a.

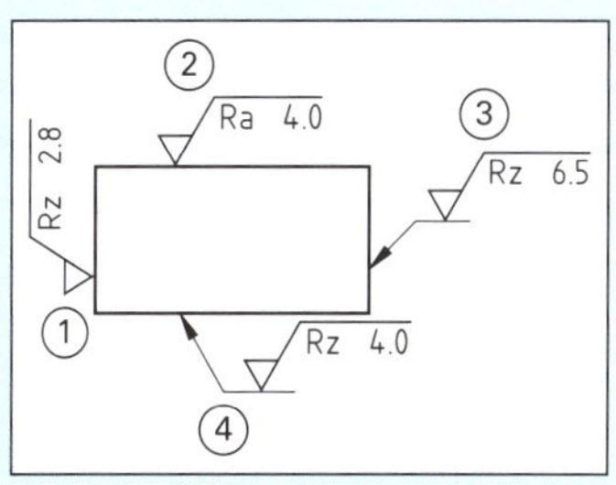

1.7 Fits

A fit is the dimensional relationship of two mating construction components. The components have the same nominal size at the fitting location. They differ in the quantity and range of the tolerance.

There are three different kinds of fits, depending on the dimensional difference between the matching components. The choice of the different fit is determined either by the use or by the production of the parts.

Clearance fit (figure)

Clearance fit always enables some space between the hole and shaft. The lower limit size of the hole is greater or at least equal to the upper limit size of the shaft.

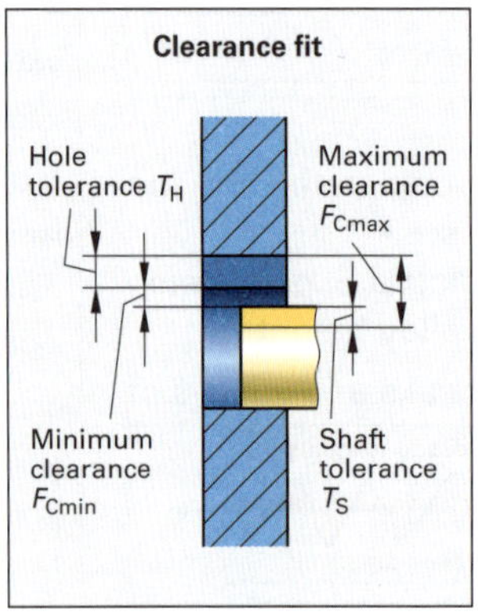

The maximum clearance (F_{Cmax}) equals the hole maximum dimension (G_{UH}) minus the shaft minimum dimension (G_{IS}).

$\Rightarrow$ $\mathbf{F_{Cmax} = G_{UH} - G_{IS}}$

The minimum clearance (F_{Cmin}) is calculated by the hole minimum dimension (G_{IH}) minus the shaft maximum dimension (G_{US}).

$\Rightarrow$ $\mathbf{F_{Cmin} = G_{IH} - G_{US}}$

Interference fit (figure)

It is a type of fit which always has some excess material between the hole and shaft. The upper limit size of the hole is smaller or at least equal to the lower limit size of the shaft.

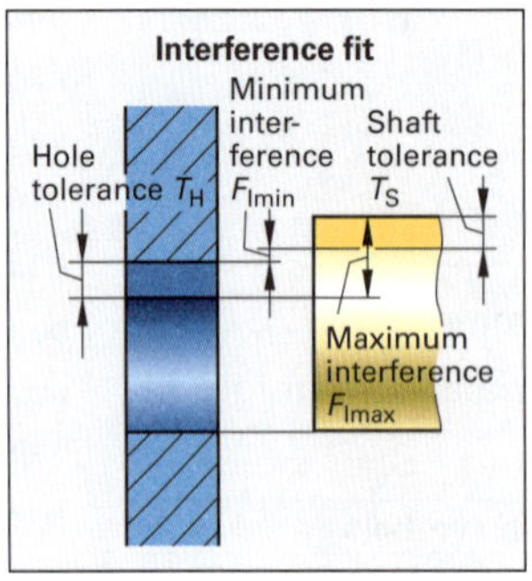

The maximum interference (F_{Imax}) is calculated by the hole minimum dimension (G_{IH}) minus the shaft maximum dimension (G_{US}).

$\Rightarrow$ $\mathbf{F_{Imax} = G_{IH} - G_{US}}$

The minimum clearance (F_{Cmin}) equals the hole maximum dimension (G_{UH}) minus the shaft minimum dimension (G_{IS}).

$\Rightarrow$ $\mathbf{F_{Imin} = G_{UH} - G_{IS}}$

Transition fit (figure)

It is a fit where both types of fit may occur. The tolerance zones of the hole and shaft partly or completely interfere. There can be a clearance fit or an interference fit.

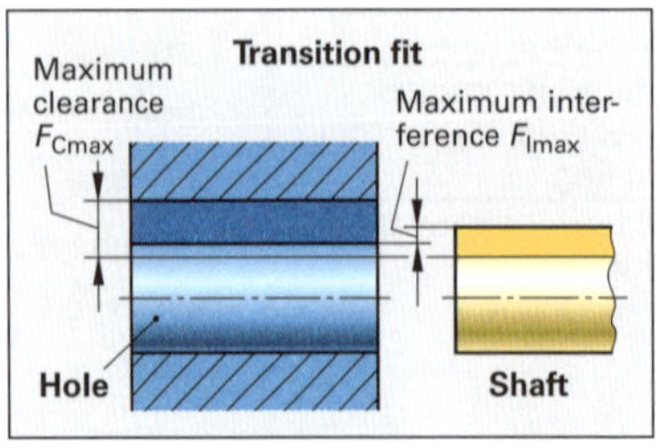

Words

English	German
fit	Passung
dimensional relationship	Größenbeziehung
mating	passend
construction component	Bauteil
nominal size	Nenngröße
to differ	sich unterscheiden
range	Spannweite
tolerance	Toleranz
to depend on	abhängig sein von
difference	Unterschied
matching	zusammengehörend
choice	(Aus-)wahl
to determine	bestimmen
use	Einsatz
production	Herstellbarkeit
clearance fit	Spielpassung
to enable	ermöglichen
space	Spiel/Raum
hole	Bohrung
shaft	Welle
lower limit size	Mindestmaß
at least	mindestens
upper limit size	Höchstmaß
hole max. dimension	Höchstmaß Bohrung
shaft max. dimension	Höchstmaß Welle
hole minimum dimension	Mindestmaß Bohrung
shaft minimum dimension	Mindestmaß Welle
interference fit	Übermaßpassung
excess	Überschuss
transition fit	Übergangspassung
to occur	vorkommen
to interfere	überlagern
criteria	Kriterium
to select	auswählen
expression	Begriff
abbreviation	Abkürzung

Exercises

1. Answer the following questions in English.
   a) What is a fit?
   b) Which two criterias are given to select the type of fit?
   c) What are the dimensions of the hole and shaft, when a clearance fit is given?
   d) Which three types of fits are possible? Explain!
2. Find the correct expressions and match them to the abbreviation.
   a) F_{Imin}/F_{Imax}
   b) G_{IH}/G_{UH}
   c) T_H/T_S
   d) G_{IS}/G_{US}
   e) F_{Cmin}/F_{Cmax}

1.8 Fit Systems

Fit systems are needed to limit the amount of tolerances of two mating parts. In a fit system one of the parts is produced with a basic tolerance and the other part has the tolerance according to the specific fit system.

Fit system: Basic hole system

When the basic hole system is used, the diameter of the hole is produced with the fundamental deviation H **(figure)**. The basic hole system is attached to different basic sizes of the shaft, e.g. d, e or k, m. The basic hole system is widely used in mechanical engineering and in the automotive industry.

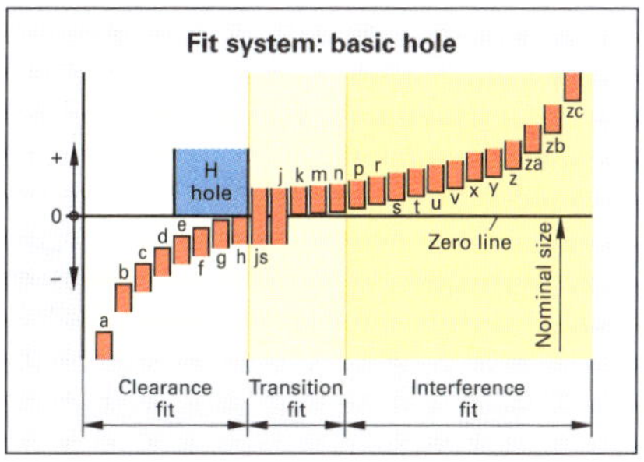

Range for type of fits

There are three general type of fits according to the different basic sizes of the shaft **(figure beside).**

Clearance fits: H/a…h
Transition fits: H/j…n or p
Interference fits: H/n or p…z

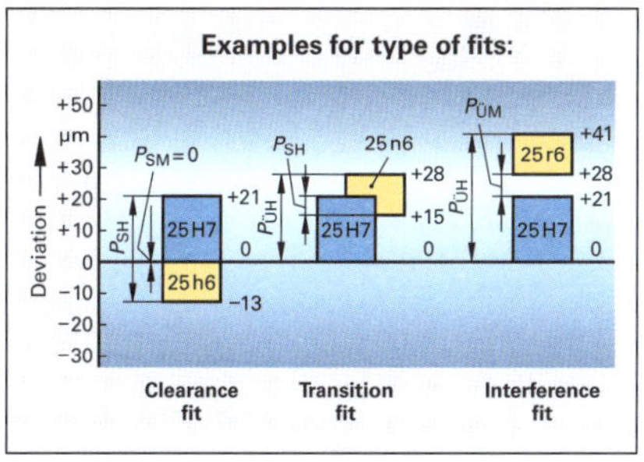

Fit system: Basic shaft system

When the basic shaft system is applied, all shaft dimensions have the fundamental deviation h **(figure),** e.g. clearance fit: h/A…H

The basic shaft system is used for shafts that are produced in standard sizes; the mating hole must be calculated.

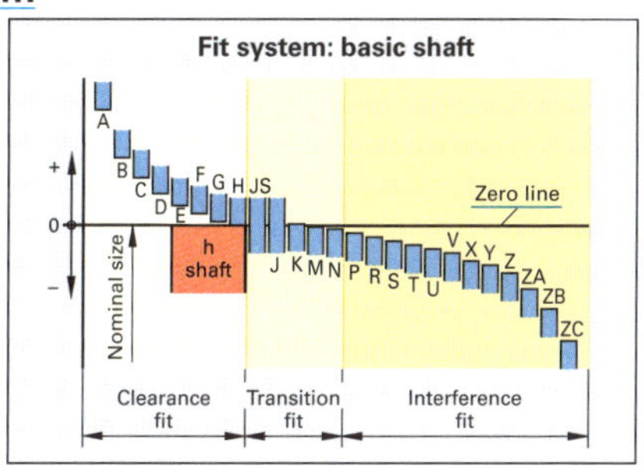

Words	
fit system	Passungssystem
to limit	begrenzen
mating	passend
basic tolerance	Grundtoleranz
diameter	Durchmesser
basic hole system	Einheitsbohrung
fundamental deviation	Grundabmaß
to attach	zuordnen
basic size	Grundabmaß
widely	weitgehend
mechanical engineering	Maschinenbau
automotive industry	Automobilindustrie
according	entsprechend
range for type of fits	Bereiche der Passungsarten
basic shaft system	Einheitswelle
to apply	anwenden
zero line	Nulllinie
standard size	Normgröße
to create	erzeugen
nominal size	Nennmaß
letters	Buchstaben
to determine	bestimmen
required	erforderlich

Range for the type of fits

The different type of fits are achieved by different fundamental deviations of the hole.

Clearance fits: h/A…H Transition fits: h/J…N or P Interference fits: h/N or P…Z

Example of the calculation of a fit:

Which important values need to be calculated to create a fit of 8.2 H7/d9?

*Use the tables of a **Metal Trades Handbook** to look up the different limits of the shaft and hole.*

8.2 H7/d9 ⇒ clearance fit Nominal size $N = 8.2$ mm

Hole limits: maximum dimension (G_{UH}) = 8.215mm; minimum dimension (G_{IH}) = 8.200 mm

Shaft limits: maximum dimension (G_{US}) = 8.160 mm; minimum dimension (G_{IS}) = 8.124 mm

Clearance limits: Maximum clearance (F_{Cmax}) = $G_{UH} - G_{IS}$ = 8.215 mm – 8.124 mm = 0.091 mm

Minimum clearance (F_{Cmin}) = $G_{IH} - G_{US}$ = 8.200 mm – 8.160 mm = 0.040 mm

Exercises

1. Answer the questions in German.
   a) Which difference do the two basic systems have?
   b) Where is the basic hole system used?
   c) Which letters are used in the basic hole system for interference fits?
2. Determine the type of fit of the following fits:
   a) 8H9/d9 b) 24H7/s6 c) 9K7/h6 d) 153 H11/c11
3. a) Read the required values for the fit of Nr. 2 a) to d) from a **Metal Trades Handbook.**
   b) Calculate the maximum and minimum clearance or interference, by using your **Metal Trade Handbook.**

2 Quality management

2.1 Basics of quality management

If a company wants to be successful on the market, the product quality must match the satisfaction of the customer. Customer's requirements are e.g. an appealing design, performance, functionality, reliability, maintainability and a good customer service.

Therefore, many companies have become certified and implemented a quality management system according to ISO 9000 standards.

Operating areas of quality management

Modern quality management encompasses all activities in a company, e.g. quality planning, quality control, quality assurance and quality improvement **(figure).**

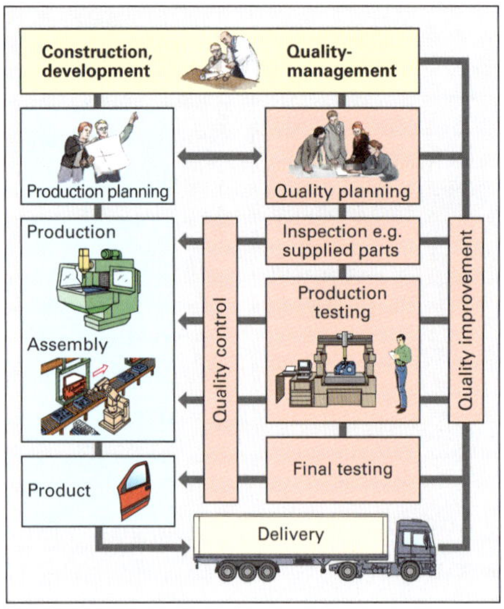

It is carried out successfully if all employees follow the guidelines of the ISO standards. In this way the quality of work processes can be controlled. Errors can be detected as early as possible so that production costs can be decreased.

Quality characteristics and errors

There are two different categories of quality characteristics:

- **Quantitative (variable) characteristics**
  can be measured or counted, e.g. the length of a workpiece or the diameter of a shaft.
- **Qualitative (attributive) characteristics**
  describe a quality, e.g. the quality of the painting of a vehicle.

Errors are present when one or more quality requirements are not fulfilled, e.g. a dimension is not correct or there is a malfunction in production.

The 1-10-100 rule **(figure)** states that when a product moves through a production sequence, the cost of correcting an error multiplies by 10 from stage to stage.

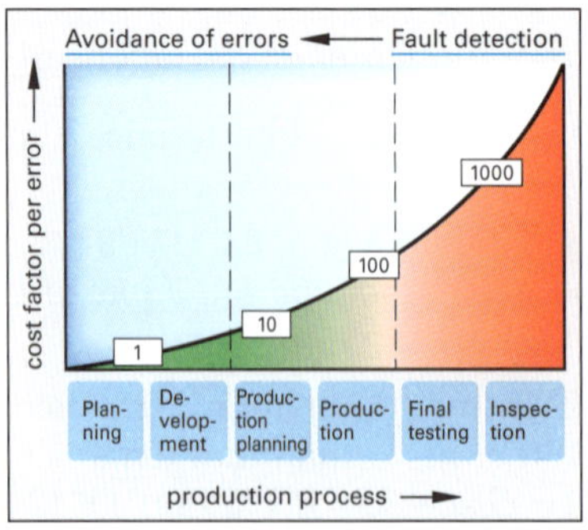

Words	
quality management	Qualitätsmanagement
successful	erfolgreich
to match	erfüllen
satisfaction	Zufriedenheit
customer	Kunde
requirement	Anforderung
appealing	ansprechend
performance	Leistungsfähigkeit
reliability	Zuverlässigkeit
maintainability	Instandhaltungsfähigkeit
customer service	Kundendienst
to certify	zertifizieren
to implement	umsetzen
operating area	Arbeitsbereich
to encompass	umfassen
quality assurance	Qualitätssicherung
quality improvement	Qualitätsverbesserung
to carry out	durchführen
employee	Arbeitnehmer
guideline	Richtlinie
error	Fehler
to detect	erkennen
to decrease	vermindern
quality characteristics	Qualitätsmerkmale
quantitative	mengenmäßig
present	vorhanden
to fulfill	erfüllen
malfunction	Störung
to state	aussagen
sequence	Abfolge
to correct	korrigieren
to multiply by	multiplizieren mit
stage	Phase
avoidance of error	Fehlervermeidung
fault detection	Fehlerentdeckung

Exercises

1. Working with words. Which words from the text are described here?
   a) If the product looks really good, the design is very ______________.
   b) If the device runs without a problem for a long time, it is very ______________.
   c) If the product can be used in many different ways, the ______________ is very high.
2. Translate the definition of quantitative and qualitative characteristics.
3. Answer the following questions in English.
   a) Which 3 quality characteristics (= requirement of the customer) should your next smart phone have?
   b) Which system supports the quality process in companies?
   c) What does the 1-10-100 rule describe?
   d) Which different stages appear in a product circle?

2.2 Quality tools

In order to fulfill the quality requirements in a company, quality tools are used. They are often graphical aids, such as diagrams and charts, because they are easy to understand for the staff members and give a quick overview about the process or the measuring results. Besides, the employees are involved in the improvement process.

Graphical aids

The **defect chart** is a simple method to list and detect different errors in a production process **(figure)**. The tally marks of the errors are sorted and counted up. This information forms the base for the Pareto analysis.

Defect chart

Type of defect	Oct.	Nov.	Dec.	Σ
workpiece tilted	𝍸 |||	|||	𝍸 ||	18
handling defect	𝍸 𝍸		𝍸 𝍸 ||	𝍸 𝍸 𝍸	38
control defect	|||	||||	||	9
loose workpiece	𝍸 𝍸 𝍸		𝍸 𝍸 𝍸 ||	𝍸 𝍸 ||	45
torn-off e-cable					1
Total defects	38	37	36	111

The **Pareto chart** shows the frequency of different defects **(figure)**. They are sorted by their importance. The bars indicate the type and the frequency of the defects. The line displays the cumulative total of the errors. The purpose of the chart is to highlight the most freuently occurring error. It gives an idea of which problems should be solved immediately to improve the process most efficiently.

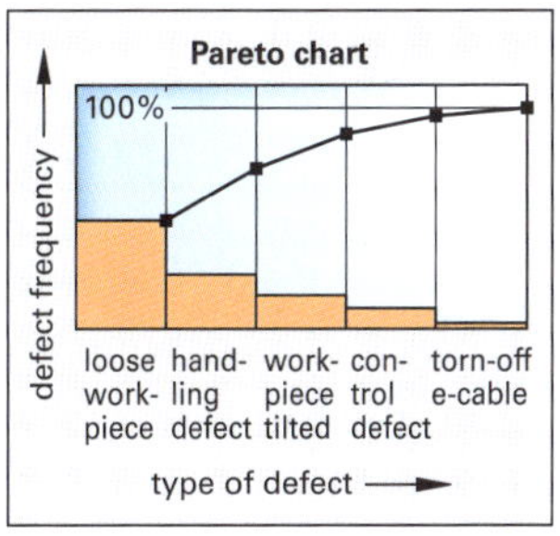

The **cause-and-effect diagram**, also called fishbone chart or Ishikawa diagram is used to find the causes of problems. It combines the techniques of brainstorming with a type of mind map. It considers all possible causes of a problem rather than just the ones that are most obvious. The main branches of the fishbone-skeleton are for example the 6 Ms: **m**anpower, **m**achine, **m**ethod, **m**aterial, **m**ilieu, **m**easurement.

In order to draw a histogram, a **tally sheet** to summarise data is used **(figure)**. In a tally sheet all the classes with their values are listed. The tally marks are added, sorted according to the values and counted up.

Tally sheet (extract)

class nr.	measured value *D* in mm	frequency	Σ
1	8.00 – 8.02			1
2	8.02 – 8.04	𝍸 ||||	9
3	8.04 – 8.06	𝍸 𝍸 𝍸		16

The **histogram** is a bar chart and shows the distribution of measured results **(figure)**. It indicates the frequency of data within a range of values, called a class. The frequency of the data that falls in each class is displayed by the height of the bar.

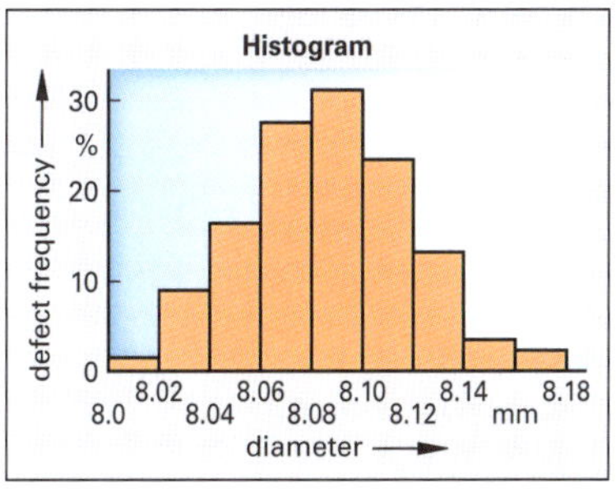

Words

English	German
quality tools	Qualitätswerkzeuge
requirement	Anforderung
graphical aids	zeichnerische Hilfsmittel
chart	Schaubild
staff member	Mitarbeiter
employee	Arbeitnehmer
to be involved	miteinbezogen sein
improvement	Verbesserung
defect chart	Fehlersammelliste
to list	aufführen
to detect	erkennen
tally marks	Zählstriche
Pareto analysis	Paretoanalyse
frequency	Häufigkeit
importance	Wichtigkeit
bar	Balken
cumulative total	kumulierte Gesamtzahl
purpose	Zweck
to highlight	hervortreten
to occur	auftreten
immediately	sofort
cause-and-effect diagram	Ursache-Wirkungs-Diagramm
fishbone	Fischgräte
brainstorming	Ideensammlung
mind map	Gedankenstütze
cause	Ursache
obvious	offensichtlich
main branch	Hauptast
skeleton	Skelett
manpower	Arbeitskraft
histogram	Histogramm
tally sheet	Strichliste
to summarise	zusammenfassen
to count up	aufaddieren
bar chart	Säulendiagramm
distribution	Verteilung
frequency	Häufigkeit
range	Spannweite
to display	anzeigen

Exercises

1. Answer the questions:
   a) Which two type of graphs are used in a Pareto chart?
   b) Why is the Ishikawa diagram also fishbone diagram?
   c) What is meant by the 6 Ms?
   d) Which function has a tally sheet?
   e) What is shown in a histogram?
   f) What shows the height of a bar in a histogram?
2. Draw a histogram on an extra sheet of paper by using the data below.

Length of the shaft in mm

Measured values	14.990	14.995	15.000	15.005	15.010	15.015	15.020	15.025	15.030	15.035
Frequency n_i	2	5	10	13	15	16	13	9	6	3

2.3 Normal distribution

If you look at nature or your working environment you realise that the values of some quantities do not have all an exact number, e.g. the height of humans or the measured size of produced components. Their values are distributed around a mean value.

The mathematician *Carl Friedrich Gauss* recognised, that data, which only depends on random influences is distributed in a certain way. It is called normal distribution or Gaussian distribution.

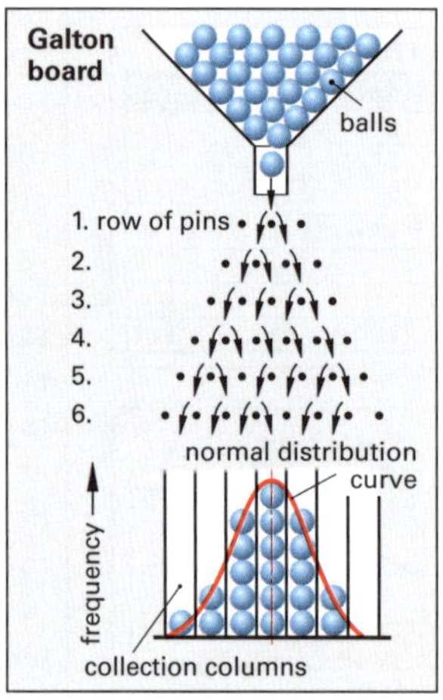

Another scientist, *Francis Galton*, demonstrated this phenomenon by a machine called the Galton board **(figure)**.

The machine consists of a vertical board with rows of pins, which are arranged in staggered order. The front of the device is covered with a glass pane to allow watching the different paths of the balls. Then balls are dropped from the top, and bounce randomly either to the left side or the right side as they touch the pins. At the end, they are collected into one-ball-wide columns at the bottom.

The different heights of the ball columns show a curve in the shape of a bell. It is named the bell curve, the Gaussian distribution curve or the normal distribution curve.

The **normal distribution curve** is reached when measured data values are only influenced by random parameters.

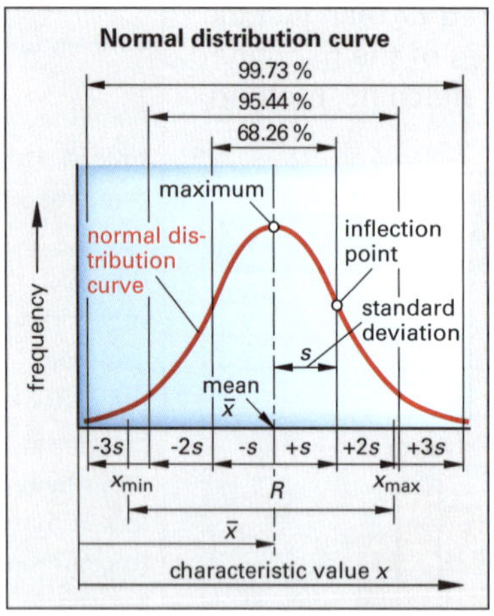

The curve is symmetrical with a maximum at the mean value, decreasing to both sides **(figure)**. They have an inflection point at each side.

The bell-shaped curve is defined by two characteristic parameters:

a) The mean $\bar{x}$ at the peak of the curve.

b) The standard deviation *s* represents the distance from the mean to the inflection point and shows how values deviate from the mean.

The height of the normal distribution curve characterizes the frequency of the values. The area below the curve from $-s$ to $+s$ includes 68.28 % of the values, from $-2s$ to $+2s$ there are 95.44 %.

Words	
normal distribution	Normalverteilung
working environment	Arbeitsumfeld
quantity	Mengen
number	Wert
height	Größe
human	Mensch
to distribute	verteilen
random influences	zufällige Einflüsse
normal distribution	Normalverteilung
Gaussian distribution	Gauß'sche Verteilung
scientist	Wissenschaftler
phenomenon	Phänomen
Galton board	Galton Brett
row of pins	Nagelreihe
staggered order	versetzt angeordnet
front	Vorderseite
device	Gerät
to cover	bedecken
glass pane	Glasscheibe
to allow	erlauben
path	Weg, Pfad
to drop	herunterfallen
top	oberes Ende
to bounce	abprallen
randomly	zufallsbedingt
to touch	berühren
to collect	sammeln
bottom	unteres Ende
shape of a bell	Glockenform
to decrease	abnehmen
inflection point	Wendepunkt
application	Anwendung
to propose	aufstellen
mean	Mittelwert
peak	Höchstwert
standard deviation	Standardabweichung
bell-shaped curve	Glockenkurve
to deviate	abweichen
frequency	Häufigkeit
construction	Aufbau
procedure	Durchführung
result	Ergebnis

Exercises

1. Give three examples of nature or technology in which data can be normally distributed.
2. Explain the experimental principle of a Galton board in German. Use the following structure:
   a) Construction of the board b) Experimental procedure c) Experimental result
2. Translate the sentences according the normal distribution into English:
   a) Die Normalverteilung entsteht, wenn viele zufallsbedingte Einflüsse wirksam sind.
   b) Sie zeigt eine typische Glockenkurve der Häufigkeit über dem Merkmal $\bar{x}$.
   c) Der Mittelwert $\bar{x}$ liegt beim Kurvenmaximum und zeigt die Lage der Verteilung.
   d) Die Standardabweichung kennzeichnet die Streuung, d.h. die Verteilung um den Mittelwert.

2.4 Statistical characteristics of data quantities

If a list of measured values results in a normal distribution curve, you can define and calculate statistical characteristics. They are helpful to display an average value or the spreading of data values.

Characteristics for describing the average value of a quantity of data give a representative mean value of data. The most common are the arithmetic mean and the median value.

The **arithmetic mean** $\bar{x}$ of a row of data is calculated as the sum of the individual data divided by the number of the data.

Arithmetic mean $\bar{x}$
$\bar{x} = \dfrac{x_1 + x_2 + x_3 + \ldots + \bar{x}_n}{n}$

$x_1, x_2, \ldots$ are the individual values of a row of data
n is the number of data

The **median** $\tilde{x}$ is the middle value of a row of data which are arranged in ascending sequence. For odd number of data, it is the value in the middle of the sequence (marked in red).

For even number of data, the median is calculated by the mean of the two values in the middle of the sequence.

Median $\tilde{x}$
For odd number of values:
$x_1, x_2, x_3, x_4, x_5, x_6, x_7, x_8, x_9$
$\tilde{x} = x_5$
For even number of values:
$x_1, x_2, x_3, x_4, x_5, x_6, x_7, x_8$
$\tilde{x} = \dfrac{(x_4 + x_5)}{2}$

Example: The following values of the density of an alloyed steel are listed in kg/dm³:

7.862 7.873 7.852 7.879 7.857 7.866 7.869

Which arithmetic mean $\bar{x}$ does the row of data have?

Solution:

$$\bar{x} = \frac{x_1 + x_2 + x_3 + \ldots}{7} = \frac{7.862 + 7.873 + 7.852 + \ldots}{7} = \mathbf{7.865}$$

Characteristics for the spreading of the data values are the range and the standard deviation.

The **range** R is the difference between the highest (x_{max}) and the lowest value (x_{min}).

Range R
$R = x_{max} - x_{min}$

The **standard deviation** s is a measure for the amount of variation from the average. A low standard deviation indicates that the measured values tend to be very close to the mean; a high standard deviation indicates that the values are spread out over a large range.

s standard deviation
x_1, x_2 individual values
n number of values

Standard deviation s
$s = \sqrt{\dfrac{(x_1 - \bar{x})^2 + (x_2 - \bar{x})^2 + \ldots + (x_n - \bar{x})^2}{n - 1}}$

Words (English)	Words (German)
statistical	statistisch
characteristic	Kennwert
data quantity(ies)	Datenmenge(n)
list of measured values	Messwertreihe
to define	definieren
spreading	Streuung
data value	Datenwert
average value	Mittelwert
quantity of data	Datenmenge
representative	repräsentativ
mean value	Mittelwert
most common	häufigste
arithmetic mean	arithmetisches Mittel
median value	Medianwert
row of data	Datenreihe
individual data	Einzelwert
to divide	teilen
number	Anzahl
to arrange	ordnen
ascending	aufsteigend
sequence	Reihenfolge
odd number	ungerade Zahl
even number	gerade Zahl
density	Dichte
solution	Lösung
range	Spannweite
standard deviation	Standardabweichung
measure	Maß
amount	Betrag, Höhe
variation	Abweichung
to tend	neigen
close	eng
spread out	weit verteilt
sampling test	Stichprobe
diameter	Durchmesser
nominal value	Nennwert

Exercises

1. Translate the definition in German of
   a) the arithmetic mean b) the median c) the range

2. Your company inspects the diameter of produced shafts, nominal value = 19 +/– 0.001 mm.
   The result of a sampling test is presented in the following table:

Diameter of shafts						
Measured value in mm	18.999	19.000	19.001	19.002	19.003	19.998
Number of values	3	6	8	5	2	4

Calculate the following values by using a calculator:
a) the mean value $\bar{x}$ b) the range R c) the standard deviation s d) the median $\tilde{x}$

2.5 Machine capability

A machine capability describes the capability of an automatic production machine to manufacture faultless parts within the required tolerance limits under constant production conditions in a preliminary run.

The **machine capability test (MCT)** is necessary to start and use quality control charts within a statistical process control (SPC). It is carried out after the set-up or installation of a new machine, after the repair of an existing machine or in a new process before the release of series production.

The MTC is a short term study with at least 50 manufactured parts in a test run. The measured values, e.g. the diameter of a produced shaft, are recorded and evaluated. If the values are normal distributed, you can determine characteristic values such as e.g. the arithmetic mean $\bar{x}$ or the standard deviation s. They are necessary to calclulate the machine capability indexes C_m and C_{mk} within the required tolerance limits (LLV and ULV).

The **machine capability index C_m** is a characteristic, if the measured values of the produced parts are:

- arranged in the middle of tolerance
- within the tolerance limits LLV and ULV **(figure)**

It is calculated by the formula:

$$C_m = \frac{T}{6 \cdot s} = \frac{ULV - LLV}{6 \cdot s}$$

T tolerance (ULV–LLV)

ULV upper limit value

LLV lower limit value

s standard deviation

For fulfilling the machine capability condition, the index C_m must be: $C_m \geq 1.67$

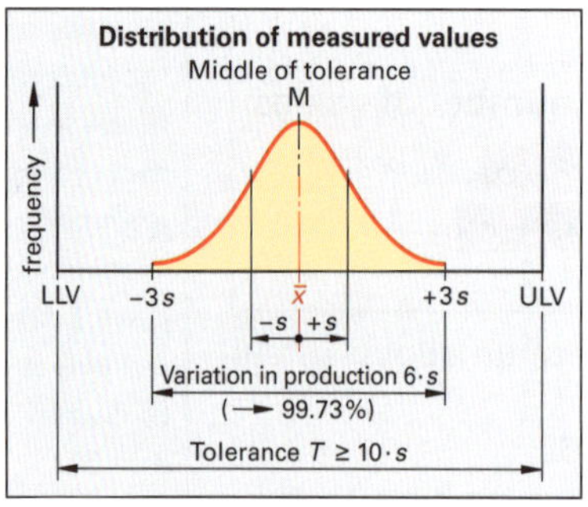

The **machine capability index C_{mk}** is a characteristic, if the measured values of the produced parts lie in the middle of the tolerance range **(figure)**.

It is calculated by the formula:

$$C_{mk} = \frac{\Delta crit}{3 \cdot s}$$

$\Delta crit$ the smallest value between mean $\bar{x}$ and a tolerance limit

For fulfilling the machine capability condition, the index C_{mk} must be: $C_{mk} \geq 1.67$

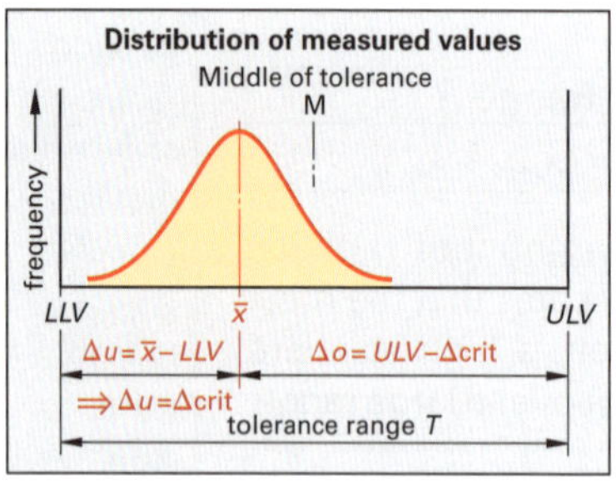

If the conditions $C_m \geq 1.67$ and $C_{mk} \geq 1.67$ are fulfilled, the automatic production machine is capable to produce parts with dimensions within the required tolerance.

Words	
machine capability	Maschinenfähigkeit
faultless parts	fehlerfreie Teile
required	gefordert
tolerance limit	Toleranzgrenze
preliminary run	Probelauf
machine capability test (MCT)	Maschinenfähigkeits-untersuchung (MFU)
necessary	notwendig
machine capability index	Maschinenfähigkeits-index
characteristic	Kennwert
quality control chart	Qualitätsregelkarte
statistical process control	Statistische Prozess-regelung (SPC)
set-up	Einrichten
repair	Reparatur
release of series production	Serienfreigabe
short term study	Kurzzeituntersuchung
at least	wenigstens
to record	erfassen
to evaluate	auswerten
to determine	bestimmen
to arrange	(an)ordnen
formula	Formel, Gleichung
upper limit value	oberer Grenzwert
lower limit value	unterer Grenzwert
to fulfill	erfüllen
to lie (lay, lain)	liegen

Exercises

1. Translate the following sentences into English:
   a) Maschinenfähigkeitsuntersuchungen (MFU) werden vor dem Einsatz von Maschinen, bei Maschinenabnahme sowie nach umfangreichen Wartungsarbeiten und Reparaturen eingesetzt.
   b) Die MFU wird über einen längeren Zeitraum durchgeführt.
   c) Bei der MFU werden in einem Vorlauf zur Fertigung mindestens 25 Teile gefertigt und ihre Maße geprüft.
   d) Der Mittelwert, die Spannweite und Toleranz sind wichtige Werte zur Auswertung der MFU.
   e) Zur Auswertung der MFU werden die gemessenen Maße der gefertigten Teile als Normalverteilungskurve in ein Koordinatensystem gezeichnet und der Mittelwert $\bar{x}$, die Spannweite R, die Standardabweichung s und die Toleranz T eingetragen.
2. In the sentences of exercise 1 are three wrong statements. Find and correct them.

2.6 Process capability

The process capability gives some information, if an automatic production process is capable to produce faultless and accurate components over a long-term period. The process capability test is carried out before introducing a new production process or before starting to control a process by quality control charts.

The **process capability test (PCT)** respects the influence of the five 5 Ms in production: **m**an, **m**achine, **m**ethods, **m**aterial, and **m**easurements of the environment.

In order to carry out the PCT, you take at least 25 random samples out of the current production process with an amount of 5 parts each sample. After the parts have been measured and the data have been documented, the statistical values are calculated: the mean value $\bar{x}$ and the standard deviation s. Next, the process capability can be calculated by taking the required tolerance T into account.

The **process capability C_p** describes the distribution of the measured values along the tolerance range, which are mostly accumulated around the centre. C_p is calculated by the tolerance range T divided by six times of the standard deviation s.

$$C_p = \frac{T}{6 \cdot s} = \frac{ULV - LLV}{6 \cdot s}$$

The process is **capable**, if the index C_p is greater than $C_p > 1.33$.

The process capability C_p does not consider if the process is off-centre. Therefore you use a second characteristic, the **critical process capability C_{pk}**.

It describes how centred the measured values are. It is calculated by the formula adjacent.

$$C_{pk} = \frac{\Delta crit}{3 \cdot s}$$

The process is **consistent**, if the index C_{pk} is greater than $C_{pk} > 1.33$.

The figure below shows different possible values for the process capability indizes C_p and C_{pk} and its position in the tolerance range.

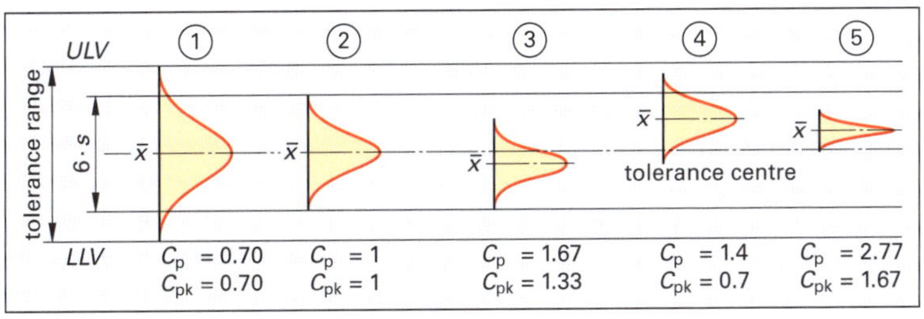

① The curve has a wide, centric distribution and reaches outside of the tolerance limits.
→ The process is **not capable** and **not consistent.**

② + ③ + ⑤ The curves have a narrow distribution, lie partially off-centre but inside the tolerance limits.
→ The process is **capable** and **consistent**.

④ The curve has a narrow, off-centre distribution and reaches outside of the tolerance limits.
→ The process is **capable** but **not consistent**.

Words (English)	Words (German)
process capability	Prozessfähigkeit
capable	fähig
faultless	fehlerfrei
accurate	genau
long-term period	langfristiger Zeitraum
process capability test	Maschinenfähigkeits-untersuchung
to carry out	durchführen
to introduce	einführen
to control	steuern
quality control charts	Qualitätsregelkarte
to respect	berücksichtigen
influence	Einfluss
environment	Umwelt
random sample	Zufallsstichprobe
current	laufend
amount	Menge
next	als Nächstes
to take into account	beachten
distribution	Verteilung
tolerance range	Toleranzbereich
to accumulate	sich häufen
off-centre	außermittig
centred	zentriert
adjacent	nebenstehend
consistent	beherrscht
wide	breit
centric	mittig
narrow	eng
required	gefordert

Exercises

1. Find the missing word from the text above:
   a) The "*C*" in the process capability indexes C_p and C_{pk} stands for ______________________.
   b) The process capability is carried out within a ______________________ period.
   c) The difference between the upper limit value (*ULV*) and the lower limit value (*LLV*) is called the ______________________.
   d) If parts are produced in the required quality without faulty ones in a long term the process is ______________________.
   e) The process capability C_p doesn't consider if the curve is off- ________.

2. Explain, why the curve (4) in the figure above is capable but not consistent.

2.7 Statistical process control with quality control chart

Statistical process control (SPC) is used in series production for measuring and controlling quality during the manufacturing process. It is a procedure which uses statistical calculations and graphical aids such as quality control charts.

With the representation of measured values in a control chart the process can be assessed if it is stable or unstable and if the products fulfil the specifications within the limits of the tolerances.

Structure of a quality control chart

A quality control chart is a special diagram to control the quality of produced parts. It has a typical structure **(figure).** The x-axis represents the sample number or the time.

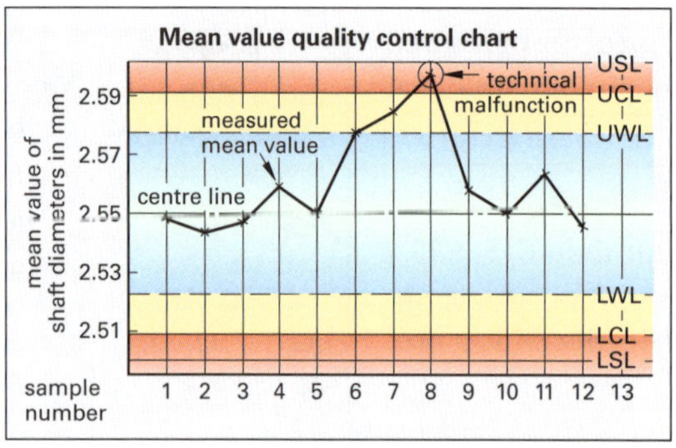

The y-axis shows the measured values. A horizontal central line is a reference to mark shifts or trends of the process.

The limit lines limit the diagram: an upper and lower warning line (UWL, LWL) an upper and lower control line (UCL, LCL) and an upper and lower customer specification line (USL, LSL).

The measured values are marked by a cross and connected by a line. ⇒ The course of the graph can be recognized immediately.
The purpose of SPC by quality control charts is:
- to reduce variability of the produced dimensions and scrap
- to improve productivity by reducing costs and production time
- to react immediately to process deviation (faulty parts)

Types of quality control charts

The **raw data chart** is a documentation of all measured values. Samples with 5 values each are entered in the chart. It is used if only a few values are present and if a quick overview of the process is necessary.

In the **mean chart** (figure above) statistical quantities such as the mean value $\bar{x}$ of several samples are calculated and plotted along the y-axis. The **standard deviation chart** shows the calculated standard deviation along the y-axis.

Very common are two-track control charts with one chart on top of the other. The **mean $\bar{x}$ – standard deviation s – control chart** or the **median value $\tilde{x}$ – range R control chart.**

Words (English)	Words (German)
statistical process control (SPC)	statistische Prozessregelung
quality control chart	Qualitatsregelkarte
series production	Serienproduktion
procedure	Verfahren
graphical aid	grafisches Hilfsmittel
representation	Darstellung
to assess	beurteilen
stable	stabil
to fulfil	erfüllen
specification	Anforderungen
structure	Aufbau
sample number	Stichprobennummer
reference	Bezug
shift	Veränderung
limit line	Grenzlinie
warning line	Warngrenze
control line	Eingriffsgrenze
customer specification	Kundenanforderung
cross	Kreuz
course	Verlauf
to recognize	erkennen
immediately	sofort
purpose	Zweck
variability	Schwankung
scrap	Ausschuss
to improve	verbessern
deviation	Abweichung
raw data chart	Urwertkarte
to enter	eintragen
mean chart	Mittelwertkarte
standard deviation chart	Standardabweichungskarte
two-track	zweispurig
on top of the other	übereinander

Exercises

1. Translate the purpose of using control charts in series production into German.
2. Your company produces shafts at CNC turning machine. The diameter of the shaft can be taken out of the technical drawing: 30 ± 0.05 mm. Besides you have the following limits given below:
   Upper control limit: 29.07 mm Upper warning limit: 29.08 mm
   Lower control limit: 30.03 mm Lower warning limit: 30.02 mm

   The mean diameter from each sampling lot can be taken out of the table below:

sampling lot	1	2	3	4	5	6	7	8	9	10	11	12
mean diameter	30.01	30.02	29.08	30.00	29.08	29.09	30.01	30.02	30.01	30.00	29.09	29.09

   a) Draw a mean chart (see figure in text above) and label the different axis and limits.
   b) Add the measured values of the table into the chart and connect them by lines.

The most common control charts use a two-track control chart. One chart to control the average process course and the second chart to show the variations in the process. So you have two aids to describe the same process. This increases the chance to check if the process is out of control or to mark the causes of variations.

Median value – range-chart ($\tilde{x}$ – *R-chart*)

Inspect characteristic: diameter	Control dimension: 5±0.05			
Sample size: $n = 5$	Control-interval: 60 min			
Measurem. values mm x_1	4.98	4.96	5.03	4.97
x_2	4.97	4.99	5.01	4.96
x_3	4.99	5.03	5.02	5.01
x_4	5.01	4.99	4.99	4.99
x_5	5.01	5.00	4.98	5.02
Σx	24.96	24.97	25.03	24.95
$\tilde{x}$	4.99	4.99	5.01	4.99
R	0.04	0.07	0.05	0.06

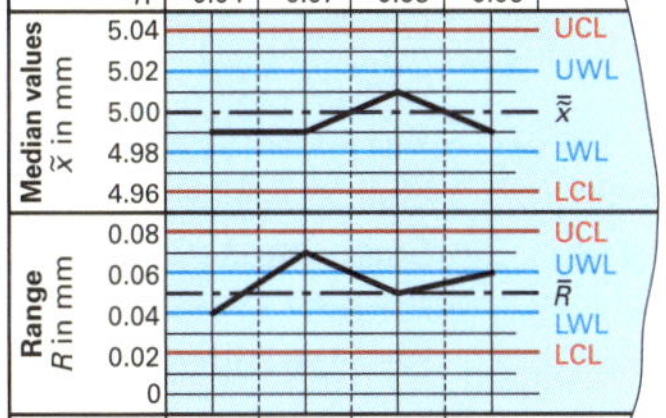

Sample no.	1	2	3	4
Time	6⁰⁰	7⁰⁰	8⁰⁰	9⁰⁰

The upper chart shows the individual measured median value $\tilde{x}$ of mostly small sample sizes of odd number **(figure)**. The lower chart plots the range values. These values can be easily calculated. This combination control chart is widely used to examine the stability of processes in many industries and can be used for manual control chart management.

Mean-standard deviation-chart ($\bar{x}$ – *s-chart*)

Inspect characteristic: diameter	Control dimension: 5±0.05			
Sample size: $n = 5$	Control-interval: 60 min			
Measurem. values mm x_1	4.98	4.96	5.03	4.97
x_2	4.97	4.99	5.01	4.96
x_3	4.99	5.03	5.02	5.01
x_4	5.01	4.99	4.99	4.99
x_5	5.01	5.00	4.98	5.02
$\bar{x}$	4.992	4.994	5.006	4.990
s	0.018	0.025	0.021	0.025

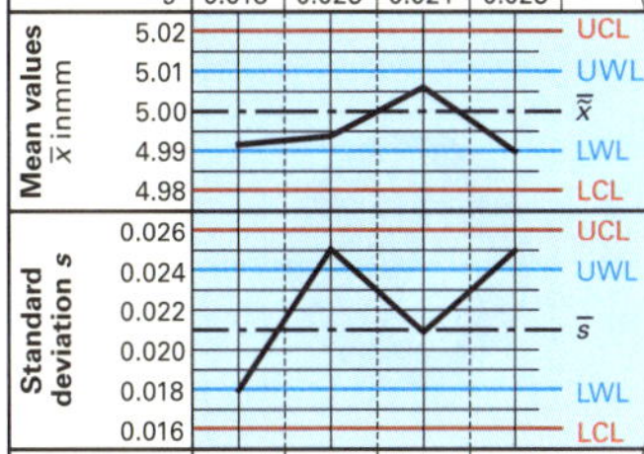

Sample no.	1	2	3	4
Time	6⁰⁰	7⁰⁰	8⁰⁰	9⁰⁰

The upper chart indicates the calculated mean value $\bar{x}$ of large sample sizes of even number **(figure)**. The lower chart shows how the data is spread and used to study system variability. This combination control chart exhibits more sensitivity than the $\tilde{x}$ – *R*-chart but it is more complex to calculate and therefore used for computer-aided control chart management.

Interpreting control charts

The course of measured values in quality control charts is not always random (figure on page 24). Sometimes there are typical courses. The process trend helps to identify the cause of the error.

Typical process course	Course name, observation	Possible causes
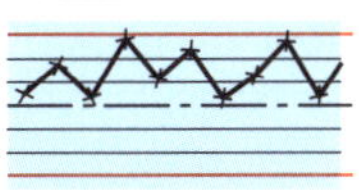 UCL $\bar{x}$ LCL	**Run** 7 or more sequential values lie on one side of the mean line.	– Tool wear – Other material – New tool – New staff
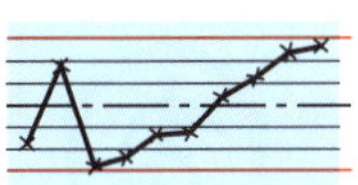 UCL $\bar{x}$ LCL	**Trend** 7 or more sequential values show an increasing or decreasing trend.	– Tool wear – Wear on measuring devices – Operator fatigue
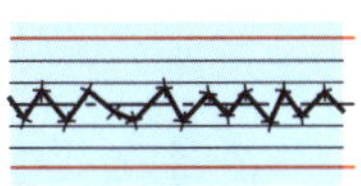 UCL $\bar{x}$ LCL	**Middle Third** At least 15 sequential values lie within the standard deviation s	– Improved production – Better supervision – manipulated test results
 UCL $\bar{x}$ LCL	**Cyclicals** The values cross the mean line periodically	– Oscillating measuring devices – Systematic spread of data

Words	
most common	gebräuchlichst
two-track	zweispurig
average	durchschnittlich
process course	Prozessverlauf
variation	Abweichung
aid	Hilfsmittel
to increase	erhöhen
out of control	unkontrollierbar
to mark	hervorheben
cause	Grund
median value	Medianwert
upper	obere
sample size	Stichprobengröße
odd number	ungerade Zahl
lower	untere
to plot	ausgeben, zeichnen
to calculate	berechnen
to examine	untersuchen
stability	hier: Maßhaltigkeit
manual	manuell
even number	gerade Zahl
to spread	sich verteilen
variability	Schwankungen
to exhibit	darstellen
sensitivity	Empfindlichkeit
complex	kompliziert
computer-aided	rechnergestützt
random	zufällig
process trend	Prozessentwicklung
sequential value	aufeinanderfolgende Werte
mean line	Mittellinie
decreasing trend	fallende Tendenz
cyclicals	Perioden, Zyklen
to cross	überschreiten
tool wear	Werkzeugverschleiß
operator fatigue	Personalermüdung
to improve	verbessern
supervision	Überwachung
manipulated	geschönt
oscillating	schwingend
spread of data	Streuung der Daten

Exercises

1. Answer the following questions in English.
   a) Why are two-track charts, showing two different statistical values, used in control charts?
   b) When do you use a $\tilde{x}$ – *R*-chart and when are $\bar{x}$ – *s*-charts used? Explain!
2. Explain three typical courses in control charts in German by using the information in the table above.

3 Production engineering

3.1 Safety at work

In order to work safely in a workshop or production hall and prevent accidents, every staff member has to follow the accident prevention regulations. These safety rules are issued by the trade associations. These rules will protect you and your colleagues from injury at work and reduce the danger of damaging or breaking the tools or machines.

An important aid to prevent accidents are safety signs.

Safety signs

The safety rules are presented in the form of safety signs with symbols. There are different safety signs.

Mandatory signs

The circular mandatory signs have a blue background and a white symbol, showing necessary safety equipment. They must be used to ensure worker's safety. For example you have to wear protective gloves while spraying **(figure)**.

Prohibitive signs

These round signs show forbidden actions in black on a white background. The rim of the sign is red and it has a red crossbar. For example: In a hall, where highly explosive gases are used, it is prohibited to operate with open flames or to smoke **(figure)**.

Warning signs

The triangular signs are normally yellow with a black symbol and a black rim. They warn of certain hazards or dangerous conditions. In warehouses they indicate where combustible, explosive or toxic substances are stored **(figure)**.

Escape and rescue signs

These signs are square or rectangular with the colours green and white. They point to escape routes and show the emergency exit. They indicate locations, where first aid boxes, defibrillators or other emergency equipment are stored **(figure)**.

Words	
production engineering	Fertigungstechnik
safety	Sicherheit
production hall	Produktionshalle
accident	Unfall
staff member	Mitarbeiter
accident prevention regulation	Unfallverhütungs-vorschrift (UVV)
to issue	erlassen
trade association	Berufsgenossenschaft
to protect	schützen
injury	Verletzung
danger	Gefahr
to damage	beschädigen
safety sign	Sicherheitszeichen
mandatory sign	Gebotszeichen
safety equipment	Sicherheitsausrüstung
circular	rund
protective gloves	Schutzhandschuhe
to spray	lackieren
prohibitive sign	Verbotszeichen
forbidden	verboten
rim	Randzone
crossbar	Querbalken
to prohibit	verbieten
open flames	offene Flamme
warning sign	Warnzeichen
triangular	dreieckig
hazard	Gefahr
warehouse	Lagerhalle
combustible	brennbar
toxic	giftig
escape and rescue sign	Rettungszeichen
square	quadratisch
rectangular	rechteckig
emergency exit	Notausgang
first aid box	Erste-Hilfe-Kasten
rinsing	spülen
fire extinguisher	Feuerlöscher
pedestrian access	Fußgängerdurchgang

Exercises

1. Translate the descriptions.
   Then match it to the signs, e.g. 1 → ***h***.
   *(Use your **Metal Trades Handbook** if necessary)*
   (1) Wear protective gloves
   (2) Eye rinsing equipment
   (3) Fire extinguisher
   (4) Warning: Hazardous area
   (5) No cell phones
   (6) Warning: Corrosive substances
   (7) Wear face protection
   (8) Pedestrian access prohibited
   (9) No forklifts
   (10) Warning: Toxic substances

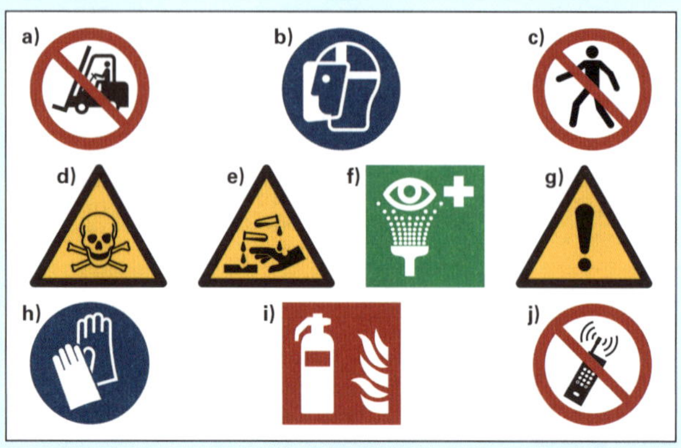

2. Complete the table and describe the safety signs. Give one example of each category.

Safety sign	Geometrical form	Colour	Meaning	Example
Mandatory sign	*round/circular*	***blue**/white*	*You **must wear** the item.*	*Wear gloves*
Prohibitive sign	...	...	...	...

3.2 Prevention of accidents

Accidents are caused by human failure such as unawareness of danger and carelessness but also by technical failure. They can be prevented by respecting any dangers at work.

Human failure
Not every worker is skilled enough or has the appropriate training to use complex tools or machines. Therefore, machine guards or two-hand controls are used to limit the danger of injuries.

Technical failure
It can be caused by material fatigue or wear of a machine component. Maintenance must be carried out in certain intervals and documented.

Safety measures
To keep the amount of accidents in work places as low as possible, safety measures are taken. Therefore any risks of accidents are minimized, hazardous areas are indicated and any danger is reduced.

The three main groups of safety precautions are:

Elimination of hazards
- Any defects on machines, tools and equipment must be reported to the person in duty. They have to be repaired or taken out of service.
- Emergency routes have to be kept free.
- Sharp tools are not allowed to be carried in clothing.
- Jewellery, watches and rings should not be worn while working.

Indication of hazardous areas
- Hazardous areas have to be indicated by safety devices and safety signs. They are not allowed to be removed.
- Components, such as gears and shafts at machine tools are not allowed to rotate without a guard.
- Containers with flammable, explosive or toxic substances inside, have to be indicated and stored in a safe area.

Prevention of dangers
- Safety clothes have to be worn against heat, noise, radiation and flying sparks.
- Face and eyes are protected by wearing safety glasses, face shields, hair net and dust mask or respirator.
- Hands can be protected by safety gloves.
- Ear plugs or ear muffs are necessary against loud noises.
- Safety shoes and an overall or dungarees should be worn the whole time in the workshop.

Words	
prevention	Vermeidung
to cause	verursachen
human failure	menschliches Versagen
unawareness	Unbewusstsein
carelessness	Leichtsinn
technical failure	technisches Versagen
to respect	berücksichtigen
skilled	qualifiziert
appropriate	angemessen
guard	Schutz
injury	Verletzung
material fatigue	Werkstoffermüdung
wear	Verschleiß
maintenance	Wartung
safety measure	Sicherheitsmaßnahme
to minimize	minimieren
precaution	Vorsichtsmaßnahme
elimination	Beseitigung
to report	melden
person in duty	verantwortliche Person
to take out of service	außer Betrieb nehmen
to keep free	freihalten
jewellery	Schmuckstück
indication	Bezeichnung
safety device	Sicherheitseinrichtung
to remove	entfernen
gear	Getriebe
heat	Hitze
noise	Lärm
radiation	Strahlung
spark	Funken
eye	Auge
face shield	Gesichtschutz
hair net	Haarnetz
dust mask	Staubmaske
respirator	Atemschutzgerät
ear plug	Ohrstöpsel
ear muff	Gehörschutz
safety shoes	Sicherheitsschuhe
dungarees	Latzhose
safety device	Sicherheitseinrüstung
milling tool	Fräswerkzeug
to catch	(sich) fangen

Exercises

1. The skilled worker is grinding a workpiece (figure). Label the safety device (1) to (6).

2. Find the three wrong statements and correct them in German.
   a) Accidents are always caused by human failure.
   b) Rotating drills or milling tools can catch long hair into a machine.
   c) Adequate training prevents accidents at the workplace.
   d) Machine guards can reduce the amount of accidents.
   e) Taking medicine or drugs increase your concentration when operating machines.
   f) Material fatigue or the fatigue of the operator are technical failures.

3.3 Overview of manufacturing processes

Manufacturing changes raw materials (blanks) into usable products, for example the different components of the gear box **(figure)**.

The figure shows various parts of the gear box and how they can be produced.

Some parts require more than one manufacturing process.

These processes can be divided into 6 different main groups which create, change or keep the form of a workpiece.

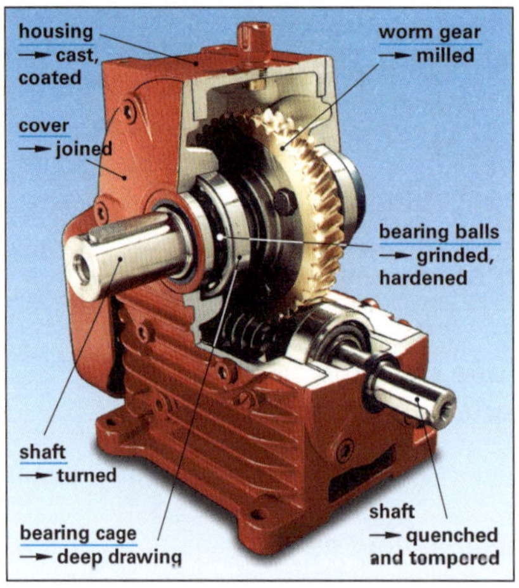

The form of the workpiece					
is created	is changed			is kept	
Primary forming 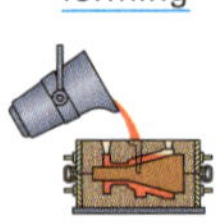	Reforming 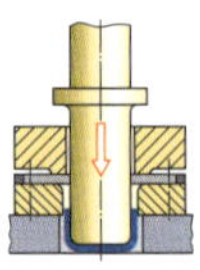	Cutting 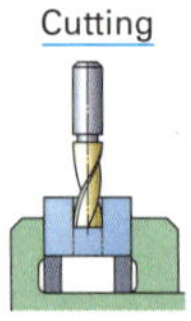	Joining 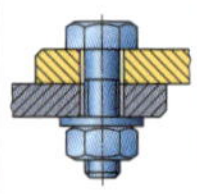	Coating 	Modification of properties 
Description of the process					
The workpiece is made of formless material. The coherence is created in the process.	The form of a solid material is changed by a plastic reforming process.	Workpieces are created by cutting material off the part.	Two or more parts are connected permanently or non-permanently.	A formless material is used to cover the upper layer of a workpiece.	By relocating or adding elements in a workpiece, the properties of the part are changed.
Samples for the manufacturing processes					
– Casting – Extruding – Sintering	– Bending – Rolling – Deep drawing	– Drilling – Milling – Grinding – Thread cutting	– Welding – Soldering – Bonding with adhesives	– Painting – Spraying – Galvanizing	– Hardening – Quenching and tempering – Decarbonisation

Another classification is to distinguish the manufacturing process into:

- **Subtractive manufacturing processes**
  create the required geometry by cutting off unwanted areas, e.g. by drilling, milling or turning
- **Formative manufacturing processes**
  reform a workpiece, e. g. by deep drawing
- **Additive manufacturing processes**
  create the required geometry by combining different atoms or building up workpieces in different layers (generative procedures), e.g. laser sintering, stereolithography, 3D-printing.

Words

manufactung process	Fertigungsverfahren
to change	verwandeln
usable	verwendbar
gear box	Getriebe
various	verschiedenartig
to require	benötigen
to be divided	aufgeteilt sein in
to create	herstellen
to keep	behalten
housing	Gehäuse
cover	Deckel
shaft	Welle
bearing cage	Lagerkäfig
worm gear	Schneckenrad
bearing balls	Lagerkugeln
primary forming	Urformen
reforming	Umformen
cutting	Trennen
joining	Fügen
coating	Beschichten
modification of properties	Stoffeigenschaften ändern
formless	formlos
coherence	Zusammenhalt
solid	fest
permanently	dauerhaft, unlösbar
to cover	bedecken
layer	Schicht
to relocate	umlagern
to add	hinzufügen
casting	Gießen
bending	Biegen
rolling	Walzen
deep drawing	Tiefziehen
drilling	Bohren
milling	Fräsen
grinding	Schleifen
thread cutting	Gewindeschneiden
welding	Schweißen
soldering	Löten
bonding with adhesives	Kleben
to galvanize	galvanisieren
to harden	härten
quenching and tempering	Vergüten
decarbonisation	Entkohlen
to distinguish	unterteilen
subtractive	abtragend
formative	formativ
additive	zusammenfügend
stereolithography	Stereolithographie
3 D-printing	3 D-Drucker
key fob	Schlüsselanhänger
machined	bearbeitet
bracket	Bügel
nut	Mutter

Exercises

1. Describe the production of a **key fob** (figure) and name the manufacturing processes (main group and exact process) which are needed here.
   a) Which processes are needed to produce the machined steel plate?
   b) Which processes are needed for the bracket?
   c) What is the reason to use a nut here?

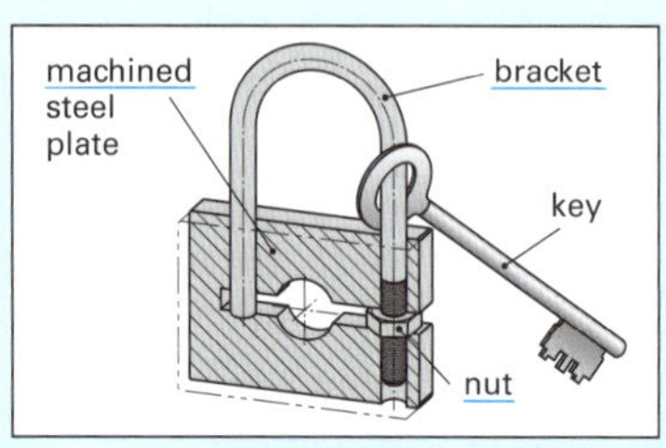

2. Translate the table of the description of the manufacturing processes into German.

3.4 Casting

Mechanical parts are produced by casting if there are several requirements:
- the part has a complex design **(figure)**
- there is no other efficient way to produce it
- the special characteristics of cast materials are important, e.g. good sliding properties.

Cast motor block

Casting means to pour molten metal into a cavity of a mould which has the shape of the desired part.

The common casting method is **expendable casting (figure).** The mould consists of a drag box and a cope box and inside a core. The mould is normally handmade of sand with a binder. The melt is poured through the downsprue in the cavity of the mould until it is filled. After solidification, the mould and core are destroyed and the casting is deformed **(figure).**

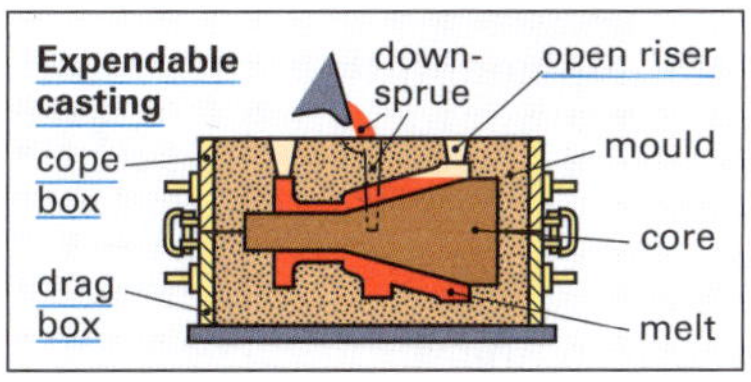

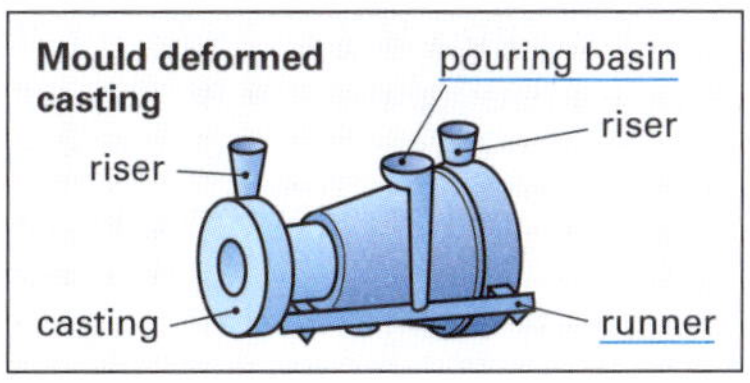

If great numbers of castings are produced, the moulding process is carried out by moulding machines. The moulding procedure is the same, but made by an automated moulding system. The moulding material is compressed evenly: the moulding form is more accurate than by hand moulding.

The cast products, poured in automatically produced casting moulds, are more accurate and have a higher surface quality than castings from hand-formed moulds.

Permanent mould casting is used, if a high number of non-metal cast are produced. The moulds are made of alloyed steel or iron-cast materials. In die casting, the molten metal is pressed into the heated form under high pressure and high speed. By this procedure, products with a small wall thickness can be manufactured e.g. motor blocks or crankcases for engines.

The different casting procedures vary if moulds are used, reused or lost **(figure).**

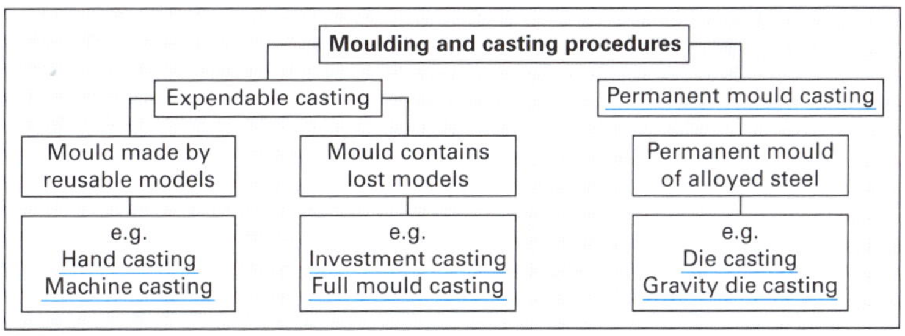

Words

English	German
casting	Gießen, Gussstück
requirement	Anforderung
efficient	effizient
sliding property	Gleiteigenschaft
to pour	gießen
cavity	Hohlraum
mould	Form
expendable casting	Gießen in verlorene Form
drag box	Unterkasten
cope box	Oberkasten
core	Kern
binder	Bindemittel
melt	Schmelze
downsprue	Einguss
solidification	Erstarren
to destroy	zerstören
casting	Gussstück
to deform	ausformen
pouring basin	Eingussstumpf
riser	Speiser
runner	Lauf
great number	große Anzahl
moulding procedure	Formverfahren
to compress	verdichten
evenly	gleichmäßig
permanent mould casting	Gießen in Dauerformen
iron-cast material	Gusswerkstoff
wall thickness	Wandstärke
motor block	Motorblock
crankcase	Kurbelgehäuse
to vary	sich unterscheiden
to reuse	wieder verwenden
to lose, lost, lost	verlieren
hand casting	Handguss
machine casting	Maschinenguss
investment casting	Feingießen
full mould casting	Vollformgießen
permanent mould casting	Gießen in Dauerformen
die casting	Druckgießen
gravity die casting	Kokillengießen

Exercises

1. Label the components in the right figure a) to g)
2. Answer the questions.
   a) What are three reasons for casting workpieces?
   b) What are the differences in expendable and permanent moulding processes?
   a) What are the advantages of automated moulding processes?

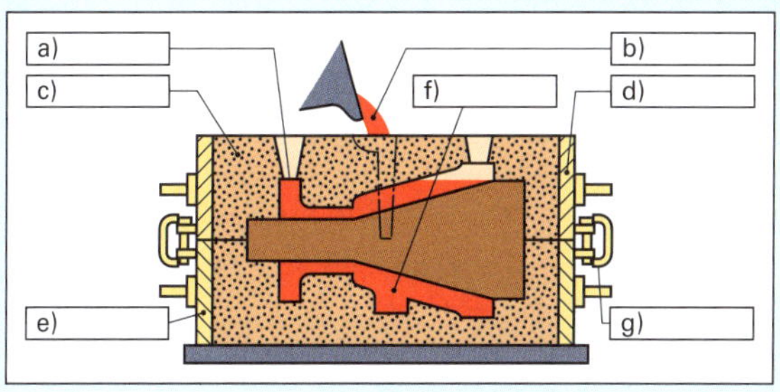

3.5 Reforming

Many pieces are produced by plastic deformation of a base part in reforming processes.

These workpieces can be produced more cost-efficiently by reforming than by other production techniques.

Besides, in case of cold reforming, the mechanical properties of the material are improved by the reforming process e.g. the yield strength or the fatigue strength.

Reforming techniques can be used with suitable materials such as unalloyed soft steels e.g. C10 or soft aluminium materials such as EN AW-AlMn1. They have a wide range of reforming strain. It is the red marked area in the stress-strain-curve **(figure)**.

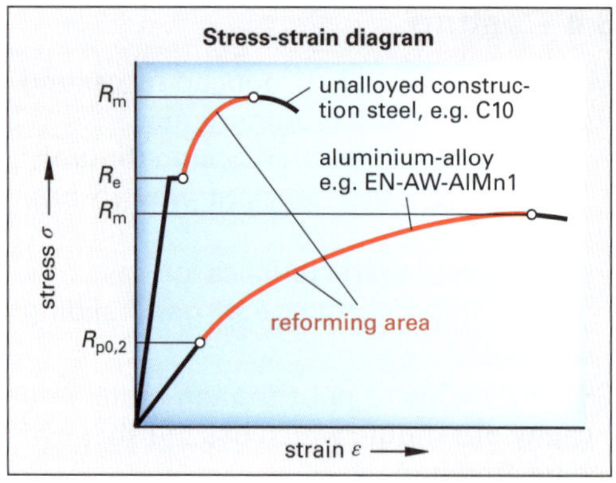

The reforming processes can be divided by the types and the direction of the operating forces:

- Bend-reforming
- Pressure reforming
- Push-pull-reforming
- Die forging, extrusion moulding

Some reforming processes are operated at room temperature, such as bend reforming. Others are processed at forging temperature of the material e.g. die forging or extrusion moulding.

Bend reforming

For producing bent components, a prepared base part is bent in the required form **(figure)**. It can be realized by hand tools, special devices or machines.

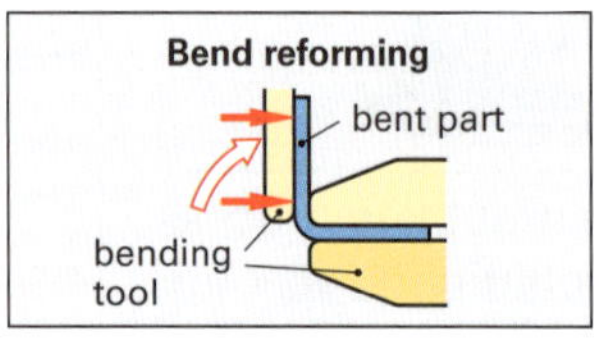

The developed length L of bent parts with small bending radii is the sum of the single parts l_1, l_2, l_3 **(figure)** and a bend allowance v :

$L = l_1 + l_2 + l_3 - n \cdot v$

n is the number of bends.

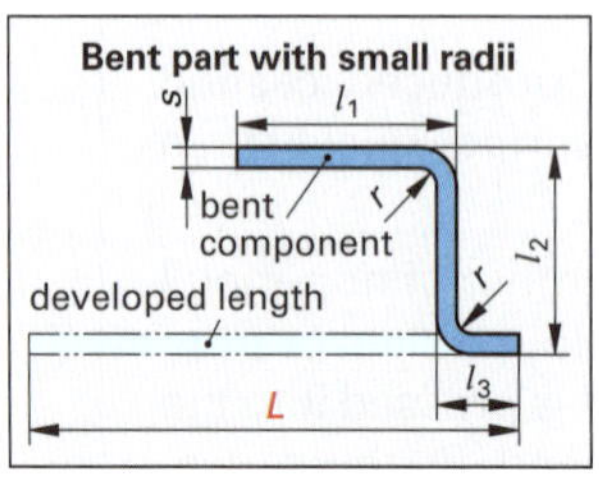

At bent components with big bending radii the developed length L is the sum of the overall length of the neutral line **(figure)**: $L = l_1 + l_2 + l_3$

To avoid cracks in the bending zone, the bending radius r has to be over a minimum radius. It depends on the material and the sheet thickness (Metal Trade Handbook).

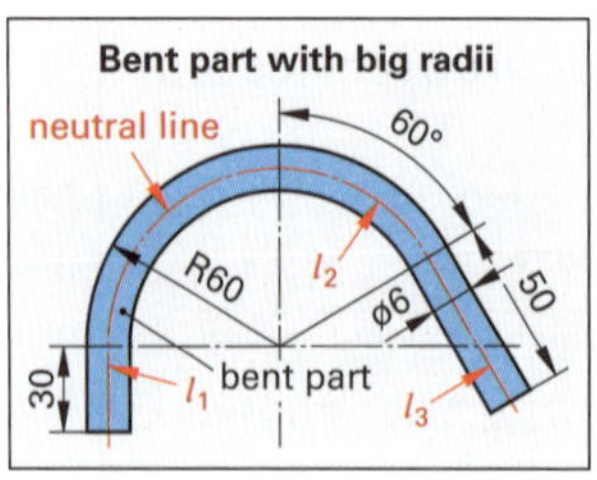

Besides, springback has to be considered to achieve the required bending angle. The component has to be over-bent including the elastic springback. A bending die with a lower bending angle has to be used.

Deep drawing

When deep drawing, a metal sheet blank is reformed in several drawing steps to create a hollow body **(figure)**. The blank diameter D of the sheet metal depends on the geometry of the component. The dimensional change in one drawing step is described by the drawing ratio β. It is represented by $\boldsymbol{\beta = D/d_1}$

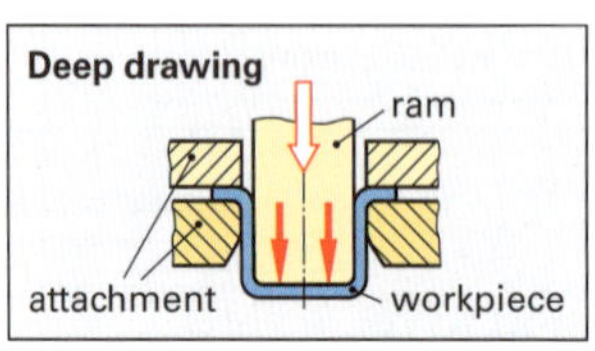

There are different drawing ratios, during certain drawing steps.

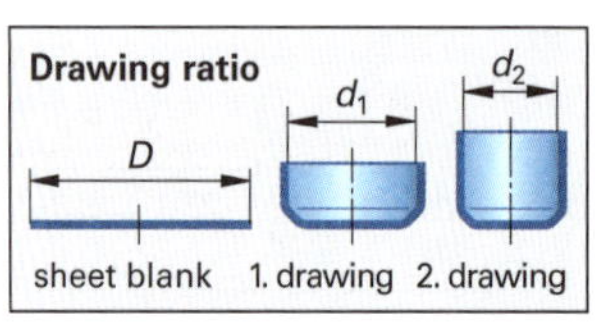

Words

reforming	Umformen
plastic deformation	plastische Verformung
base part	Ausgangsteil
cost-efficient	kostengünstig
to improve	verbessern
yield strength	Streckgrenze
fatigue strength	Dauerfestigkeit
to be used	angewendet werden
suitable	geeignet
range	Bereich
strain	Dehnung
stress-strain curve	Spannungs-Dehnungs-Kurve
to divide	unterteilen
operating force	wirkende Kraft
bend-reforming	Biegeumformen
pressure reforming	Druckumformen
push-pull reforming	Zug-Druck-Umformen
die forging	Gesenkschmieden
extrusion moulding	Strangpressen
to operate	durchführen
forging temperature	Schmiedetemperatur
bent component	Biegeteil
device	Gerät
developed length	gestreckte Länge
bending radius	Biegeradius
plural: bending radii	Plural: Biegeradien
sum	Summe
bend allowance	Biege-Ausgleichswert
neutral line	neutrale Faser
to avoid	vermeiden
crack	Riss
sheet	Blech
springback	Rückfederung
to consider	berücksichtigen
to achieve	erhalten
over-bent	überbogen
deep drawing	Tiefziehen
metal sheet blank	Blechzuschnitt
hollow body	Hohlkörper
blank diameter	Ausgangsdurchmesser
geometry	geometrische Form
dimensional change	Größenänderung
drawing ratio	Ziehverhältnis

Die forging

In die forging processes, the heated raw part is reformed in one step by dynamic pressure forces in a two-piece die **(figure)**. After removing the burr, you get the finished component. The advantages of die forging are:

- Manufacturing of difficult shapes in one step
- High repetition accuracy
- High-strength grain orientation
- Good cost efficiency for mass production components

The disadvantages are the high costs of the forging die.

Extrusion moulding

By extrusion moulding **(figure)** only metal materials with a good flowing behaviour can be processed, such as aluminium or zinc materials.

The raw material is a material block, which is heated at high forging temperature. The ram presses the plastic-flowing material through the moulding tool, which forms the profile. By using a mandrel, it is possible to form hollow profiles.

Internal pressure reforming

In this process, base tube sections are reformed by a hydraulic fluid in a two-piece die **(figure)**. The base tube is placed in the opened moulding die. The die is closed slowly and the tube is filled simultaneously with hydraulic fluid up to a pressure of 4000 bar. The tube gets the internal shape of the die and an open inner face. Complex moulded pipes can be produced.

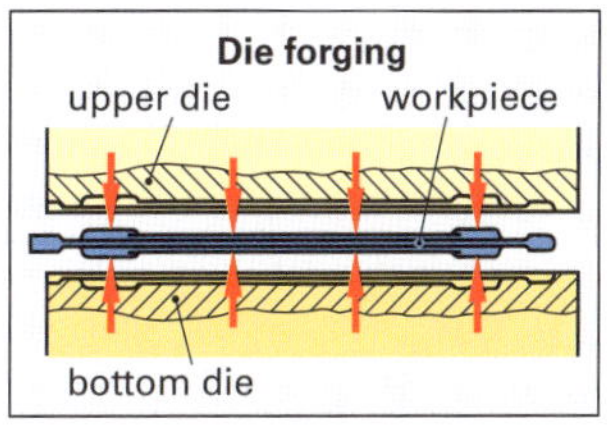

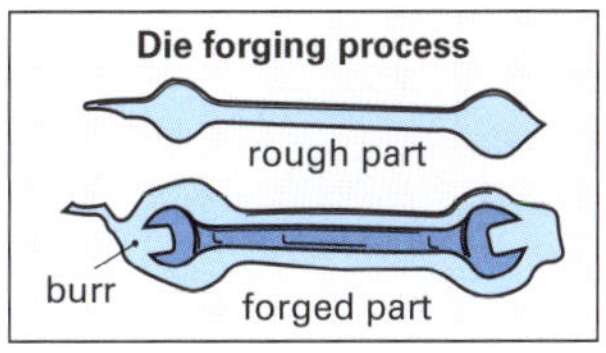

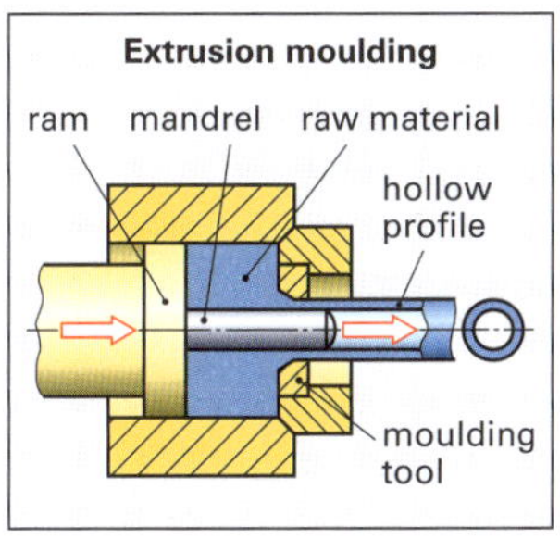

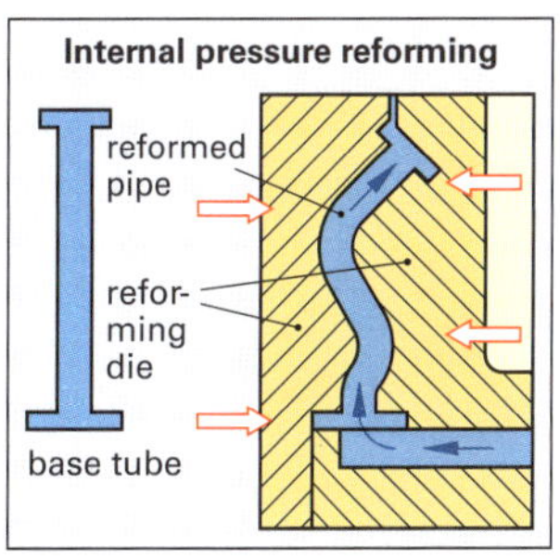

Words

die forging	Gesenkschmieden
raw part	Rohteil
two-piece	zweiteilig
to remove	entfernen
burr	Grat
finished	fertig bearbeitet
advantage	Vorteil
shape	Form
repetition accuracy	Wiederholgenauigkeit
grain orientation	Faserverlauf
mass production	Massenprodukt
component	
disadvantageous	nachteilig
forging die	Schmiedegesenk
extrusion moulding	Strangpressen
flowing behaviour	Fließverhalten
to process	verarbeiten
ram	Druckstempel
moulding tool	Formwerkzeug
profile	Profil
mandrel	Dorn
internal pressure reforming	Innendruck-Umformen
base tube section	Ausgangs-Rohrabschnitt
hydraulic fluid	Hydraulikflüssigkeit
to place	einlegen
simultaneous	gleichzeitig
internal shape	Innenform
inner face	Innenseite
moulded	geformt
pipe	Rohrleitung

Exercises

1. Name the English technical terms for
   a) Plastische Verformung b) Streckgrenze c) Biegeumformen d) Gesenkschmieden
   e) Biegeteil f) Neutrale Faser g) Tiefziehen h) Ausgangsdurchmesser
2. Complete the following sentences
   a) Die forging is processed at _______________ temperature.
   b) The partial springback of a bent sheet section is called _______________.
   c) To get the finished part by die forging, you have to remove the _______________.
   d) By internal pressure reforming, tube sections are reformed to _______________.
3. Answer the following questions in English:
   a) Which mechanical values (stress-strain diagram) are important for reforming?
   b) Which mechanical properties of the material are improved by cold reforming?
   c) Which components are usually produced by deep drawing?
4. Calculate the length of the bent components shown in a) and b). Use your Metal Trade Handbook.

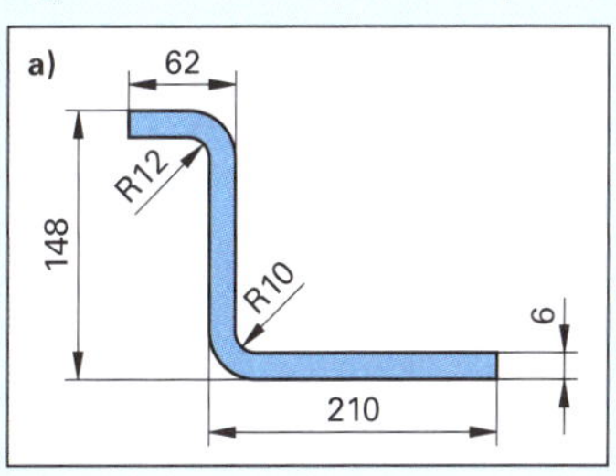

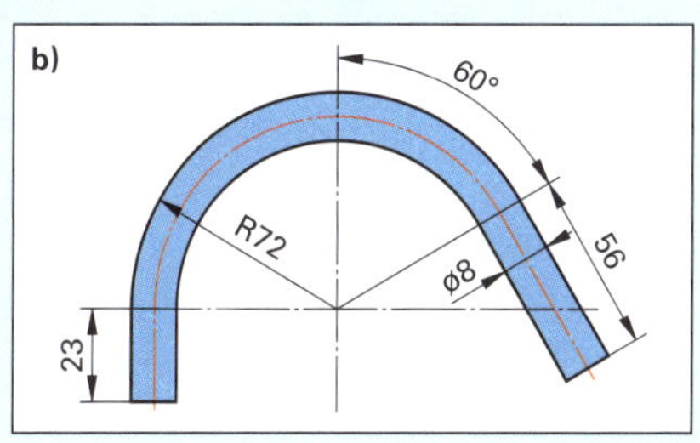

3.6 Basics of metal-cutting manufacturing

All metal-cutting manufacturing processes use tools which have a cutting edge with a wedge profile e.g. files, saw blades, drills etc. **(figure at right hand).**

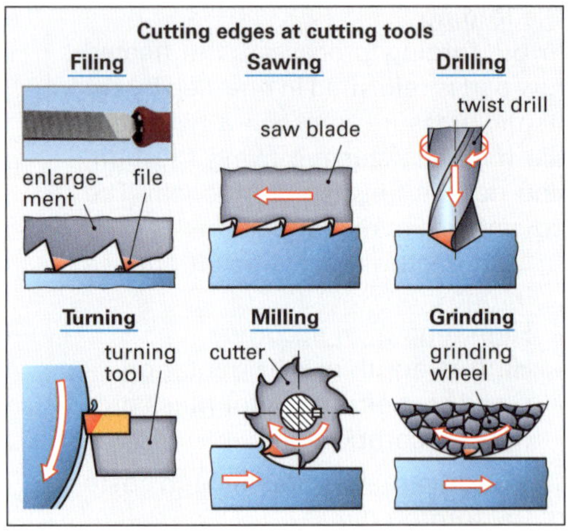

The cutting wedge penetrates the material and cuts off chips **(figure).** The tool wedge has a cutting face and a tool flank. They shape the wedge angle β.

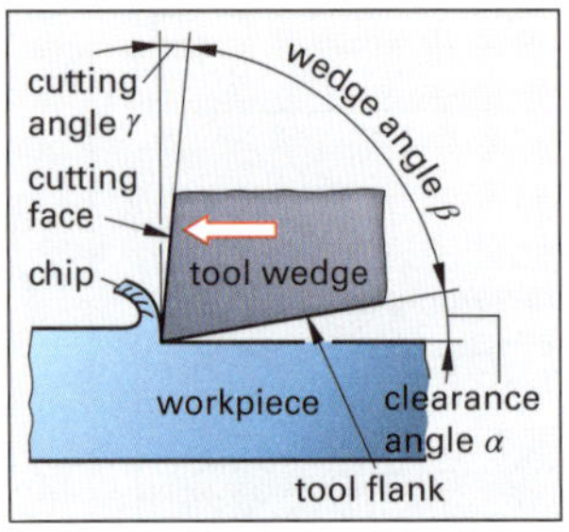

Between the wedge, and the workpiece, there is the clearance angle α. Between the wedge and the vertical line, there is the cutting angle γ.

The cutting wedge penetrates much easier into the material, the smaller the wedge angle β is. But the wedge angle must have a certain minimum value, so that the cutting wedge does not break when cutting harder material.

The cutting angle γ essentially determines the chip formation. The softer the material, the greater the cutting angle γ. A great cutting angle leads to long chips.

The clearance angle α guarantees that the cutting wedge does not rub against the workpiece.

Preparing by marking

In the basic manufacturing processes, like filing, sawing or drilling, the dimensions of the workpiece drawing have to be marked on the raw material.

The marking lines must be thin and should not damage the workpiece surface. To make the marking line visible, the surface of the raw material is coated by whiting or marking paint.

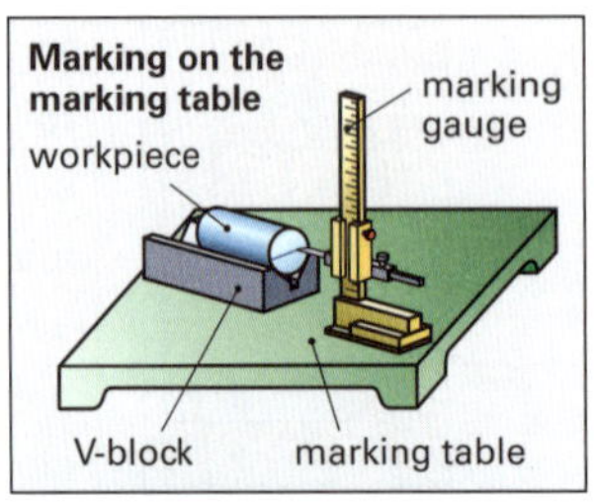

The marking is carried out by using special marking tools on a levelled marking table **(figure).**

Marking tools for steel materials are a scriber, centre punch, divider and marking gauge **(figure).** Aluminium workpieces are marked with a pencil.

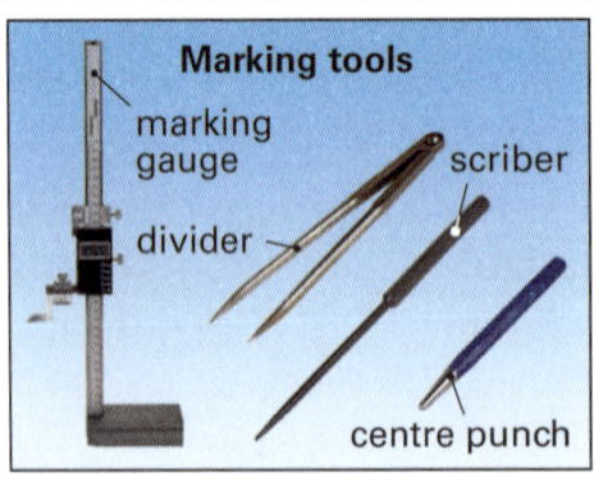

With the scriber you mark lines. For marking circles or distances you use a divider. The centre point of a circle is hammered with a centre punch. Round workpieces are fixed for marking in a magnetic V-block **(figure).**

Exercises

1. Mark and name the different angles of the tool wedge in the figure beside:
   a) wedge angle
   b) cutting angle
   c) clearance angle

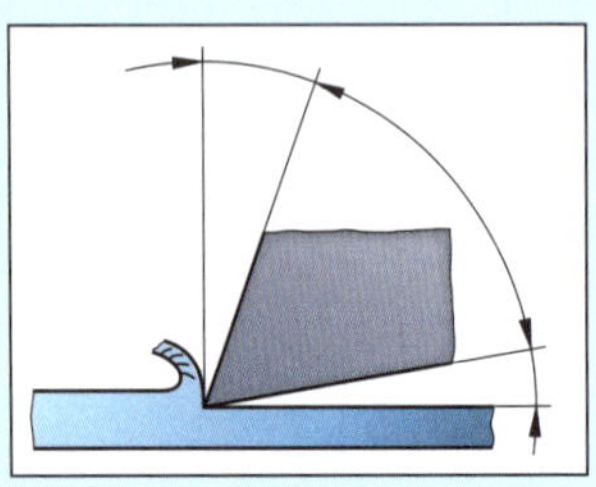

2. Complete the sentences:
   a) The chip formation is determined by the ________________ angle.
   b) The cutting angle is shaped by the ________________ and the ________________.
   c) Marking tools are: ________________________________.

Words

English	German
basics	Grundlagen
metal cutting manufacturing process	spanendes Fertigungsverfahren
cutting edge	Werkzeugschneide
wedge profile	Keilform
filing	Feilen
sawing	Sägen
drilling	Bohren
turning	Drehen
milling	Fräsen
grinding	Schleifen
cutting wedge	Schneidkeil
to penetrate	eindringen
to cut off	abtrennen
chip	Span
cutting face	Spanfläche
tool flank	Freifläche
to shape	formen, bilden
wedge angle	Keilwinkel
clearance angle	Freiwinkel
vertical line	Senkrechte
cutting angle	Spanwinkel
to determine	bestimmen
chip formation	Spanbildung
to guarantee	garantieren
to rub	reiben
marking	Anreißen
dimensions	Maße
drawing	Zeichnung
to damage	beschädigen
whiting	Schlämmkreide
marking paint	Anreißlack
to carry out	ausführen
levelled	ausgerichtet
marking table	Anreißtisch
scriber	Reißnadel
centre punch	Körner
divider	Spitzzirkel
marking gauge	Höhenreißer
pencil	Bleistift
circle	Kreis
to hammer	einschlagen

3.7 Filing and sawing by hand

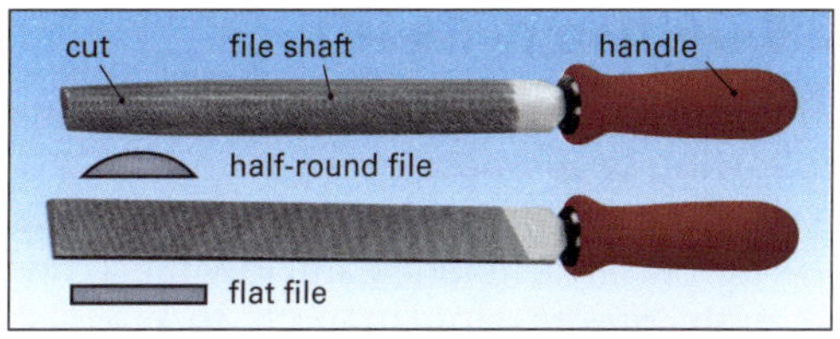

Filing

A file is a multi-edged tool to remove thin layers of material in form of small chips. It consists of a steel file-shaft and the plastic handle **(figure).** The file-teeth are hammered or milled into the shaft and hardened afterwards.

The linear teeth-rows are called **cut**. There are files with different types of cuts, e.g. one-cut or cross-cut **(figure).** Most of the files have a cross cut to avoid filing marks.

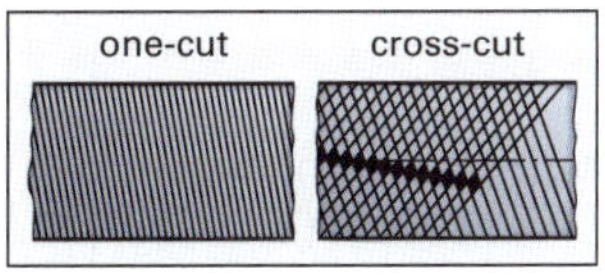

Files are suitable for steels, cast iron, brass, hard plastics and wood.

The number of cuts per centimetre is the **cut number**. Usual workshop files have cut numbers from 2 to 12.

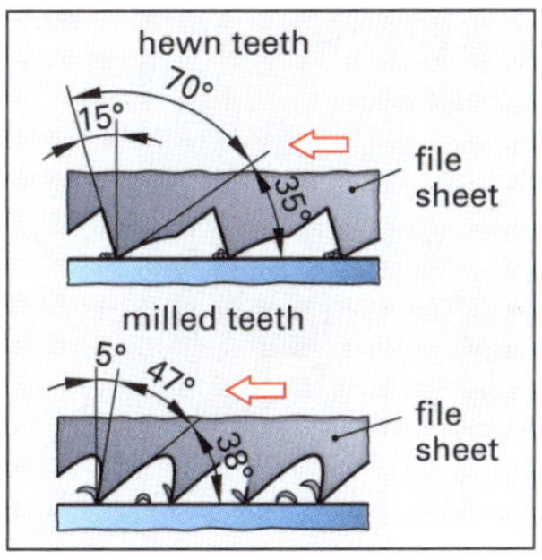

The cut number defines the use of the files, e.g. rough working (2 to 4) or fine finishing (5 to 12).

Hewn file teeth have a negative cutting angle, milled file teeth a positive cutting angle and a lower cut number **(figure).**

Rough filing is called **roughing**, fine filing means **finishing**.

Sawing per hand

The most usual tool for sawing per hand is the **metal hacksaw (figure).** The hacksaw cuts in pushing direction. The sawing blade is clamped in the studs, so that the sawing teeth point in pushing direction.

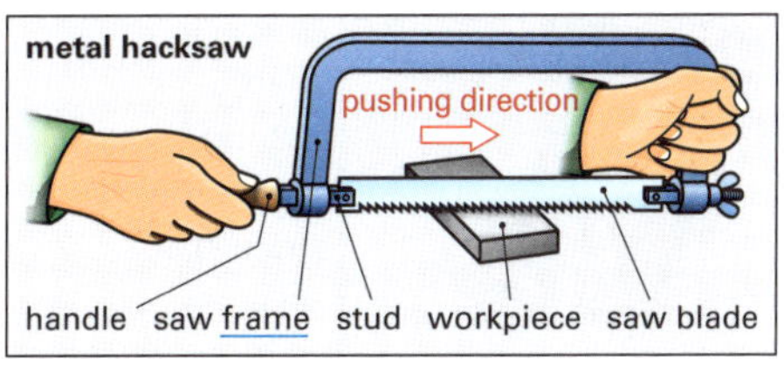

The sawing blades are 0.6 mm to 1 mm thick. They have a teeth or wave offset. The sawing gap is wider than the blade thickness, so the saw cuts freely.

The sawing blade is a multi-cutting tool. The wedge-shaped teeth cut chips off the material **(figure).** They are pushed out with every pass of the saw blade. The distance of two teeth in inch is called **tooth pitch**. Identically you count the number of teeth per inch (25.4 mm).

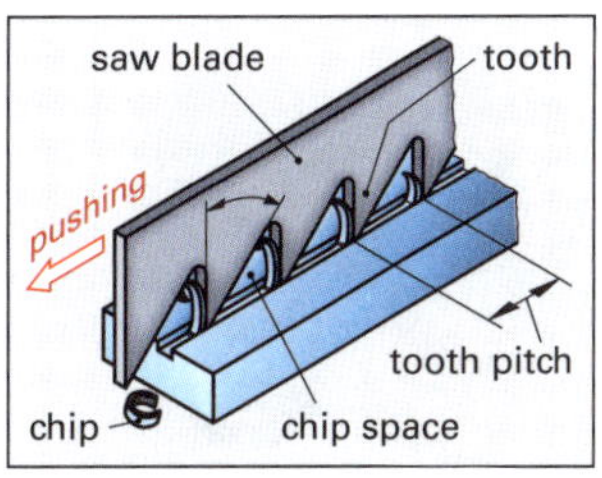

Sawing blades with small tooth pitch (12 to 16) are used for soft materials e. g. aluminium. Wide tooth pitches (20 to 32) are suitable for hard materials such as construction steels **(figure).**

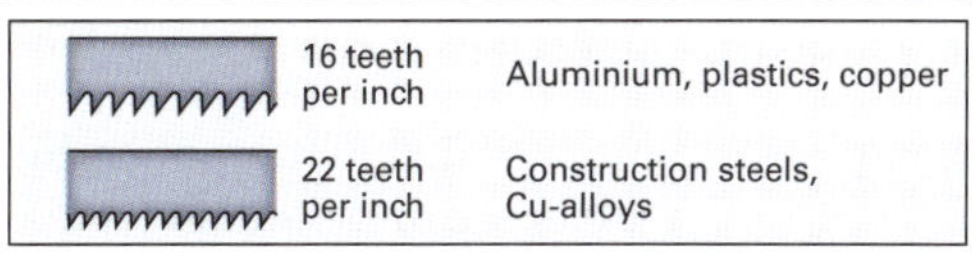

Words

multi-edged	vielschneidig
to remove	abtragen
file shaft	Feilenschaft
handle	Handgriff
file tooth, pl. teeth	Feilenzahn
to hammer	schlagen
hardened	gehärtet
linear	linienförmig
teeth row	Zähnereihe
cut	Hieb
cross-cut	Kreuzhieb
filing marks	Riefen
brass	Messing
cut number	Hiebzahl
workshop file	Werkstattfeile
rough working	Grobbearbeitung
fine finishing	Feinbearbeitung
hewn file teeth	gehauene Feilenzähne
roughing	Schruppen
finishing	Schlichten
sawing per hand	Sägen von Hand
hacksaw	Bügelsäge
pushing direction	Stoßrichtung
to clamp	einspannen
stud	Zapfen
frame	Rahmen
wave offset	Wellenschränkung
sawing gap	Sägespalt
to cut freely	freischneiden
wedge shaped	keilförmig
tooth pitch	Zahnteilung
identically	gleichlautend
to count	zählen
suitable	geeignet
construction steel	Baustahl

Exercises

1. Answer the following questions in English:
   a) Why do files have a cross cut?
   b) Which cut numbers do workshop files have?
   c) In which direction do you have to clamp the sawing blade?
   d) Why do the sawing blades have an offset?
   e) Which tooth pitch should a saw blade have for sawing construction steels?
2. Translate the first paragraphs of the chapter *filing* and the chapter *sawing* into German.
3. A saw blade has a tooth pitch of 14. For which materials can you use this saw blade?
4. What kind of offset does the figure beside show?

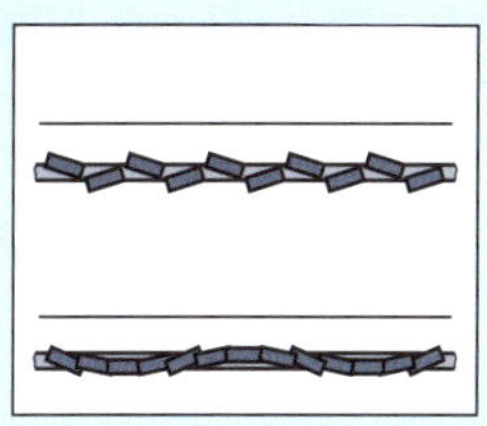

3.8 Cutting materials

The cutting tools are made of cutting materials. They have the following properties:

- High hot hardness, i.e. high hardness also at high temperatures
- High wear resistance, i.e. low mechanical abrasion
- High compression strength, to avoid crumbling of the edge
- Sufficient toughness, to stand abrupt loads.

There are different cutting materials for various applications.

High speed steels (HSS)

The high speed steels are alloyed tool steels with the main alloying elements tungsten (W), molybdenum (Mo), vanadium (V) and cobalt (Co). Their percentages are named in the designation code.

Example: HS6-5-2-5 is a HS-steel with 6% W, 5% Mo, 2% V and 5% Co.

HSS are used, if the cutting edge has to be very sharp, e. g. for drills and cutters **(figure)**. The hardness and wear resistance are improved by coating the tool.

High speed steels (HSS)

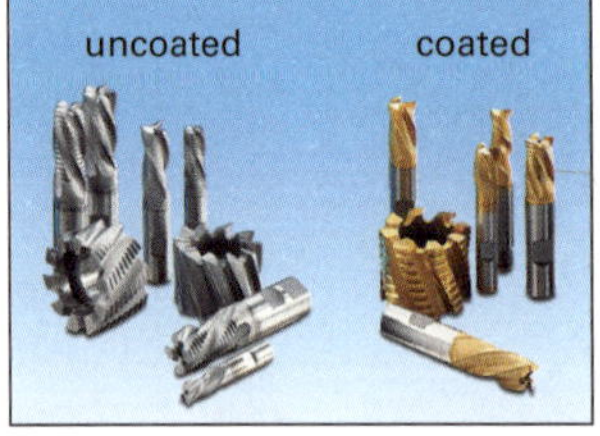

Carbide metals

Carbide metals, also called hard metals or carbides, are composite materials that consist of 75% to 90% microscopic hard material grains (about 1 µm to 10 µm) of tungsten carbide (WC) and a cobalt matrix.

Carbide metals are used as cutting inserts for drilling-, turning-, sawing- and milling tools **(figure)**.

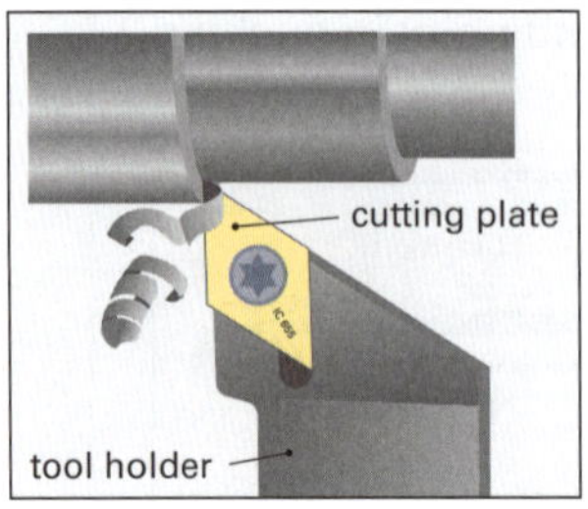

Carbide metals can consist of different component percentages and grain sizes. A high percentage of metal carbides improves the wear resistance and the hot hardness.
A high percentage of the binding cobalt leads to high toughness.

By coating the cutting inserts of carbide metals with a thin layer of hard titanium carbon nitride (TiCN), the wear resistance is increased. They have a grey or golden surface **(figure)**.

Coated cutting inserts have a longer life time than uncoated tools.

Standardisation and designation of carbide metals

The carbide metals are standardised and designated, first by the components in carbide metal groups and secondly by the main cutting groups with the application group.

The carbide metal groups are:

HW Uncoated carbide metals, with the main component tungsten carbide WC

HT Uncoated carbide metals, consisting of titanium carbide TiC or titanium nitride TiN

HC Carbide metals, coated with titanium carbon nitride (TiCN)

The designation of a carbide metal consists of two characters for the carbide metal group plus the cutting and application group.

Example: HW-P40: Uncoated carbide metal, cutting and application group P40 (for roughing of steels).

Words

English	German
cutting material	Schneidstoff
hot hardness	Warmhärte
i.e. , von lat. id est	d. h. (das heißt)
wear resistance	Verschleißfestigkeit
abrasion	Abrieb
compression strength	Druckfestigkeit
crumbling	ausbröckeln
edge	Schneidkante
sufficient	ausreichend
toughness	Zähigkeit
to stand	ertragen
load	Belastung
different	verschieden
various	unterschiedlich
application	Verwendung
high speed steel	Schnellarbeitsstahl
tungsten	Wolfram
molybdenum	Molybdän
vanadium	Vanadium
cobalt	Cobalt
percentage	Prozentgehalt
designation code	Kurzbezeichnung
coating	Beschichtung
carbide metal, hard metal, carbide	Hartmetall
to consist of	bestehen aus
microscopic	mikroskopisch
hard material grain	Hartstoffkorn
tungsten carbide	Wolframcarbid
matrix	Grundgerüst
cutting insert	Schneidplatte
component	Bestandteil
grain size	Korngröße
layer	Schicht
to increase	erhöhen
life time	Standzeit
standardisation	Normung
character	Buchstabe
roughing	schruppen
long chipping	langspanend
finishing	schlichten

Classification of carbide metals

main group	application group	metal cutting
P for long chipping materials e.g. steels malleable cast iron	P10 : P30 : P50	finishing : : : roughing
M for long- and short chipping materials e.g. stainless steels	M10 M20 M30 M40	finishing : : roughing
K for short chipping materials e.g. cast iron non-ferrous metals	K01 K10 K20 K30	finishing : : roughing

Cutting ceramics

Cutting ceramics are hot sintered materials with ceramic properties. They are very hard, hot wear resistant, but sensitive against thermal shock and abrupt load.

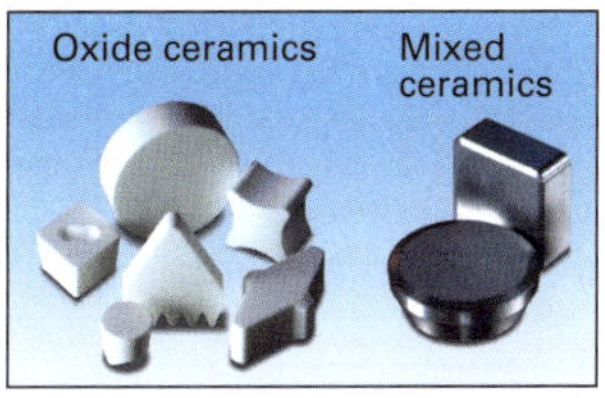

There are three cutting ceramics:

- **Aluminium oxide** (Al_2O_3), also called **oxide ceramics (figure).**
- **Mixed ceramics** have an aluminium oxide base and other components, such as titanium carbide TiC. It is tougher than pure aluminium oxide ceramic.
- **Silicium nitride** (Si_3N_4) has similar ceramic properties but a better toughness as the other ceramics.

The cutting ceramics are used for cutting cast iron and hardened steels at high cutting velocity v_c.

Words	
cutting ceramics	Schneidkeramik
hot sintered	heiß gesintert
sensitive	empfindlich
thermal shock	Temperaturwechsel
abrupt	schlagartig
aluminium oxide	Aluminiumoxid
oxide ceramics	Oxidkeramik
mixed ceramics	Mischkeramik
base	Basis
silicium nitride	Siliciumnitrid
similar	ähnlich
cutting velocity	Schnittgeschwindigkeit
instructor	Ausbilder

Exercises

1. Name the English technical terms:
   a) Schnellarbeitsstahl b) Hartmetall
   c) Schneidkeramik d) Mischkeramik
2. Answer the following questions in English:
   a) Which tools are made of high speed steels?
   b) For which applications are carbide metals and cutting ceramics used?
   c) What is the reason for the coating of cutting inserts?
   d) What are the special properties of cutting ceramics and what are their applications?
3. You have to order for your instructor:
   60 cutting plates of coated carbide metal, application group P30.
   Name the standardised designation of these tools.
4. Choose the suitable carbide metal for turning (roughing) malleable cast iron by using your **Metal Trade Handbook.**

3.9 Cooling lubricants for cutting

In cutting processes the cooling lubricant decreases the friction between cutting tool and the cut surface **(figure).** Additionally it dissipates the heat energy that is generated by the cutting process. Besides, the chips are flushed away from the cutting space.

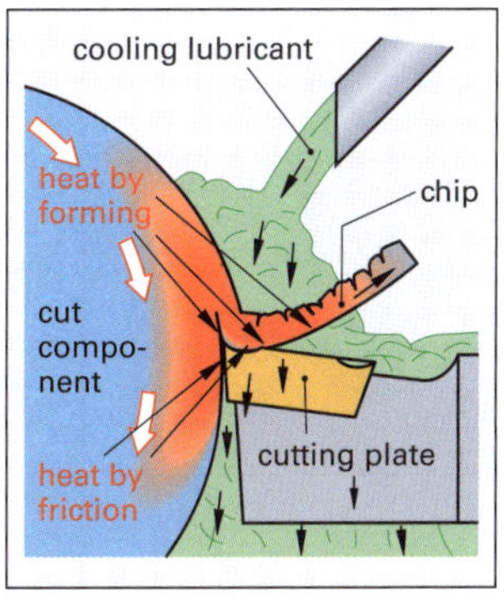

A suitable cooling lubricant improves the life time of the tools and the surface quality of the product.

There are different types of cooling lubricants:

Cooling lubricant emulsions are mixtures of 2% to 20% emulsive lubricant in water. They are mixed to a milky-looking fluid. The emulsions contain additives for protection against corrosion, affection of microorganism and skin disease. They are used for turning, drilling and sawing, when a good cooling effect is required.

Cutting oils are mineral oils with additives to increase the lubricant performance. They are applied for tapping, milling and reaming, where good lubrication is necessary. Additives protect the workpiece against corrosion and prolongs the life time of the oil.

Words	
cooling lubricant	Kühlschmierstoff
to decrease	vermindern
friction	Reibung
to dissipate	ableiten
to generate	erzeugen
to flush away	fortspülen
to improve	verbessern
surface quality	Oberflächengüte
emulsion	Emulsion
emulsive	emulgierbar
milky-looking	milchartig
to contain	enthalten
additive	Zusatz
protection	Schutz
affection	Befall
skin disease	Hautkrankheit
to be required	erforderlich sein
cutting oil	Schneidöl
performance	Leistungsfähigkeit
tapping	Gewindeschneiden
reaming	Räumen
lubrication	Schmierung

Exercises

1. Name the English technical terms for
   a) Kühlschmierstoff b) Reibung c) Zusätze
2. Which are the functions of cooling lubricants for cutting?
3. For which cutting processes do you use cutting lubricant emulsions?
4. Find a suitable cooling lubricant for tapping in your **Metal Trade Handbook.**

3.10 Drilling

Drilling machine

The most common drilling machine to produce workpieces in a workshop is a pillar drill **(figure)**. It consists of a base plate with a column or pillar, the drive unit with the drill and the drilling table with height adjustment.

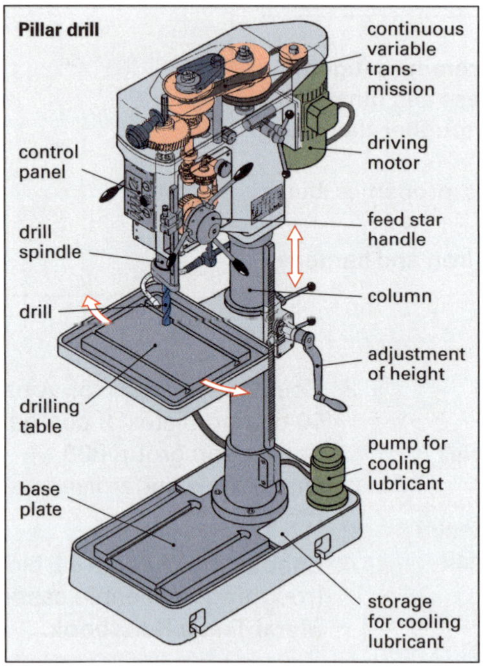

The drive unit has an electric motor and a variable transmission. The rotary frequency of the drill is set at the control panel. The feed of the drill is performed by the star handle.

The drill is fixed in the drill chuck of the spindle.

The base plate includes the pump and the storage tank of the cooling lubricant und carries the column.

Drilling process

Blind or through holes in a workpiece are produced by drilling. When drilling, the drill executes the rotary cutting motion and the linear feed motion **(figure)**.

The feed power causes the drill penetration into the material, the rotational cutting power takes chips off.

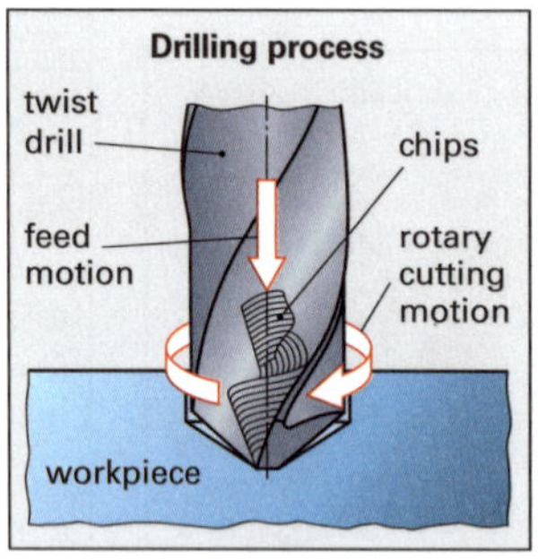

The most commonly used drill for holes up to 25 mm diameter is the twist drill **(figure)**. It has two helical notches, which form the cutting angle γ at the drill point.

The shape and the pitch of the helical notches determine the cutting angle γ. It has its greatest value at the outer diameter and decreases to the drill point.

The helix angle γ_F is used as a characteristic angle for the cutting process. The angle at the drill point is called point angle σ.

For drilling different materials, the point angle σ and the helix angle γ_F have different values.

There are three types of twist drills: Type N, type H and type W **(figure)**. Each drill type is suitable for drilling different materials.

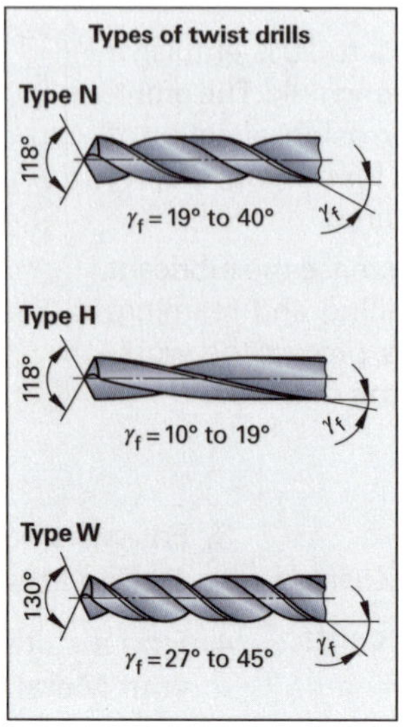

Words	
drilling	Bohren
pillar drill	Ständerbohrmaschine
to consist of	bestehen aus
base plate	Grundplatte
column	Säule
drive unit	Antriebseinheit
drilling table	Bohrtisch
height adjustment	Höhenverstellung
variable transmission	stufenloses Getriebe
rotary frequency	Drehfrequenz
to set (set, set)	einstellen
control panel	Bedienfeld
feed of the drill	Bohrervorschub
to perform	ausführen
star handle	Drehkreuz
to fix	befestigen
drill chuck	Bohrfutter
spindle	Spindel
to include	beinhalten, enthalten
pump	Pumpe
storage tank	Vorratsbehälter
cooling lubricant	Kühlschmiermittel
to carry	tragen
drilling process	Bohrvorgang
blind hole	Grundloch
through hole	Durchgangsloch
to execute	ausführen
rotary cutting motion	rotierende Schnittbewegung
linear	geradlinig
feed motion	Vorschubbewegung
feed power	Vorschubkraft
penetration	Eindringen
to take off	abtragen
diameter	Durchmesser
twist drill	Spiralbohrer
helical	wendelförmig
notch	Nut
cutting angle	Spanwinkel
drill point	Bohrerspitze
shape	Form
pitch	Steigung
to determine	bestimmen
outer diameter	Außendurchmesser
to decrease	vermindern
helix angle	Drallwinkel
characteristic	charakteristisch
point angle	Spitzenwinkel
different	verschieden

Drilling characteristics

The correct cutting velocity v_c depends on several conditions: the drill type, the materials of the drill and workpiece and the required surface quality of the hole. The **table** below e.g. shows the suitable values of the cutting velocity for a drilling task with HSS-drill. It is given by the drill manufacturer.

The required rotary frequency n of the drill can be read off a **cutting velocity diagram** (see below).

Alternatively it can be calculated with the cutting velocity v_c divided by the drill diameter d and π:

$$n = \frac{v_c}{\pi \cdot d}$$

The feed speed v_f (mm/min) is equal to the rotary frequency n times feed f:

$$v_f = n \cdot f$$

Example: You use a HSS-drill for drilling holes with a diameter of 12 mm and 42 mm length in a workpiece of structural steel (tensile strength 620 N/mm²)

a) Which cutting velocity and speed can you read off the table?

b) Which rotary frequency can you read off the diagram or can be calculated?

Solution: a) From the table you read: $v_c = 30$ m/min; $f = 0.13$ mm;

b) From the diagram you read off with v_c and d: $n = 750\ \text{min}^{-1}$;
You calculate: $\boldsymbol{v_f} = n \cdot f = 750\ \text{min}^{-1} \cdot 0.13\ \text{mm} = \mathbf{97.5\ mm/min}$.

Words

English	German
drilling characteristic	Bohrer-Kennwert
cutting velocity	Schnittgeschwindigkeit
to depend on	abhängen von ...
required	erforderlich
manufacturer	Hersteller
to read off	ablesen
rotary frequency	Drehfrequenz
to calculate	berechnen
divided by	geteilt durch
feed speed	Vorschubgeschwindigkeit
is equal to	ist gleich
times	mal
depth	Tiefe
to label	benennen
tensile strength	Zugfestigkeit
formula	Formel

Table: Cutting data for coated HSS-twist drill for drilling depths up to 5 x drill diameter

material of the workpiece	v_c m/min	f mm for drill diameter > 3...6	> 6...12	> 12...25	cooling lubricant
Steels $R_m \le 600$ N/mm²	40	0.10	0.15	0.28	emulsion cutting oil
Steels $R_m > 600$ N/mm²	30	0.09	0.13	0.22	
Steels $R_m > 800$ N/mm²	20	0.08	0.10	0.15	
Stainless steels $R_m \ge 800$ N/mm²	12	0.06	0.08	0.12	emulsion cutting oil
Cast iron materials ≤ 250 HB	20	0.20	0.30	0.40	emulsion or dry
Aluminium alloys $R_m \le 350$ N/mm²	45	0.20	0.30	0.40	emulsion cutting oil
Thermoplastics	50	0.15	0.30	0.40	dry

Cutting velocity diagram

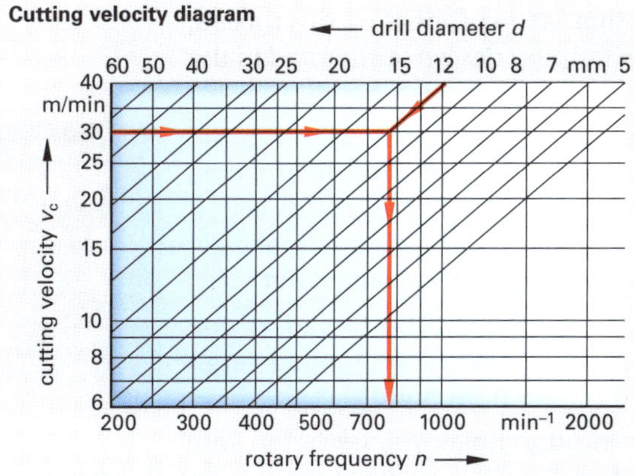

Exercises

1. Label the machine parts in the figure below.

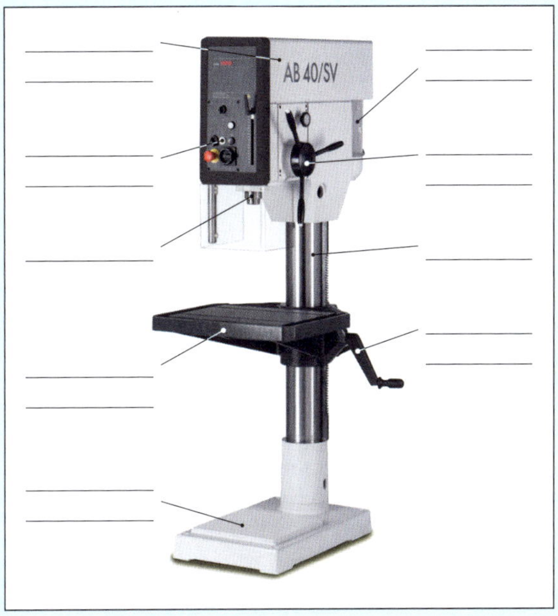

2. Twist drill
   a) Label the parts and angles ① to ⑤ of the drill in the figure beside.
   b) Describe the edges of the drill, which form its characteristic angles.

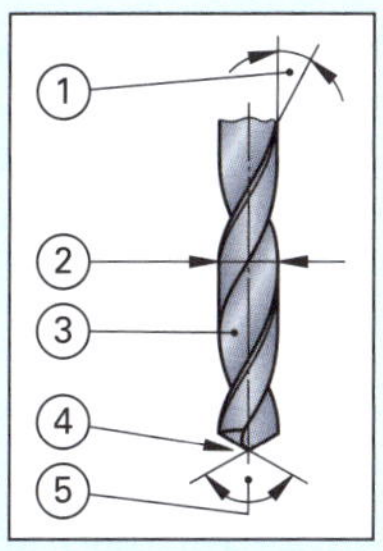

3. For which materials are these types of drill used?
   a) Type N b) Type H c) Type W
4. Name the formulas for calculating the following **characteristics** and describe it in a complete English sentence.
   a) Rotary frequency n of the drill b) Feed speed v_c of the drill
5. a) Determine the cutting velocity and the feed speed for drilling a 15 mm hole in a workpiece made of cast iron.
   b) Read the suitable rotary frequency off the cutting velocity diagram.
   c) Calculate the feed speed for this task.

3.11 Tapping

Internal threads can be produced by hand or by a drilling machine. Before tapping, the core hole has to be drilled **(figure)**. Its diameter d_k is the nominal diameter minus the thread pitch. $d_K = d - P$

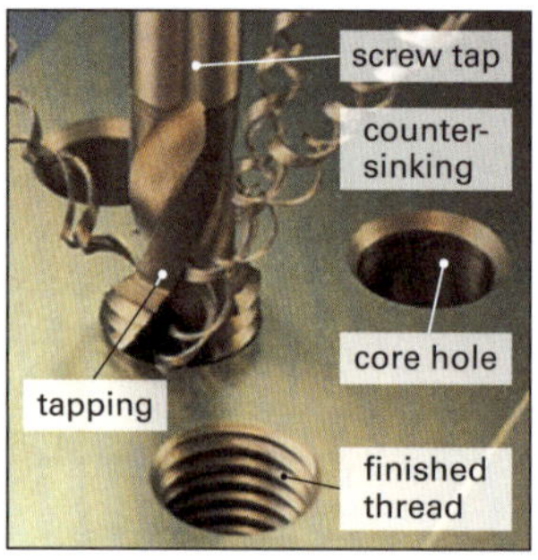

The core hole has to be countersunk with a 90°-countersink. Then the tapping can start.

For **tapping by hand** you need a three-part screw tap set **(figure)**.

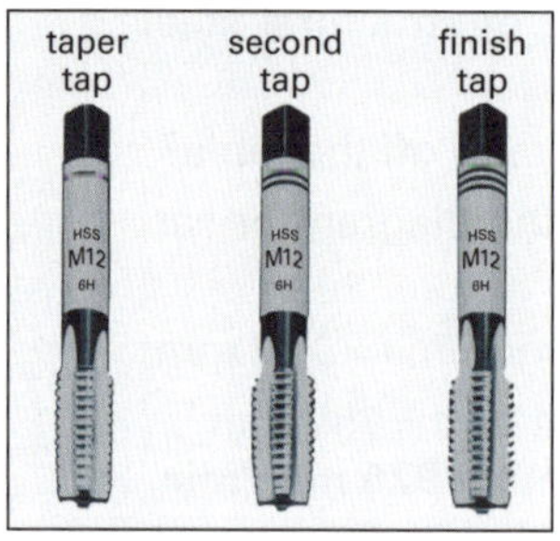

The little conic taper lead enables the vertical insertion into the core hole. The rotations of the tap pull it into the hole and cut the thread pitches. With each tap the pitches are cut deeper.

If the tap is stuck, it is turned back to break the chips. A suitable cutting oil has to be used.

The **tapping with a drilling machine** facilitates the production of a thread. The tapping device is clamped in the drill chuck **(figure left hand)**.

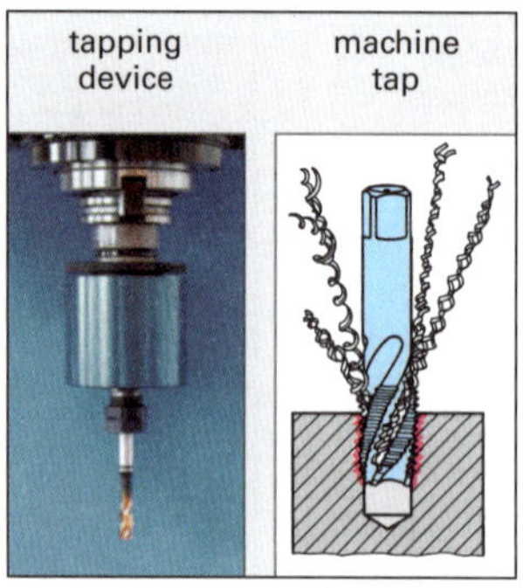

The screw tap moves right into the hole with constant velocity and cuts the thread. At the end, the direction of rotation changes automatically and the screw tap is pulled out.

Machine taps cut the thread in one step. They have a prolonged taper lead **(figure right hand)**.

For through holes you use a tap with left-hand twist; it pushes the chips out of the hole. For blind holes you use a tap with right-hand twist; it pulls the chips out of the hole.

3.12 Countersinking (counterboring)

Countersinking is a drilling process for deburring or to produce a conical or cylindrical recess in a drilled hole **(figure)**.

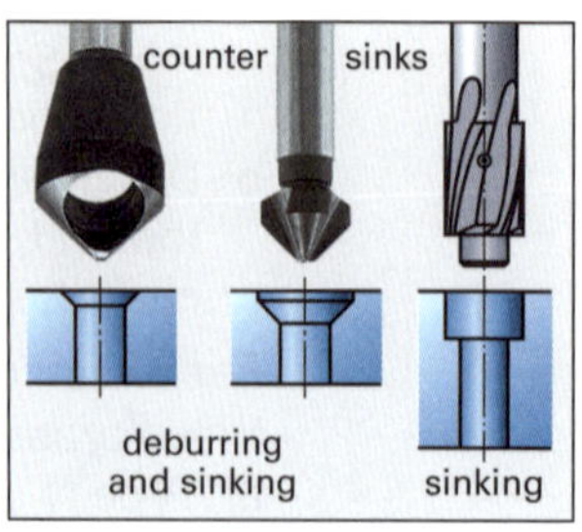

You use different sinking tools for the diverse sinks. For tapping as preparation or for flat head screws you need a conic sink. For the head of a socket screw you need a cylindrical sink.

Words

English	German
tapping	Innengewindebohren
internal thread	Innengewinde
core hole	Kernloch
nominal diameter	Nenndurchmesser
thread pitch	Gewindesteigung
countersink	Senker
three-part	dreiteilig
screw tap set	Gewindebohrersatz
conic	konisch
taper lead	Anschnitt
to enable	ermöglichen
vertical insertion	senkrechtes Einführen
thread pitch	Gewindegang
to be stuck	festbohren, festsetzen
to turn back	zurückdrehen
to facilitate	erleichtern
tapping device	Gewindeschneid-apparat
to clamp	einspannen
drill chuck	Bohrerfutter
direction of rotation	Drehrichtung
machine tap	Maschinen-gewindebohrer
prolonged	verlängert
through hole	Durchgangsloch
left-hand twist	Linksdrall
to push	stoßen
blind hole	Grundloch
to pull	ziehen
to countersink, countersank, countersunk	ansenken
to counterbore	senken
to deburr	entgraten
recess	Aussparung
diverse	verschieden
sink	Senkung
flat head screw	Senkschraube
socket screw	Inbusschraube
cylindrical	zylindrisch
individual	einzelne
purpose	Zweck

Exercises

1. Summarise in German:
   a) The first paragraph of *Tapping*.
   b) The first paragraph of *Countersinking*.
2. Complete the sentences:
   a) The production of a thread can be made by ______________ or with a ______________.
   b) Countersinking is made for ______________ or to produce a ______________.
3. Answer the following questions:
   a) How are the individual three-part screw taps called for tapping by hand?
   b) How does a tapping device for tapping with a drilling machine **(figure above)** works?
   c) What purpose does the process of countersinking have?
4. Describe the three steps to produce a thread in a through hole.

3.13 Turning

Turning is a machining process with a turning tool on a turning machine.

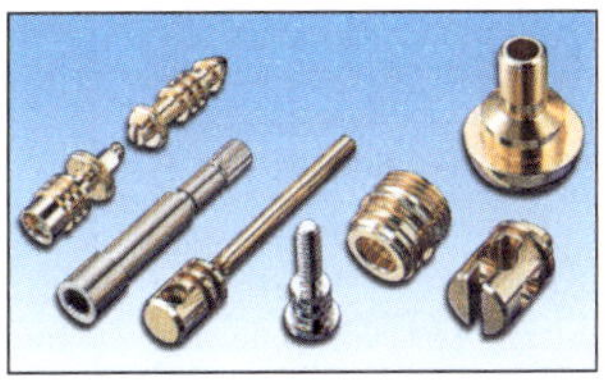

By turning a lot of components are produced: e. g. drive shafts, spindles, bolts, discs, bushes etc. **(figure)**.

Turning machine

Turning is executed on a turning machine, also called turning lathe or shortly lathe. The figure below shows a conventionel lathe.

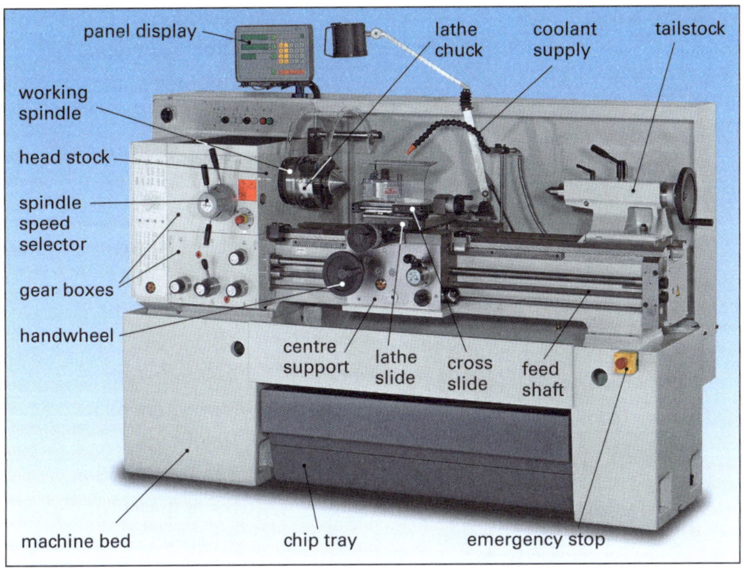

The basis of a turning machine is the **machine bed**. It carries the functional assemblies. It contains a tray for the chips and the drain for cooling lubricant. With an emergency stop the machine can be stopped when a hazard occurs.

The main functional components of a lathe are:

The **head stock** with the working spindle. It is driven by a continuous variable electric motor with gear box. It provides the rotational energy for the turning process. The working spindle includes the lathe chuck with the clamped workpiece.

The **centre support** consists of the lathe slide and the cross slide with the clamping device for the turning tool. The lathe and the cross slide are directly operated by handwheels and execute the feed motion.

The mechanical feed energy for the lathe slide and the cross slide is delivered by the feed gear.

The slide positions are measured by a position measuring system and indicated on a display.

The **tailstock** serves for the support of long workpieces or for clamping drilling tools.

Words	
turning	Drehen
machining process	spanender Bearbeitungsvorgang
turning tool	Drehwerkzeug
drive shaft	Antriebswelle
spindle	Spindel
bolt	Bolzen
disc	Scheibe
bush	Buchse
lathe	Drehmaschine
machine bed	Maschinenbett
functional assembly	Funktionsbaugruppe
tray	Wanne
drain	Abfluss
emergency stop	Not-Aus-Schalter
hazard	Gefahr
head stock	Spindelstock
working spindle	Arbeitsspindel
continuous variable	stufenlos einstellbar
gear box	Getriebe
to provide	liefern
lathe chuck	Drehmaschinenfutter
to clamp	einspannen
centre support	Werkzeugschlitten
lathe slide	Bettschlitten
cross slide	Querschlitten
clamping device	Spannvorrichtung
turning tool	Drehmeißel
to operate	verstellen
handwheel	Handrad
feed gear	Vorschubgetriebe
slide position	Schlittenposition
to measure	Messen
position measuring system	Wegmesssystem
to indicate	anzeigen
display	Anzeige, Display
tailstock	Reitstock
support	Abstützen

Exercises

1. Label the numbered functional assemblies of the lathe in the figure beside.
2. Which components are produced by turning?
3. Describe the functions of
   a) a lathe chuck
   b) a working spindle
   c) a lathe slid
   d) a cross slide
   e) a tailstock
   f) an emergency stop

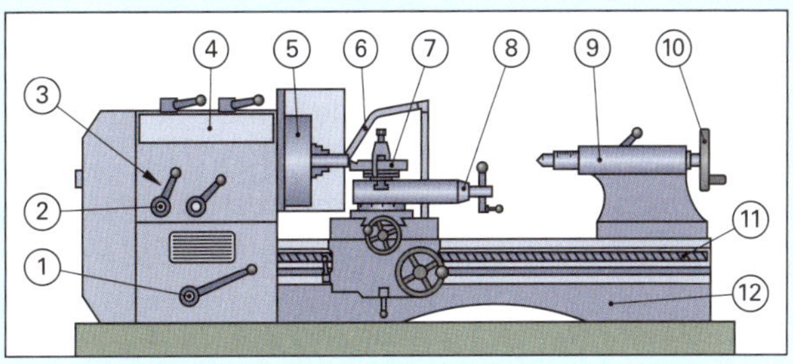

Turning techniques

When turning, the rotating workpiece provides the energy for the cutting motion. The cutting tool performs the feed motion.

The turning techniques are classified by the direction of the feed motion.

During **longitudinal turning**, the feed motion proceeds in direction of the z-axis **(figure)**. After one longitudinal turning step is finished, the turning tool is led back to the start. Then the tool is set by the cutting depth in the direction of the centre (infeed) and the next turning step starts.

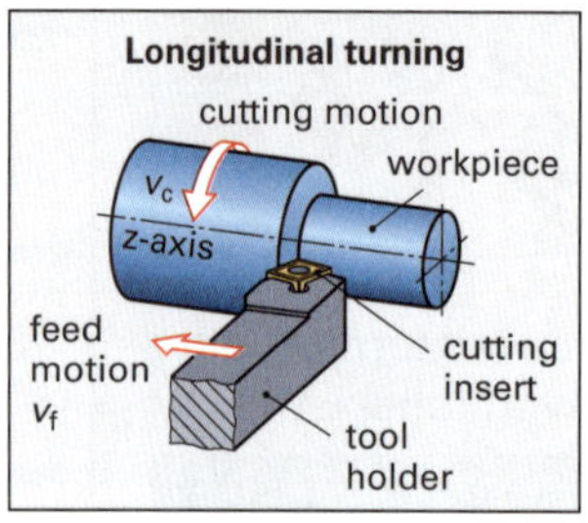

When **facing**, the feed motion proceeds in direction to the centre of the workpiece, in x-direction **(figure)**. By facing you turn flats at the end of the workpiece.

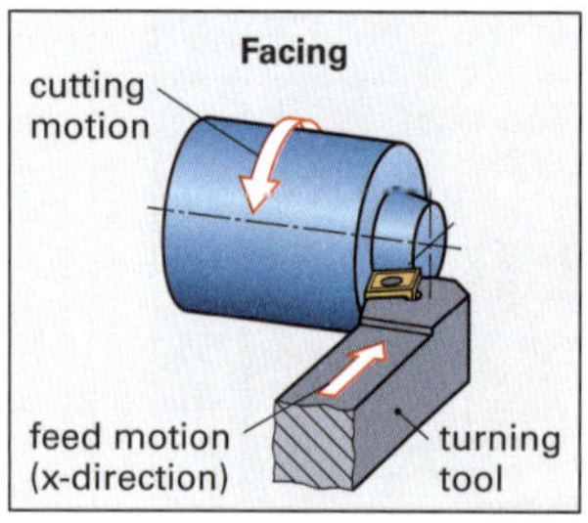

Other turning techniques are contour turning, thread turning and parting off.

Turning techniques, which are performed outside of the workpiece, are called **external turning** techniques. In contrary the **internal turning** works inside an opening of the workpiece **(figure)**.

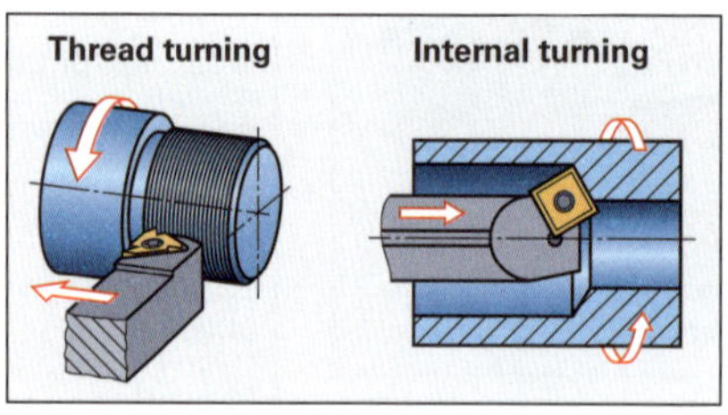

Machining variables

The main machining variables, when turning, are the **cutting velocity** v_c and the **feed** f **(figure)**.

The cutting velocity is determined by the workpiece rotatory speed and its external diameter. The feed f is the range which the cutting tool performs in one revolution of the workpiece.

The cutting depth a_p, is set after each turning step by the infeed.

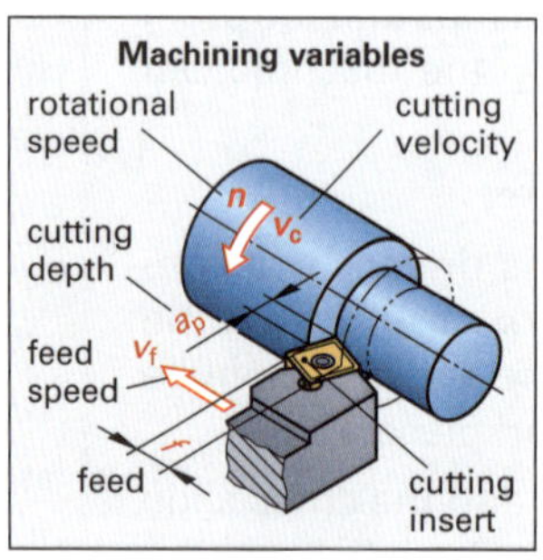

Roughing means turning with a high feed velocity v_f. The purpose of roughing is to cut as much as possible with the largest feed and high cutting velocity. It leads to a rough surface.

By **finishing** you cut with high turning frequency and small feed velocity. The purpose is to get the final workpiece shape with the required surface finish and dimensional tolerances.

Turning tools

For turning you use the **turning tool**. It consists of the tool holder and the cutting insert **(figure)**.

The cutting edge of the cutting insert is formed by the cutting face and the tool flank of the insert.

The determining angles at the cutting insert are the cutting angle γ, the wedge angle β, the clearance angle α and the corner angle ε **(figure)**.

Also important for the turning process is the cutting wedge angle κ, which is formed by the main cutting edge and the workpiece axis.

The **choice** of the tool holder and the cutting inserts depends on the turning operations to be processed.

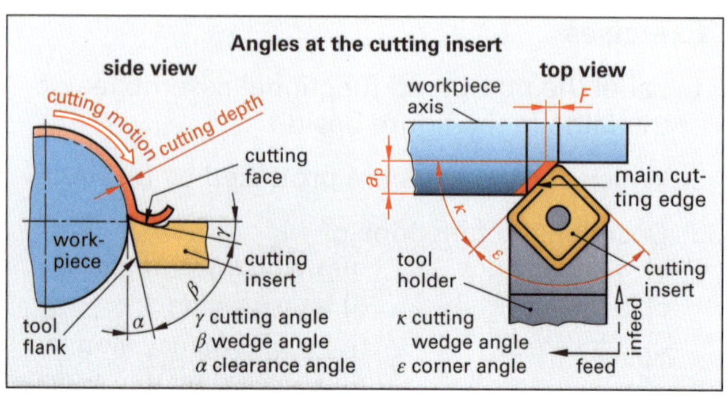

Words

English	German
turning techniques	Drehverfahren
rotating	rotierend
to provide	bereitstellen
cutting motion	Schnittbewegung
to perform	durchführen
feed motion	Vorschubbewegung
longitudinal turning	Längsdrehen
to proceed	verlaufen
direction	Richtung
turning step	Dreharbeitsgang
to lead back (led, led)	zuführen
cutting depth	Schnitttiefe
direction of the centre	Zentrumsrichtung
infeed	Zustellung
facing	Plandrehen
flat	ebene Fläche
contour turning	Formdrehen
thread turning	Gewindedrehen
parting off	Abstechen
external turning	Außendrehen
internal turning	Innendrehen
opening	Hohlraum
machining variables	Spanungsgrößen
cutting velocity	Schnittgeschwindigkeit
feed	Vorschub
rotational speed	Drehfrequenz
range	Strecke
revolution	Umdrehung
roughing	Schruppen
purpose	Zweck
finishing	Schlichten
surface finish	Oberflächengüte
dimensional tolerance	Maßtoleranz
lathe chisel	Drehmeißel
turning tool	Schneidplatte
cutting edge	Schneidkeil
tool flank	Freifläche
cutting angle	Spanwinkel
wedge angle	Keilwinkel
clearance angle	Freiwinkel
corner angle	Eckenwinkel
cutting wedge angle	Einstellwinkel
choice	Auswahl
turning operation	Dreharbeit
to process	ausführen

The tool holder should be compact and rigid. It must have the suitable space for the cutting insert.

The cutting inserts have different base shapes **(figure)**.

The square, the triangular and the round inserts are suitable for longitudinal turning. The rhombic inserts are suitable for contour turning.

For the attachment of the cutting inserts there are clamping systems, e. g. the screw joint or the toe dog **(figure)**.

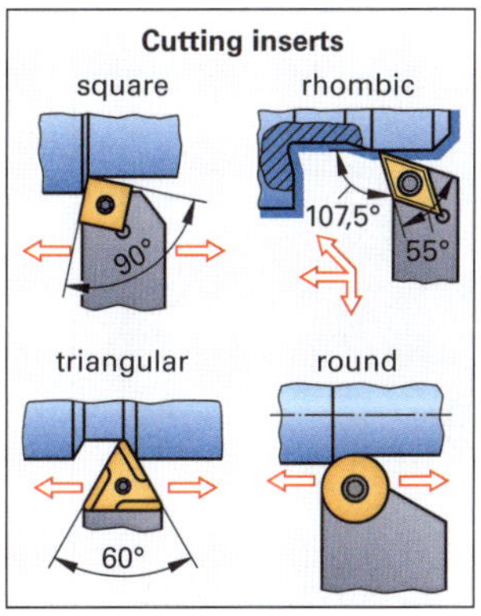

Cutting inserts

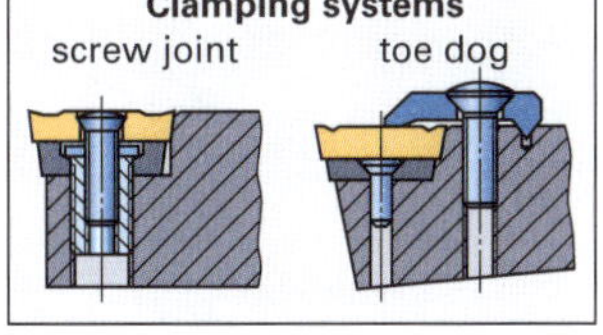

Clamping systems

Words (English)	Words (German)
rigid	starr
space	Aussparung
base shape	Grundform
square	quadratisch
triangular	dreieckig
rhombic	rautenförmig
attachment	Befestigung
clamping system	Spannsystem
screw joint	Schraubverbindung
toe dog	Spannfinger
cutting data	Schnittdaten
peripheral speed	Umfangsgeschwindigkeit
rotational speed	Drehzahl
extract	Ausschnitt
standard value	Richtwert
gear shaft	Getriebewelle
to sketch	einzeichnen

Cutting data

The cutting data for turning are the cutting velocity v_c, the feed f and the cutting depth a_p.

The cutting velocity v_c is the peripheral speed of the workpiece surface at the working point of the cutting insert. It is calculated by the workpiece diameter d times the rotational speed n of the lathe spindle: $v_c = \pi \cdot d \cdot n$

The suitable cutting velocity for turning a specific material at defined turning conditions is taken from tables which are determined by the insert manufacturer. You can find it in your **Metal Trade Handbook.** The table above shows an extract.

The **rotational speed *n*** of the lathe spindle can be determined from a rotary speed diagram **(figure)**.

Table: Standard values for turning (extract)

workpiece	coated carbide HC-P35
steel type of the workpiece	feed in mm 0.6...0.8
	cutting velocity in m/min
Unalloyed: C35	195 – 170
Alloyed steel:	
tempered	110 – 95
hardened	60 – 50

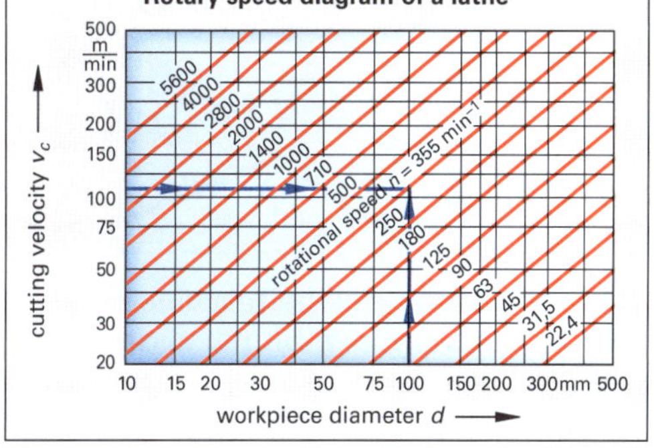

Rotary speed diagram of a lathe

Example of a turning task:

A gear shaft of tempered alloyed steel with a diameter of 100 mm has to be cut by longitudinal turning with a feed of 0.6 mm. The cutting insert consists of coated carbide HC-P35.

Which rotary speed do you have to set at the lathe?

Solution: Cutting velocity taken out of the table above: v_c = 110 m/min.
Rotary speed from the diagram above: $n \approx 350\ \text{min}^{-1}$.

The **feed *f*** (in mm per revolution) times the **cutting depth a_p** equals the cutting area: $A = f \cdot a_p$. Maximum allowed values for f and a_p can be taken of your **Metal Trade Handbook** and the extract of the table above.

Exercises

1. Complete the figure below:
   a) Label
      – the cutting motion
      – the feed motion
   b) Name
      – the tool holder
      – the cutting insert
      – the workpiece

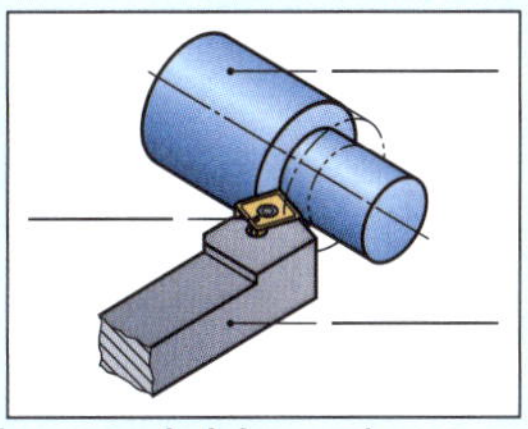

2. Name the main machining variables when turning and sketch it in the figure.
   a) ______________________
   b) ______________________
   c) ______________________
3. Name the three angles in the next figure.
4. Calculate the cutting velocity from a workpiece with 62 mm diameter and a frequency of 500 min^{-1}.

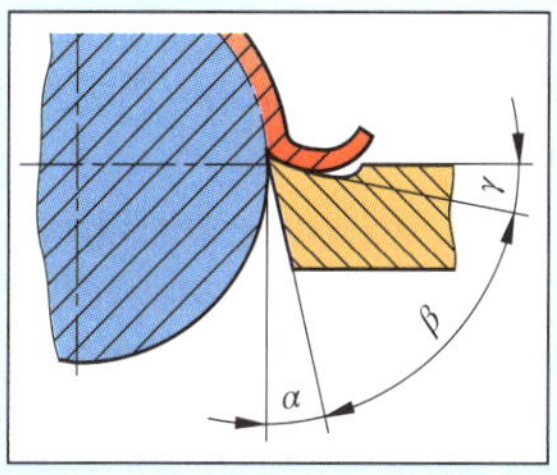

5. You have to turn a workpiece with the following data: Longitudinal turning (finishing) of a spindle of a tempered and quenched steel with 800 mm diameter; normal cutting conditions. Determine the turning data:
   a) cutting velocity b) feed c) cutting depth

   Use your **Metal Trade Handbook.**

3.14 Milling

Milling is a production technology using multi-blade milling cutters to create even surfaces or contours of a workpiece **(figure).**

During the milling process, the blades of the cutter alternately cut and run free.

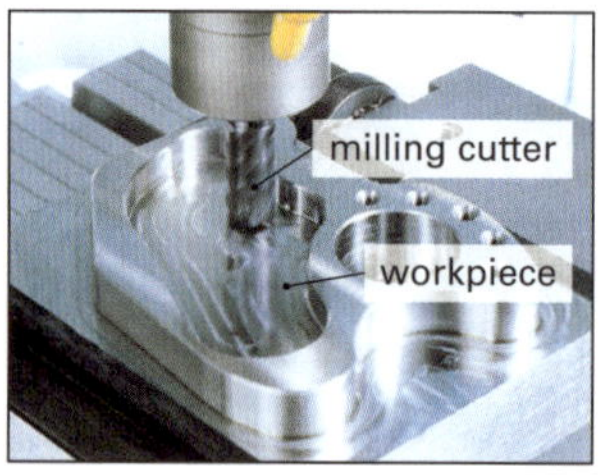

Milling machines

There are different types of milling machines.

The **universal milling machine** is used for small-series applications, for prototypes and vocational training **(figure).**

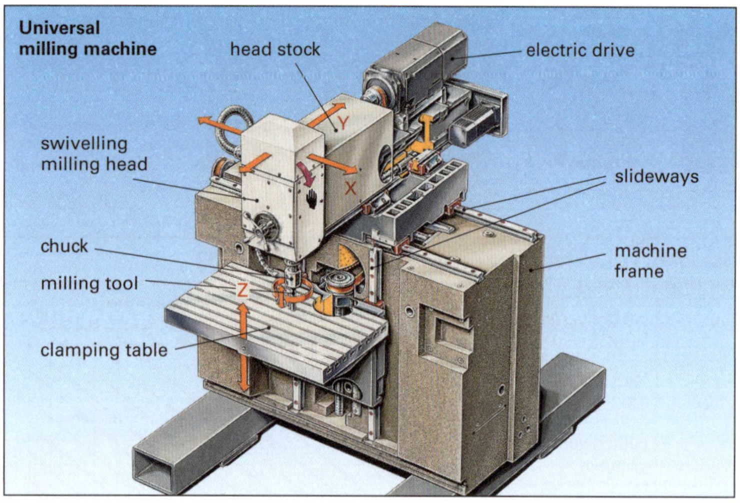

The basis of the milling machine is the machine frame. The assembly groups move on the slideways: The cross slide (x-axis) with the head stock (y-axis) horizontally and the clamping table (z-axis) vertically. The milling head is movable in x-, y- and z-direction. It can also be swivelled and moved along this direction. The milling cutter is fixed in the chuck.

Milling techniques

Milling techniques are classified according to their mode of operation **(figure).**

Peripheral milling: The blade at the periphery of the cylinder cutter produces the surface of the workpiece **(figure).** There are two techniques; the difference is the feed direction.

During **up-cut milling**, the cutting direction of the blade and the feed direction run in contrary directions. The chip is initially thin and becomes thicker when the milling tool leaves the material. The cutting force tries to lift the fixed workpiece from the clamping table.

During **down-cut milling** (synchronous milling), the cutting direction of the blade and the feed direction of the workpiece run in the same direction **(figure).** At the beginning, the blade cuts with the full chip thickness into the material and gets continuously thinner. The surface quality is better than with up-cut milling.

Front side face milling: The blades at the front side and at the periphery of the face milling cutter cut the material and produce even surfaces. During **corner milling**, the end milling cutter produces a workpiece with a shoulder.

Form milling, contour milling: It is possible to produce difficult shapes, such as notches, cavities and contours with an end milling cutter with round end **(figure).**

Words

English	German
milling	Fräsen
multi-blade	mehrschneidig
milling cutter	Fräser
even	eben
contour	Kontur
alternately	abwechselnd
vocational training	Berufsausbildung
machine frame	Maschinengestell
slideway	Führungsbahn
cross slide	Querschlitten
head stock	Spindelkasten
horizontal	waagrecht
clamping table	Aufspanntisch
vertical	senkrecht
milling head	Fräskopf
to swivel	schwenken
chuck	Spannkopf
mode of operation	Arbeitsweise
peripheral	Umfangsfräsen
cylinder cutter	Walzenfräser
up-cut milling	Gegenlauffräsen
contrary	entgegengesetzt
initial	anfänglich
down-cut milling	Gleichlauffräsen
front side face milling	Stirn-Planfräsen
corner milling	Eckfräsen
end milling cutter	Schaftfräser
shoulder	Absatz
major edge	Hauptschneide
minor edge	Nebenschneide
notch	Nut

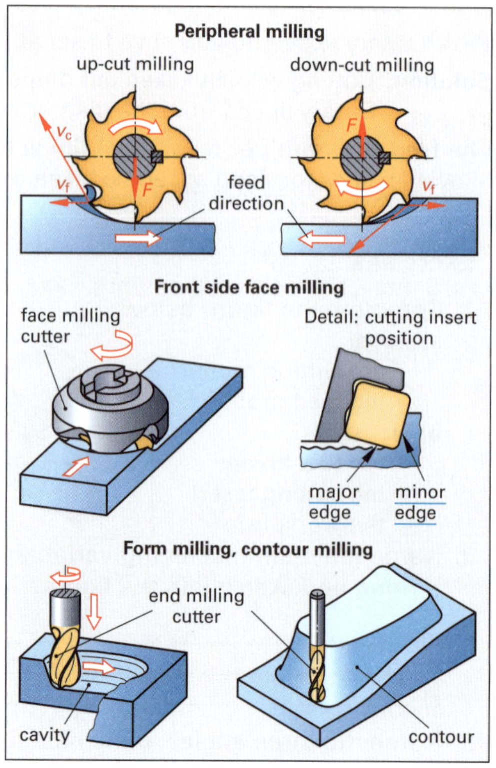

Milling tools

Milling tools **(figure)** can be classified by several aspects: Depending on the material, the shape of the blade, the mode of operation or the milling task.

Shell-type milling cutters (figure) are attached on a milling shaft. They are made of coated speed steels (HSS) or soldered on carbide metals. The feed motion is usually executed by the clamping table.

End milling cutters (figure) are clamped in the chuck. The feed motion is usually performed by the milling head **(see figure page 42)**. The material of the end milling cutters are HSS or carbide metals.

Milling tools with insert tips are used for high material removal rates **(figure)**. The insert tips are made of coated carbide metals or cutting ceramics (page 34). They are wearproof and heat resistant, which allow to cut with high cutting velocity.

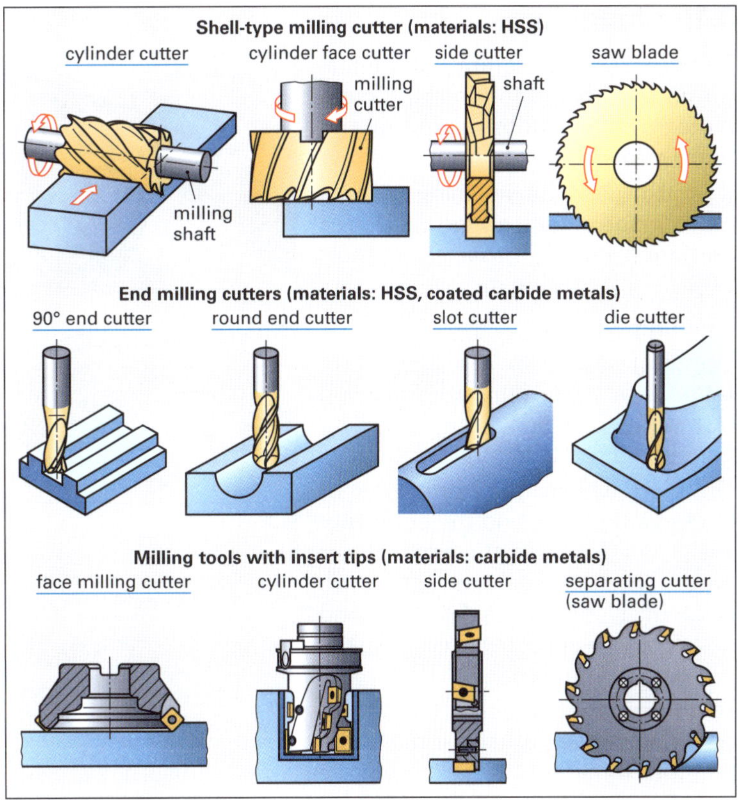

Machining variables

The main machining variables for face milling are the cutting velocity v_c, the feed per revolution f or per milling tooth f_z and the radial milling depth a_e.

Feed speed v_f: $v_f = f \cdot n$

$v_f = f_z \cdot z \cdot n$

Cutting velocity v_c: $v_c = \pi \cdot d \cdot n$

Material removal rate Q: $Q = a_p \cdot a_e \cdot v_f$

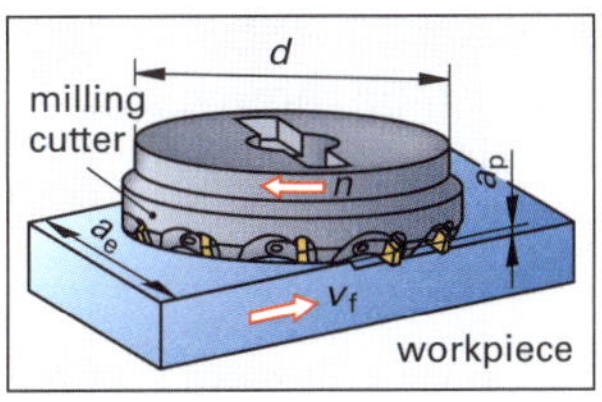

Example of a milling task

A workpiece of 42CrMo4 is face milled according to the cutting values of the **Metal Trade Handbook**. The width of the workpiece is 100 mm, the cutter has 8 insert tips and a diameter of 125 mm. The cutting depth is 5 mm. The cutting dimensions: a_p = 5 mm; a_e = 100 mm; Determine or calculate: v_c, f_z, n, v_f, Q;

Solution:

From the **Handbook** you read: v_c = 120 m/min; f_z = 0.2 mm;

$$n = \frac{v_c}{\pi \cdot d} = \frac{120\ \text{m/min}}{\pi \cdot 0.125\ \text{m}} \approx \mathbf{305\ min^{-1}}$$

$$v_f = f_z \cdot z \cdot n = 0.2\ \text{mm} \cdot 8 \cdot 305\ \text{min}^{-1} \approx \mathbf{489\ mm/min}$$

$$Q = 5\ \text{mm} \cdot 100\ \text{mm} \cdot 489\ \text{mm/min} \approx \mathbf{244 \cdot 10^{-3}\ cm^3/min}$$

Words

aspect	Gesichtspunkt
shell-type milling cutter	Aufsteckfräser
cylinder cutter	Walzenfräser
side cutter	Scheibenfräser
saw blade	Sägeblatt
end milling cutter	Schaftfräser
90°-end cutter	90° Schaftfräser
round end cutter	Kugelschaftfräser
slot cutter	Nutenfräser
die cutter	Gesenkfräser
insert tip	Wendeschneidplatte
face milling cutter	Planfräser
separating cutter	Trennfräser
removal rate	Zerspanvolumen
width	Breite
flat steel	Flachstahl

Exercises

1. Name the English terms for the components:
   a) Fräskopf b) Spannfutter c) Führung
   d) Aufspanntisch e) Fräsmaschinen-Gestell
2. Name the machine variables shown in the figure in English.
   a) b) c)

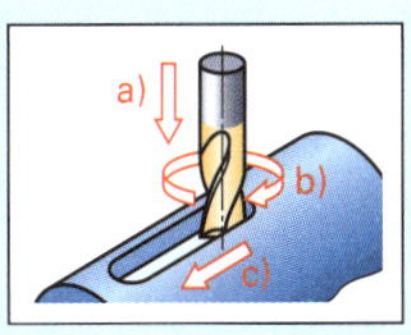

3. Which milling technique is used to produce a plane surface on a flat steel?
4. Which milling tool and milling technique is used in the figure?

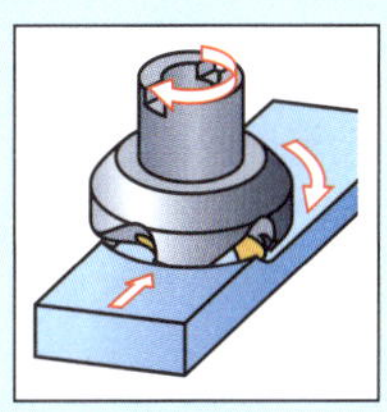

5. Label the milling variables in the figure.
   a) frequency
   b) feed velocity
   c) cutting velocity
6. A 72 mm wide flat steel of C45 has to be milled by a face milling cutter (d = 94 mm) with 6 insert tips. The cutting depth is 3.5 mm.
   Determine: a) v_C b) f c) n d) Q

3.15 Grinding

Grinding is a chip removal manufacturing technology for finishing components with smooth surfaces and narrow tolerances **(figure).**

It is also used for finishing components made of hard materials such as hardened steels, or to sharpen tools of HSS and carbide metals.

Grinding wheels

Grinding wheels are disc-shaped rotational wheels **(figure)**. They are clamped between the chucking flange and rotate at high frequency.

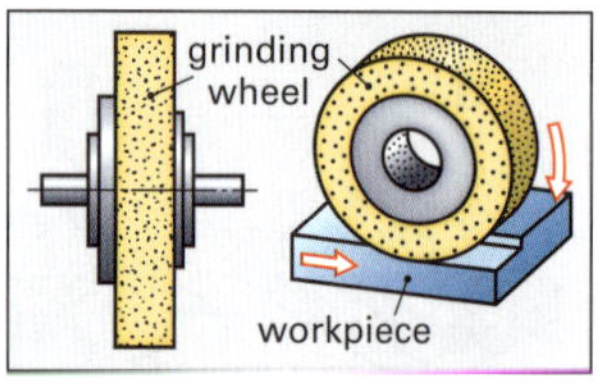

Grinding wheels are composed of abrasive particles and the bond **(figure).** The abrasive particles consist of hard materials such as corundum Al_2O_3 or silicon carbide SiC. The bond is synthetic resin or ceramics. It keeps the particles together.

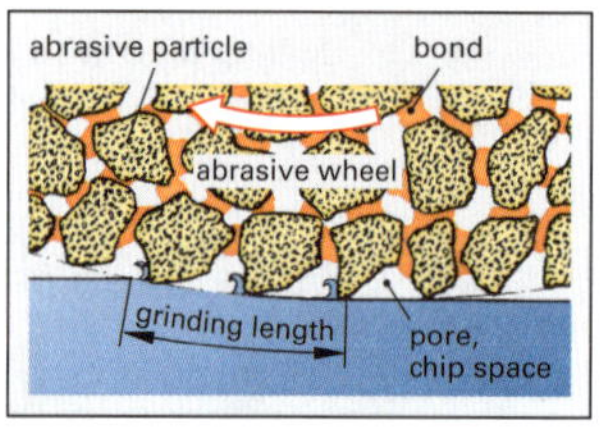

At the grinding process the sharp-edged abrasive particles remove the workpiece material by taking off many small chips. They are collected in the pores and thrown out by the high frequency.

The particle size of the grains has an influence on the metal removal rate and the surface quality. Big grains have a high removal rate and generate low surface quality. Small grains have a low removal rate and a high surface quality.

Machining variables

The main grinding techniques are peripheral face grinding and cylindrical grinding **(figure).** They have typical movements and machining variables **(table)**, which lead to machine settings.

The **cutting velocity v_c** of the grinding wheel $v_c = \pi \cdot D \cdot n$ is the peripheral velocity.

The maximal frequency n_{max} is shown on the label of the wheel. The common cutting velocity v_c for grinding steels is 30 m/s. Higher velocities are possible with special grinding wheels.

The **feed speed v_f** is the velocity of the workpiece. During peripheral face grinding it is the feed of the table; during cylindrical grinding it is the peripheral turning of the workpiece.

The **cross feed f** is the movement across to the grinding wheel. The **cutting depth a_e** is vertically set to the feed direction.

Example: A clamping table of cast iron has to be cut by peripheral face grinding. Determine the machine variables and calculate the frequency for a grinding wheel, with a diameter of 320 mm.

Solution: From the table beside you read: v_c = 30 m/s;
v_f = 10... 35 m/min;

$$v_c = \pi \cdot D \cdot n \Rightarrow \frac{v_c}{\pi \cdot D} = \frac{30 \text{ ms}}{\pi \cdot 0.32 \text{ m}} \approx \mathbf{29.8\ s^{-1}}$$

Words	
grinding	schleifen
to grind, ground, ground	schleifen, schliff, geschliffen
chip removal	spanabhebend
to finish	endbearbeiten
smooth	glatt
narrow	eng
tolerance	Toleranz
to sharpen	schärfen
grinding wheel	Schleifscheibe
disc-shaped	scheibenförmig
chucking flange	Spannflansch
to be composed of	bestehen aus
abrasive particle	Schleifkorn
bond	Bindung
chip space	Spankammer
corundum	Korund
silicon carbide	Siliciumcarbid
synthetic resin	Kunstharz
sharp edged	scharfkantig
grain	Korn
machining variable	Zerspanungsgröße
peripheral face grinding	Umfangs-Stirn-schleifen
cylindrical grinding	Rundschleifen
movement	Bewegung
machine setting	Maschinen-Einstell-größe
label	Etikett
common	üblich
feed of the table	Tischvorschub
cross feed	Quervorschub
cutting depth	Zustelltiefe

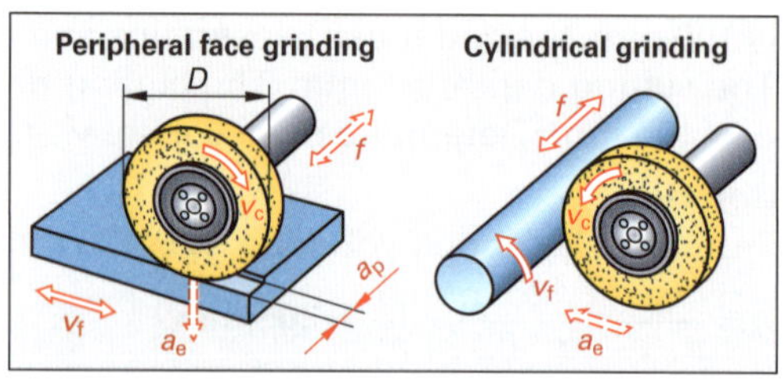

Table: Standard values for machining variables

material	peripheral face grinding		cylindrical grinding	
	v_c m/s	v_f m/min	v_c m/s	v_f m/min
steel	30	10–35	35	10
cast iron	30	10–35	25	11
Al-alloys	18	15–40	18	24–30

Exercises

1. Answer the following questions:
   a) Which applications are common for grinding?
   b) Which are the different components of a grinding wheel?
2. Why is a grinding wheel not allowed to rotate at a frequency over the maximum frequency?
3. Determine the cutting velocity and the feed speed for grinding a tool of carbide metal, by using your **Metal Trade Handbook.**

3.16 Overview of joining technologies

Machines, devices and equipments are composed of several components. They have to be joined (connected). There are many joining technologies for the diverse purposes. They can be divided according to their mode of function in form-locking, force-locking and material-locking joining methods. Form-locking connections are e.g. feather keys, snap connections and partially screw joints.

Feather key joint

A feather key transfers the torque from the driving shaft to the hub and then to the component fitted at it, e.g. a gear-wheel **(figure)**.

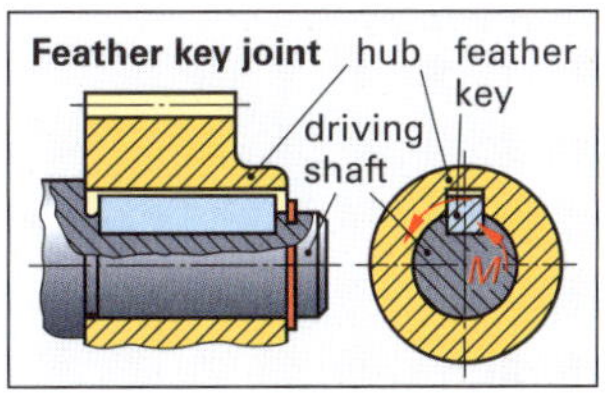

Screw joint

A screw joint consists of a screw, a screw nut and a locking ring **(figure)**. It connects two components by the threads of the screw and nut. By tightening the nut, the components are pressed together by the preload force F_p. The friction between the components carries the load F_L. To get a high enough frictional force, the screw nut has to be tightened by a torque wrench.

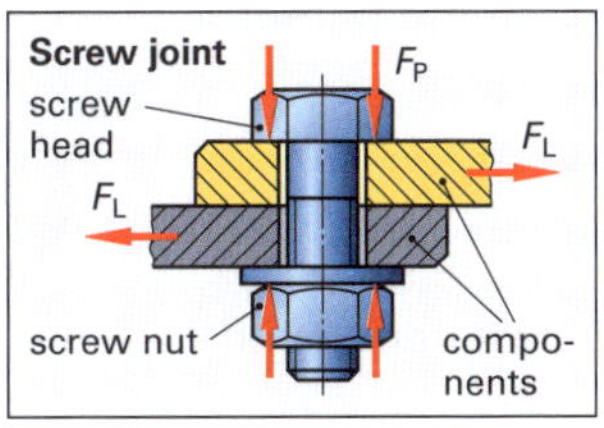

Snap-connection

A snap-connection fixes two components in an assembly group. It consists of hooks at one component and back tapers at the other component **(figure)**. Snaps are not suitable to transfer great forces and torques.

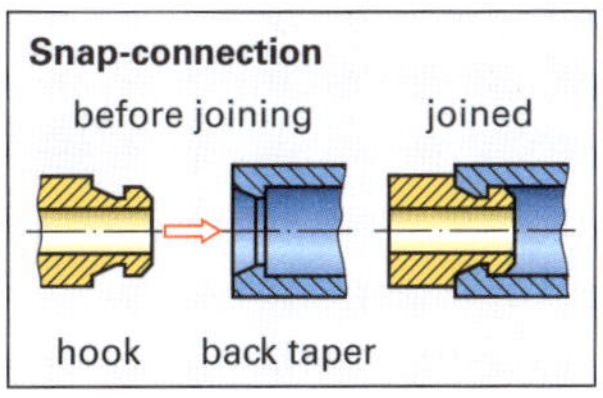

Shrink joint (connection)

A shrink joint is generated, when two fitting surfaces with oversize are pressed together.

At a shaft-hub-shrink joint e.g. the shaft has a minor greater diameter than the bore **(figure)**. The components are joined together by assembling the cooled shaft on the heated hub.

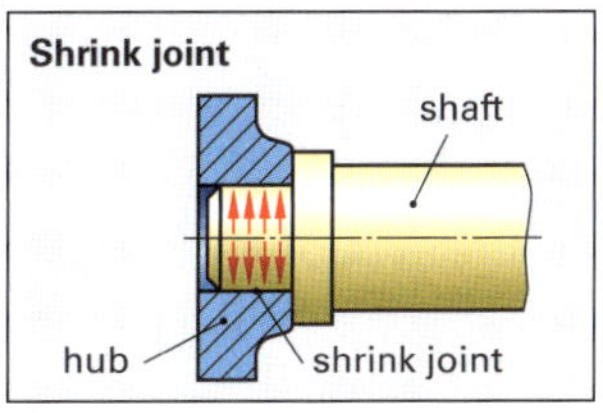

Adhesive joint (Bonding)

The bonding joint of two components is generated by an adhesive **(figure)**. The covers of a sandwich panel are e.g. bonded with the intermediate layer.

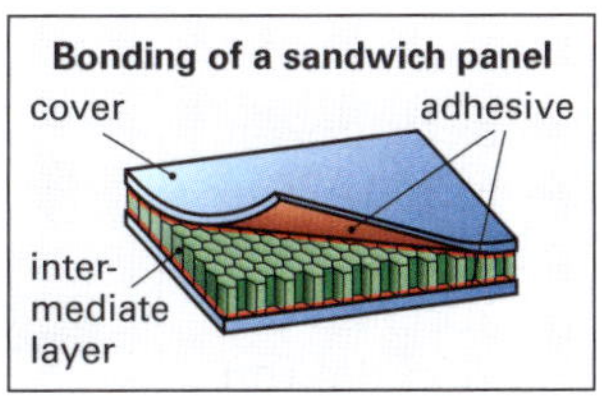

Soldering

The soldering connection between two metal components is generated by a low melting solder, e.g. of tin-lead **(figure)**. The soldering point is heated and the solder flows into the soldering fit. A flux supports the flow of the soldering alloy.

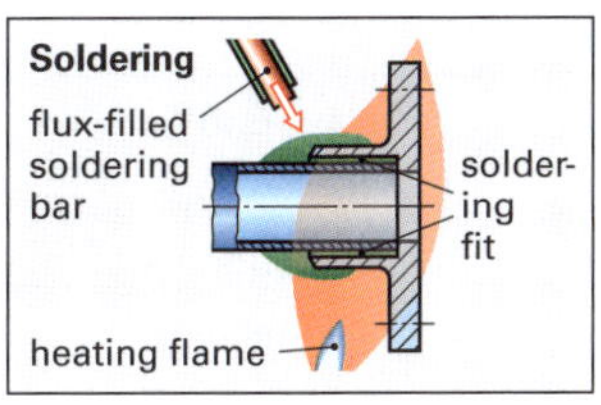

Welding

By welding, two components are connected non-detachable by melting the material at the welding gap **(figure)**. The solidified welding seam connects the components.

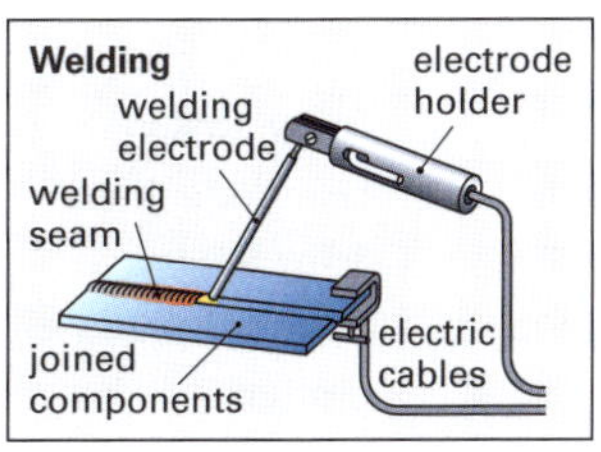

Words	
joining technology	Fügeverfahren
device	Gerät
equipment	Vorrichtung
to compose of	bestehen aus
to join, to connect	fügen, verbinden
diverse	unterschiedlich
purpose	Zweck
mode of function	Wirkungsweise
form-locking	formschlüssig
force-locking	kraftschlüssig
material-locking	stoffschlüssig
feather key	Passfeder
to transfer	übertragen
torque	Drehmoment
driving shaft	Antriebswelle
hub	Nabe
gear-wheel	Zahnrad
screw joint	Schraubenverbindung
screw nut	Mutter
locking ring	Sicherungsring
thread	Gewinde
to tighten	festziehen
preload force	Vorspannkraft
friction	Reibung
torque wrench	Drehmomentschlüssel
snap-connection	Schnappverbindung
assembly group	Baugruppe
hook	Haken
back taper	Hinterschneidung
shrink joint	Schrumpfverbindung
to generate	erzeugen
fitting surface	Passfläche
oversize	Übermaß
adhesive joint	Klebeverbindung
bonding	Klebung
adhesive	Klebstoff
cover	Deckschicht
sandwich panel	Sandwichplatte
intermediate layer	Mittellage
to solder	löten
low-melting solder	niedrig schmelzendes Lot
tin-lead	Zinn-Blei
soldering point	Lötstelle
soldering fit	Lötspalt
flux	Flussmittel
to support	unterstützen
to weld	schweißen
non-detachable	unlösbar
welding gap	Schweißfuge
to solidify	erstarren
welding seam	Schweißnaht

3.17 Welding

Welding is the most common joining method to connect steel components permanently. By welding, usually components of similar steel types are joined together.

Before welding, the components are loosely fixed. Then they are heated up to the melting temperature at the gap together with filler metal. After filling the welding gap solidifies and forms the welding seam. It connects the components non-detachably by the solidified material.

There are several welding techniques.

Gas fusion welding (autogenous welding)

The flame of a welding torch heats and melts the edges of the joining components and the filler metal **(figure)**. After solidifying, it connects the two components by the welding seam.

The fuel gas for the torch is acetylene. It is mixed in the welding torch with oxygen and burns at a 2500 °C welding flame.

For the correct welding procedure you require:

- a suitable welding torch (according to the thickness of the components)
- the correct flame adjustment (by the mixing ratio of acetylene and oxygen). Preferably you need a neutral flame with equal portions of acetylene and oxygen.
- a suitable welding rod (the right diameter and filler metal).

Standard values of the operating data and the welding rods are taken from a Metal Trade Handbook. By gas fusion welding only thin components of unalloyed steels are welded.

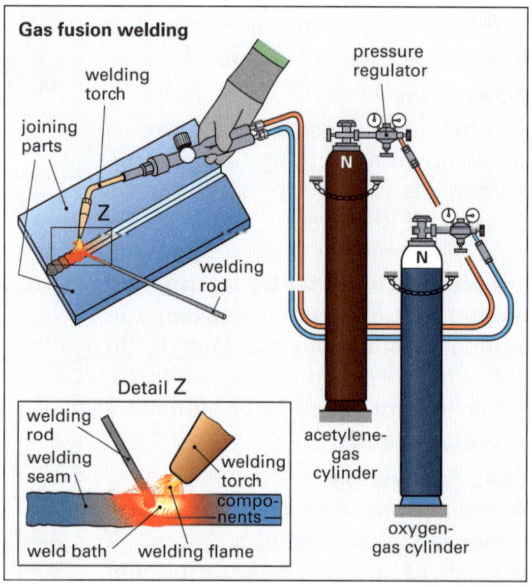

Manual arc welding

For manual arc welding, a welding equipment consists of a welding power source, an electrode holder and the covered electrode **(figure)**.

By touching the joining components at the welding gap with the electrode rod, a very hot electric arc (4.000 °C) starts between the electrode rod and the components. It melts the material of the component edges and of the electrode rod and generates the welding bath. During this process, the evaporating electrode covering forms a gas cloud around the welding point and a cleaning slag on the welding bath. It shields the welding metal against oxidation by the oxygen of the atmosphere. After solidifying, the slag is struck off and the welding seam is visible.

DC- and AC-current can be used. The standard values for power are 15 V to 30 V, the current should be about 200 A to 300 A. The welding power and the welding rods are chosen according the components' thickness and the welded material. You find the suitable values in your **Metal Trade Handbook** and in the rod manufacturers' instructions.

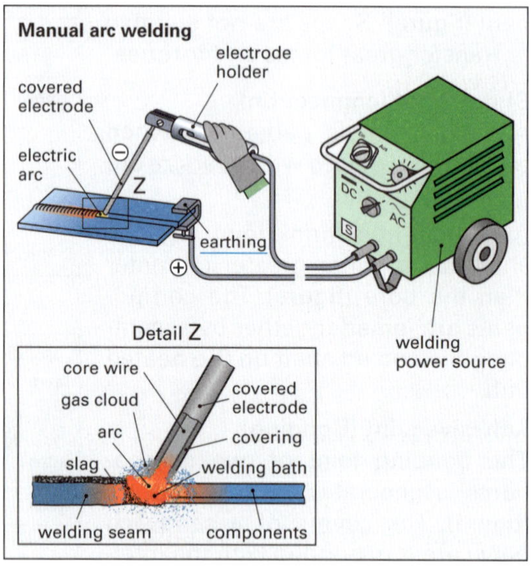

Words

welding	Schweißen
permanent	unlösbar
loosely fixed	lose fixiert
filler metal	Zusatzstoff
gas fusion welding	Gasschmelz-schweißen
autogenous	autogen
welding torch	Schweißbrenner
pressure regulator	Druckminderventil
fuel gas	Brenngas
acetylene	Acetylen
oxygen	Sauerstoff
to burn	brennen
to require	benötigen
adjustment	Einstellung
mixing ratio	Mischverhältnis
preferably	bevorzugt
neutral flame	neutrale Flamme
welding rod	Schweißstab
manual arc welding	Lichtbogenhand-schweißen
power source	Spannungsquelle
covered	umhüllt
covering	Umhüllung
electrode rod	Stabelektrode
arc	Lichtbogen
to evaporate	verdampfen
cloud	Wolke
cleaning slag	Reiningungs-schlacke
to shield	schützen
to strike off (struck, struck)	abschlagen
earthing	Erdung
DC-current	Gleichstrom
AC-current	Wechselstrom

Gas-shielded arc welding

For gas-shielded arc welding you need a welding equipment with a power source, a shielding gas supply, an electrode tracking and a hand-held welding torch **(figure).**

The electric arc melts the welding bath; the flowing gas shields the metal bath against oxidation by atmospheric oxygen. Shielding gases are argon (Ar), nitrogen (N_2), carbon dioxide (CO_2), oxygen (O_2), hydrogen (H_2) and mixtures of it.

Depending on the shielding gas and the electrode type, there are different welding technologies available.

MAG- and MIG-welding

In these welding technologies a thin wire electrode and the shielding gas is fed through the welding holder to the welding point **(figure, detail).** The wire electrode together with the components edges melt by the arc and form the welding bath. After solidifying it becomes the welding seam.

In **MAG-welding** (MAG: metal active gas) a mixture of active gases, like CO_2, O_2 in an Argon-based gas, is fed to the welding point. The active gas reacts with the welding bath and shields it from the atmosphere.

The suitable gas-mixture and wire electrode can be chosen from a **Metal Trade Handbook** or the manufacturers' instructions. When using MAG-welding, it is possible to weld unalloyed and alloyed steel, such as CrNi-steels.

In **MIG-welding** (MIG: metal inert gas) inert gases, such as Argon (Ar), Helium (He) and Hydrogen (H_2) shield the welding bath.

With MAG- and MIG-welding technologies great welding capacities can be reached. They are suitable for automatic welding.

TIG-welding (TIG: tungsten inert gas)

In this welding technology, the electric arc performs between the non-melting tungsten electrode and the melting bath (figure, detail TIG-welding).

The shielding gas is inert (which means it is not reactive), the welding rod is fed manually. The TIG-welding is applied for CrNi-steels and non-ferrous metals, such as aluminium or titanium, especially for thin sheet metals.

Gas shielded arc welding

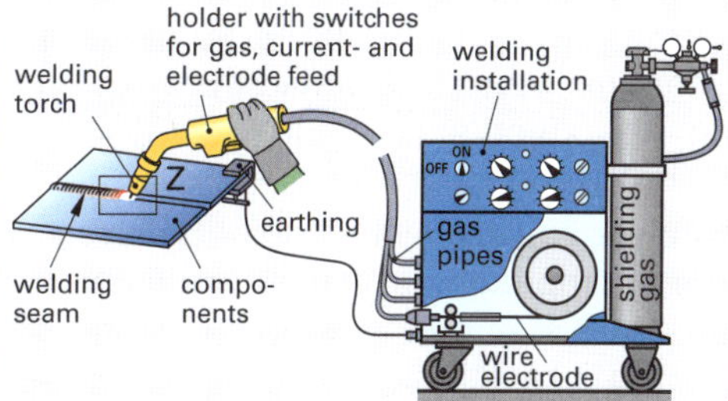

Detail: MAG- and MIG-welding

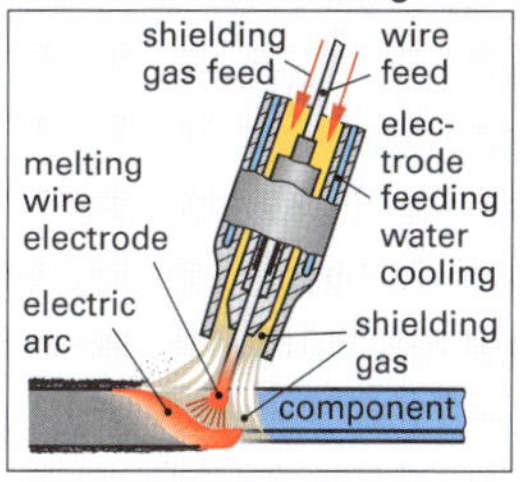

Detail: TIG-welding

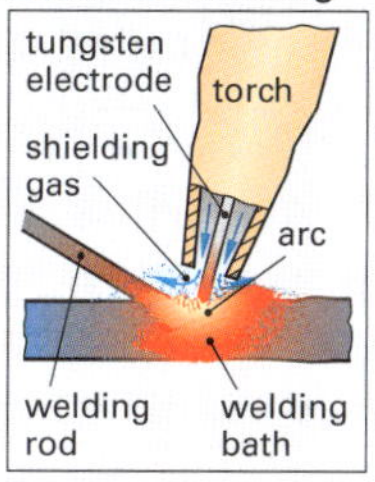

Words

English	German
gas-shielding arc welding	Schutzgas-Lichtbogen-schweißen
gas supply	Gasversorgung
tracking	Nachführung
to shield	abschirmen
nitrogen	Stickstoff
carbon dioxide	Kohlenstoffdioxid
hydrogen	Wasserstoff
depending on	je nach
wire electrode	Drahtelektrode
to feed (fed, fed)	zuführen
welding capacity	Schweißleistung
sheet metal	Blech
to match	zuordnen
assembly drawing	Montagezeichnung
abbreviation	Abkürzung

Exercises

1. Summarise in English the paragraph about the feather key joint from page 45.
2. Match the joining technologies – feather key, screw joint, snap-joint, shrink joint, bonding, soldering, welding – according to the mode of function of
   a) form-locking b) force-locking
   c) material-locking.
3. Which joining technologies can be used in the assembly drawing of the numbers 1 to 5?

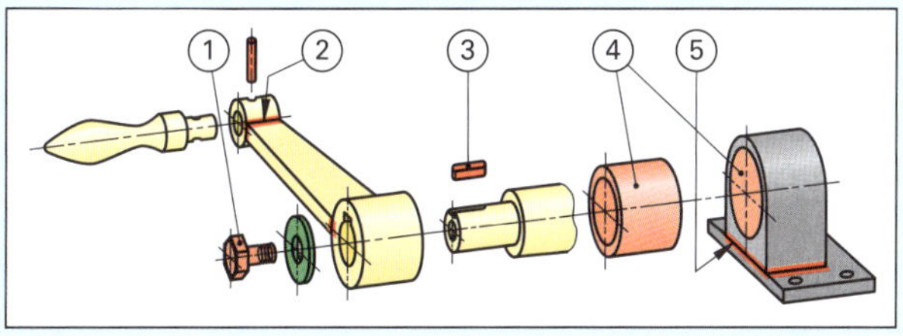

4. Name two differences between the joining methods soldering and welding.
5. Name the English terms of manual arc welding for the numbers in the figure at right hand.
6. Which gases do you need for gas fusion welding?

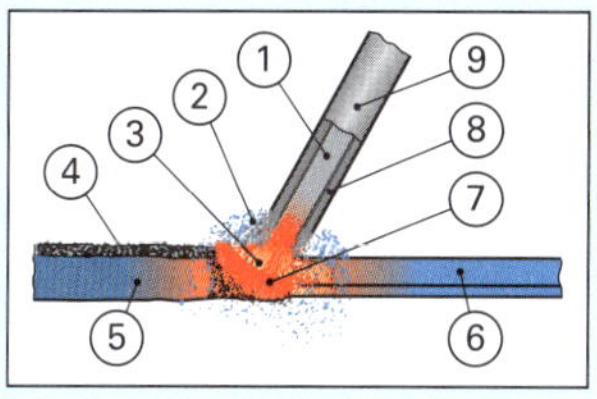

7. What do the abbreviations mean?
   a) MAG-welding
   b) TIG-welding
   c) MIG-welding
8. a) Which welding technology does the figure show?
   b) Name the terms of the numbers.

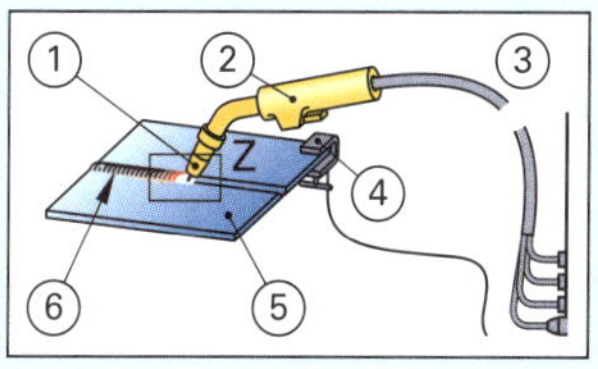

3.18 Assembly technique

During the assembly, the components are connected and form a functional product. Right at the beginning of the construction of the components, care has to be taken, that the assembly steps are quick and simple to operate.

Example: The shaft with the continuous step **(figure)** was constructed inappropriately, because the roller bearing must be pushed over the entire step during assembly. If the shaft in front of the roller bearing is constructed with a shoulder and a smaller diameter, the bearing can be assembled easier and faster on the shaft.

Design of a shaft

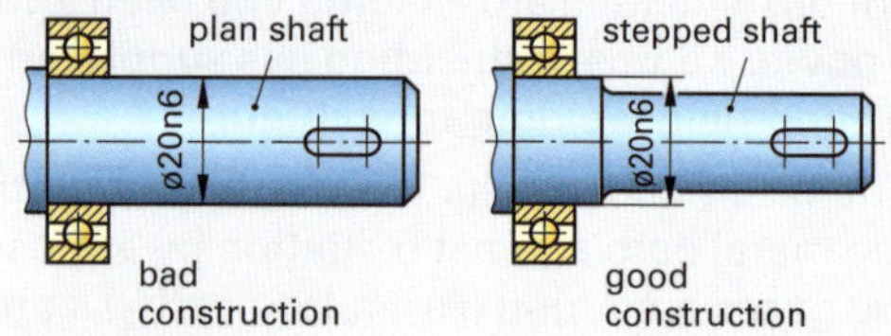

Assembly plan

For a procedure of the systematic assembly you need to establish an assembly plan **(figure)**. The order of assembly is listed. With the respective assembly processes the required working materials (machines, jigs, tools and auxiliary materials) are named as well. For the functional control of the assembly, the measuring instruments are specified in the assembly plan.

Assembly plan for an assembly group (example)

Nr.	assembly process	working material measuring instrument	assembly notice
1	Deburr edges of the components, clean them and check for completeness. Measure the main dimensions	file, cloth calliper	take the bill of the material
2	Assemble the key (16) on the shaft (15)	soft-head hammer	carefully hit the key

For the inspection, the repair or the transport, products must be disassembled partially or completely, especially in cases of large dimensions, e.g. machine tools. The disassembly also has to be planned carefully and to be documented in a disassembly plan gradually.

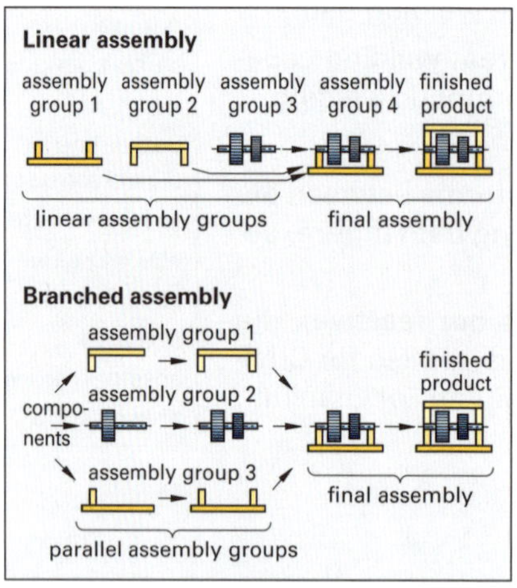

Assembly form of organisation

There are different methods of organising the assembly **(figure)**.

In the linear assembly the work steps are made one after the other.

In branched assembly parallel assembly groups are connected for its own. The different assembly groups are finally mounted to the product.

Mass product articles are usually assembled in automatic line of production. Large and complex products, e.g. a machining center, are produced first in group assembly and then in branched assembly.

Words

assembly technique	Montagetechnik
component	Einzelteil
functional product	Gebrauchserzeugnis
to take care	Sorge tragen
to operate	durchführen
shaft	Welle
step	Absatz
to construct	konstruieren
inappropriate	ungünstig
roller bearing	Wälzlager
diameter	Durchmesser
to assemble	montieren
assembly plan	Montageplan
respective	jeweilig
assembly process	Montagevorgang
working material	Betriebsmittel
jig	Vorrichtung
tool	Werkzeug
auxiliary material	Hilfsmittel
measuring instrument	Prüfmittel
to deburr	entgraten
file	Feile
cloth	Tuch
soft-head hammer	Schonhammer
inspection	Überprüfung
repair	Reparatur
to disassemble	demontieren
disassembly	Demontage
linear assembly	unverzweigter Montageablauf
work steps	Arbeitsschritte
branched assembly	verzweigte Montage
to mount	zusammenbauen
mass product articles	massengefertigte Produkte
machining center	Bearbeitungszentrum
group assembly	Gruppenmontage
measure	Maßnahme

Exercises

1. Answer the following questions in English.
   a) Which information is listed in an assembly plan?
   b) What are the advantages of an assembly group?
   c) For which application do you need the disassembly?
2. Summarize the paragraph about assembly techniques into German.
3. Name a constructive measure, which leads to an easier assembly process.
4. Complete the following sentences:
   For a procedure of the ______________ you need to build ______________________.
   The ______________________ must be listed.

Example: Final assembling of an air cylinder

The air cylinder consists of the assembly groups A (cylinder head), B (cylinder bottom), C (piston and piston rod) and the individual parts, cylinder D, cylinder flange E, sealing rings, wiper rings, and screws **(figure).** Additionally you need lubrication for the assembly.

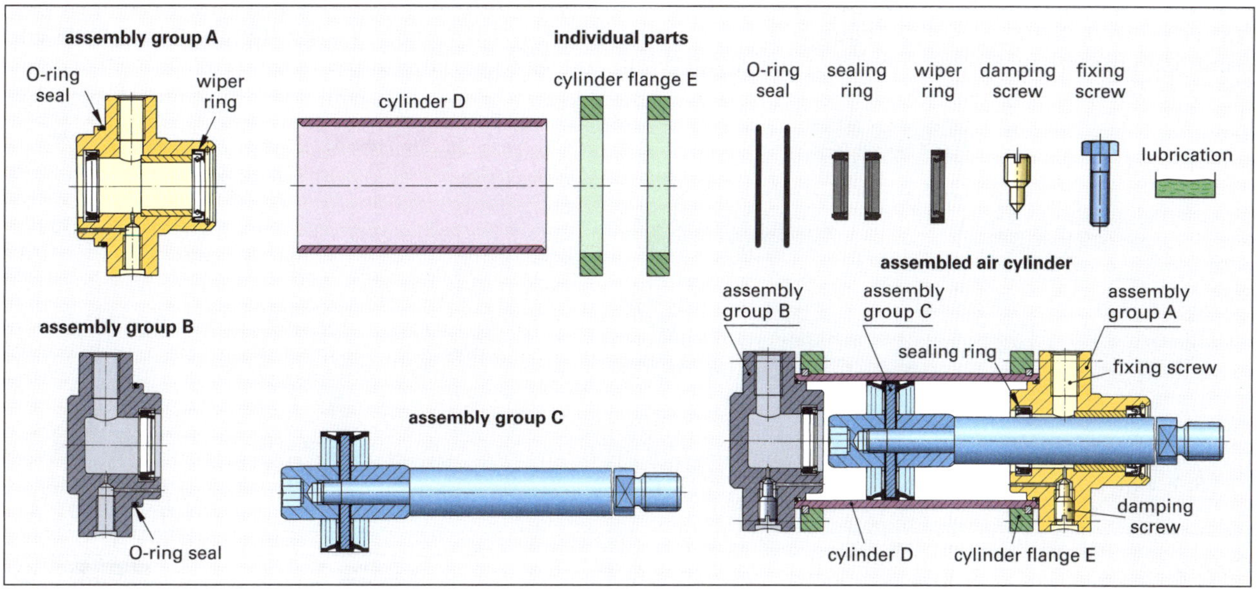

At first the assembly groups A, B and C including the O-ring seals and the wiper ring, are assembled on its own and laid out.

As well, the cylinder, the cylinder flanges, sealing rings, screws and the lubrication are produced, provided and laid out.

Then the final assembly starts.

Next the cylinder flanges E and the sealing rings are pushed over cylinder D.

Before assembly group C (piston rod and piston) can be installed in assembly group A, the piston rod has to be greased and to be inserted in the guide bush of assembly group A.

Then the piston of assembly group C will be filled with lubrication.

Now the assembly groups A and C are inserted together into the cylinder D carefully. Both assembly groups are pressed down into the bore until assembly group A is in contact with cylinder D. Then assembly group A and the cylinder flange are connected with four fixing screws. Finally, assembly group B is screwed to the second cylinder flange.

The final check begins with testing the ease of motion. The piston rod is moved to the final position by axial displacement. Then leakproofness is made at a piston pressure of 6 bar.

In the final functional check the damping of the final position is set with damping screws.

Words

air cylinder	Druckluftzylinder
cylinder head	Zylinderkopf
cylinder bottom	Zylinderboden
piston	Kolben
piston rod	Kolbenstange
cylinder flange	Zylinderflansch
sealing ring	Dichtring
wiper ring	Abstreifring
screw	Schraube
lubrication	Schmierstoff
to lay out (laid, laid)	bereitlegen
greased	eingefettet
to insert	einsetzen
guide bush	Führungsbuchse
bore	Bohrung
fixing screw	Befestigungsschraube
final check	Endkontrolle
ease of motion	Leichtgängigkeit
final position	Endlage
leakproofness	Dichtheit
piston pressure	Kolbendruck
functional check	Funktionsprüfung
damping screw	Dämpfungsschraube
to explain	erklären

Exercises

1. Complete the following sentence in regard to the final assembly:
   Both assembly groups are pressed down into the ________________ until assembly group A is in contact with ________________.
2. Answer the following questions:
   a) Which assembly groups and parts are laid out for the final assembly?
   b) What has to be done with the piston before installing assembly group C?
   c) By which joining elements are the assembly group A and B fixed to the cylinder flange?
3. Explain the various test procedures during the final check.

4 Material engineering

4.1 Overview of materials

In order to get an overview of the variety of materials, they are arranged in material groups according to their composition or their properties **(figure).** The three main groups of the materials are metals, non-metals and composite materials. Further more they are divided into special material groups.

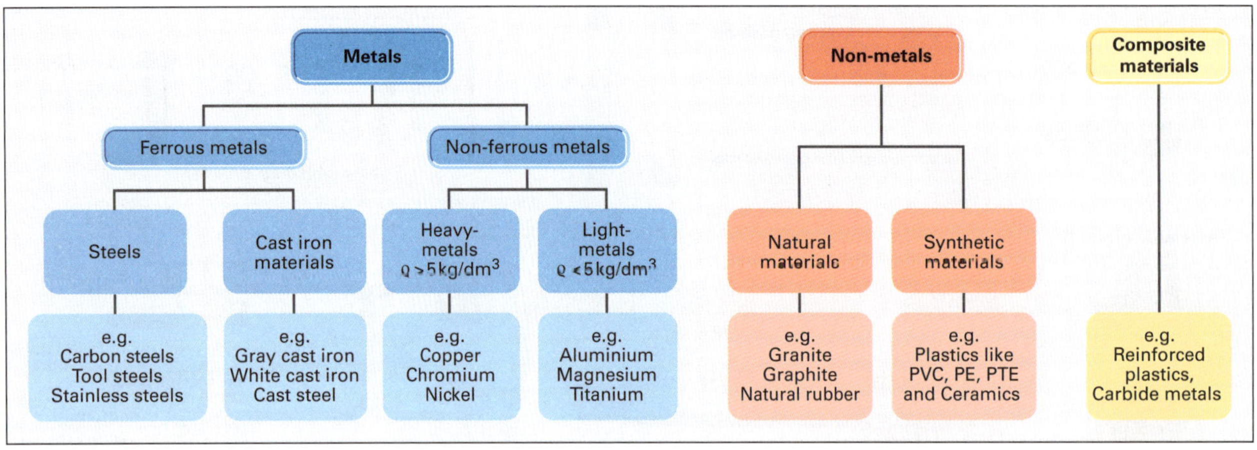

Steels

Steels are the most important materials for mechanical engineering. They are iron-based materials with high strength.

They are used for machine components which have to bear and transfer power: screws, bolts, shafts and gear wheels **(figure)**. There are about 2000 standardised steels. The most common types of steels are carbon steels, quenched and tempered steels, tool steels and stainless steels **(figure)**.

Semi-finished products of carbon steel

Camshaft ofquenched and tempered steel

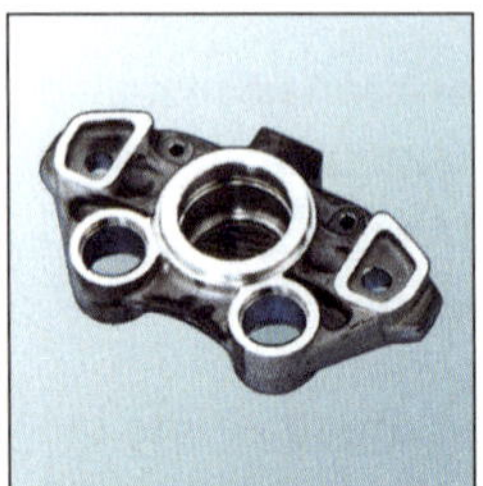

Housing-cover of gray cast iron

Cast iron

Cast iron are easily castable iron-based materials. They are cast into components of difficult shapes, for example housings **(figure above)**.

Words

material engineering	Werkstofftechnik
variety of material	Vielfalt der Werkstoffe
composition	Zusammensetzung
properties	Eigenschaften
metal	Metall
composite material	Verbundwerkstoff
to divide	unterteilen
steel, steels	Stahl, Stähle
mechanical engineering	Maschinenbau
strength	Festigkeit
machine component	Maschinenbauteil
screw, bolt	Schraube, Bolzen
shaft	Welle
gear wheel	Zahnrad
standardised	genormt
carbon steel	unlegierter Baustahl
quenched and tempered steel	Vergütungsstahl
stainless steel	Nichtrostender Stahl
camshaft	Nockenwelle
housing-cover	Gehäusedeckel
cast iron	Gusseisen
easily castable	gut vergießbar
shape	Form
to arrange	zuordnen

Exercises

1. Give an answer in English.
   a) Which are the most important steels in mechanical engineering?
   b) Which construction elements are made of cast iron?
   c) What is the main difference between heavy metals and light metals?
   d) Name three light metals and give an application.
   e) Name two composite materials of your professional field.
2. Arrange the following materials into the groups below:
   Graphite, gray cast iron, zinc, stainless steel, carbids, metals, natural rubber, magnesium, carbon steel, copper, aluminium, plastic, titanium, granite, reinforced plastic, lead, ceramic, quenched and tempered steel.

steels	cast iron	heavy metals	light metals	natural materials	synthetics	composites

Heavy metals

Heavy metals are metal materials with a density over 5 kg/dm^3, e.g. copper, zinc, lead, chromium and nickel. They are used for their typical material properties:

- Copper e.g. for its excellent electric conductivity for motor coils **(figure right hand).**
- Chromium and nickel as alloying elements in stainless steels increase the corrosion resistance **(figure right hand).**

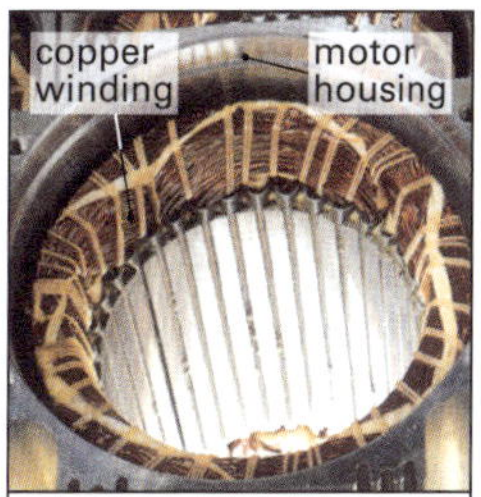

Electric coil of copper for a driving motor

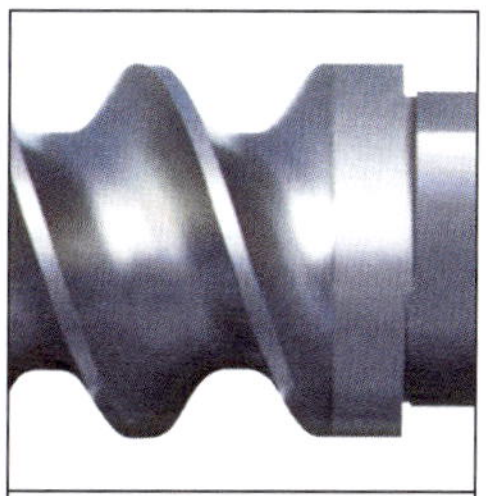
Homoginising screw of chromium steel for an extruder

Light metals

Light metals are metal materials with a density under 5 kg/dm^3: aluminium ϱ_{Al} = 2.7 kg/dm^3, magnesium ϱ_{Mg} = 1.8 kg/dm^3, titanium ϱ_{TI} = 4.5 kg/dm^3.

The light metal alloys have a high strength and can be used for construction elements.

Their main field of application are light weight components for cars and planes **(figure, left hand and middle).**

Aeroplane-parts of aluminium alloy

Wheel-rim of aluminium alloy for a car

O-seals of silicone-rubber for machines

Plastics

Plastics are light and electrically insulating materials. They are available in types from soft rubber **(figure above, right hand)** to stiff construction parts. Their use is extremely manifold. It reaches from material for tyres to engine components **(figure below, left hand).**

Small gear-box of plastic for a car wiper

Cutting inserts of industrial ceramic in a milling head

Grinding wheel of hard particle/plastic-composite

Synthetic and composite materials are mainly used because of their hardness, e.g. as cutting inserts **(figure above).**

Composites are composed of several materials, e.g. fiber reinforced plastics of glass fibers and a plastic matrix or grinding wheels of hard-particles and a plastic bonding **(figure).**

Words

heavy metal	Schwermetall
density	Dichte
copper, zinc, lead	Kupfer, Zink, Blei
chromium, nickel	Chrom, Nickel
electric conductivity	elektrische Leitfähigkeit
electric coil	elektrische Wicklung
alloying element	Legierungselement
corrosion resistance	Korrosionswiderstand
motor coil	Motorwicklung
driving motor	Antriebsmotor
homogenising screw	Knetschnecke
light metal	Leichtmetall
aluminium	Aluminium
magnesium, titanium	Magnesium, Titan
construction element	Konstruktionsbauteil
application	Anwendung
plane	Flugzeug
wheel-rim	Radfelge
O-seal	O-Ring
plastic	Kunststoff
electrically insulating	elektrisch isolierend
soft rubber	Weichgummi
stiff construction parts	steife Formteile
manifold	vielfältig
tyre	Reifen
gear-box	Getriebe
car wiper	Scheibenwischer
industrial ceramic	Industriekeramik
hardness	Härte
cutting inserts	Schneideplatte
milling head	Fräskopf
composite	Verbundwerkstoff
fiber reinforced	glasfaserverstärkt
plastic matrix	Kunststoffbindung
grinding wheel	Schleifscheiben
bonding	Bindung

Exercises

1. Translate the first two sentences of this page in German.
2. Test your material knowledge. Give an answer in English for the questions:
   a) What is the main property for the application of copper?
   b) What are light metals used for?
   c) Which types of steel contain chromium and nickel as alloying elements?
   d) What are typical properties of plastics?
   e) Name three applications for plastics.
   f) What are cutting inserts made of?
   g) Name two composites and the materials they consist of.

4.2 Important properties of materials

Physical properties

Physical properties describe the mass of the material and the modification of its condition while temperature changes.

The **density** of a material gives an idea of the weight of a component **(figure)**. The density of a body is calculated by the mass m divided by the volume V.

$$\varrho = \frac{m}{V}$$

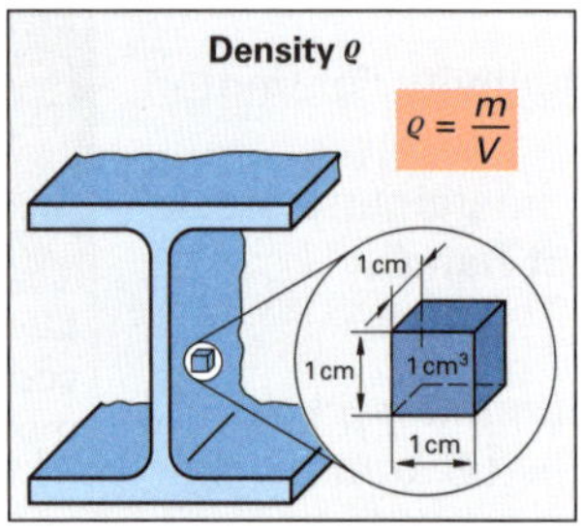

The **melting point** δ_b is the temperature when a material begins to melt **(figure)**.

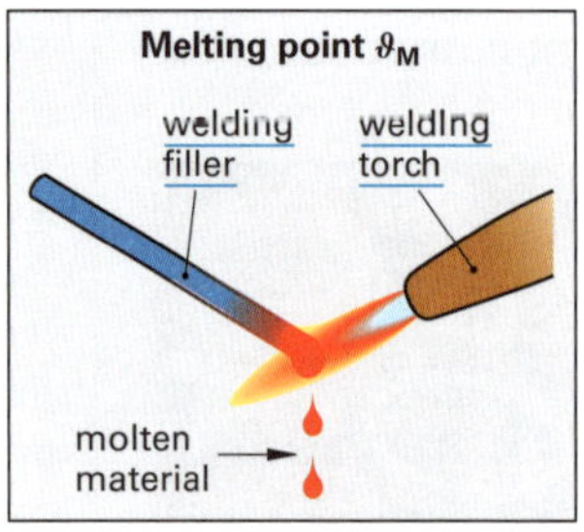

The melting point is important for welding and soldering.

The **thermal expansion** describes the elongation of a component by a temperature change **(figure)**.

It is calculated by the **thermal expansion coefficient** α, the length l of the component and the temperature increase $\Delta\vartheta$.

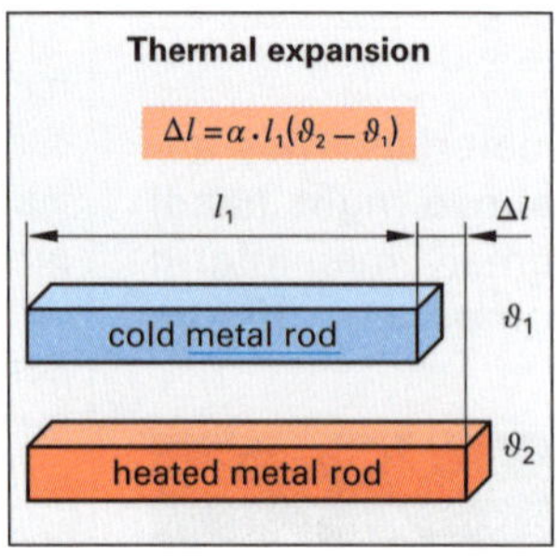

The thermal expansion is needed for the measuring and the assembly of engine components.

You find the values of the physical properties of the materials in your **Metal Trade Handbook**.

Chemical properties

Corrosion is the attack and the damage of metal materials, caused by chemical and electrochemical reactions with active agents of the environment **(figure)**.

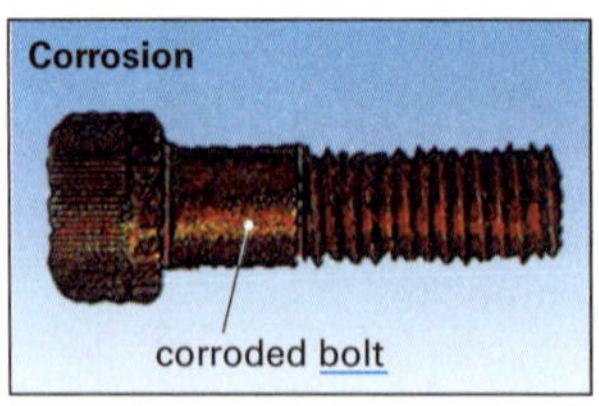

You need the corrosion properties of materials to choose one material to use in a corrosive environment.

Scaling is another chemical property. It happens e.g. while forging.

Words

English	German
property	Eigenschaft
physical	physikalisch
material	Werkstoff
modification	Änderung
condition	Zustand
to change	ändern
density	Dichte
idea	Vorstellung
weight	Gewicht
component	Bauteil
to calculate	berechnen
mass	Masse
volume	Volumen
melting point	Schmelzpunkt
welding	Schweißen
soldering	Löten
welding filler	Schweißstab
welding torch	Schweißbrenner
thermal expansion	thermische Ausdehnung
elongation	Verlängerung
expansion coefficient	Ausdehnungskoeffizient
increase	Erhöhung
measuring	Messen
assembly	Zusammenbau
engine	Motor
metal rod	Metallstab
chemical	chemisch
corrosion	Korrosion
attack	Angriff
damage	Zerstörung
to cause	verursachen
electrochemical reaction	elektrochemische Reaktion
active agent	Wirkstoff
environment	Umgebung
to choose, chose, chosen	auswählen
bolt	Schraube
scaling	verzundern
forging	Schmiedestück
statement	Erklärung
to indicate	angeben
application	Anwendung

Exercises

1. Fill in the missing words:
   a) The density of a material is defined as a quotient of ______________ and the ______________.
   b) The melting point is the temperature when ______________________________.
   c) The thermal expansion is needed for ______________________________.
   d) The attack of a metal material by electrochemical reactions is called ______________________.

2. Test your knowledge of material properties. Give an answer in English:
   a) Which statement for the weight of a component can you make when you know its density?
   b) What does the melting point of a material indicate?
   c) For which applications do you need a special knowledge on thermal expansion?
   d) Which consequences can the corrosion of a metallic component cause?

Technical properties

The technical properties of the materials characterise the material behaviour under the influence of forces during the applications.

The most important technical properties are measured by the **tensile test (figure opposite).** By loading a specimen and measuring the force and the elongation, you get a stress-strain-diagram showing the mechanical values.

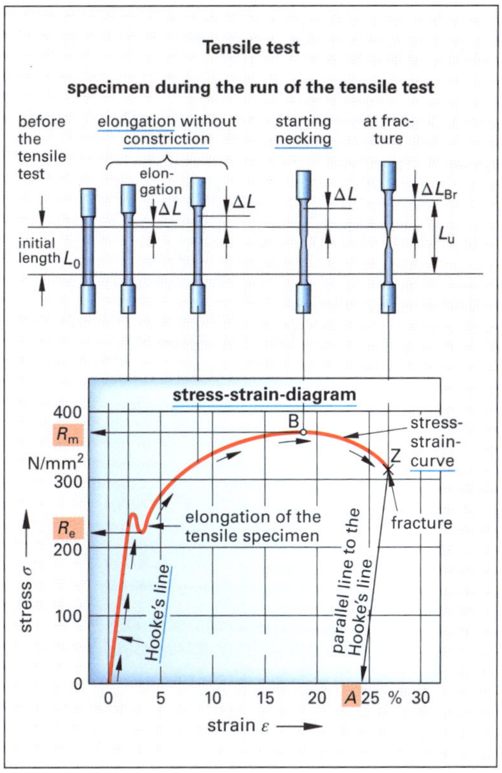

The **tensile strength** R_m is the highest tensile stress which can occur in a material. It is calculated by the maximum force F_m, a specimen can withstand, divided by the initial cross section area S_0.

$$R_m = \frac{F_m}{S_0}$$

The **yield point** R_e is the tensile stress which can resist a material, right before the material begins to deform permanently under the influence of the force F_e:

$$R_e = \frac{F_e}{S_0}$$

The **elongation at fracture** *EL* is the quotient of the permanent deformation $L_u – L_0$ which a specimen has undergone after the mechanical load up to the fracture and the initial length L_0.

$$EL = \frac{L_u - L_0}{L_0} \cdot 100\,\%$$

The **hardness** of a material is the resistance force caused by the indentation of a test specimen.

It is measured by a **hardness test (figure).** Hard materials are hardened steels or carbide metals. Materials, which are not so hard, are aluminium and copper.

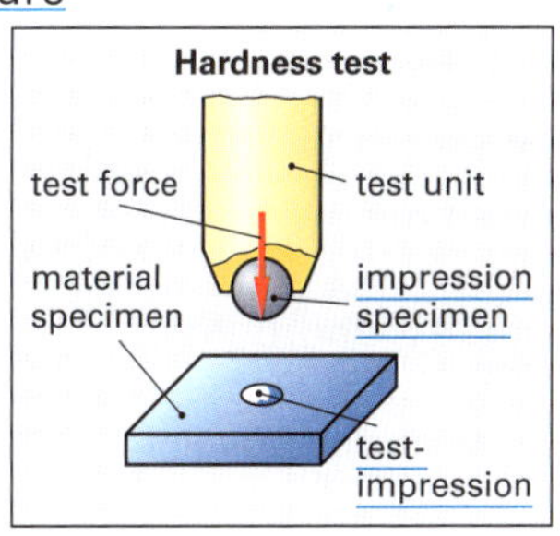

Words	
technical properties	technische Eigenschaften
to characterise	bestimmen
material behaviour	Werkstoffverhalten
influence	Wirkung
force	Kraft
hardness	Härte
resistance force	Widerstandskraft
indentation	Eindrücken
specimen	Prüfkörper
hardness test	Härteprüfung
hardened steel	gehärteter Stahl
carbide metal	Hartmetall
copper	Kupfer
impression specimen	Eindrückkörper
test-impression	Prüfeindruck
tensile test	Zugversuch
loading	Belastung
stress-strain-diagram	Spannungs-Dehnungs-Diagramm
tensile strength	Zugfestigkeit
tensile stress	Zugspannung
to occur	auftreten
maximum force	Höchstkraft
to divide	teilen
initial cross-section area	anfänglicher Bauteilquerschnitt
yield point	Streckgrenze
right before	kurz vor
to deform permanently	bleibend verformen
elongation at fracture	Bruchdehnung
elongation	Verlängerung
permanent deformation	bleibende Verformung
to undergo	ertragen
mechanical load	mechanische Belastung
fracture	Bruch
necking	Einschnürung
initial length	Anfangsmesslänge
curve	Kurve
Hooke's line	Hooke'sche Gerade
initial length	Anfangslänge
pressing	Eindrücken
quantity(ies)	Größe(n)

Exercises

1. Fill in the missing terms:
   a) By pressing an indentation body into a material specimen you determine its __________________.
   b) The tensile strength R_m is calculated by the maximum force F_m divided by the __________________.
   c) The tensile strength of a material at the beginning of its permanent deformation, is called ____________________________________.
   d) The permanent deformation of a loaded specimen after its fracture is called __________________.

2. Test your knowledge on material properties. Give an answer in English:
   a) Which quantities are necessary to calculate the tensile strength?
   b) What is the yield point of a material?

4.3 Designation system for steels

Steels are designated by codes. This designation system for steels is standardised in the German and European standard DIN EN 10027-2.

There are two material categories of designation codes.

Designation by application and mechanical and physical properties

The designation code in this category is composed of main symbols and supplemental symbols.

The **main symbol** consists of a code letter for the steel grade, for example S, P, L, E and the minimal yield strength R_e in the unit N/mm².

The code letters identify a special steel group:

S structural steels for steel construction
E steels for engineering
P steels for pressure vessel construction
D steels for flat rolled products for cold forming

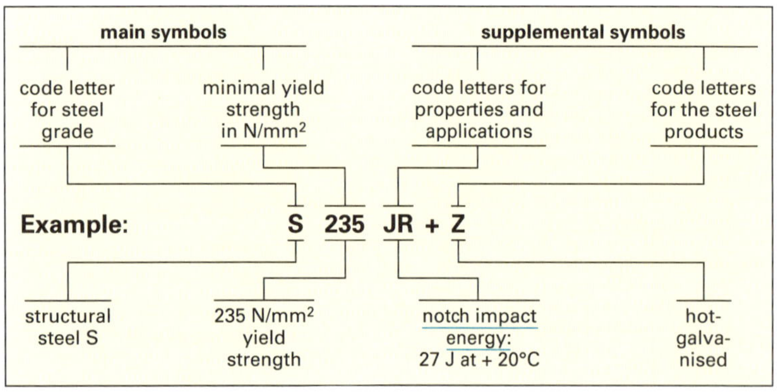

The **supplemental symbols** for unalloyed structural steels are code letters for the notch impact energy and for the further treatment of the steel product.

Designation by the chemical composition

The steels for this designation are classified in 4 sub-groups.

1. Unalloyed steels with a manganese percentage ≤ 1 %

The designation code of these steels is composed of
- the code letter C (for carbon steel)
- a carbon code number for the carbon percentage (hundredfold the carbon percentage)
- a supplemental symbol for special percentages or/and special applications.

Words (English)	Words (German)
designation system	Bezeichnungssystem
to designate	bezeichnen
code	Kurzzeichen
standardised	genormt
standard	Norm
category (-ries)	Gruppe (Gruppen)
application	Anwendung
composed	zusammengesetzt
main symbol	Hauptsymbol
supplemental symbol	ergänzendes Symbol
to consist (of)	bestehen (aus)
code letter	Kennbuchstabe
steel grade	Stahlgruppe
minimal yield strength	Mindest-Streckgrenze
unit	Einheit
to identify	kennzeichnen
structural steels	Baustähle
steel for engineering	Maschinenbaustahl
flat rolled	flach gewalzt
pressure vessel	Druckbehälter
notch impact energy	Kerbschlagarbeit
treatment	Behandlung, Veredelung
chemical composition	chemische Zusammensetzung
to classify	unterteilen
sub-group	Untergruppe
unalloyed steel	unlegierter Stahl
manganese percentage	Mangangehalt
carbon code number	Kohlenstoffkennzahl
carbon percentage	Kohlenstoffgehalt
hundredfold	hundertfach
to recognise	erkennen
concerning	betreffend

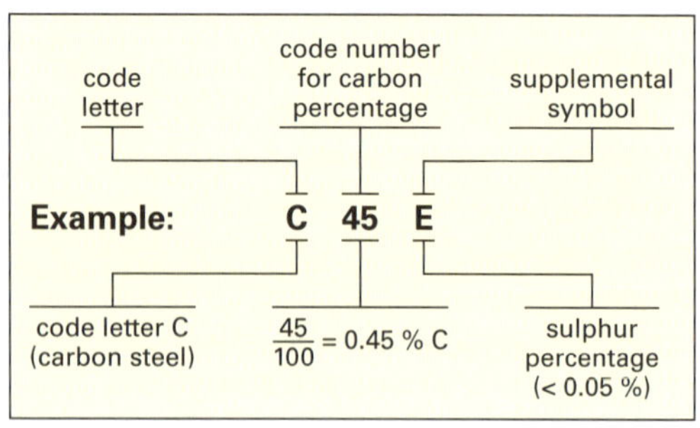

Exercises

1. Summarize the first two sentences of this page into German.
2. Test your material knowledge. Give an answer in German and then in English.
   a) What are the main symbols in a code for an unalloyed structural steel?
   b) What is the code letter of a steel for machine constructions?
   c) How do you calculate the carbon percentage using the carbon code number?
3. Answer the following questions in English:
   a) A steel has the designation code S275JR. Which data can you take of the code?
   b) Which code does a steel for engineering have with a minimal yield strength of 335 N/mm²?
   c) A steel code is C60E. What data can you recognise of the code, concerning
      - the steel grade
      - the carbon percentage
      - a special percentage?

2. Unalloyed steels with Mn ≥ 1 %, free cutting steels and alloyed steels with one alloying element content < 5 %

The designation code of these steel grades consists of:
- a carbon code number for the carbon content (hundredfold of the carbon content)
- the chemical symbols for the alloying elements in the order of their percentage
- the code numbers of the alloying elements in the same order.

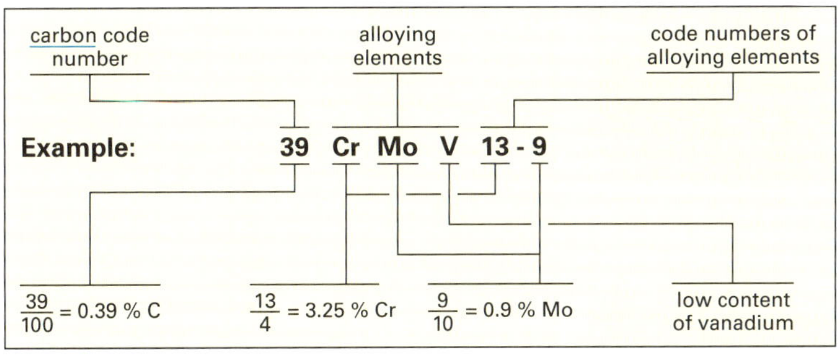

You can calculate the content of the alloying elements by dividing the element code number by the code number factor **(table)**.

Examples: Carbon code number 39: That means a carbon content of $\frac{39}{100}$ = 0.39 % carbon

Chromium code number 13: → $\frac{13}{4}$ = 3.25 % Cr

Alloying elements for steels are: chromium (Cr), nickel (Ni), manganese (Mn), cobalt (Co), Silicium (Si), tungsten (W), molybdenum (Mo), vanadium (V) e.c.

Words	
unalloyed steel	unlegierter Stahl
free cutting steel	Automatenstahl
alloyed steel	legierter Stahl
designation code	Bezeichnungs-Kurzzeichen
carbon code number	Kohlenstoffkennzahl
chemical symbol	chemisches Symbol
in the order	in der Reihenfolge
percentage	Prozentanteil
carbon	Kohlenstoff
to calculate	berechnen
code number factor	Kennzahlfaktor
except	außer
high-speed steel	Schnellarbeitsstahl
at least	wenigstens
code letter	Kennbuchstabe
main	Haupt-

Table: Code number factor for alloying elements

factor 4	Cr	Mi	Mn	Co	Si	W
factor 10	Al	Cu	Mo	Ta	Ti	V
factor 100	C	P	S	N	Ce	

3. Alloy steels (except high speed steels)

(at least one alloying element is over 5 %)

The designation codes of these steels consist of
- the code letter **X** (for alloyed steel)
- the carbon code number for the carbon content (the hundredfold of the carbon content)
- the chemical symbols of the alloying elements
- the percentage of the alloying elements in % in the same order.

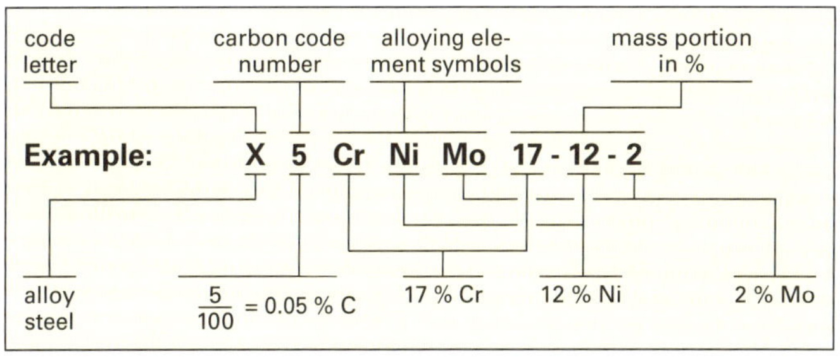

4. High speed steels (HSS steels)

The designation codes of the high-speed steels consist of
- the code letters **HS**
- the numbers, which show the percentage of the main alloying elements in the order tungsten (W) – molybdenum (Mo) – vanadium (V) – cobalt (Co)

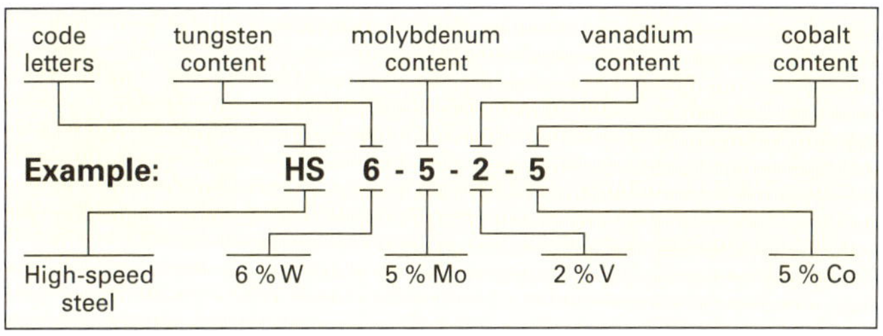

Exercises

1. Test your material engineering knowledge on designation codes for steels.
   a) Which alloying elements do the alloying elements code factor 4 have?
   b) Which steel grade does an **X** in front of the designation code have?
   c) Which alloying elements are designated by the numbers in the code for high-speed steels? Name the alloying elements in the right order.
2. Name the steel group, the properties, the alloying elements and the percentage of the alloying elements you can read off the following material codes:
   a) S275JR b) 42CrMo4 c) C60 d) X5CrNiMo18-10
   e) S355 f) HS10-4-3-10 g) X37CrMoV5-1

4.4 Steel groups and their applications

There are more than 2000 standardised steels. They are divided in steel groups in order to get an overview. The main steel groups are structural steels, steels for engineering, tool steels and corrosion resistant steels.

Structural steels

Steel constructions are produced of structural steels.

Unalloyed structural steels

They are low cost steels for structural steel engineering **(figure)**.
They have a moderate yield strength and tensile strength and are used for basic applications with moderate load. They are traded as hot rolled sheets, bars, profiles und I-beams.
Examples: S185, S235JR, S275JR

Weldable fine-grained structural steels

These steels have a low carbon content (for weldability) and low contents of Cr, Ni, Cu and V. They are used for high loaded welded constructions.
Examples: S355M, S460N

Steels for engineering

By these steels components for engines, cars, ships and vessels are produced.

Quenched and tempered steels

They have a carbon content from 0.2% to 0.65% and other alloying elements. By hardening and tempering they get a high yield strength and toughness.
They are used for dynamic high loaded engine components, e.g. shafts **(figure)**.
Examples: C45E, 25CrMo4

Free cutting steels

They have a high content of sulphur (S) and partially lead (Pb). The alloying elements S and Pb have the effect, that the machining chips break in short pieces. Components of these steels are produced in large number on automatic lathes **(figure)**.
Examples: 10SPb20 , 11SMn30

Case hardened steels

These steels have a low content of carbon, e.g. 0.1%. By case hardening the workpiece gets a carburised layer, which is hardened. You produce components of these steels, which need a tough core und a hardened skin **(figure)**.
Examples: C10E , 16MoCr5

Building frame of unalloyed structural steel

Shafts of quenched and tempered steel

Components of free cutting steel

Wheel gear of case hardened steel

Words

steel group	Stahlsorte
structural steel	Stahlbaustahl
steel for engineering	Maschinenbaustahl
tool steel	Werkzeugstahl
corrosion-resistant steel	korrosionsbeständiger Stahl
vessel	Reaktor
low cost	preiswert
structural steel engineering	Stahlhochbau
basic	einfach
building frame	Gebäudeskelett
moderate load	mittlere Belastung
to be traded	gehandelt werden
hot rolled sheet	warm gewalztes Blech
bar	Stab
profile	Profil
I- beam	I-Träger
weldable fine-grained structural steel	Schweißgeeigneter Feinkornbaustahl
welded construction	Schweißkonstruktion
quenched and tempered steel	Vergütungsstahl
hardening and tempering	vergüten
toughness	Zähigkeit
free cutting steel	Automatenstahl
partially	teilweise
to effect	bewirken
machining chips	Späne
piece	Stückchen
component	Bauteil
automatic lathe	Drehautomat
case hardened steel	Einsatzstahl
case hardening	Einsatzhärten
carburised layer	Kohlenstoffangereicherte Randschicht
to harden	härten
tough core	zäher Kern
hardened skin	gehärtete Randschicht
term	Fachausdruck
semi-finished steel product	Stahl-Halbzeug

Exercises

1. Name the German term for the following steel groups:
   a) case hardened steel
   b) unalloyed structural steel
   c) steel for engineering
   d) quenched and tempered steel
   e) weldable fine-grained structural steel
   f) free cutting steel
2. Name an application for each steel group mentioned above.
3. Answer the following questions:
   a) In which product form are semi-finished steel products available?
   b) Which special elements do free cutting steels have?
   c) Which mechanical properties do quenched and tempered steels have?

Tool steels

Tools are made of tool steels. Most of the tool steels are alloyed steels. They are classified into sub-groups according to the application temperature.

Cold work steel

Tools made of cold work steels can be used until an application temperature of 200 °C. Hammers, pliers, hand chisels, cutting punches, injection moulds e.g. are made of these steels **(figure)**.

There are unalloyed and alloyed cold work steels. They have a relatively high content of carbon (0.45% to 2.10%) and partly low percentages of the alloying elements chromium (Cr), manganese (Mn) and vanadium (V).

Examples: C80 U, 90MnCrV8

Hand tools of cold work steels

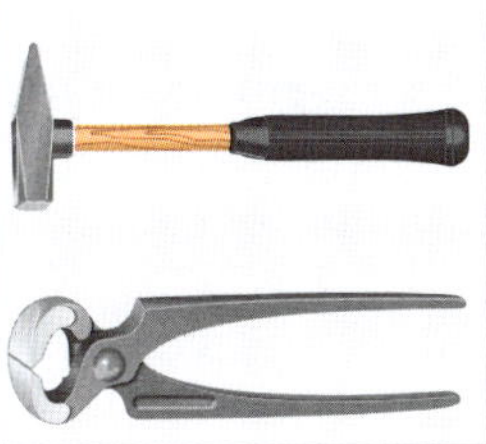

Hot work steels

These steels are used, if the application temperature for the tool is allowed to have 400 °C.

Main products are e.g. extrusion dies, forging dies, mandrels etc. **(figure)**. Alloying elements are minimum 0.3% carbon and Cr, Ni, Mo and V.

Example: 35NiCrMoV7

Forging die of hot work steel

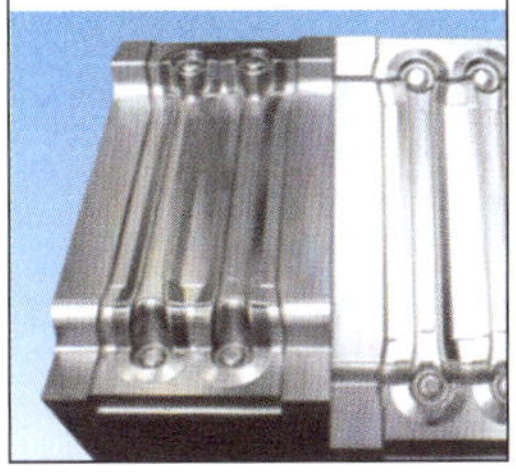

High speed steels

These steels are high performance steels with high hardness and wear resistance at temperatures up to 600 °C.

Applications are drills, milling cutters, lathe tools **(figure)**. They are alloyed steels with a content of W, Mo, V and Co.

Example: HS10-4-3-10 with 10% W, 4% Mo, 3% V, 10% Co.

Cutting tools of high speed steel

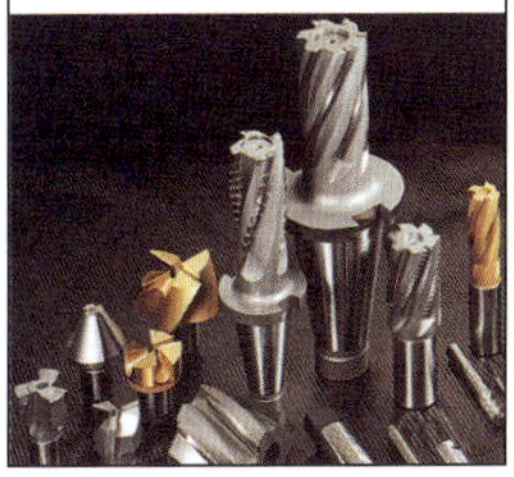

Corrosion-resistant steels

These steels have a high content of the alloying elements Cr and Ni, sometimes additional Mo and Ti. Every steel has a particular content of carbon.

According to the carbon content, there are two groups of steels. The **ductile** corrosion-resistant steels (austenitic steels) have a low carbon content of 0.05%, e.g. X5CrNiMo17-12-2.

Vessels and pipes for the chemical industry and decorative components for cars are made of these steels **(figure)**.

The **hard** corrosion-resistant steels (martensitic steels) have a higher carbon content and mainly a high chromium content, e.g. X46Cr13 with 0.46% C and 13% Cr. Machine knives, spindles, extruder screws etc. are made of these steels **(figure)**.

Words	
tool steel	Werkzeugstahl
according to	entsprechend
cold work steel	Kaltarbeitsstahl
application temperature	Anwendungstemperatur
hammer	Hammer
pliers	Zange
hand chisel	Handmeißel
cutting punch	Schneidstempel
injection mould	Spritzgießform
relatively	relativ
partly	zum Teil
hot work steel	Warmarbeitsstahl
extrusion die	Pressstempel
forging die	Schmiedegesenk
mandrel	Biegerolle
high speed steel	Schnellarbeitsstahl
high performance steel	Hochleistungsstahl
wear resistance	Verschleißfestigkeit
drill	Bohrer
milling cutter	Fräser
lathe tool	Drehwerkzeug
corrosion-resistant	korrosionsbeständig
particular	bestimmt, eigen
according	entsprechend
ductile	zäh, dehnbar
austenitic steel	austenitischer Stahl
martensitic steel	martensitischer Stahl
machine knife (knives)	Maschinenmesser
spindle	Spindel, Achse
extruder screw	Extruderschnecke

Vessel of austenitic CrNi-steel

Extruder screw of martensitic Cr-steel

Exercises

1. Complete the following sentences:
   a) A tool steel which can be used to an application temperature of 400 °C is called ________________.
   b) Corrosion-resistant steels have the alloying elements ________________________________.
2. Determine the alloying elements of the steel with the designation code X4CrNiTi18-12.
3. Answer the questions first in German and then in English.
   a) Which tools are made of high speed steels?
   b) Up to which temperature can cold work steels be used?

4.5 Semi-finished steel products

Skilled workers in mechanical engineering process steel materials as semi-finished steel products. They are produced by rolling and pulling. Most of the steel products are standardised. Additionally there are a lot of special non-standardised steel products.

In the standards, the dimensions, the scaling, the materials, the finish and the designation are determined.

For the mail order of a steel product you use an **identification code**. It is determined in the standard of the steel product.

The following example shows a typical identification code.

	Symbol or name of the steel product	Number of the standard	Main dimensions	Standard of the material	Designation code of the material
Example:	**IPB-Profile**	**EN 10024**	**- IPB 180**	**- steel EN 10025**	**- S235JR**
	Wide I-beam IPB type	According to DIN EN 10024	Base height 180 mm	Unalloyed steel DIN EN 10025	Steel type S235JR

Steel products are classified in long rolled products and flats.

Long rolled products are hot rolled bars, profiles, hollow profiles, tubes and wires.

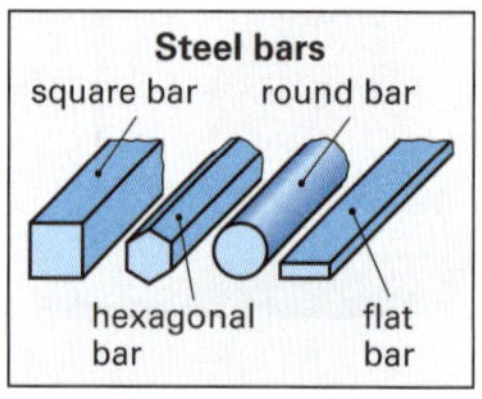

Hot rolled bars can have a circular, a square, a rectangular, a hexagonal and an octagonal cross section **(figure).**

Example: **Round bar EN 10060 – 60 × 5000 steel EN 10025-2 – S235J0**

is a hot rolled round steel bar, d = 60 mm, length l = 5.000 mm, unalloyed structural steel S235J0, standard EN 10025-2.

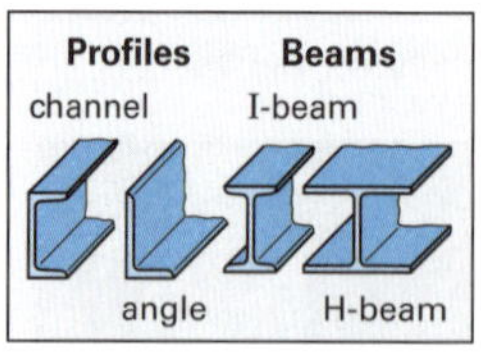

Hot rolled profiles are small profiles in tee-, zed-, channel- and angle form as well as large profiles such as I-beams and H-beams **(figure). Example:**

Channel DIN 1026-1 – U80 – S235JR

is a steel channel DIN 1026-1, height h = 80 mm, unalloyed structural steel S235JR.

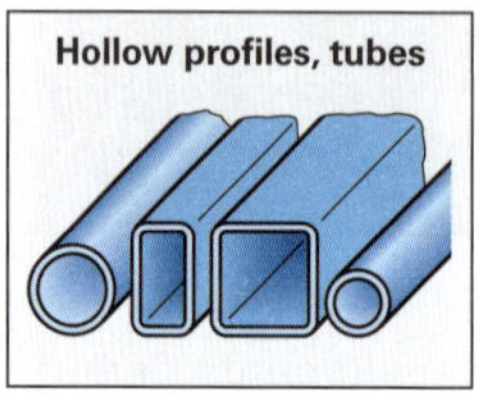

Hot rolled hollow profiles have a circular, a square or a rectangular cross section **(figure). Tubes** are mostly round.

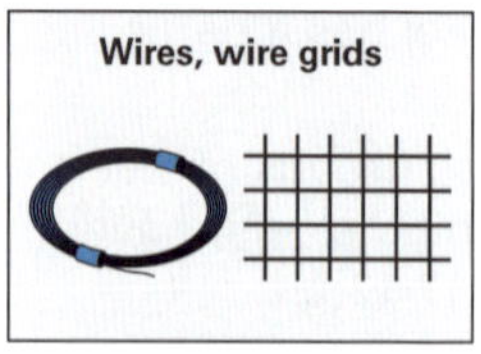

Wires are produced in different diameters, **wire grids** in different wire diameters and mesh sizes **(figure).**

Flat products are wide flat steels, sheet metals and coils **(figure). Example:**

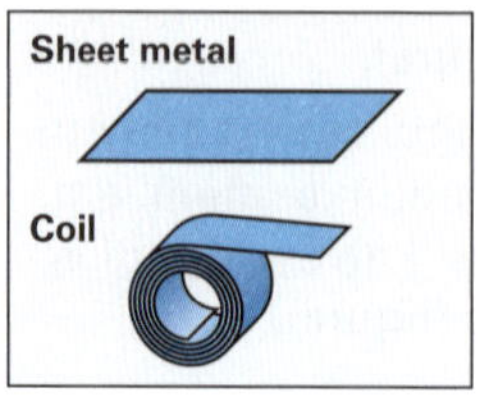

Sheet metal EN 10130 – DC03 – A – m

is a hot rolled sheet metal standardised in EN 10130, soft steel DC03, surface type A, surface finish: matt.

Words	
semi-finished steel product	Stahl-Halbzeug
skilled worker	Facharbeiter
mechanical engineering	Maschinenbau
to process	verarbeiten
rolling	Walzen
pulling	Ziehen
standardised	genormt
additional	zusätzlich
standard	Norm
dimensions	Maße
scaling	Größenstufung
finish	Endbehandlung
designation	Bezeichnung
to determine	festlegen
mail order	Bestellung
to use	verwenden
identification code	Kennzeichnungscode
main dimension	Hauptabmessung
wide T-beam	breiter T-Träger
according	gemäß
base height	Steghöhe
unalloyed structural steel	unlegierter Baustahl
to classify	einteilen
long rolled product	Langerzeugnis
flat	Flacherzeugnis
hot rolled bar	warm gewalzter Stabstahl
hollow profile	Hohlprofil
tubes	Rohre
wires	Drähte
circular	kreisförmig
square	quadratisch
rectangular	rechteckig
hexagonal	sechseckig
octagonal	achteckig
cross section	Querschnitt
angle	Winkelstahl
T-beam	T-Träger
H-beam	Breitflanschträger
steel channel	U-Stahl
tube	Rohr
wire grid	Drahtgitter
mesh size	Maschenweite
wide flat steel	Breitflachstahl
sheet metal	Blech
coil	Bandrolle
soft steel	weicher Stahl
matt (surface)	matt (Oberfläche)

Exercises

1. Translate these terms for the steel products in German: Hot rolled flat bar, equal leg steel angle, I-beam.
2. In a manufacturing program you find the following steel product: Hot rolled square bar EN 10059 – 50 × 4000 – quenched and tempered steel EN 10083-3 - 34Cr4. Name the steel product and the material in German.
3. Name the identification code for the semi-finished steel product: Hot rolled equal flange T-profile T70, according DIN EN 10055, material S235JR according EN 10025-2.

4.6 Cast iron materials

Construction components with a complex and multiform shape, such as motor blocks or pump housings, are produced most efficiently by casting. The materials for these components are cast iron materials.

There are several cast materials for different applications. The properties of the cast iron materials depend on their carbon content and the segregation of the carbon particles in the material.

Cast iron with lamellar graphite (Grey cast iron)

Cast iron with lamellar graphite contains about 3% carbon in form of graphite. It is segregated in fine graphite lamellas in the basic iron Perlit-texture **(figure)**.

Machine housing of cast iron with lamellar graphite

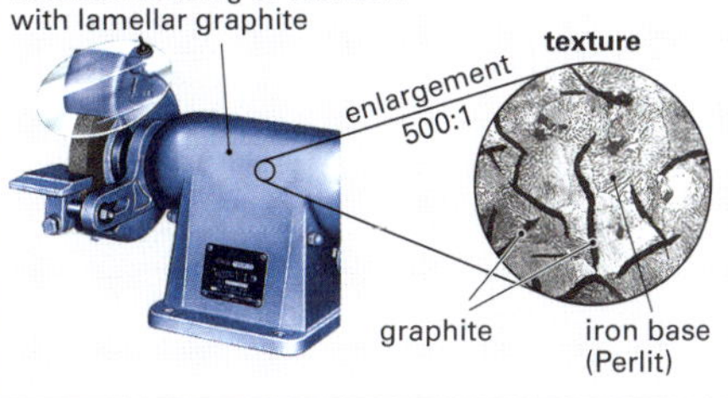

The graphite lamellas cause the low tensile strength and the brittleness of the material. The positive effect of the graphite lamellas is the absorption of vibrations and the slippage of the surface. Lamellar-graphite cast iron is an economic material for housings and tool machine bases.

Cast iron with spheroidal (nodular) graphite

This cast iron is also called **ductile cast iron.**

It contains 3% carbon, which is dispersed in microscopic small graphite spheres in the basic Ferrit-iron **(figure)**.

Machine housing of cast iron with nodular graphite

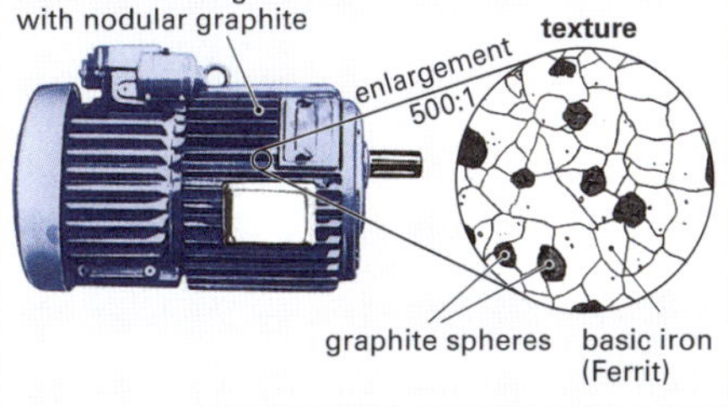

Ductile cast iron has a tensile strength and a ductility comparable with basic structural steel. It is produced to motor blocks and housings, which need a high strain capacity.

Malleable cast iron

Malleable cast iron originally contains 3% carbon. The parts are tempered in an inert or decarbonising furnace for several days. Afterwards the parts have steel-like properties. Malleable cast iron is cast to small machine or tool parts **(figure)**.

Tool elements of malleable cast iron

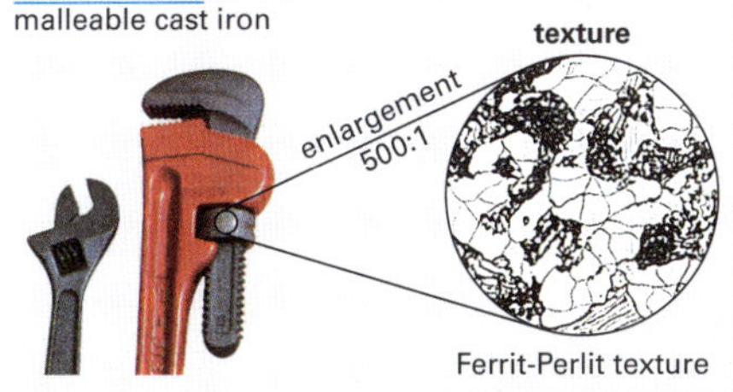

Cast steels

Cast steels are special steel materials with good casting behaviour and the properties of steel: high tensile strength and ductility. There are unalloyed and alloyed cast steel materials.
For example: GE200, G17Mn5, GX5CrNi13-4.

Words

cast iron materials	Gusseisenwerkstoffe
construction components	Konstruktionsbauteile
complex	kompliziert
multiform	vielgestaltig
shape	Bauform
pump housing	Pumpengehäuse
efficient	kostengünstig
casting	Gießen
application	Anwendung
property	Eigenschaft
to depend on	abhängen von
carbon content	Kohlenstoffgehalt
segregation	Ausscheidung
particles	Teilchen
lamellar graphite	Lamellengrafit
grey cast iron	Grauguss
to contain	enthalten
to cause	verursachen
Perlit-texture	Perlit-Gefüge
tensile strength	Zugfestigkeit
brittleness	Sprödigkeit
absorption of vibrations	Dämpfung von Schwingungen
slippage	Gleitfähigkeit
economic	kostengünstig
tool machine base	Werkzeugmaschinenbett
spheroidal	kugelförmig
nodular	kugelig
ductil	zäh
sphere	Kugel
strain capacity	Belastungsfähigkeit
malleable cast iron	Temperguss
malleable	schmiedbar
tool elements	Werkzeugteile
to temper	glühen
inert	inert (nicht reagierend)
decarbonising	entkohlend
furnace	Glühofen
cast steel	Stahlguss

Exercises

1. Complete the following sentence:
   Grey cast iron has a texture with __________ graphite; ductile cast iron with __________ graphite.
2. Name three types of cast materials.
3. Answer the following questions in English:
   a) Which construction elements are made of cast iron with spheroidal graphite (ductile cast iron)?
   b) Which texture do grey cast iron and ductile cast iron have?
   c) Which parts are produced of malleable cast iron?

4.7 Light metals

Non-ferrous metals are classified by their density: Light metals have a density below 5 kg/dm³, heavy metals above 5 kg/dm³.

The most important light metals are aluminium (ϱ_{Al} = 2.7 kg/dm³), magnesium (ϱ_{MG} = 1.7 kg/dm³) and titanium (ϱ_{TI} = 4.5 kg/dm³).

Light metals are important materials for light weight construction components for vehicles, aircrafts and articles of daily use.

Aluminium materials

The most important properties of aluminium materials are its low density of 2.7 kg/dm³, good processing properties like formability and weldability as well as weathering resistance. Additionally, aluminium has a good current conductivity and is non-toxic. Unalloyed aluminium is used for foils and conductors. Aluminium alloys have wider applications. They are classified in aluminium wrought alloys and aluminium casting alloys.

The aluminium materials are grouped in series, e.g. series 3000: AlMn-alloys, series 6000: AlMgSi-alloys.

The designation code of aluminium materials consists of the letters EN AW and a serial number. Besides, the alloying elements and their percentage can be given in brackets.

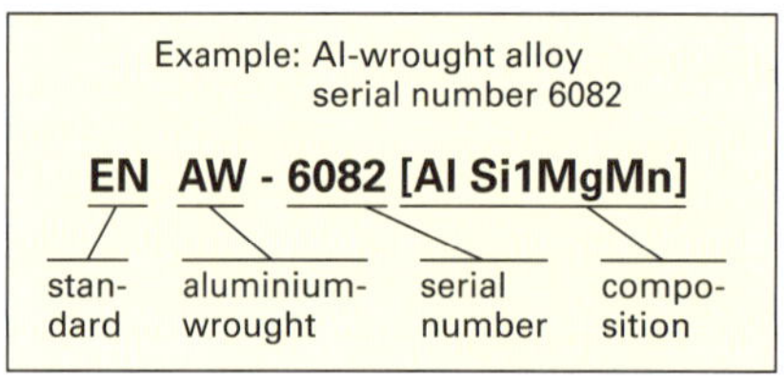

Aluminium wrought alloys

These alloys contain magnesium (Mg), manganese (Mn), silicium (Si), zinc (Zn) or copper (Cu). They have the light weight of aluminium and the high tensile strength as an unalloyed construction steel: R_m = 200...550 N/mm².

An example for a hardenable Al-wrought alloy with high tensile strength is EN AW-2024 [Al Cu4Mg1], used e.g. for car components **(figure)**.

Body frame for a car of high strength Al wrought alloy

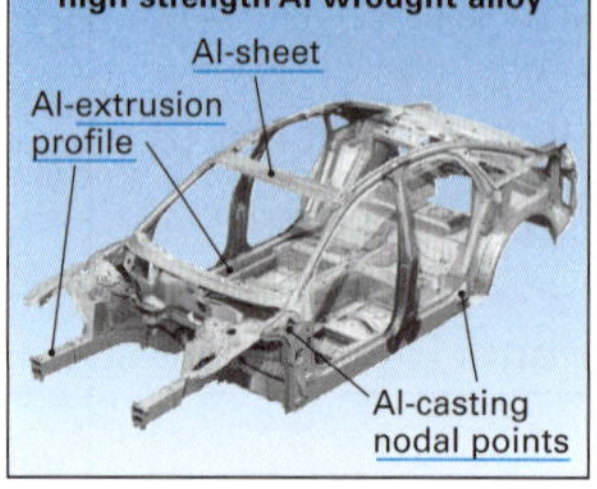

Aluminium free cutting alloys

These alloys contain beside their alloying elements an addition of lead (Pb). Example: EN AW-2030 [Al CuPbMg].

Aluminium casting alloys

The most common aluminium casting alloy for mechanical engineering is EN AC-4410 [Al Si12].

Housings, car body nodal points and motor blocks are produced of this alloy **(figure)**.

Motor block of aluminium casting alloy

Words

light metal	Leichtmetall
non-ferrous metal	Nichteisenmetall
to classify	unterteilen
density	Dichte
light weight construction	Leichtbaukonstruktion
vehicle	Fahrzeug
aircraft	Flugzeug
article of daily use	Gebrauchsgegenstand
processing property	Verarbeitungseigenschaft
formability	Formbarkeit
weldability	Schweißbarkeit
weathering resistance	Wetterbeständigkeit
additional	zusätzlich
current conductivity	Stromleitung
non-toxic	ungiftig
foil	Folie
conductor	Stromleiter
wide	breit, umfangreich
wrought alloy	Knetlegierung
casting alloy	Gusslegierung
to be grouped in	in Gruppen unterteilt sein
series	Serie
designation code	Kurzbezeichnung
to consist of	bestehen aus
letter	Buchstabe
percentage	Gehalt
bracket	Klammer
to contain	enthalten
body frame	Karosserierahmen
Al-sheet	Al-Blech
extrusion profile	Strangpressprofil
free cutting alloy	Automatenlegierung
addition	Zusatz
lead	Blei
mechanical engineering	Maschinenbau
housing	Gehäuse
car body nodal point	Karosserieknoten
heading	Überschrift
production	Herstellung

Exercises

1. Translate the headings of the text and the figures into German.
2. Answer the following questions in German and in English:
   a) What are the most important properties of aluminium materials?
   b) In which two groups are aluminium alloys classified according to their production?
   c) Which components does a designation code of aluminium alloys consist of?
   d) What special alloying element do aluminium free cutting alloys contain?
3. Give a solution for the following task:
   a) Name an application for aluminium wrought alloys and for aluminium casting alloys.
   b) Give an example for the designation code of an aluminium wrought alloy and an aluminium casting alloy.

Hardening of aluminium alloys

The hardening of aluminium alloys is carried out in three steps: solution annealing at 500 °C, quenching in water and ageing. After several days, the hardened workpieces have a tensile strength up to 550 N/mm^2, such as the alloy EN AW-7075 [Al Zn5, 5MgCu].

Processing of aluminium materials

Aluminium materials can be processed by the usual manufacturing methods of metal materials: bending, moulding, cutting such as drilling, turning, milling and welding.

Aluminium semi-finished products

Aluminium materials are available in the standard long rolled products and flats: bars, profiles, tubes, sheets and coils (page 58).

Magnesium materials

Magnesium materials have a density from 1.8 to 2.0 kg/dm^3. They are the lightest technical metal materials, which are about 40% lighter than aluminium materials.

Unalloyed magnesium has no application as construction material. Technically important are magnesium alloys. They are in appearance, in corrosion resistance and in tensile strength comparable to aluminium alloys, but even lighter.

Magnesium casting alloys are often used in mechanical engineering, e.g. the alloy EN MC-MgAl8Zn1.

They are formed by pressure die casting and finished by cutting.

They are used for device and gear housings, motor blocks and handheld machines **(figure)**.

The processing of magnesium materials is similar to aluminium alloys.

Housing of a chain saw of magnesium casting alloy

Titanium materials

Titanium materials have a density of about 4.5 kg/dm^3. That means that a titanium workpiece is 40% lighter than a steel workpiece (ϱ_{st} = 7.8 kg/dm^3) which has the same dimension. They have high tensile strength, high ductile values and high corrosion resistance. It is used for high grade components, because titanium is an expensive material. In mechanical engineering only titanium alloys are used. Important alloys are Ti Al6V4 or Ti Al4Mo4Sn2.

These titanium alloys have a comparable tensile strength to alloyed tempered steels up to 1.000 N/mm^2. Construction components for aircrafts and machines with high mechanical load capacity are made of titanium alloys **(figure)**.

Turbine blades of an aircraft jet engine of titanium alloy

Words	
hardening	Härten
solution annealing	Lösungsglühen
quenching	Abschrecken
ageing	Auslagern, Altern
to process	verarbeiten
usual	üblich
bending	biegen
moulding	Formpressen
cutting	Spanen
drilling	Bohren
turning	Drehen
milling	Fräsen
welding	Schweißen
available	verfügbar
appearance	Aussehen
corrosion resistance	Korrosionsbeständigkeit
comparable	vergleichbar
even	noch, sogar
pressure die casting	Druckguss
to finish	endbearbeiten
device	Gerät
gear housing	Getriebegehäuse
handheld	handgeführt
chain saw	Kettensäge
to be similar to	ähnlich sein zu ...
to mean	bedeuten
dimension	Größe
ductile values	Zähigkeitswerte
high grade	hochwertig
expensive	teuer
high mechanical	mechanisch hoch
load capacity	belastbar
turbine blade	Turbinenschaufel
jet engine	Strahltriebwerk

Exercises

1. Complete the following sentences:
   a) Aluminium alloys are hardened in three steps: ______
   b) The lightest technical metallic material is ______.
   c) The values of the density of aluminium, magnesium and titanium are:
   d) ϱ_{Al} = ______ ϱ_{Mg} = ______ ϱ_{Ti} = ______
   e) The magnesium material EN MC – Mg Al8Zn1 contains the alloying elements: ______
2. Answer the following questions in English:
   a) Which cutting methods are used to process aluminium materials?
   b) Which titanium alloys are used for structural components with high mechanical load capacity?

4.8 Heavy metals

Materials with a density above 5 kg/dm³ and which are not iron based, belong to heavy metals.

The most important heavy metal materials for construction components are copper alloys. The other heavy metals are mainly alloying elements such as zinc, tin, lead, chromium, nickel, vanadium, cobalt, tungsten, molybdenum.

Unalloyed copper

Unalloyed copper has a density of ϱ_{Cu} = 8.9 kg/dm³ and a melting temperature of 1,083 °C. Its special property is the good electrical and thermal conductivity. Unalloyed copper is used for heat exchangers, electric conductors and coils **(figure).** It is unusable for construction components because of its low strength.

Conductor of electric-copper

Copper alloys

The most commonly used copper alloy materials are copper-zinc alloys, also called **brass**, and copper-tin alloys, also called **bronze**.

Copper alloys have a special designation code with the element symbols and the percentage. The copper alloy shown adjoining consists of 38 % zinc (Zn) and 2 % lead (Pb).

Free cutting copper-zinc-lead alloy
CuZn38Pb2

Copper-zinc alloys (brass) have 5 % to 40 % zinc and partially small percentage of other alloying elements such as manganese (Mn), aluminium (Al) or lead (Pb). Brasses have a medium strength, good corrosion resistance and low sliding friction. You use it e. g. for screws which are often removed and reassembled **(figure).**

Screws and nuts of brass

Copper-tin alloys (bronze) have 2 % to 15 % tin. They have corrosion resistance, strength, wear resistance and high slippage. They can get spring elasticity and hardness by rolling. You use it e. g. for bearing bushes **(figure).**

Bearing bushes of bronze

Words

English	German
heavy metals	Schwermetalle
copper alloy	Kupferlegierung
mainly	überwiegend
tin	Zinn
tungsten	Wolfram
melting temperature	Schmelzpunkt
thermal conductivity	Wärmeleitfähigkeit
heat exchanger	Wärmetauscher
electric conductor	Stromleiter
coil	Wicklung
unusable	unbrauchbar
most commonly	häufigste
brass	Messing
bronze	Bronze
percentage	Prozentgehalt
medium	mittlere
sliding friction	Gleitreibung
screw	Schraube
small parts	Kleinteile
to remove	demontieren
to reassemble	zusammenbauen
wear resistance	Verschleißfestigkeit
spring elasticity	Federelastizität
bearing bush	Lagerbuchse
low melting	niedrig schmelzend
solder	Lot
otherwise	andererseits
importance	Bedeutung
to process	verarbeiten
stainless steel	rostfreier Stahl
high speed steel	Schnellarbeitsstahl
term	Begriff
non-standard	nicht genormt

Alloying metals

Zinc (Zn) (δ_m = 418 °C), tin (Sn) (δ_m = 232 °C) and lead (Pb) (δ_m = 327 °C) are **low melting metals.** They are used for special applications, such as tin-lead-alloys for solders, and also as alloying elements in copper alloys (see above) and steels.

The **high melting metals** chromium (Cr), nickel (Ni), vanadium (V), cobalt (Co), tungsten (W) and molybdenum (Mo) have no importance as pure metals. They are processed as alloying elements for steels.

Commonly used steel alloys, containing these alloying elements are **chromium-nickel-steels (called stainless steels)**, for example X5CrNiMo17-12-2, or **high speed steels**, for example HS6-5-2-5 (see page 57).

Exercises

1. Find the German terms for the following English words:
   a) density b) current conductivity c) corrosion resistance d) wear resistance e) sliding friction
2. Name two low melting alloying elements and three high melting alloying elements.
3. Name the alloying elements and their percentage in the corrosion resistant steel X5CrNiMo17-12-2.
4. Answer the following questions:
   a) What is the non-standard name for copper-zinc alloys and for copper-tin-alloys?
   b) What is the reason for the application of brass materials for screws and often removed nuts?
   c) Copper-tin-alloys are used for bearing bushes. Which material properties does this material have?

4.9 Sintered materials

Sintered materials are produced in a three-step production process by mixing metal powders, moulding it in a press to blanks and sintering them above 1000 °C to formed parts **(figure)**.

The properties of the sintered parts depend on the powder material, the powder particle size, the moulding pressure and the sintering temperature. Low moulding pressure and low sintering temperature produce porous parts. High moulding pressure and high sintering temperature lead to compact material with good loading capacity.

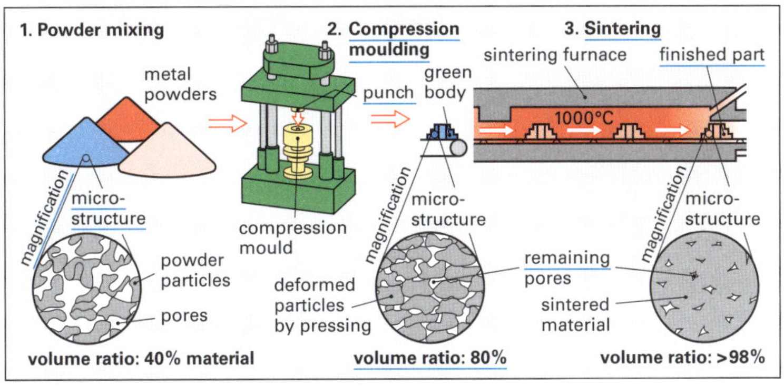

The advantage of the sintering process is, that the produced components are ready for use after the process without any finishing. Sintered components are low cost products if they are manufactured in high numbers.

The disadvantage of the sintering technique is that you can only produce mass components with relatively small size.

Sintered metals for slide bearings

The slide bearings are made of bronze and have a fine-porous microstructure. The pores of the finished slide bearing are filled by pressure with lubricant. In use, the bearing is heated by friction and the lubricant leaves the pores: the bearing is self-lubricating **(figure)**.

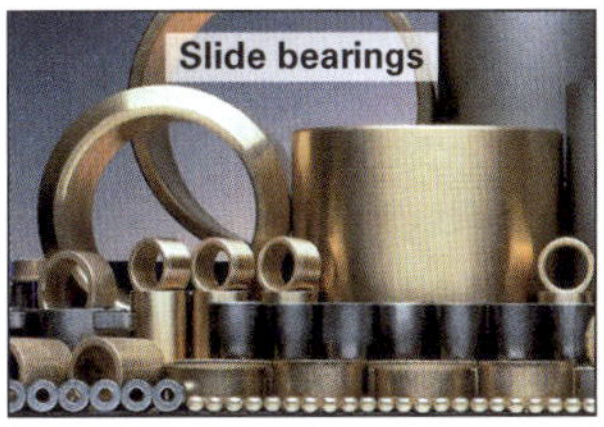

Sintered metals for machine parts

Small sized machine parts for medium loading capacity, such as gears, levers, cams etc. **(figure)** are sintered from different structural steels.

These components are produced in great number and you find them in each machine.

Carbides (Hard metals)

Carbides are sintered material composed of two components: small sharp-edged particles of very hard materials such as tungsten carbide (WC) or titanium carbide (TiC) and the tough-elastic bonding metal cobalt (Co). Cutting tips are made of carbides **(figure)**.

Words

sintered material	Sinterwerkstoff
metal powder	Metallpulver
to mould	formpressen
blank	Rohling
formed part	Formteil
to depend on	abhängen von
particle size	Teilchengröße
porous	porös
to lead to	führen zu
compact	kompakt, fest
loading capacity	Belastbarkeit
magnification	Vergrößerung
compression moulding	Formpressen unter Druck
sintering	Sintern
punch	Stempel
microstructure	Mikrostruktur
finished part	Fertigteil
remained	verbleibend
volume ratio	Volumenanteil
advantage	Vorteil
ready for use	gebrauchsfertig
finishing	Endbearbeitung
disadvantage	Nachteil
mass components	Massenteile
slide bearing	Gleitlager
lubricant	Schmiermittel
to heat	erwärmen
friction	Reibung
to leave	austreten
self-lubricating	selbstschmierend
small sized parts	Kleinteile
cam	Nocke
carbide	Hartmetall
composed	bestehend
sharp-edged	scharfkantig
hard material	Hartstoff
bonding metal	Bindemetall
cutting tip	Schneidplättchen

Exercises

1. The production of sintered material consists of three production stepsa)
   a) Name the three steps.
   b) Explain the advantages of sintered metals.
   c) Name the disadvantages of the sintering production technique.
2. Answer the following questions in English:
   a) What is the advantage of a self-lubricating bearing?
   b) Which small sized machine parts of sintered steels are produced in great number?
   c) Which materials contain carbides?

4.10 Heat treatment of steels

The purpose of heat treatments is to adapt the properties of materials for a certain application or to improve the hardness, the strength and the ductility of steel components.

The modification of the steel properties are induced by the microstructural change of the material, which is caused by heating.

There are several kinds of heat treatments:

- Tempering
- Hardening
- Quenching and tempering
- Surface hardening

They are realised in heat treatment workshops **(figure)**.

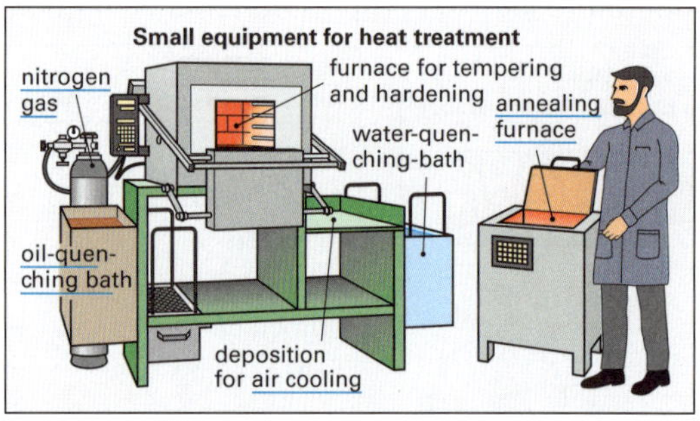

Tempering

In order to temper the workpiece, it is slowly heated in the furnace, held at tempering temperature and finally cooled slowly at the air. There are tempering techniques with different tempering temperatures and periods.

Internal stress and cold-formed embrittlement is decreased in the workpiece by **stress-relief-tempering** and **recrystallisation-tempering** at 550 °C to 650 °C for two hours. By **soft-tempering** at 600 °C to 750 °C, the steel can be processed easier by metal cutting.

Normalising is applied to reform a steel with coarse grain to fine grain microstructure. It is tempered at 730 °C to 830 °C.

Hardening

Steels get hard and wear resistant by hardening. It is applied for tools which need a hard surface: drills, chisels, scribers or slideways **(figure)**.

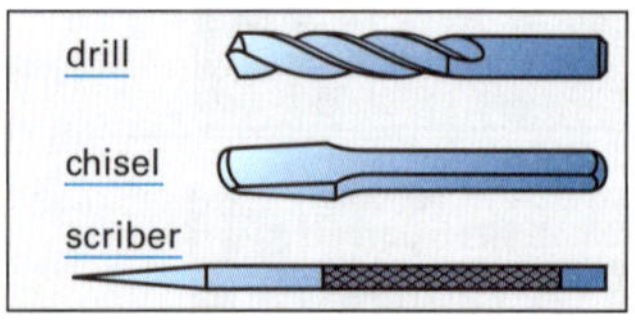

The work sequences while hardening are shown in the **figure** below. Hardening consists of

- heating up to the hardening temperature
- holding for a time
- quenching in water, oil or blasting with air
- annealing to application hardness.

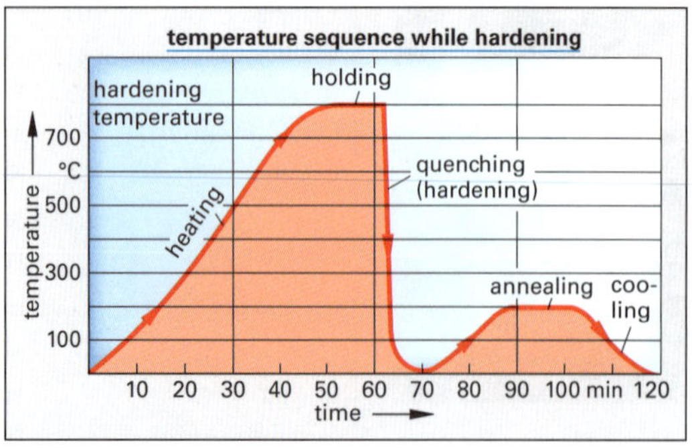

Words	
heat treatment	Wärmebehandlung
purpose	Zweck
to adapt	anpassen
to improve	verbessern
ductility	Zähigkeit
to induce	erzeugen
microstructural change	Gefügeänderung
to cause	verursachen
heating	Erwärmung
tempering	Glühen
hardening	Härten
quenching and tempering	Vergüten
surface hardening	Randschichthärten
to realise	durchführen
workshop	Werkstatt
nitrogen gas	Stickstoffgas
oil-quenching bath	Öl-Abschreckbad
air cooling	Luftabkühlung
annealing furnace	Anlassofen
period	Dauer
embrittlement	Versprödung
to decrease	vermindern
stress-relief tempering	Spannungsarmglühen
recrystallisation	Rekristallisation
soft-tempering	Weichglühen
normalising	Normalglühen
to apply	anwenden
to reform	rückbilden
coarse grain	Grobkorn
drill	Bohrer
chisel	Meißel
scriber	Reißnadel
slideway	Gleitbahn
temperature sequence	Temperaturverlauf
work sequence	Arbeitsablauf
to consist of	bestehen aus
annealing	Anlassen
application hardness	Gebrauchshärte

Exercises

1. Answer the following questions:
   a) What is the reason of the modification of properties by heating?
   b) Which devices do you need in a small workshop for heat treatment?
   c) Which tempering methods can you name?
   d) What is the purpose of soft-tempering?
   e) Which work sequences are important when hardening?

2. Complete the following sentences:
   a) The purpose of normalising is to reform a steel with coarse grain to ______________________.
   b) Hardening is applied for the following tools: ______________________.
   c) The purpose of hardening is to get ____________________ workpieces.

The values of the hardening and annealing temperatures depend on the steel type **(table).**

Unalloyed tool steels are hardened at about 800 °C, alloyed steels at 800 °C to 900 °C and high speed steels at about 1200 °C.

Table: Values of hardening and annealing temperature

steel type tool steel	hardening temperature in °C	annealing in °C	quenching medium	Surface hardness in HRC after hardening	after annealing 100 °C	200 °C	300 °C	400 °C	500 °C
unalloyed steel C80U	780...800	100...300	water	58	58	54	48	–	–
alloyed steel 90MnCrV8	780...800	200...550	oil	65	65	62	56	50	42
high speed steel HS6–5–2C	1200...1220	200...550	oil	64	65	62	62	62	65

Quenching and tempering

By quenching and tempering you get construction components with high tensile strength and good ductility. Shafts of motors or gear boxes, bolts, screws and levers need these properties and are quenched and tempered **(figure).**

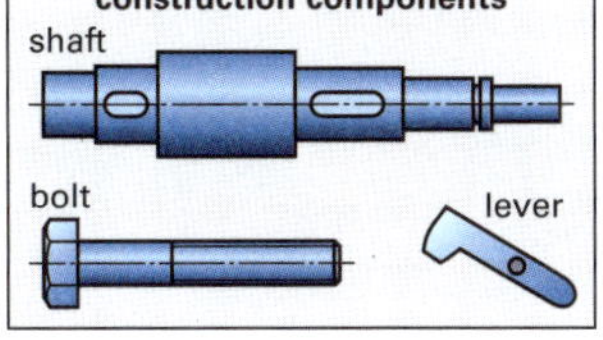

Quenched and tempered construction components

The work sequences for quenching and tempering are similar to the sequences of hardening (**figure** on the left page):
Heating to hardening temperature – quenching – reheating – tempering – finally cooling.
Different is the higher tempering temperature at 540 °C to 680 °C.

If you temper at a low temperature of 580 °C you get a component with high tensile strength; if you temper at 650 °C high ductility is achieved.

The necessary temperature to achieve the desired tensile strength R_m, yield strength R_e and ductility (strain to rupture A) for a specified steel you can read off its tempering diagram **(figure).**

Tempering diagram for the steel 34Cr4

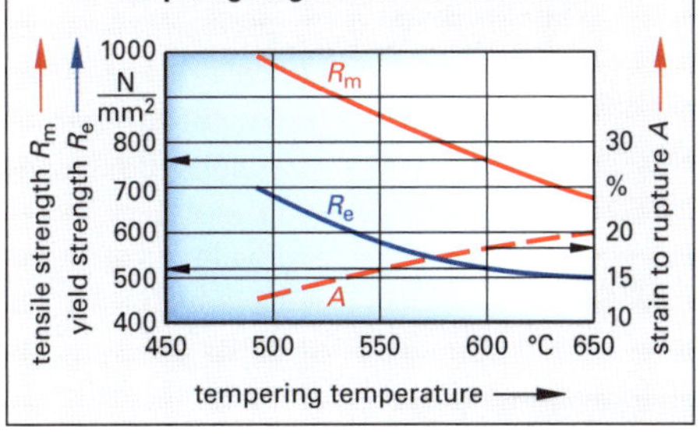

Example: A shaft of the steel 34Cr4 is quenched and tempered at 600 °C. How great is its tensile strength R_m, yield strength R_e and strain to rupture A?

Solution: You read off the tempering diagram:
$R_m = 760$ N/mm², $R_e = 520$ N/mm², $A = 18\%$.

Surface hardening

If you need structural components which must have a tough-elastic core and a hard, wear-resistant and good sliding surface, the steel components will be surface hardened.

Such components are cable drums, roller guides or large bolts. For surface hardening, the component is at first quenched and tempered. The preprocessed component is then heated quickly in a thin surface layer and quenched at once **(figure).** The thin surface layer is hardened, the components' core keeps its tough-elastic properties from quenching and tempering.

Words

English	German
steel type	Stahlsorte
quenching and tempering	Vergüten
shaft	Welle
gear box	Getriebe
bolt	Bolzen, Schraube
lever	Hebel
necessary	erforderlich
to achieve	erreichen
desired	gewünscht
yield strength	Streckgrenze
ductility	Zähigkeit
strain to rupture	Bruchdehnung
specified	bestimmt
to read	ablesen
tempering diagram	Anlassschaubild
tough-elastic	zähelastisch
core	Kern
to slide	gleiten
cable drum	Seiltrommel
roller guide	Rollenbahn
at once	sofort
quench head	Brausenkopf
burner nozzle	Brennerdüse
red hot	rotglühend
burner flame	Brennerflamme
equipment	Einrichtung
to expect	erwarten

Continuous surface hardening

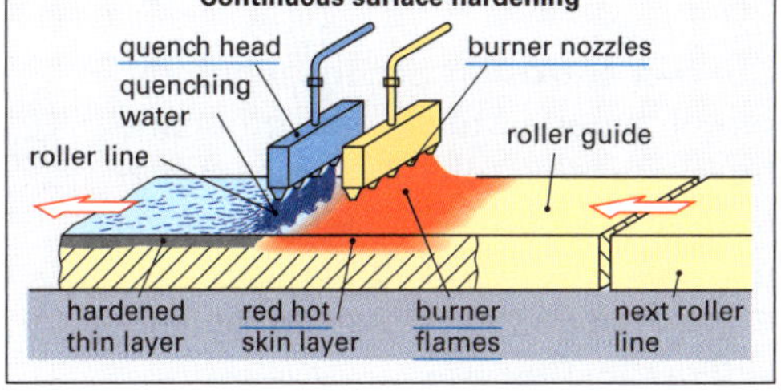

Exercises

1. Name the English words for: Glühen, Härten, Vergüten, Randschichthärten.
2. Which components are hardened and which are quenched and tempered? Give two examples.
3. Describe the surface hardening of a roller guide in a continuous hardening equipment (figure above).
4. Determine the hardening and annealing temperature and the quenching medium of the steel 90MnCrV8.
5. A quenched and tempered gearbox shaft of steel 34Cr4 is tempered at 550 °C. How high are the expected values for tensile strength, yield strength and strain for rupture after this heat treatment?

4.11 Corrosion and corrosion protection

Corrosion is the attack and the damage of metallic materials by chemical and electrochemical reactions with active agents of the environment or weathering **(figure).**

The most common corrosion damages are caused by **electrochemical corrosion.** It happens when a metallic material is in contact with water, the electrolyte **(figure).** Two materials form with water a galvanic element: A small voltage is generated. It dissolves one element of the material and destroys its structure.

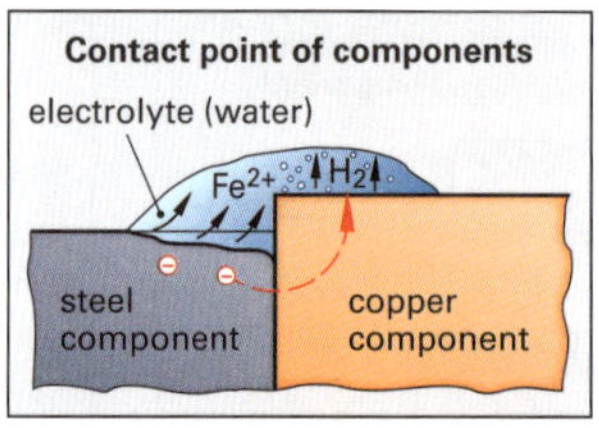

In case of steel material, the basis element iron (Fe) is dissolved. It reacts with the oxygen of the air to rust.

Other corrosion cells exist at a damaged spot of a zinc coating on steel or between the grains of an alloyed steel.

The **high temperature corrosion,** also called **scaling,** occurs with the air at temperatures above 600 °C **(figure).**

Types of corrosion

There are different types of corrosion.

Equal surface corrosion occurs on structural components of unalloyed structural steels (carbon steels) at outdoor weathering **(figure).** It is characterised by corrosion abrasion.

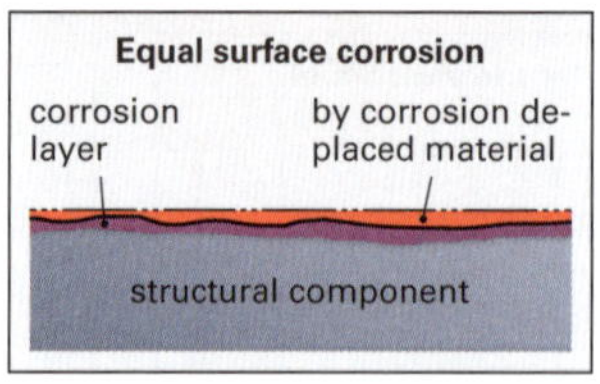

Crater corrosion shows deepenings at the surface of steels **(figure).**

Pitting corrosion exists at stainless steels in contact with chloride-containing active agents, like sea-water or chlorinated pool water. The material shows microscopical cracks **(figure),** which are invisible by the naked eye.

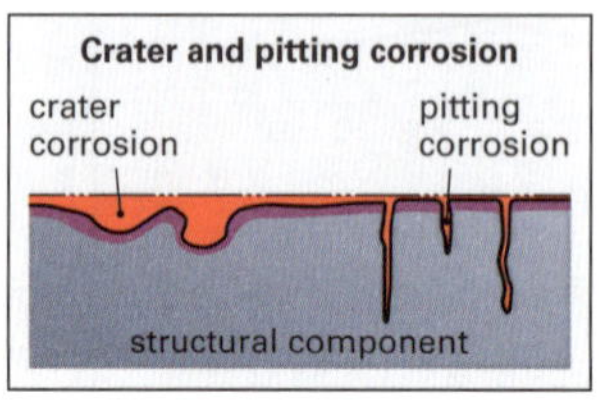

Contact corrosion occurs, when different materials touch each other and humidity (electrolyte) is present **(figure).** At this corrosion cell, one of the materials is dissolved and destroyed. Contact corrosion exists e.g. between the screw connection and the components or in a sliding bearing.

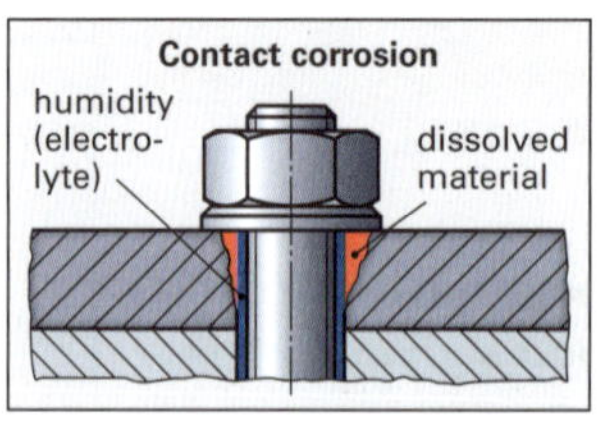

Words

corrosion	Korrosion
corrosion protection	Korrosionsschutz
attack	Angriff
damage	Beschädigung
active agent	Wirkstoff
environment	Umgebung
weathering	Bewitterung
to happen	stattfinden
electrolyte	Elektrolyt
to form	bilden
galvanic element	galvanisches Element
voltage	elektrische Spannung
to generate	erzeugen
to dissolve	auflösen
to destroy	zerstören
structure	Struktur, Aufbau
in case of	im Fall von
iron	Eisen
to react	reagieren
oxygen	Sauerstoff
rust	Rost
corrosion cell	Korrosionselement
damaged spot	Schadstelle
zinc coating	Zinkbeschichtung
grain	Gefügekorn
scaling	Verzundern
type of corrosion	Korrosionsart
equal surface corrosion	gleichmäßige Flächenkorrosion
unalloyed structural steel (carbon steel)	unlegierter Baustahl (Kohlenstoffstahl)
abrasion	Abtrag
crater corrosion	Muldenkorrosion
deepening	Vertiefung
pitting corrosion	Lochfraß-Korrosion
chloride-containing	chloridhaltig
sea-water	Meerwasser
chlorinated	gechlort
crack	Riss
invisible	unsichtbar
by the naked eye	mit bloßem Auge
humidity	Feuchtigkeit
sliding bearing	Gleitlager

Exercises

1. Answer the questions in English:
   a) What is the definition of the term corrosion? b) What is the cause of most corrosion damages?
   c) At which temperatures does scaling (high temperature corrosion) take place in the atmosphere?
   d) Which materials are commonly corroded by equal surface corrosion?

2. Name the English words for:
   a) gleichmäßige Flächenkorrosion b) Lochfraß c) Kontaktkorrosion.

3. Complete the following sentences:
   a) In a galvanic cell a small ________________ is generated.
   b) Rust is formed by a reaction between ________________ and ________________.
   c) Chloride-particles in the pool water cause the ________________ corrosion of stainless steels.

Corrosion protection

The corrosion and the corrosion damages can be avoided or decreased by suitable protective measures.

The **proper selection of the material** is the most effective corrosion protection. The structural steel S235JR, is e.g. suitable as steel girder in a dry workshop, while e.g. in a chemical plant the corrosion-resistant steel X5CrNiMo17-12-2 is the right selection.

Anti-corrosion engineering is also important to avoid corrosion. Construction components and machines need to be manufactured without susceptible areas, such as gaps between components, rough surfaces and welding seams.

Corrosion protection of bare components

The surface of many components of machines must be bare, to achieve their function, like slideways or pillar guides **(figure).** The corrosion resistance is achieved by a ground surface and greased with a corrosion-protection lubricant.

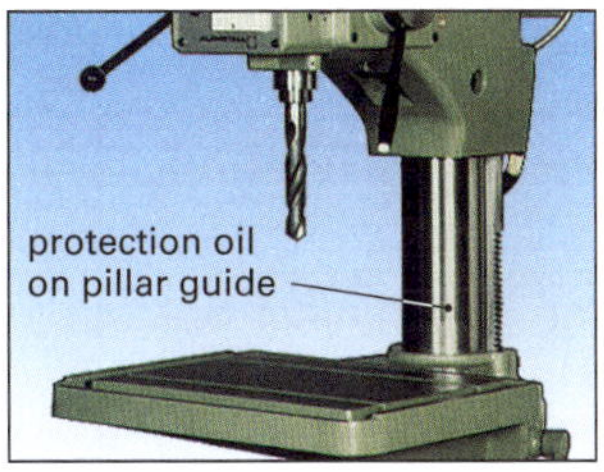

Newly-fabricated workpieces are dipped in corrosion-protection oil or coated with a clear varnish.

Corrosion protection paints

The paints consist of several layers, which are sprayed one after the other on car sheet metals and machine housings **(figure).** For a good bonding on the component and a long life time of the paints, the surface must be clean and free of grease. Rusty components have to be derusted. Basic paints have two layers; long life paints e.g. on car sheets have six layers. They consist of alkyd resin or polyurethane resin.

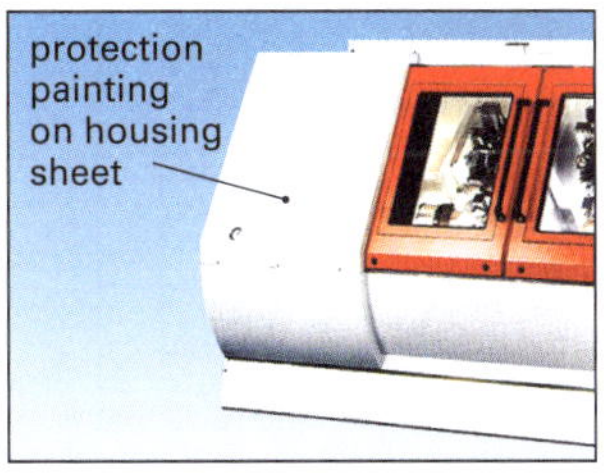

Metal coatings

A very effective and low cost metal coating for corrosion protection against weathering is **hot-dip zinc galvanisation** of structural components **(figure).**

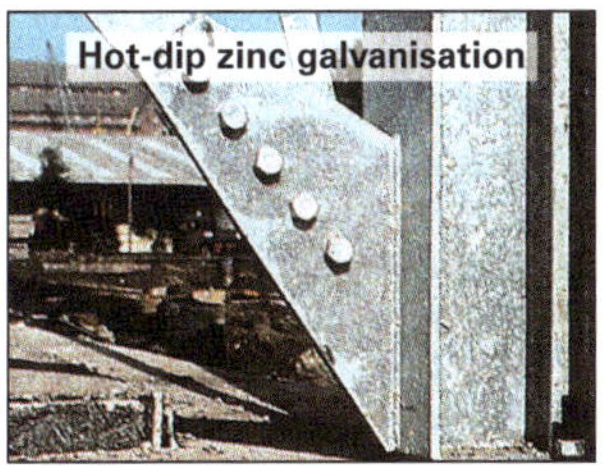

Protection of aluminium components

Aluminium components are protected against corrosion by **anodic oxidation.** The components get a corrosion-resistant layer of aluminium oxide Al_2O_3 in a galvanic process. It has a metallic shine on its surface **(figure).**

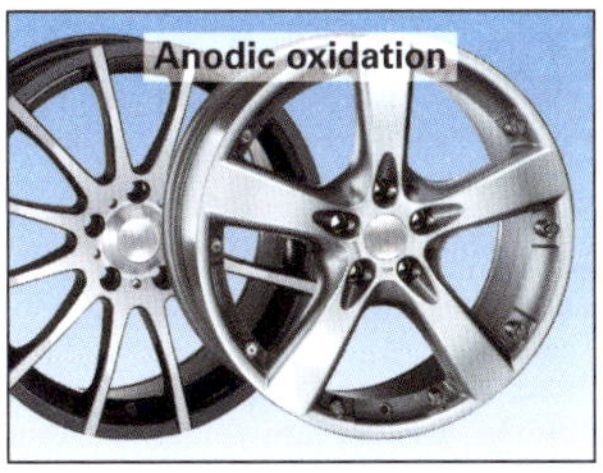

Words	
corrosion protection	Korrosionsschutz
to avoid	vermeiden
to decrease	vermindern
proper selection	richtige Auswahl
most effective	effektivste
steel girder	Stahlträger
chemical plant	Chemieanlage
corrosion-resistant	korrosionsbeständig
anti-corrosion	korrosionsverhindernd
enginneering	Konstruktion
susceptible areas	Schadstelle
gap	Spalt, Lücke
rough	uneben, rau
welding seam	Schweißnaht
bare	blank
to achieve	erfüllen, erreichen
slideway	Gleitbahn
pillar guide	Säulenführung
ground	geschliffen
to grease	schmieren
lubricant	Schmiermittel
newly-fabricated	neu gefertigt
to dip	tauchen
to coat	beschichten
clear varnish	Klarlack
protection paint	Schutzanstrich
to consist	bestehen aus
layer	Schicht
to spray	aufspritzen
car sheet metal	Autoblech
bonding	Haftung
life time	Lebensdauer
rusty	rostig
to derust	entrosten
alkyd resin	Alkydharz
polyurethane resin	Polyurethanharz
metal coating	Metallbeschichtung
hot-dip zinc coating	Feuerverzinken
anodic oxidation	anodische Oxidation
shine	Glanz
to apply	einsetzen
turning lathe	Drehmaschine
car body frame	Karosserierahmen

Exercises

1. Answer the following questions in English:
   a) Which corrosion resistant material must be applied for tanks in a chemical plant?
   b) How do you protect newly-fabricated workpieces against immediate corrosion?
   c) How do you prepare the surface of metals for a good bonding of a corrosion painting?
   d) Which process protects aluminium components against corrosion?
2. Select the suitable metallic material for a component in sea air with your **Metal Trade Handbook.**
3. Name the suitable corrosion protection for the following applications:
   a) Slideway of a turning lathe
   b) Housing of a milling machine
   c) Steel girder in a football stadium
   d) Car body-frame of steel.

4.12 Plastics

Plastics are synthetically produced, organic materials with a wide range of applications. They are made from the raw material crude oil by synthetic processes in chemical plants.

Plastics have replaced many metal applications, e.g. barrels for liquids, and have conquered a lot of new applications e.g. housings of power tools, small gears, electric-insulating tool grips, car tyres etc. **(figure)**.

Plastics have fundamental different properties than metals.

- low density: 0.9 to 1.4 kg/dm³
- low thermal resistance
- stiff, flexible or elastic
- electric insulating
- low tensile strength
- resistant against weathering

Technical classification

According to their molecular structure and the mechanical behaviour while heating, the plastics are divided into three groups.

Thermoplastics have a microscopic filamentary structure **(figure)**. At room temperature they are hard and stiff. When heating to 120 °C they get flexible and at about 180 °C they become liquid. At 250 °C they will be thermally destroyed. By cooling at room temperature they get their original hardness and strength. Thermoplastics are weldable.

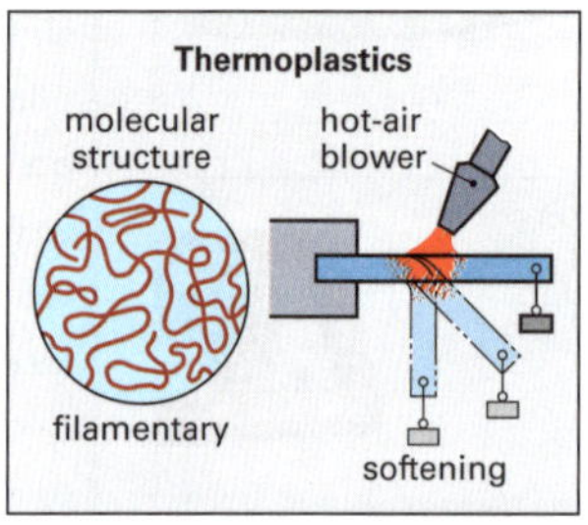

Thermosetting plastics (Thermosets) have a microscopical structure of dense networked macromolecules **(figure)**. At room temperature they are hard and stiff. By heating, they do not soften or change their properties considerably. At 250 °C they will be thermally destroyed. Thermosets are not softened or melted by heating; they are not weldable.

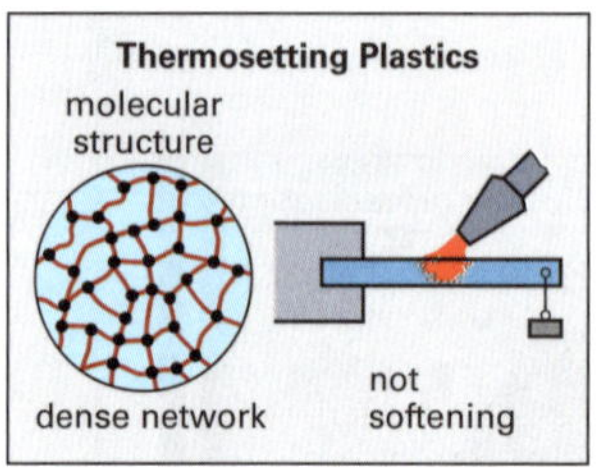

Elastomer plastics (**Elastomers** or **rubber**) have a molecular structure of wide-meshed macromolecules **(figure)**. Similar to the Thermosets they are not melted by heating. Their form can be changed significantly and they will return to their original shape when the load is released. Their most important property is great elasticity.

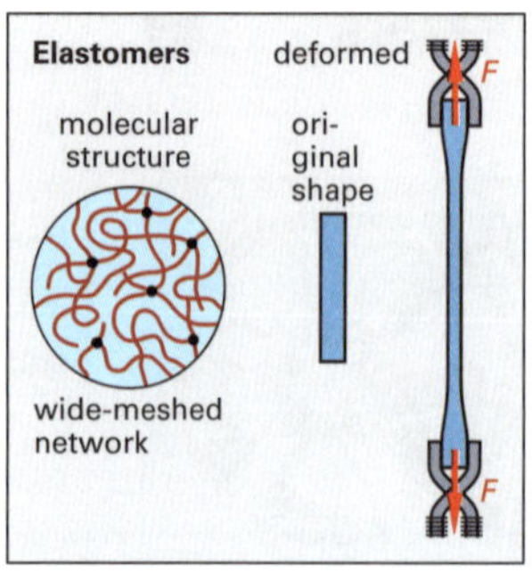

Words	
plastic	Kunststoff
synthetic	synthetisch
organic	organisch
range	Bereich
application	Anwendung
raw material	Rohstoff
crude oil	Erdöl
chemical plant	Chemiefabrik
to replace	ersetzen
barrel	Fass
to conquer	erobern
power tool	Elektrowerkzeug
tool grip	Werkzeuggriff
car tyre	Autoreifen
fundamental	grundlegend
electric insulating	elektrisch isolierend
thermal resistance	Wärmebeständigkeit
tensile strength	Zugspannung
stiff	steif
flexible	weich
weathering	Bewitterung
technical classification	technische Einteilung
according to	entsprechend
heating	Erwärmen
Thermoplastic	Thermoplast
filamentary	fadenförmig
thermal destroyed	thermisch zerstört
cooling	Abkühlen
weldable	schweißbar
hot-air blower	Heißluftgebläse
Thermosetting plastic	Duroplast
dense networked	dicht vernetzt
to soften	erweichen
considerably	beträchtlich
Elastomer Plastic	Elastomer
wide-meshed	weitmaschig
form, shape	Form
to release	entlasten
elasticity	Elastizität

Exercises

1. Answer the questions in English:
   a) What are the typical properties of plastics?
   b) In which groups are plastic materials classified?
   c) What molecular structure do they have? • Thermoplastics • Thermosets • Elastomers
   d) What is the reason for the weldability of the Thermoplastics and the non-weldability of the Thermosets?
2. Find a plastic component in your environment and verify the typical properties of plastics.
3. Name for each typical property of plastics an application from your job.

Thermoplastics

Plastic type	Properties, applications	
Poly-ethylene PE **Poly-propylene PP**	Waxy sliding surface Density: 0.92 kg/dm³ Soft-PE: flexible, tough Hard-PE: hard, stiff	
	Barrels, container, tubes	
Polyvinyl-Chloride PVC	Soft-PVC: flexible, tough Hard-PVC: hard, stiff, Resistant against acids, bases, oil, hot water	
	Pipes, tubes, hoses	

Plastic type	Properties, applications	
Poly-styrene PS **Polystyrene-Copolymers ABS, SAN**	Shiny surface, stiff, unbreakable: housings can be foamed: called Styrofoam	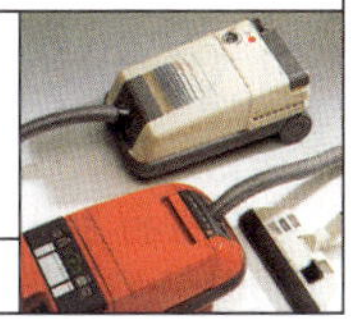
	Heat insulation	
Polyamid PA	Slipping and wear resistant surface, stiff, high strength, thermal and chemical resistant (against motor fuel)	
	Slideways, car elements	

Thermosetting plastics (Thermosets)

Polyester resin UP	Shiny surface, resistant against motor fuels, acids, bases	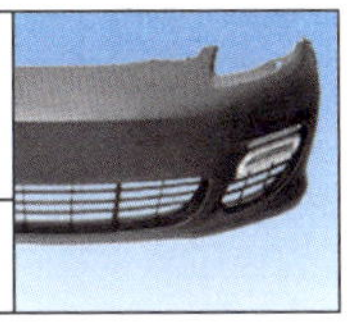
	Base-resin for fibre-reinforced plastics	
Polyurethane resin PU	Form hard and stiff to tough or elastic, chemical resistant	
	Small gears, rolls, shock-absorbing components	

Elastomers, rubber

Butadien Rubber BR	High elastic, good wear, heat and aging resistance	
	Rubber buffers, tyres, sealings	
Silicone rubber SR	Flexible-elastic or stiff-elastic, repellent against water and lubricants	
	Sealings, casting moulds for casting resin	

Fibre-reinforced plastics

Glasfiber-reinforced plastics GRP	High tensile strength to 1,000 N/mm² Density: 2.0 kg/dm³	
	Vehicle and boot components	
Carbon-reinforced plastics CRP	High tensile strength to 1,500 N/mm², light and stiff, density: 1.5 kg/dm³	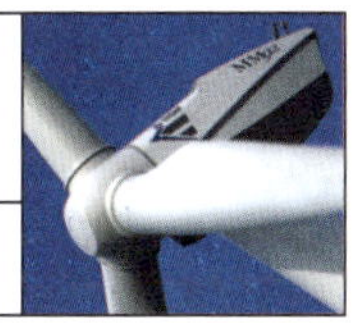
	Rotor blades, aircraft and vehicle components	

Words

waxy	wachsartig
sliding	gleitfähig
container	Behälter
polystyrene	Polystyrol
unbreakable	unzerbrechlich
to foam	schäumen
heat insulation	Wärmedämmung
acid, base	Säure, Lauge
pipe, tube	Rohr
hose	Schlauch
wear-resistant	verschleißfest
motor fuel	Kraftstoff
slideway	Gleitbahn
car element	Autobauteil
base-resin	Basisharz
fibre-reinforced	faserverstärkt
shock-absorbing	stoßdämpfend
aging resistance	Alterungsbeständigkeit
rubber buffer	Gummipuffer
repellent	abweisend
lubricant	Schmiermittel
casting mould	Gießform
rotor blade	Rotorblatt
to classify	einteilen

Exercises

1. Complete the following sentences:
   a) Polyurethane resin is processed to ______________________________.
   b) A plastic which is reinforced with glass fibres is called ______________________________.
2. Name the properties of Polyvinylcloride PVC and some applications of it.
3. Classify the following plastics to the material groups: Polyester resin, Silicon rubber, Polyamid, Polyethylene, Polyurethane resin, Butadien rubber, Polyvinylchloride, Polystyrene.

Thermoplastics	Thermosetting plastics	Elastomers

4. What applications does Styrofoam have?
5. Find components made of plastics in your work environment and name it with its technical designation.
6. What properties and applications do Carbon reinforced plastics have?

5 Mechanical engineering

5.1 Classification of machines

Workers are supported in their job by the use of machines. The machines are regulated by instructions of the machine operator or automatically by program instruction.

The main function of a machine is the transformation of energy, material or information into a technically usable workpiece. The machines are divided by the main function into three types:

- **Engines** (power machine) as energy transforming machines
- **Work machines** as material transforming machines
- **Data processing equipment** as an information transforming machine.

Engines

Engines transform the input energy for a special purpose **(figure).** Depending on the type of engine, electrical energy, fluid-flow energy or pressure energy is transformed into movement energy, also called kinetic energy.

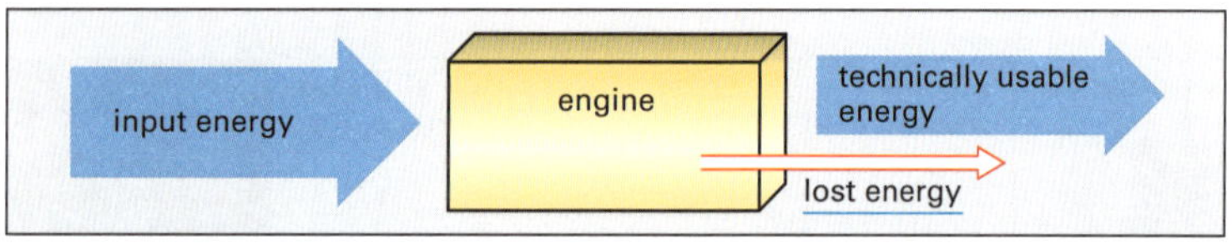

If the engine moves a workpiece, the engine performs work W. Work W is defined as the force F times the distance s: $W = F \cdot s$

The unit of work W is Joule (J). The work of 1 Joule (J) is performed when a force of 1 Newton (N) acts upon a distance of 1 m.

Examples for engines are electric motors, Diesel or Otto motors, fluid power motors, hydraulic or pneumatic cylinders.

Electric motors are the most common engines in the industrial field (**figure** below, left hand). They transform electrical energy into movement energy. They are characterised by high efficiency.

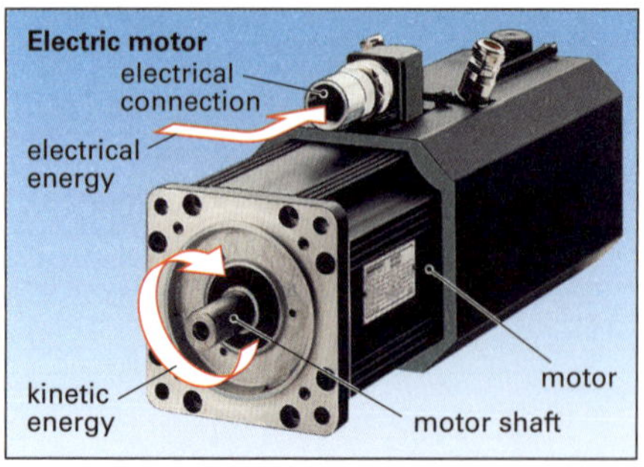

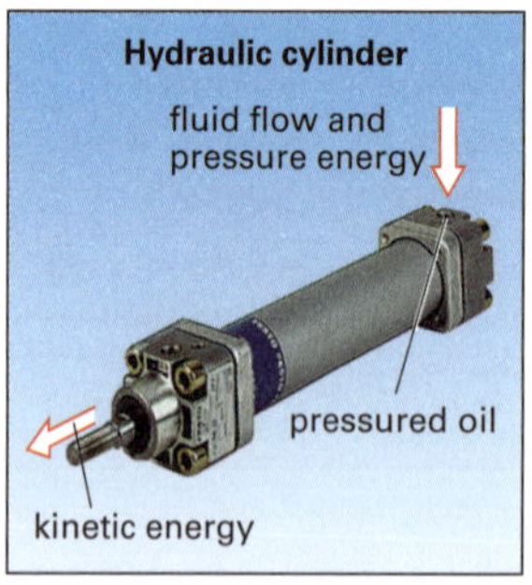

Words (English)	Words (German)
mechanical engineering	Maschinentechnik
classification	Einteilung
worker	Arbeiter
to regulate	steuern
machine operator	Maschinenbediener
program instruction	Programmanweisung
main function	Hauptfunktion
transformation	Umsetzung
information	Information
engine	Kraftmaschine
energy transforming	energieumsetzende
work machine	Arbeitsmaschine
material transforming	stoffumsetzende
data processing equipment	Datenverarbeitungs-anlage
purpose	Verwendungszweck
fluid flow energy	Strömungsenergie
pressure energy	Druckenergie
movement energy	Bewegungsenergie
kinetic energy	Bewegungsenergie
lost energy	Verlustenergie
force	Kraft
distance	Weg
to act	wirken
fluid power motor	Hydromotor
hydraulic cylinder	Hydraulikzylinder
pneumatic cylinder	Pneumatikzylinder
industrial field	industrieller Bereich
efficiency	Wirkungsgrad
combustion engine	Verbrennungskraft-maschine
to store	speichern
chemical energy	chemische Energie
thermal energy	Wärmeenergie
thermodynamic	thermodynamisch
liquids	Flüssigkeiten
air	Luft

Diesel and Otto motors are combustion engines. First they transform stored chemical energy by combustion into thermal energy which is afterwards transformed into kinetic energy by thermodynamic transformation.

In case of **hydraulic or pneumatic engines,** the fluid flow energy and pressure energy of liquids or air are transformed into kinetic energy (**figure** above, right hand).

Exercises

1. Complete the following sentences:
   a) Depending on the type of engine ____________, ____________ or fluid flow and pressure energy are transformed into ____________.
   b) The work of 1 Joule (J) is performed when ____________.
2. Answer the following questions:
   a) In to which types are machines divided?
   b) Which engines use chemical energy transformation?
   c) With which energy type are wind power stations and pneumatic cylinders moved?

Work machines

Work machines transport, transform or change the starting material by the use of energy.

The starting material is characterised by its state of aggregation as solid material, liquid or gas. In production, a distinction is made between amorphous material and material with a geometrically determinated form.

The mass of a material is expressed in kilogram (kg) or tons (t) (1 t = 1,000 kg). The density ϱ of a material represents the mass per volume unit. The density of solid materials and liquids are indicated in the unit kg/dm^3, g/cm^3 or t/m^3, the density of gases in the unit kg/m^3.

Examples for work machines are **conveyors, machine tools** and **heat treatment furnaces.**

Conveyors of solid materials are belt conveyors, lifting equipments or crane systems. Pumps are used to transport liquids. Compressors are applied to transport gases.

In **machine tools** for primary forming, a shapeless substance is placed from a molten metal, a metal powder or a plastic granulate in a solid form.

Machine tools for primary forming are used to change the solid form of workpiece without the loss of material. In this respect e.g. machines for bending, deep-drawing or forging are used.

By the use of metal cutting machine tools, workpieces are transformed into a new form **(figure).** A loss of material occurs in the form of chips during the production with these machines.

Lathe as material transforming machine

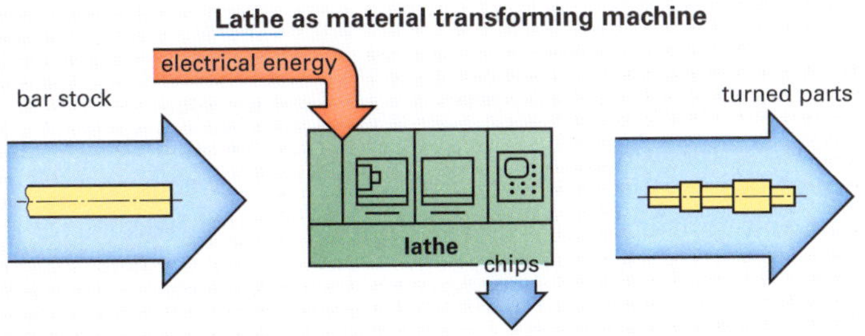

In **heat treatment furnaces** the atomic texture of a metal is changed by thermal energy. Tensile strength and hardness of steels are increased by warming and subsequent quenching.

Data processing equipments (computers)

Data processing equipments receive information by data input, process it and perform data output. Data input is implemented e.g. via keyboard or control panel of a machine tool. The processing of data is performed by a computer. Data output can be performed via a monitor or directly by a switching command to the machine tool.

Words

starting material	Ausgangsstoff
state of aggregation	Aggregatzustand
solid material	Feststoff
liquid	Flüssigkeit
distinction	Unterscheidung
amorphous material	formloser Stoff
geometrically determinated form	geometrisch bestimmte Form
mass	Masse
kilogram	Kilogramm
ton	Tonne
density	Dichte
volume unit	Volumeneinheit
to indicate	angeben
conveyors	Fördermittel
machine tool	Werkzeugmaschine
heat treatment furnace	Wärmebehandlungsofen
belt conveyor	Bandförderer
lifting equipment	Hebezeug
crane system	Krananlage
pump	Pumpe
compressor	Verdichter
primary forming	Urformen
shapeless substance	formloser Stoff
molten metal	Metallschmelze
metal powder	Metallpulver
plastic granulate	Kunststoffgranulat
solid form	feste Form
loss of material	Materialverlust
respect	Hinsicht
bending	Biegen
deep-drawing	Tiefziehen
forging	Schmieden
metal cutting machine tool	zerspanende Werkzeugmaschine
to occur	eintreten
chips	Späne
lathe	Drehmaschine
atomic texture	atomare Struktur
tensile strength	Zugfestigkeit
hardness	Härte
warming	Erwärmung
subsequent	anschließend
quenching	Abschrecken
control panel	Bedienfeld
switching command	Schaltbefehl

Exercises

1. Complete the following sentences:
   a) Examples for working machines are ________________.
   b) Machine tools for primary forming are used to ________ the solid ________ of workpiece without the loss of material.
2. Name three different metal cutting machine tools by using your **Metal Engineering Textbook.**
3. Answer the following questions:
   a) How does a working machine differ from an engine?
   b) Which conveyors can transport liquids or gases?
   c) What is the task of a heat treatment furnace?
   d) How does the data input/output of a data processing equipment work?

5.2 Functional units of machines

Machines are usually characterised according to their main task. The main task of a drilling machine for example is drilling. In order to recognise how the main task „drilling" of the pillar drilling machine is accomplished, a detailed observation is necessary **(figure)**.

The mode of operation can be illustrated easily if the system „pillar drilling machine" is divided into functional units.

Every unit, as indicated in the figure, performs a certain task.

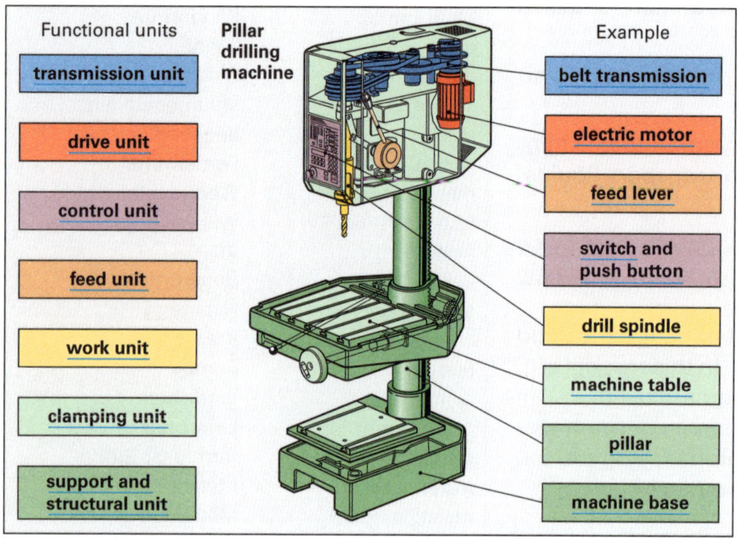

The functions of the particular units can be accomplished by different construction units. The transmission unit of a pillar drilling machine consists of a belt drive. It is used for the transmission and transformation of the rotational movement and the torque from the driving unit to the work unit. The driving unit consists of an electric motor. The work unit contains the drill spindle with the applied twist drill.

The electric motor is started and the required rotation speed of the drill spindle is adjusted by the control unit with its switches and push buttons. The drill is moved into the workpiece by the feed unit. Therefore a feed lever is operated.

The workpiece is clamped on the clamping unit, the machine table. A machine vice is used for the clamping of smaller workpieces. Big workpieces can be directly clamped on the machine table.

The support and structural unit connects the units and receives the machining forces. It consists of the machine base and the pillar. Depending on the size of the workpiece, the height of the machine table can be adjusted by a wheel of adjustment.

Words (English)	Words (German)
functional unit	Funktionseinheit
machine	Maschine
main task	Hauptaufgabe
drilling machine	Bohrmaschine
pillar drilling machine	Säulenbohrmaschine
observation	Betrachtung
to accomplish	bewältigen, erreichen
mode of operation	Wirkungsweise
transmission unit	Übertragungseinheit
gear unit	Getriebeeinheit
drive unit	Antriebseinheit
control unit	Steuereinheit
feed unit	Vorschubeinheit
work unit	Arbeitseinheit
clamping unit	Spanneinheit
support and structural unit	Stütz- und Trageeinheit
belt transmission	Riemengetriebe
electric motor	Elektromotor
switch	Schalter
push button	Taster
feed lever	Vorschubhebel
drill spindle	Bohrspindel
machine table	Maschinentisch
machine base	Maschinenfuß
pillar	Säule
construction units	Baueinheiten
to consist	bestehen
belt drive	Riementrieb
transformation	Umwandlung
rotational movement	Drehbewegung
torque	Drehmoment
twist drill	Spiralbohrer
rotation speed	Drehzahl
to adjust	einstellen
switch	Schalter
to operate	betätigen
workpiece	Werkstück
to clamp	spannen
machine vice	Maschinenschraubstock
to receive	aufnehmen
machining forces	Bearbeitungskräfte
size of the workpiece	Werkstückgröße
wheel of adjustment	Verstellrad

Exercises

1. Translate the fifth paragraph (The workpiece is clamped on the clamping unit, the...) into German.
2. Complete the following sentences:
   a) The transmission unit of a pillar drilling machine is a ______________________.
   b) The drive unit consists of ______________________.
   c) A ______________________ is used for the clamping of smaller workpieces.
3. Answer the following questions:
   a) How can the mode of operation of a pillar drilling machine be explained?
   b) What is the function of the control unit of the pillar drilling machine?
   c) How can the height of the machine table be adjusted?

Partial and basic functions of the pillar drilling machine

The main function „drilling holes into workpieces" is accomplished by the interaction of all functional units of the pillar drilling machine.

In order to achieve this main function, every functional unit has to conduct a specific task. This task is described as partial function. The drive unit with the electric motor for example has the partial function „moving the drill spindle".

In order to recognise how the partial function „moving the drilling machine" is achieved, the electric motor has to be divided into its components. Every component of the electric motor accomplishes a separate task. This is called basic function.

In the following chart, different basic functions of the listed functional units are indicated.

Functional unit	Partial function	Basic function
electric motor 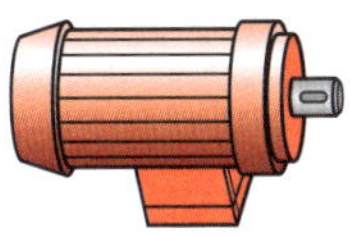	Moving the drill spindle	**Transforming** Electric energy is transformed into mechanical energy by electromagnetic inductors and the motor shaft.
belt transmission 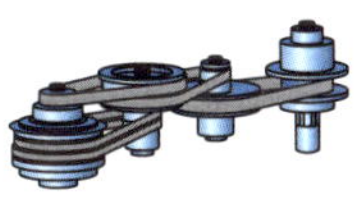	Transmitting and transferring of rotational movement	**Transmitting and transforming** Rotational speeds are transmitted by the belt transmission. The torque is transformed by wheels and belts.
drill spindle 	Taking up and moving the drill	**Taking up and moving** The drill spindle takes up the drill and moves it.
open loop control 	Calculation of cutting data and control of working steps	**Switching and controlling** The rotational speed is adjusted and the electric motor is switched on and off by push buttons, switches and displays. In case of an emergency, an emergency stop button can be pressed.
machine table 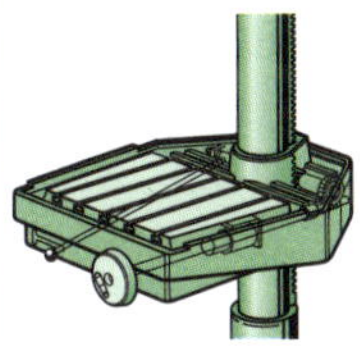	Clamping, supporting and sustaining the workpiece	**Clamping, supporting and sustaining** For drilling, workpieces are clamped on the machine table. The components of the machine are sustained and supported by the pillar.

Words	
partial function	Teilfunktion
basic function	Grundfunktion
main function	Hauptfunktion
holes	Löcher
to accomplish	erzielen
interaction	Zusammenwirken
functional unit	Funktionseinheit
to achieve	erreichen
to conduct	ausführen
task	Aufgabe
drill spindle	Bohrspindel
to recognise	erkennen
to divide	unterteilen
basic function	Grundfunktion
chart	Tabelle
different	verschiedene
to indicate	angeben
to transform	wandeln
electromagnetic inductor	elektromagnetische Spule
motor shaft	Motorwelle
rotational movement	Drehbewegung
rotational speed	Drehzahl
wheel	Rad
belt	Riemen
taking up	aufnehmen
open loop control	Steuerung
calculation	Berechnung
cutting data	Schnittdaten
to switch	schalten
to control	steuern
to adjust	einstellen
push button	Druckknopf
switch	Schalter
display	Anzeige
in case of	im Fall
emergency stop button	Not-Aus-Schalter
to clamp	spannen
to support	stützen
to sustain	tragen
Metal Engineering Textbook	Fachkunde-Buch
to dispose	beseitigen

Exercises

1. Complete the following sentences:
   a) Electric energy is transformed into mechanical energy by ______________ and ______________.
   b) For drilling ______________ are clamped on the machine table.
2. Name three functional units of a CNC machine tool by using a graphic of your **Metal Engineering Textbook.**
3. Explain with the help of your **Metal Engineering Textbook** which units are used to protect the employee and dispose of the chips regarding a CNC machine tool.
4. Answer the following questions:
   a) Which partial functions are required for the main function „drilling holes into workpieces"?
   b) Why is the partial function „moving" divided into different basic functions?

5.3 Screw connections

A connection with screws is a detachable connection.
By using screws and nuts, which are provided with a fastening thread, the components are tightened together **(figure)**.
When components are tightened with a screw and a nut, this screw connection is called through bolt.
In case of a connection with insert screws, one component contains an internal thread.
Studs do not have a screw head. The bolt is screwed in and tightened by a nut.

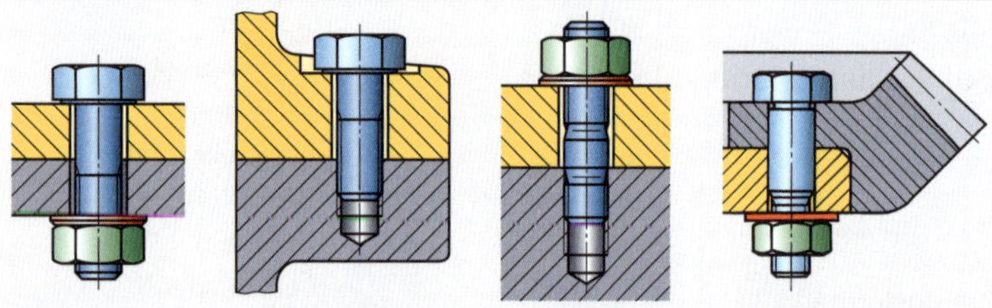

through bolt | insert screw | stud | close-tolerance bolt

The lower ends of the insert screw and of the stud are in the workpiece. The insert screw tensions the workpiece with the screw head. The stud tightens the workpiece with the nut.
Screws are only subjected to tension by tightening of the components. They are not allowed to be stressed neither on shearing nor on bending.
The close-tolerance bolt is an exception. It can also absorb lateral forces and centralise the position of two components to each other.
Screws differ according to their top form, shank form, shank dimension and other fine details. The following table shows a classification of screws according to their head form.
Hexagon head cap screws and cheese head screws are the most common screws in mechanical engineering.

Screw head form		Characteristics
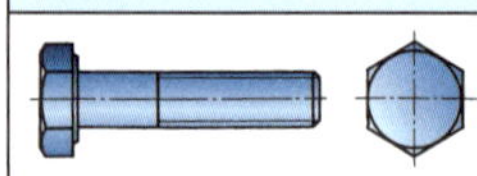	hexagon head cap screw	The external hexagon head cap screw offers a good guiding for the screw tools.
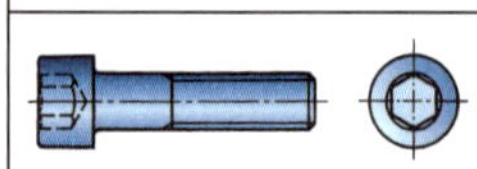	hexagon socket head screw	Their cylindrical head is located in a cavity of the workpiece and they have an internal hexagon in the head.
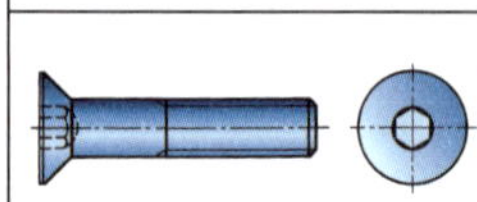	counter-sunk screw	The conical head centralises the workpiece. They have a lower head, compared to hexagon socket head screw.
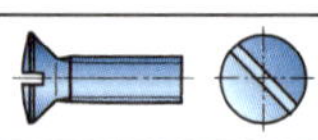	oval head screw	Oval head screws have a rounded surface at the conical head.

Words	
screw connection	Schraubenverbindung
detachable connection	lösbare Verbindung
nut	Mutter
to be provided	ausgestattet sein
fastening thread	Befestigungsgewinde
components	Bauteite
to tighten	verspannen
through bolt	Durchsteckschraube
insert screw	Einziehschraube
internal thread	Innengewinde
stud	Stiftschraube
screw head	Schraubenkopf
to tension	auf Zug spannen
to subject	belasten
tension	Zug
stressed	beansprucht
shearing	Abscherung
bending	Biegung
close-tolerance bolt	Passschraube
exception	Ausnahme
lateral forces	Querkräfte
centralise	zentrieren
top form	Kopfform
shank form	Schaftform
shank dimension	Schaftabmessung
fine detail	Einzelheit
classification	Einteilung
hexagon head cap screw	Sechskantschraube
cheese head screw	Zylinderschraube
mechanical engineering	Maschinenbau
external hexagon	Außensechskant
guiding	Führung
screw tool	Schraubwerkzeug
cylindrical head	zylindrischer Kopf
internal hexagon	Innensechskant
countersunk screw	Senkschraube
conical head	kegeliger Kopf
oval head screw	Linsenschraube
rounded	abgerundet
surface	Oberfläche

Exercises

1. Tanslate the first paragraph (A connection with screws ...) into German.
2. Complete the following sentences:
   a) Screws differ according to their ______________, ______________, ______________ and other ______________.
   b) The external hexagon head cap screw offers ______________________________.
3. Answer the following questions:
   a) How is a connection with screws called?
   b) What is the difference between a through bolt and an insert screw?
   c) What are the characteristics of a hexagon socket head screw compared to a hexagon head cap screw?

Nuts

When using screw connections with through bolts, nuts with different forms are applied (**figure** below).

Hexagon nuts are most commonly used. Cap nuts are used to prevent damage of the thread end and to protect against injuries due to sharp screw ends.

When a screw connection has to be secured, a castle nut with splint pins is used. Union nuts are needed for pipe couplings.

Wing nuts or knurled nuts are used when nuts should be tightened or loosened by hand. Lifting eye nuts have clipping eyelets in order to fasten for the transport of devices and machines.

By using groove nuts, roller bearings are fixed on shafts. They can also be used to adjust the bearing clearance.

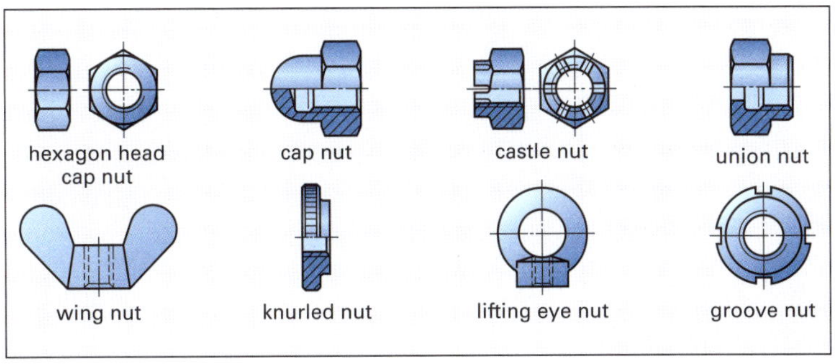

Screw locking devices

A preload force is generated in the screw by tightening. With the appropriate preload force, long screws do not need an additional lock against the release of the connection. In the course of time, the screw can set itself. This is for example known as levelling of the surface roughness under the screw head or in the thread. Setting locks are flexible washers located under the screw head. Spring lock washers, tooth lock washers or serrated lock washers prevent the unwanted decline of preload forces.

In case of highly dynamic stressed components, the screw connection may turn loose. Locking devices like e. g. ratchet screws or adhesive prevent the connection from getting loose.

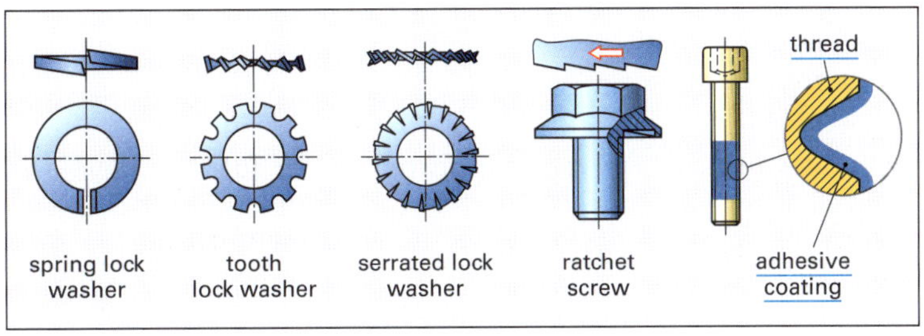

Words

nuts	Muttern
screw connections	Schraubverbindungen
forms	Formen
hexagon nut	Sechskantmutter
cap nut	Hutmutter
to prevent	verhindern
damage	Beschädigung
thread end	Gewindeende
injuries	Verletzungen
sharp	scharf
to secure	sichern
castle nut	Kronenmutter
splint pin	Splint
union nut	Überwurfmutter
pipe coupling	Rohrverschraubung
knurled nut	Rändelmutter
wing nut	Flügelmutter
tightened	angezogen
to loosen	lösen
lifting eye nut	Ringmutter
clipping eyelets	Einhängeösen
devices	Geräte
groove nut	Nutmutter
roller bearing	Wälzlager
to fix	befestigen
shaft	Welle
bearing clearance	Lagerspiel
screw locking device	Schraubensicherung
preload force	Vorspannkraft
to generate	erzeugen
appropriate	angemessen
lock	Sicherung
release	Lösen
levelling	Einebnen
surface roughness	Oberflächenrauheit
setting lock	Setzsicherung
flexible washers	federnde Scheiben
spring lock washer	Federring
tooth lock washer	Zahnscheibe
serrated lock washer	Fächerscheibe
decline	Minderung, Abnahme
dynamic stressed	dynamisch belastet
to turn loose	losdrehen
locking device	Losdrehsicherung
ratchet screw	Sperrzahnschraube
adhesive	Klebstoff
thread	Gewinde
adhesive coating	Klebeschicht

Exercises

1. Answer the following questions in English:
   a) Which nuts are tightened by hand?
   b) Which nuts are most commonly used?
   c) How does a setting lock differ from a locking device?
   d) Which screw does not need a setting lock?
2. Complete the following sentences:
   a) Cap nuts ____________________ to prevent ____________________ and to protect against ____.
   b) The screw connection may turn loose in case of ____________________ components.
3. Define three different captive screw lockings with the help of your **Metal Engineering Textbook.**

5.4 Shaft-hub connections

The purpose of a shaft-hub connection is to transfer torques e. g. between shaft and gear wheel. The gear wheel is positioned on the shaft and can be bonded in three different ways: positively, non-positively or firmly locking. Positive and non-positive shaft-hub connections are detachable. For this reason they are frequently used.

Feather key connections

Feather key connections are the mostly used positive locking shaft-hub connections. They have low manufacturing costs and can be easily installed **(figure)**. The feather key between shaft and hub is a drive type connection. The parallel lateral surfaces of the feather key are in direct contact with the shaft groove and the hub keyway. There, the torque transmission takes place. The feather key is loaded by shearing when it is stressed. There is clearance between the feather key top and the hub keyway base.

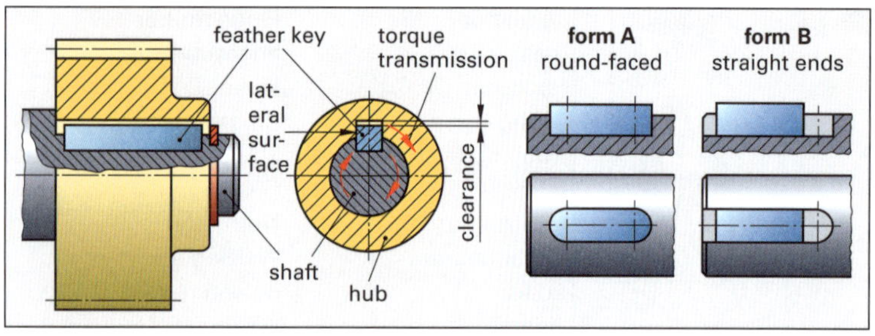

Feather key connections load the shaft and the hub on one side of the circumference. It leads to an irregular stress distribution.

This connection is not suitable for the transmission of high torques and abrupt loads. At abrupt loads the feather key and the lateral surfaces of the hub can become plastically deformed and destroyed.

Feather keys are available in different forms (**figure** above). The feather key with form A is round-faced. It connects exactly the hub to the shaft. The hub keyway base is open on both sides so that the components can be pushed over the feather key. The shaft groove is produced with an end-milling cutter, the hub keyway is usually produced by shaping or broaching.

The feather key with form B has straight ends. Only its lateral surface is in contact with the shaft groove and it is usually used with a shaft groove which is open on one side. This shaft groove can be produced with a disc milling cutter or an end-milling cutter.

Words	
shaft-hub connection	Welle-Nabe-Verbindung
torque	Drehmoment
gear wheel	Zahnrad
positively locking	formschlüssig
non-positively locking	kraftschlüssig
firmly locking	stoffschlüssig
detachable	lösbar
feather key connection	Passfederverbindung
manufacturing cost	Herstellungskosten
drive type connection	Mitnehmer-Verbindung
lateral surface	Seitenfläche
shaft groove	Wellennut
hub keyway	Nabennut
loaded	belastet
shearing	Abscherung
clearance	Spiel
circumference	Umfang
irregular	ungleichmäßig
stress distribution	Spannungsverteilung
suitable	brauchbar
transmission	Übertragung
abrupt	stoßartig
plastically deformed	plastisch verformt
destroyed	zerstört
round-faced	rundstirnig
to connect exactly	genau einpassen
hub keyway base	Nabennut-Grund
end-milling cutter	Schaftfräser
shaping	Stoßen
broaching	Räumen
straight	gerade
open on one side	einseitig offen
disc milling cutter	Scheibenfräser
bore	Bohrung
countersinking	Senkung
fixing screw	Halteschraube

Feather keys with forms C to F are, depending on the design, equivalent to form A or B; but they have one or two bores with countersinks (**figure** right hand). Those feather keys can be fixed in the shaft groove with fixing screws.

Exercises

1. The right hand **figure** shows feather keys form C and F. Name the special shape elements a) to e).

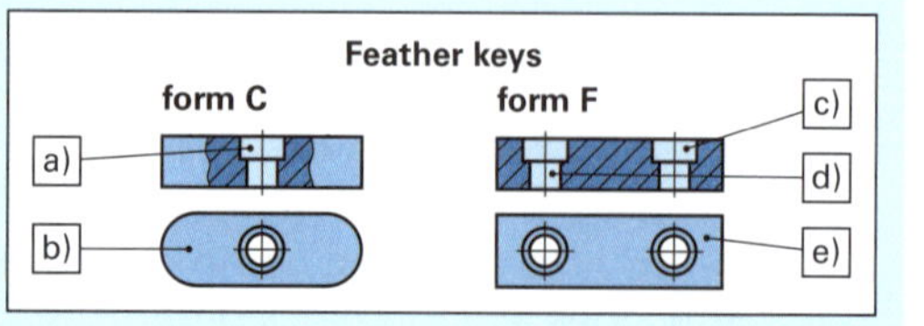

2. Complete the following sentences:
   a) The feather key is loaded to ________________ when it gets ________________.
   b) The feather key cannot be used for the transmission of high torques and abrupt loads, because the feather key and the lateral surfaces of the hub can become ________________________.
3. Answer the following questions:
   a) Which connections are detachable?
   b) Regarding a feather key connection, how is the torque transferred?
   c) Which details of the shape are different at feather key form A and feather key form B? Name them.

Spline shaft connections are used for the transmission of high torques. They are e.g. applied for manual gearboxes of machine tools. In case of the gear box, the gear wheel has a spline hub and the shaft has a spline shaft (**figure** below, left hand). They are axial movable. The torque is distributed around the circumference by an even number of grooves and feather keys.

In case of a **tooth shaft connection,** the numerous teeth evenly transfer the torque between shaft and hub. The small teeth lead to a reduced weakening of the shaft, compared to the spline shaft profile. Therefore, with the same diameter, higher torques can be transferred by the tooth shaft. Additionally, the tooth shaft connection is able to bear an abrupt load more easily.

Spline shaft connection

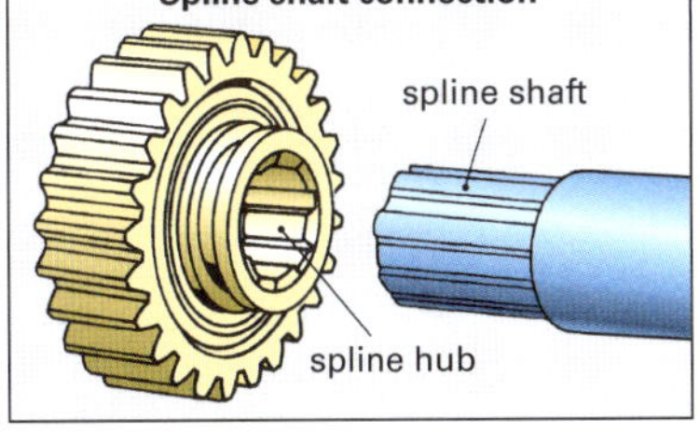

Tooth shaft connection

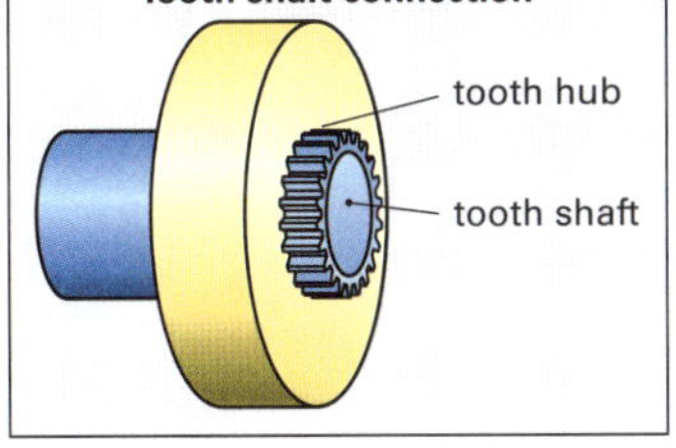

Wedge connections are produced with a wedge which has a gradient of inclination of 1:100. The wedge is hammered in the groove between the shaft and the hub and tightens the components against each other (**figure** below, left hand). Thereby, the central axes of shaft and hub become slightly shifted. A small unbalance occurs. Due to this, wedge connections are not suitable for high rotational speeds.

Circular spline connections consist of non-cylindric cross sections of shaft and hub (**figure** below, right hand). Usually the components have three circular splines. The circular spline profile of the hub is slightly bigger than the one of the shaft. The clearance is the reason why shaft and hub can be well axially joined. The torque transmission is achieved by seizing the hub and the shaft. When loaded, the parts are uptight against each other. High torques can be transferred with the circular spline connection in both directions of rotation.

Wedge connection

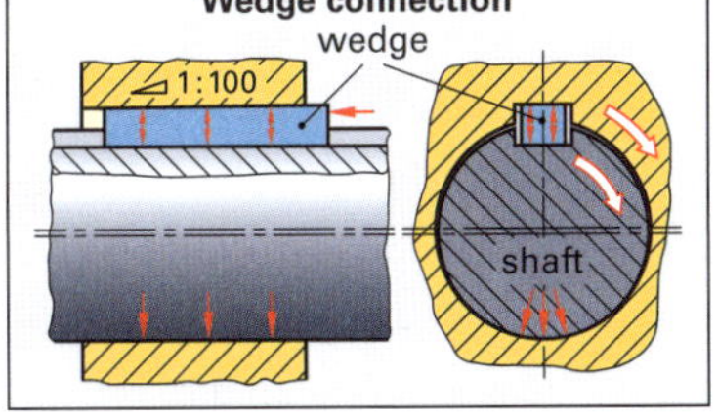

Circular spline connection

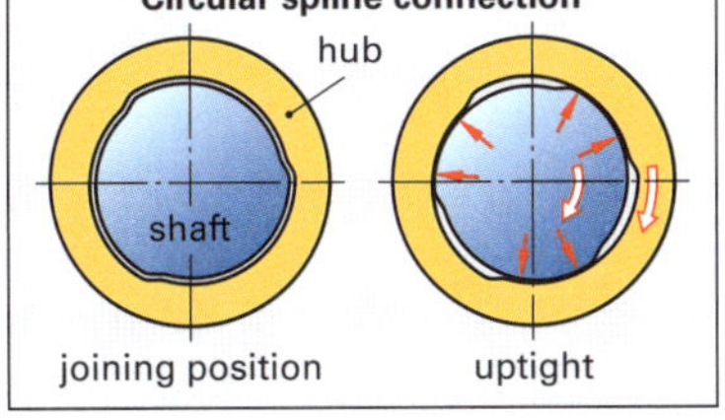

Words

spline shaft	Keilwelle
transmission	Übertragung
manual gearbox	Schaltgetriebe
machine tool	Werkzeugmaschine
gear wheel	Zahnrad
spline hub	Keilnabe
axial movable	axial verschiebbar
to distribute	verteilen
circumference	Umfang
even number	gerade Anzahl
groove	Nut
feather key	Passfeder
tooth shaft connection	Zahnwelle-Verbindung
evenly	gleichmäßig
numerous	zahlreich
weakening	Schwächung
spline shaft profile	Keilwellenprofil
to bear	tragen
abrupt load	stoßartige Belastung
wedge connection	Keilverbindung
gradient of inclination	Neigung
to hammer	einschlagen
to tighten	verspannen
to shift	verschieben
unbalance	Unwucht
to occur	auftreten
due to this	daher
suitable	geeignet
rotational speed	Drehzahl
circular spline connection	Kreiskeilverbindung
non-cylindric	unrund
cross section	Querschnitt
slightly	etwas
clearence	Spiel
to join	fügen
to achieve	erreichen
to seize	verklemmen
uptight	verklemmt
direction of rotation	Drehrichtung

Exercises

1. Complete the following sentences:
   a) In case of a ______________________ the numerous teeth evenly transfer ______________________ between ______________________________________ and hub.
   b) The circular spline profile of the hub ______________________________________ of the shaft.

2. Answer the following questions:
   a) Why is the torque evenly transferred at a spline shaft connection between spline shaft and spline hub?
   b) How does the spline shaft connection differ from the tooth shaft connection?
   c) Why is the wedge connection not suitable for high torques?
   d) How is the torque transferred between shaft and hub in a circular spline connection?

Shaft-hub connection	Torque transferring element
feather key	
spline shaft	
wedge	
tooth shaft	
circular spline	

3. Name the torque transferring component of the shaft-hub-connections in the table right hand.

5.5 Friction and lubricants

The movement of a guide carriage on a guideway causes friction **(figure)**. It counteracts the force F in moving direction.

The frictional force F_F should be reduced to a minimum by lubricants. They prevent contact between the surfaces. This reduces the friction and the surface wear of the gliding parts.

The frictional force F_F during the movement, depends on the normal force F_N, which is acting on the gliding area. Further more there are several constructive conditions such as surface texture, material combination, lubrication und friction type which have influence **(figure)**.

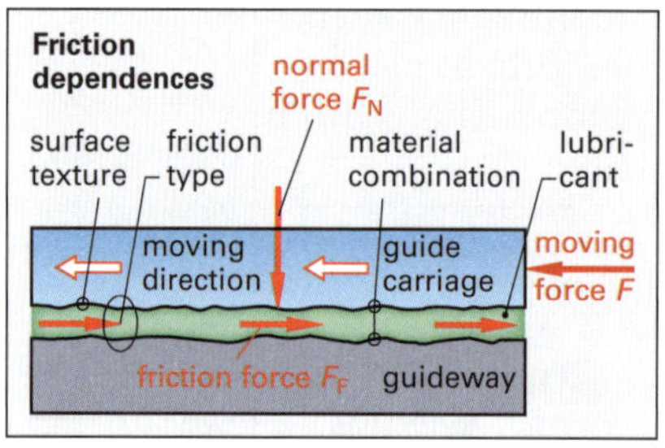

The constructive dependences are considered by the coefficient of friction μ; it is determined by experiments.

The frictional force F_F is calculated by the coefficient of friction μ and the normal force F_N.

$$F_F \ \mu \cdot F_N$$

The dimension of the friction area has no influence on the frictional force F_F as well as the force F in moving direction.

Static friction exists at downtime and at the beginning of the movement.

Sliding friction occurs when the displacement force F is greater than the static friction force F_F and the parts move against each other. In case of very slow sliding, the static friction and the sliding friction change permanently, which leads to a **stick-slip**.

States of friction

In case of **solid friction**, there is a direct contact between the sliding surfaces. When there is a lubricant, a lubricating film is built up between the surfaces. At the beginning of the movement, the surfaces are still in contact at single points. Then, **mixed friction** exists, the frictional force is smaller compared to solid friction. When there is enough lubricant between the sliding surfaces, they become completely separated by the lubricant with increasing movement. Then **fluid friction** takes place with a small frictional force.

The following table shows the coefficient of friction μ of three materials with the different types of friction.

Material combination:	Coefficient of friction μ		
	static friction dry	sliding friction dry	sliding friction lubricated
steel/grey cast iron	0.18 ... 0.20	0.15 ... 0.20	0.05 ... 0.10
steel/steel	0.15 ... 0.30	0.10 ... 0.12	0.04 ... 0.07
steel/CuSn	0.18 ... 0.20	0.15 ... 0.20	0.05 ... 0.10

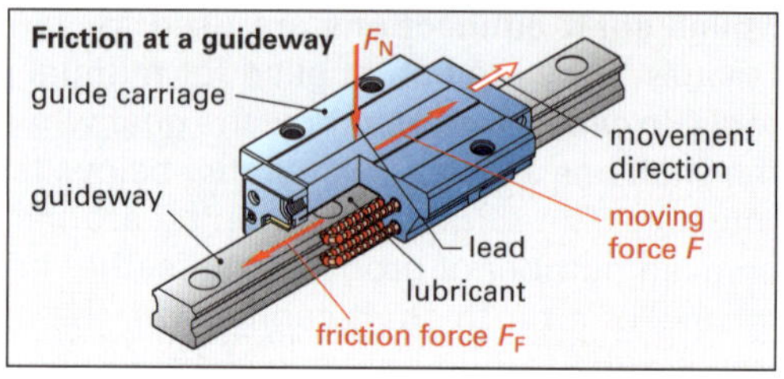

Words

English	German
friction	Reibung
lubricant	Schmierstoff
guide carriage	Führungsschlitten
guideway	Führungsbahn
to counteract	entgegenwirken
to prevent	vermeiden
contact	Berührung
to reduce	vermindern
surface wear	Oberflächenverschleiß
to depend on	abhängen von
normal force	Normalkraft
to act	wirken
gliding area	Gleitfläche
surface texture	Oberflächen-beschaffenheit
material combination	Werkstoffpaarung
lubrication	Schmierung
friction type	Reibungsart
to consider	berücksichtigen
coefficient of friction	Reibungszahl
static friction	Haftreibung
downtime	Stillstand
sliding friction	Gleitreibung
displacement force	Verschiebekraft
stick slip	Ruckgleiten
lubrication gap	Schmierspalt
state of friction	Reibungszustand
solid friction	Festkörperreibung
mixed friction	Mischreibung
to increase	steigern
fluid friction	Flüssigkeitsreibung
grey cast iron	Grauguss

Exercises

1. Complete the following sentences:
   a) The ______________________ occurs during the movement counteracts ______________________.
   b) In order to move one of the components, the ____________________________ has to be greater than the ____.

2. Answer the following questions:
   a) Which influence factors does the coefficient of friction depend on?
   b) How does the mixed friction differ from the fluid friction?
   c) A guide carriage made of steel with a weight of 250 N should be moved on a lubricated steel guideway (**figure** above). Which sliding force is needed to move the carriage?

Types of friction at machine elements

Friction is distinguished between sliding friction, rolling friction and combined sliding and rolling friction.

In case of **sliding friction**, two workpiece surfaces slide on each other. It occurs e. g. at a plain bearing **(figure)**.

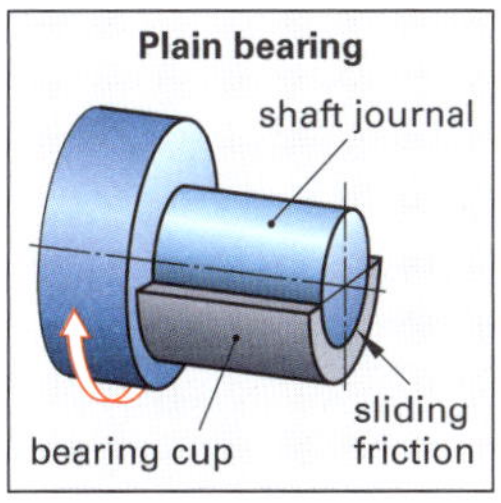

In case of **rolling friction**, cylindrical rollers or balls roll on the surface of the running surface e. g. in a roller bearing **(figure)**. Cylindrical rollers have a linear contact with the running surface, balls a single point contact on a plain surface.

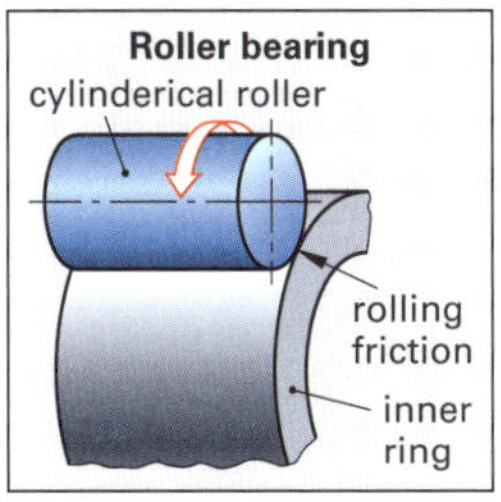

The **combined sliding and rolling friction** occurs simultaneously. The balls of a ball bearing e. g. run in a guide groove of the outer ring and therefore touch the outer ring linear **(figure)**. Along with the rolling, the balls are sliding in the outer ring. Due to this, roller bearings must necessarily be lubricated.

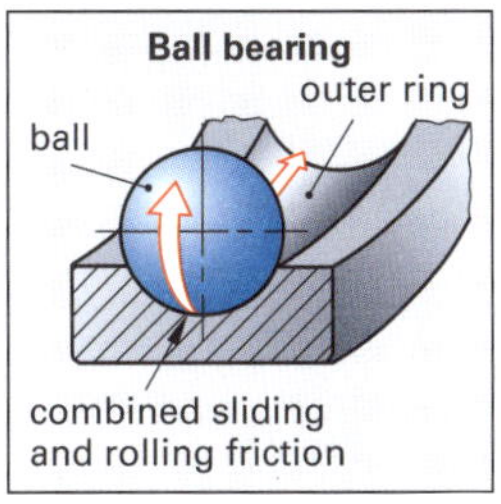

Lubricants

Lubricants have the main task of minimising friction. They can also absorb shocks, dissipate heat and wear parts and are a corrosion protection of the bare surface.

The viscosity of the lubricant is a measure for the inner friction. In case of high viscosity, the lubricant is viscous. Lubricants with low viscosity are thin fluid.

Mineral or synthetic oils are used as fluid lubricants. Additives are added to mineral oils because their viscosity decreases with increasing temperatures. As a result, the viscosity remains constant over a wide temperature range. Synthetic oils have an almost constant viscosity at different temperatures and are more resistant to ageing than mineral oils.

Lubricating greases are made of oils which had been thickened to pasty state with different soaps. They are mainly used for roller bearings and plain bearings.

Solid lubricants are used when a lubricating film of oil or grease is not able to be developed because of low sliding speeds or when the operating temperatures are too high or too low. Solid lubricants consist for example of graphite powder. The powder particles are flaky and smooth out the roughness of the workpiece surface.

Words

types of friction	Reibungsarten
to distinguish	unterscheiden
sliding friction	Gleitreibung
rolling friction	Rollreibung
combined sliding and rolling friction	Wälzreibung
workpiece surface	Werkstückoberfläche
plain bearing	Gleitlager
shaft journal	Wellenzapfen
cylindrical rollers	Zylinderrolle
ball	Kugel
running surface	Rollbahn
linear	linienförmig
single point	punktförmig
ball bearing	Kugellager
guide groove	Führungsrille
outer ring	Außenring
along with	einher mit
sliding	Gleiten
to lubricate	schmieren
trunnion	Lagerzapfen
bearing cup	Lagerschale
cylinderical roller	Zylinderrolle
shock	Stoß
to dissipate	ableiten, abführen
heat	Wärme
wear parts	Verschleißteilchen
corrosion protection	Korrosionsschutz
bare	blank
viscosity	Viskosität
viscous	dickflüssig
thin fluid	dünnflüssig
mineral oil	Mineralöl
synthetic oil	synthetisches Öl
additive	Zusatz
to decrease	verringern
ageing	Alterung
lubricating grease	Schmierfett
pasty state	pastenartiger Zustand
soap	Seife
solid lubricant	Festschmierstoff
sliding speed	Gleitgeschwindigkeit
powder particles	Pulverteilchen
flaky	plättchenförmig
to smooth out	einebnen

Exercises

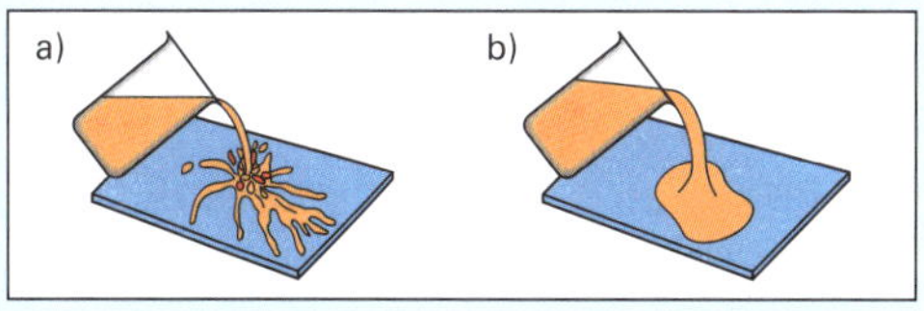

1. Answer the following questions:
   a) What are the different types of friction?
   b) In which case is a solid lubricant used?
   c) What does the term „viscosity" mean?
2. The figure right hand shows two lubricants with different viscosities.
   Describe the viscosities: a) The lubricant is ______________________.
   b) The lubricant is ______________________.
3. Complete the following sentences:
   a) In case of rolling friction ______________________ on a workpiece surface.
   b) Lubricants have the task ______________________.
4. Use your **Metal Engineering Textbook** to list, which properties lubricants should have.

5.6 Bearings

The task of a bearing is to lead and support a shaft or an axle.

Plain bearings

In a plain bearing, the shaft rotates in a bearing shell or a bearing bush **(figure).** A sufficient lubricating film has to exist between the plain bearing surfaces. Then the frictional forces are minimised.

There are hydrodynamic and hydrostatic plain bearings, depending on the type of lubrication.

In plain bearings with a **hydrodynamic lubrication**, the lubricant film is generated by the rotation of the shaft **(figure).** When starting the rotation of the shaft, the plain bearing surfaces are not completely separated by the lubricating film. This state is called mixed friction. With increasing rotation of the shaft, the lubricating oil, which is located on the unloaded bearing side, will be pulled into the narrow lubricating gap. Thereby, the shaft is raised at this point, forming an ever-growing lubricating film on the loaded side of the bearing. At a certain speed level, the shaft floats completely on the lubricating film: liquid friction exists.

Hydrodynamic plain bearing

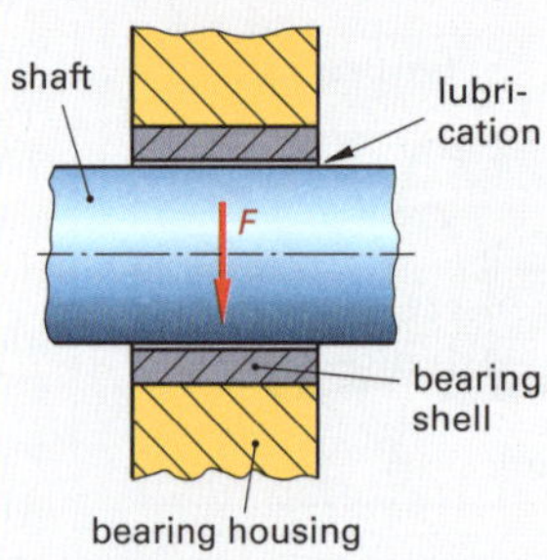

Generating of the lubricant film at hydrodynamic lubrication

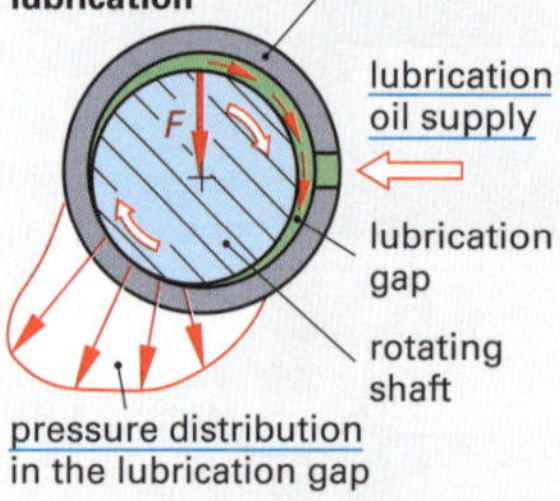

Hydrostatik plain bearing

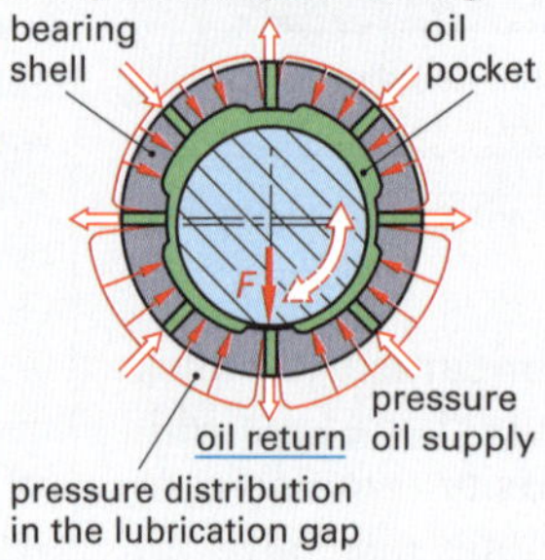

In a **hydrostatic lubrication bearing** several oil pockets are positioned on the inner surface **(figure).** The lubricating oil is pumped into every oil pocket with a constant volume flow by an external pump. If the gap becomes narrower by the external load of the shaft, the oil pressure pushes the shaft back into the bearing centre.

Advantages of hydrostatic plain bearings:
- immediatly lubrication, no wear at start-up and warming-up
- high concentricity and no stick-slip.

Disadvantages of hydrostatic plain bearings:
- expensive lubrication equipment
- monitoring of the lubrication system is necessary.

Materials for plain bearings are alloys of copper, tin, lead, zinc and aluminium as well as the plastic polyamid.

Words	
bearing	Lager
to lead	führen
to support	stützen
shaft	Welle
axle	Achse
plain bearing	Gleitlager
bearing shell	Lagerschale
bearing bush	Lagerbuchse
sufficient	ausreichend
lubrication film	Schmierfilm
to minimise	minimieren
hydrodynamic	hydrodynamisch
hydrostatic	hydrostatisch
lubrication	Schmierung
to generate	erzeugen
mixed friction	Mischreibung
lubricating oil	Schmieröl
unloaded bearing side	unbelastete Lagerseite
to narrow	verengen
lubrication gap	Schmierspalt
to raise	abheben
to float	schwimmen
liquid friction	Flüssigkeitsreibung
lubricating oil supply	Schmierölzufuhr
pressure distribution	Druckverteilung
oil pocket	Öltasche
volume flow	Volumenstrom
external pump	externe Pumpe
load	Belastung
bearing centre	Lagermitte
wear	Verschleiß
start-up	Anlauf
warming-up	Warmlaufen
oil return	Ölrücklauf
concentricity	Rundlaufgenauigkeit
stick-slip	Ruckgleiten
lubrication equipment	Schmiereinrichtung
monitoring	Überwachung
lubrication system	Schmiersystem

Exercises

1. The figure right hand shows the cross section of a small plain bearing. Name the components with the numbers ① to ⑤.

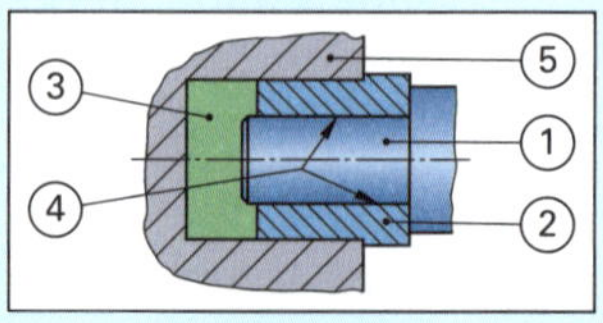

2. Complete the following sentences:
   a) In case of plain bearings with a hydrodynamic lubrication, the _______________ is generated by the _______________ shaft.
   b) In a hydrostatic lubrication _________________________ are positioned on the inner surface. The _____________ is pumped into _____________ with a constant volume flow by an external pump.
3. Answer the following questions:
   a) Describe the functionality of a hydrodynamic plain bearing.
   b) What are the advantages and disadvantages of a hydrostatic plain bearing?

Roller bearing

A roller bearing has rolling elements between the inner and the outer race **(figure)**. These rolling elements run between two bearing races, which are inserted on the shaft and in the bearing housing. The cage keeps the rolling elements in an even distance to each other.

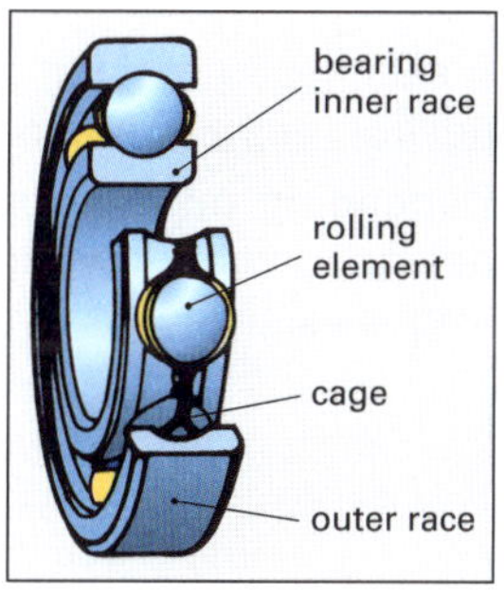

Balls and rollers are used as rolling elements (**figure** below). There are single row and double row roller bearings.

Due to the rolling elements, the rolling friction of a roller bearing is smaller than the sliding friction of a plain bearing. Roller bearings have a low friction at low speeds and need less lubricant. Disadvantages of roller bearings compared with plain bearings are the larger mounting diameters, the increased noise development and lower load capacity for the same construction size.

Depending on the basic form of the rolling elements, roller bearings are distinguished in ball bearings and roller bearings.

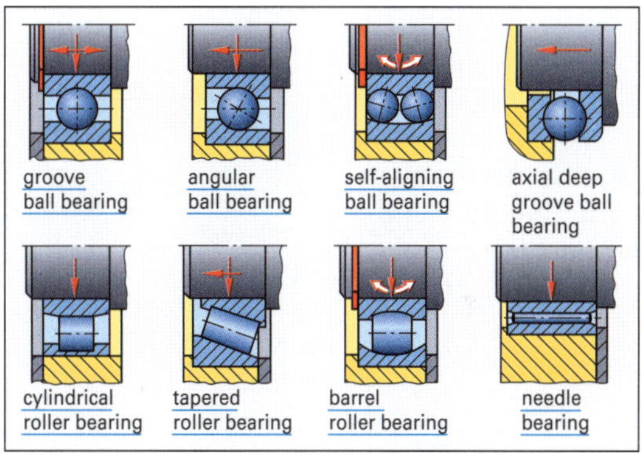

According to the loading direction and type of rolling elements, the bearing races are designed differently. Types of ball bearings are deep groove ball bearings, angular ball bearings and self-aligning ball bearings. The bearing races are fixed tightly or loosely in the housing or on the shaft.

The bearing of a shaft in a transmission, shown in the **figure** below, has a fixed bearing on the left and a floating bearing on the right side. In this case, deep groove ball bearings are used. At a higher axial force, tapered roller bearings are often installed with mutual guide.

Bearing of a gear shaft

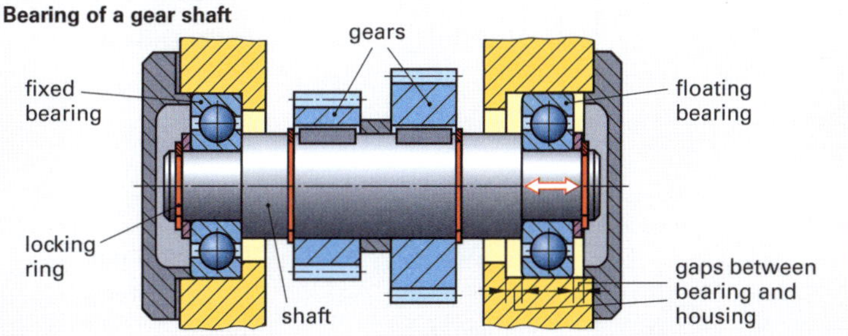

Words

roller bearing	Rollenlager
rolling element	Wälzkörper
inner race	innerer Laufring
outer race	Außenring
cage	Käfig
single row	einreihig
double row	zweireihig
due to	aufgrund
mounting diameter	Einbaudurchmesser
noise development	Geräuschentwicklung
load capacity	Tragfähigkeit
groove ball bearing	Rillenkugellager
angular ball bearing	Schrägkugellager
self-aligning ball bearing	Pendelkugellager
cylindrical roller bearing	Zylinderrollenlager
tapered roller bearing	Kegelrollenlager
barrel roller bearing	Tonnenrollenlager
needle bearing	Nadellager
ball bearing	Kugellager
tight	fest
transmission	Getriebe
fixed bearing	Festlager
floating bearing	Loslager
axial force	Axialkraft
mutual guide	gegenseitige Führung
radial force	Radialkraft
loading	Belastung
to indicate	angeben

Exercises

1. Answer the following questions:
   a) What components does a roller bearing have?
   b) What are the advantages of a roller bearing versus a plain bearing?
   c) What task has the cage in a roller bearing?

2. There are differences between the axial force and the radial force by the loading of roller bearings. Indicate in the table below which of the two forces (axial or radial) can be carried by the particular roller bearing.

Bearing type	**Kind of possible load**	**Bearing type**	**Kind of possible load**
Grooved ball bearing		Cylindrical roller bearing	
Angular ball bearing		Tapered roller bearing	
Self-aligning ball bearing		Barrel roller bearing	

5.7 Seals

A seal has to prevent the entry and discharge of fluid, gas or a solid substance, e.g. dirt or dust at the disconnection point of two components.

Depending on the application, a distinction is made between static seals and dynamic seals. They can be designed with or without sealing material **(figure)**.

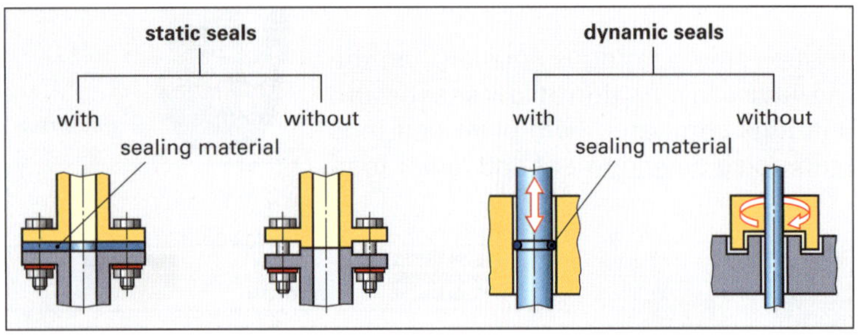

Static seals

A static seal is used at parts that do not move against each other. If the disconnection point is connected without sealing material, the contact surfaces must be very smooth and form-exact. Static seals with sealing material are deformed elastically or plastically during installation.

Flat seals and profile seals are often used. Flat seals have a wide supporting surface and usually consist of plastic material **(figure)**. At high contact pressures, metals e.g. soft steel, copper or lead are applied. The most common profile seals are round O-rings.

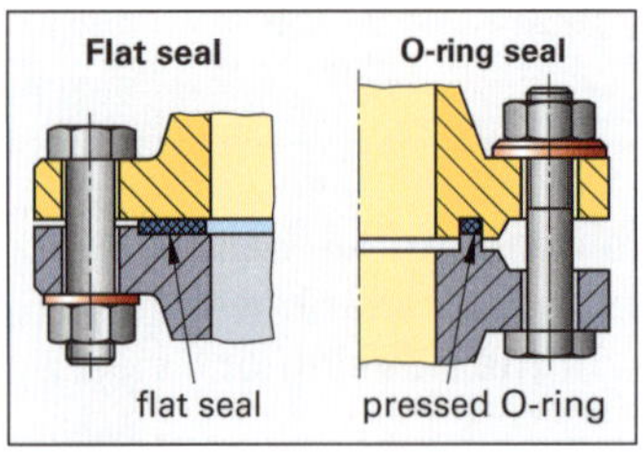

Liquid elastic sealing material is also used **(figure)**. It is spread on the surfaces and fills the roughness depths at the connection area. Then it hardens and becomes elastic.

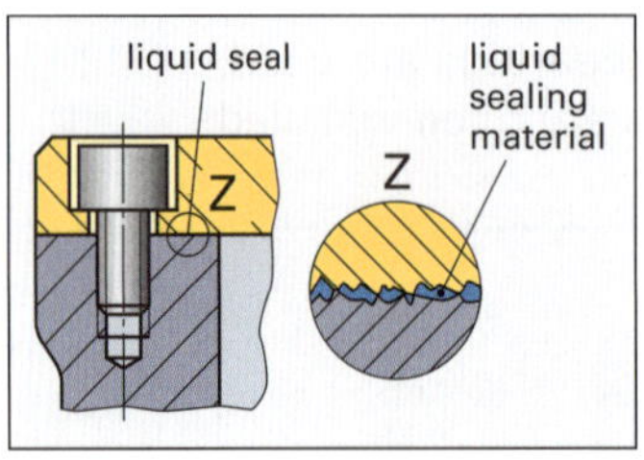

Dynamic seals

If two parts move against each other, dynamic seals will be inserted. These seals are not absolutely leak-proof.

Grooved rings (lip seals) e.g. are applied to seal the plunger in a hydraulic cylinder **(figure)**. The sealing effect occurs by the sealing lips which are pressed to the plunger.

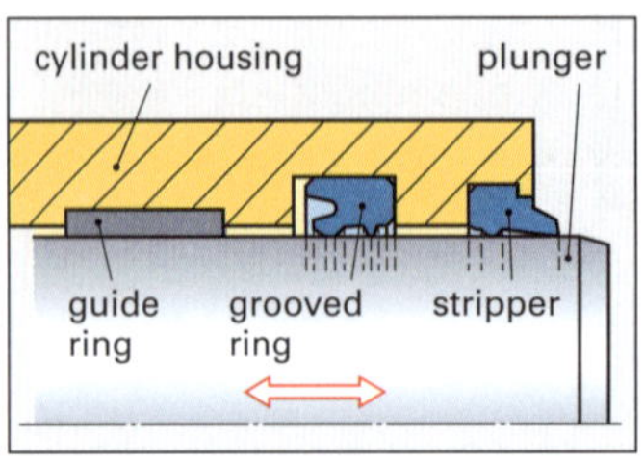

Words

seal	Dichtung
to prevent	verhindern
entry	Eindringen
discharge	Austritt
fluid	Flüssigkeit
gas	Gas
solid substance	fester Stoff
dirt	Schmutz
dust	Staub
disconnection point	Trennstelle
static seal	ruhende Dichtung
dynamic seal	Bewegungsdichtung
sealing material	Dichtungswerkstoff
contact surface	Berührungsfläche
smooth	glatt
form-exact	formgenau
installation	Einbau
elastic	elastisch
plastic	plastisch
flat seal	Flachdichtungen
profile seal	Profildichtungen
supporting surface	Auflagefläche
plastic material	Kunststoff
contact pressure	Anpressdruck
soft steel	weicher Stahl
copper	Kupfer
lead	Blei
to apply	anwenden
round O-ring	runder O-Ring
liquid	flüssig
roughness depth	Rautiefe
to harden	aushärten
to insert	einsetzen
leak-proof	dicht
grooved ring	Nutringdichtung
lip seal	Lippendichtung
plunger	Kolben
sealing effect	Dichtwirkung
to occur	entstehen
to select	auswählen

Exercises

1. Complete the following sentences:
   a) According to the movable or non-movable components you apply __________ or __________ seals.
   b) Liquid sealing materials fill the ______________________ at the disconnection point completely.
   c) If two parts move against each other ___________________________ will be inserted.
2. Translate the first paragraph into German.
3. What is the difference between static and dynamic seals?
4. Use your **Metal Trade Handbook** to determine what kind of profile seals are commonly used.

The **rotary shaft seal** is a special seal for preventing the discharge of lubricant at a shaft exit **(figure).**

It consists of a rubber body, stiffened by a metal ring and a round spiral spring. It is pressed into a groove of the housing. The sealing lips and the protection lips are pressed against the rotating shaft by the internal pressure of the lubricant. Rotary shaft seals are only suitable for low pressures.

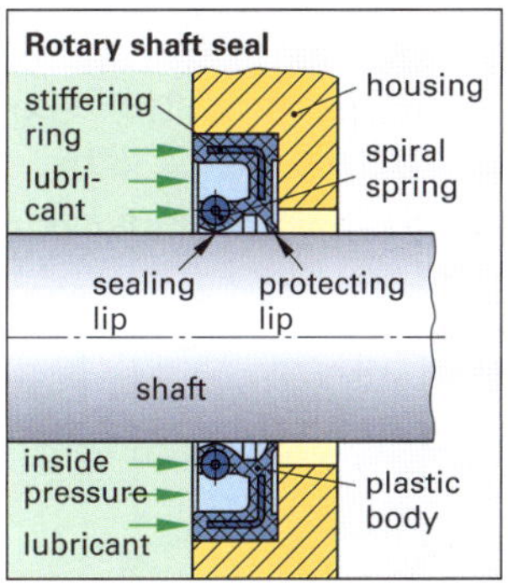

Packing boxes are seals for slowly oscillating or rotating shafts of plunger rods **(figure).** The packing consists of several square strings of plastic fibre, impregnated by a stiff lubricant grease. The seal is pressed by the gland into the housing and against the rotating shaft. A spring in the gland retensions the packing. Packing boxes have a great friction and a leakage.

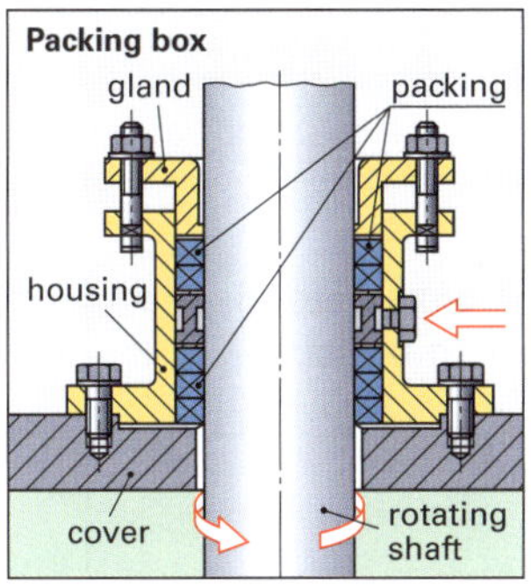

The **labyrinth seal** generates its sealing effect by the narrow gaps of a labyrinth between two parts which are connected with the shaft and the housing **(figure).** These seals are applied for bearings with lubricant grease. They have a leakage.

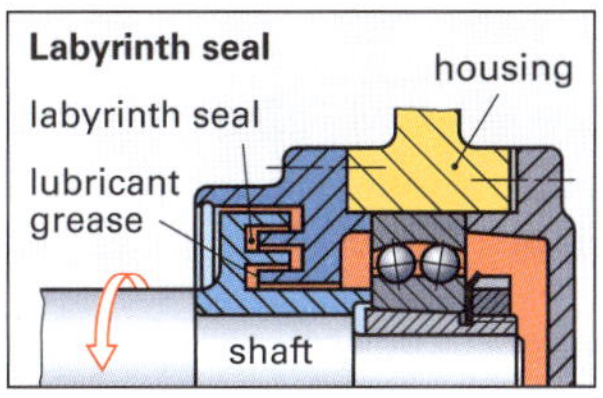

Axial face seals, also called **mechanical seals**, are used for sealing rotating shaft exits against the high pressure area within the housing **(figure).** This seal consists of two flat-ground rings; one is the pressure sliding ring, the other one is the opposite sliding ring. The rings consist e. g. of plastic material, ceramic or hard metal.

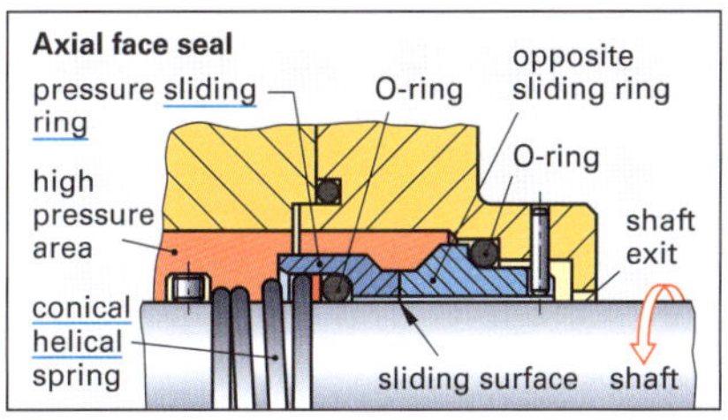

The pressure sliding ring rotates with the shaft; the opposite sliding ring is tightly fit with the housing. The pressure sliding ring is sealed by an O-ring against the shaft, the opposite sliding ring by an O-ring against the housing. The pressure sliding ring is pressed against the opposite sliding ring by a helical spring. The sliding surfaces seal the area inside and outside the housing.

Words	
rotary shaft seal	Radial-Wellendichtung
to prevent	verhindern
discharge	Auslaufen
shaft exit	Wellenaustritt
rubber body	Gummikörper
stiffened	ausgesteift
spiral spring	Spiralfeder
groove	Fuge
sealing lip	Dichtlippe
protection lip	Schutzlippe
internal pressure	Innendruck
suitable	geeignet
packing box	Stopfbuchsdichtung
oscillating	hin und her gehend
plunger rod	Kolbenstange
square	quadratisch
string	Schnur
plastic fibre	Kunststofffaser
impregnated	getränkt
lubricant grease	Schmierfett
gland	Stopfbuchsbrille
to retension	nachspannen
leakage	Leckverlust
labyrinth seal	Labyrinthdichtung
narrow gap	enger Spalt
bearing	Lager
axial face seal, mechanical seal	Gleitringdichtung
shaft exit	Wellenaustritt
flat-ground	plangeschliffen
pressure sliding ring	Druck-Gleitring
opposite sliding ring	Gegengleitring
plastic material	Kunststoff
ceramic	Keramik
hard metal	Hartmetall
to fit tightly	fest anliegen
O-ring	Runddichtung
helical spring	Spiralfeder
to specify	angeben

Exercises

1. Translate the terms into German and specify which of the seals are static or dynamic.
   a) O-ring b) Labyrinth seal c) Liquid sealing material
   d) Rotary shaft seal e) Flat seal f) Groove-ring
2. Describe the functional principle of the axial face seal in German.
3. Answer the following questions:
   a) Which dynamic seal is suitable for low pressures?
   b) What dynamic seals are suitable for rotating shafts?
   c) Which materials are used for the sliding rings of face seals?
4. For which applications are the named seals applied for?
   a) Packing bo b) Labyrinth seal c) Axial face seal

5.8 Shafts, axles, couplings

The most common motions in machines are rotary motions. They transfer the kinetic energy from a driving component, e.g. an electric motor, to a machine tool, such as a lathe.

Important components for the transfer of kinetic energy are shafts, couplings and axles.

Shafts

Shafts transfer kinetic energy of rotating components in a machine **(figure).**

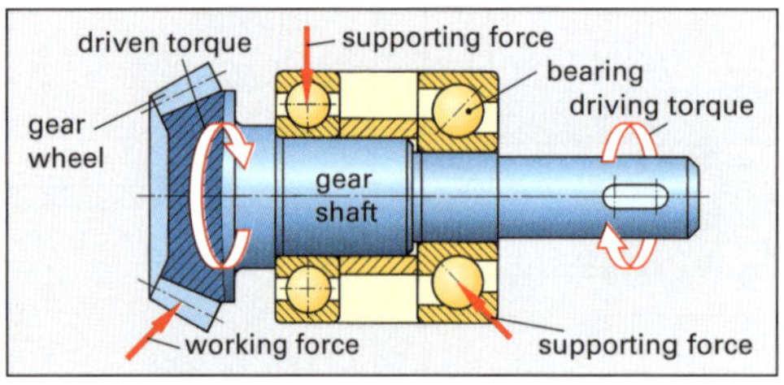

The shaft rotates with these components, e.g. gear-wheels.

The rotating motion and the torque of the driving component are transferred to the driven component.

Shafts are usually mounted in two bearings **(figure** below). The bearings transfer the radial and axial forces to the housing.

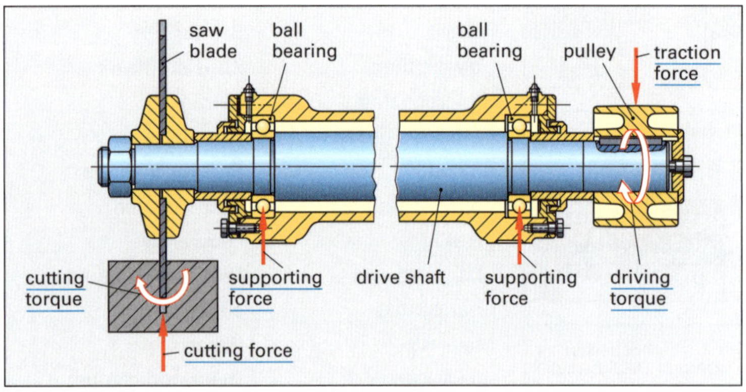

Shafts are classified in different groups according to their function. Mainly, there are drive shafts, gear shafts and spindles. Universal joint shafts, crankshafts and camshafts are shafts with a specific function, often used in automobile technology.

Drive shafts pass the torque on to other shafts, machines or tools. The drive shaft shown in the **figure above,** transfers the energy of the pulley to the saw blade of a circular saw. A belt and a motor power the pulley. The ball bearings carry the resulting radial and axial forces of the drive shaft.

Gear shafts are connected with gear wheels and change the rotation speeds and torques between the different shafts.

Shafts are called spindles if they perform cutting motion or feed motion in machine tools. Thus, e.g. the drive spindle of a lathe creates a cutting motion for a workpiece.

Words	
shaft	Welle
axle	Achse
coupling	Kupplung
most common	häufigsten
rotary motion	Drehbewegung
to transfer	übertragen
driving component	Antriebsbauteil
machine tool	Werkzeugmaschine
lathe	Drehmaschine
torque	Drehmoment
to drive (driving)	antreiben (antreibend)
driven	angetrieben
to mount	befestigen, lagern
bearing	Lager
to classify	unterteilen
drive shaft	Antriebswelle
gear shaft	Getriebewelle
spindle	Spindel
universal joint shaft	Gelenkwelle
crankshaft	Kurbelwelle
camshaft	Nockenwelle
automobile technology	Kraftfahrzeugtechnik
to pass on	weitergeben an
pulley	Riemenscheibe
saw blade	Sägeblatt
circular saw	Kreissäge
to power	antreiben
gear wheel	Zahnrad
spindle	Spindel
cutting motion	Schnittbewegung
feed motion	Vorschubbewegung
drive spindle	Antriebsspindel

Exercises

1. Name the machine components ① to ⑥ in the figure.
2. Answer the following questions:
   a) How can the resulting forces in a shaft be carried?
   b) Which are the different groups, shafts can be classified in, according to their function?
   c) What is the function of a gear shaft?
3. Use your **Metal Engineering Textbook** to determine which shafts need more than two bearings for carrying the forces.

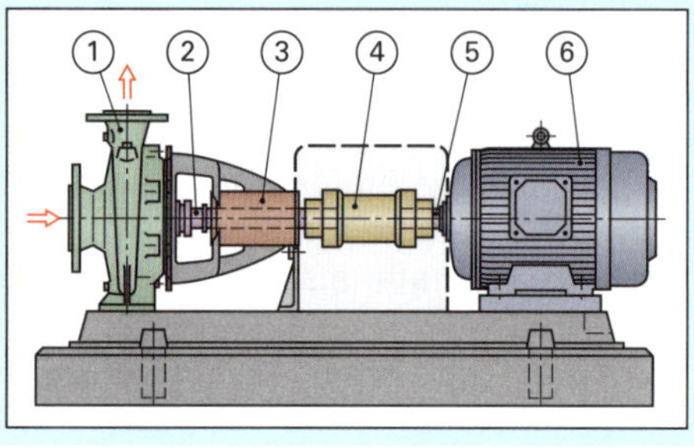

Axles

Axles function as carriers of rotating components, e.g. wheels **(figure)**. They are not engineered to transfer torque.

Axles are classified in fixed and rotating axles. Small fixed axles are also called pivot bolts (**figures** below).

The rotating axles and the rotating components form a fixed unit with the axle. The entire unit rotates in two bearings of the fixed bearing housing.

Axles, which are not driven, are used in cars and wagons. Fixed axles are secured against rotation. Rotating components are located on the fixed axle. The axle is supported by bearings.

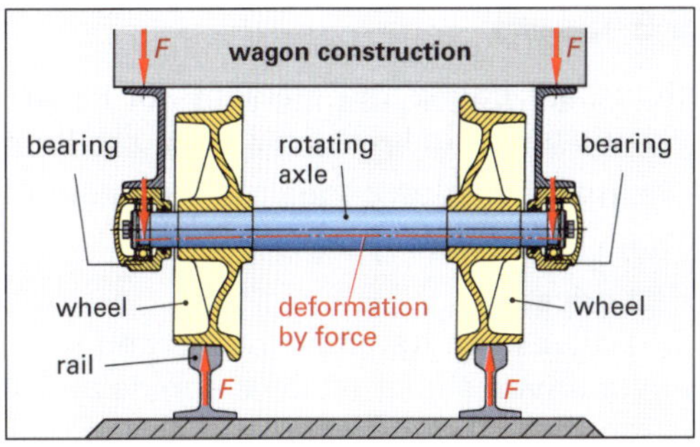

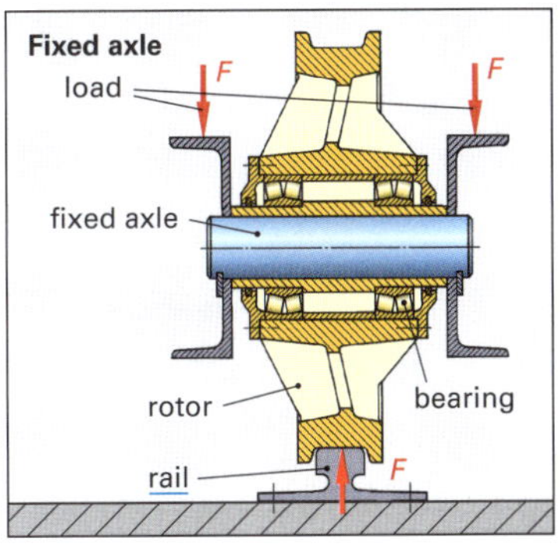

Fixed axle

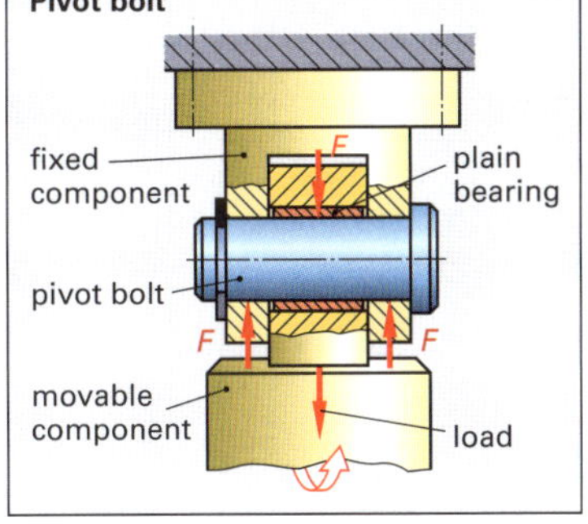

Pivot bolt

Couplings

A coupling connects two shafts and transfers the rotary motion and the torque. Usually the torque is transferred from a driving machine, like an electric motor, to a working machine such as a pump (**figure** on the bottom of the page before).

There are switchable and non-switchable couplings.

A further distinction is made between rigid and elastic couplings.

Rigid couplings cannot be separated during the operating time. They are suitable for the permanent connection of shafts which align each other.

Elastic couplings have an elastic coupling element, e.g. of rubber **(figure)**. They have a smoother running and can compensate small axial displacements.

The **claw coupling (figure)** is switchable while stopping and non-switchable while running. It establishes a positively locking connection.

Metal spring coupling
(non switchable, elastic)

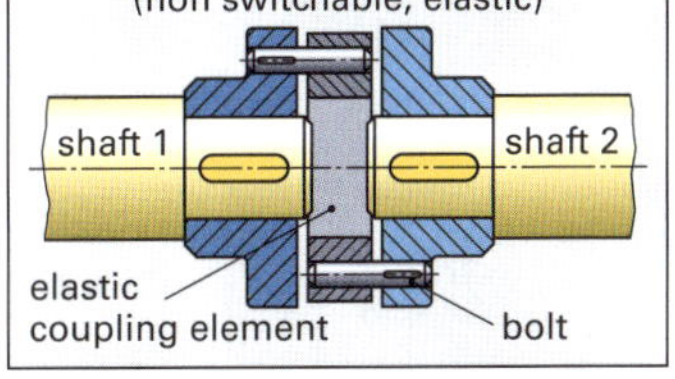

Claw coupling
(switchable, form locking)

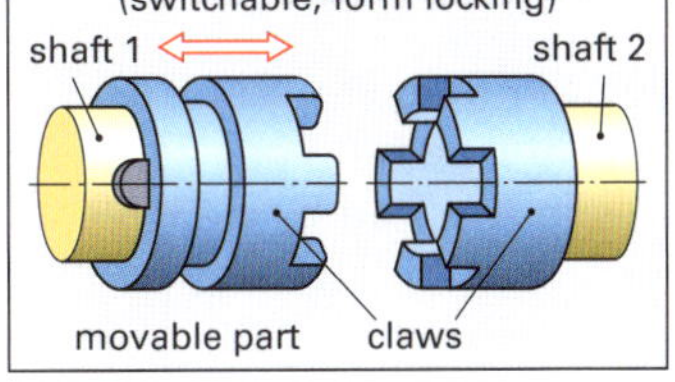

Clutch couplings are switchable and force-locking couplings. They can couple and decouple while running.

Words (English)	Words (German)
axle	Achse
to function	wirken, dienen
carrier	Träger
to engineer	gestalten
torque	Drehmoment
wagon construction	Waggonaufbau
to classify	unterteilen
fixed	feststehend
to rotate	rotieren
pivot bolt	Gelenkbolzen
to secure	sichern
fixed unit	starre Einheit
entire	gesamt
bearing housing	Lagergehäuse
to locate	anordnen
to support	unterstützen
rail	Schiene
coupling	Kupplung
switchable	schaltbar
non-switchable	nicht schaltbar
rigid	starr
elastic	elastisch
to separate	trennen, entkuppeln
operating time	Betriebszeit
to align	ausrichten, fluchten
smooth running	weicher Lauf
to compensate	ausgleichen
displacement	Versetzung
claw coupling	Klauenkupplung
to establish	herstellen
positively locking	formschlüssig
connection	Verbindung
clutch coupling	Schaltkupplung
force locking	kraftschlüssig
to balance	ausgleichen

Exercises

1. Answer the following questions:
   a) Which function does the coupling have?
   b) What is the difference between a fixed and a rotating axle?
2. What can axial shaft displacement be balanced with?
3. Distinguish the couplings listed below by form-locking and force-locking as well as switchable and non-switchable.
   a) Metal spring coupling
   b) Claw coupling
   c) Rigid coupling
   d) One-disc clutch coupling
4. Describe the function of claw coupling in German.

5.9 Gears

Gears are connected elements of electric motors **(figure).** They transform the high rotation speed of the electric motor in low speed of application or for speed adjustment.

The main function of gears is the transmission of rotary motions and torques.

There are several types of gears.

Belt drives

Belt drives can transmit speeds and torques between a driving and a driven shaft that have a midsize distance **(figure).** The belt is tensioned on a driving and driven pulley. For tensioning the belt, it is necessary to increase the distance between the discs or to press a tension roller against the belt. During the operation of the belt drive, the lower side of the belt is loaded by tension. This side is called the tight side. The unloaded side of the belt is the slack side. Belts are classified according to the type of slaving of the pulley.

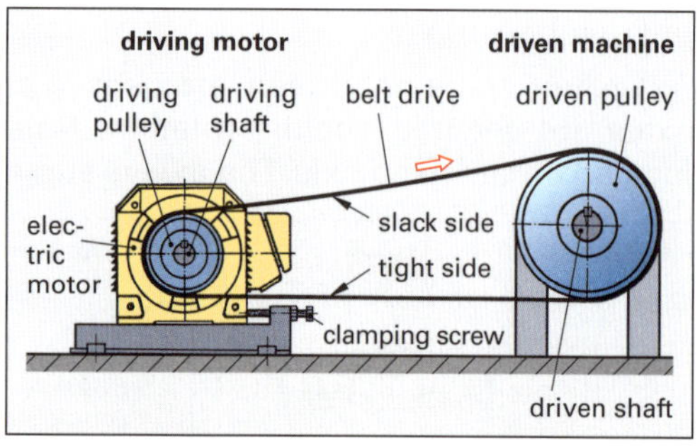

Flat belts and **V-belts** transfer the traction force locking by the friction between the running surfaces of the belt and the pulleys.

Flat belts are running on a flat disc **(figure)** and are used generally where the distance between shafts is small.

Flat belt

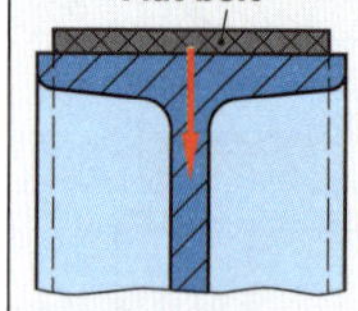

V-belts are drawn into the pulley groove by the belt force **(figure).** Due to the larger frictional forces, greater torques can be transmitted.

V-belt

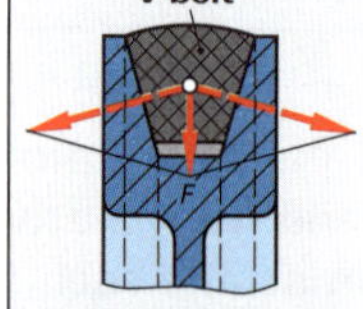

Toothed belts transfer the traction positively by the teeth of the belt **(figure).** In contrast to flat belts and V-belts, the toothed belt has no slippage.

Toothed belt

Chain drives

Chain drives **(figure)** are applied at tough operation conditions, when great traction forces without slippage have to be transferred.

Chain drive

The **transmission ratio** ***i*** of a drive is calculated by the speeds *n* or the effective diameters *d* of the pulleys.

$$i = \frac{n_{driving}}{n_{driven}}$$

$$i = \frac{d_{driven}}{d_{driving}}$$

Comparison

An advantage of flat and V-belt drives is the elastic transfer of the motions and torques. They dampen shocks and vibrations. The disadvantage is the slippage of the belt drives. An exact transmission ratio is not possible. This is reached by a toothed belt or a chain drive.

Exercises

1. Answer the following questions.
   a) What is the main function of a gear?
   b) How can the belt of a belt drive be tensioned?
2. What is meant by „slippage" of a belt drive?
3. Match the terms – positive locking, force locking, with slippage, without slippage – to the different belts or drives.
   a) Flat belt b) Toothed belt
   c) V-belt d) Chain drive
4. Explain the calculation formula for the transmission ratio ***i*** with your own words in English.

Words

gear	Getriebe
connected	nachgeschaltet
to transform	umwandeln
rotation speed	Drehzahl
speed of application	Gebrauchsdrehzahl
speed adjustment	Drehzahlverstellung
torques	Drehmomente
belt drive	Riementrieb
to transmit	übersetzen
midsize	mittelgroß
to tension	spannen
driving	treibend
driven	angetrieben
pulley	Riemenscheibe
tension roller	Spannrolle
loaded by tension	auf Zug belastet
tight side	Lasttrum
slack side	Leertrum
slaving	Mitnahme
flat belt	Flachriemen
V-belt	Keilriemen
traction	Zugkraft
force locking	kraftschlüssig
friction	Reibung
running surface	Lauffläche
pulley groove	Scheibenrille
toothed belt	Zahnriemen
positively	formschlüssig
slippage	Schlupf
chain drive	Kettentrieb
tough operation condition	raue Betriebsbedingung
transmission ratio	Übersetzungsverhältnis
comparison	Vergleich
advantage	Vorteil
to dampen	abschwächen
shock	Stoß
vibration	Schwingung

Gear wheel drives

Gear wheel drives transfer torques by gear wheels from a driving shaft to a driven shaft **(figure).**

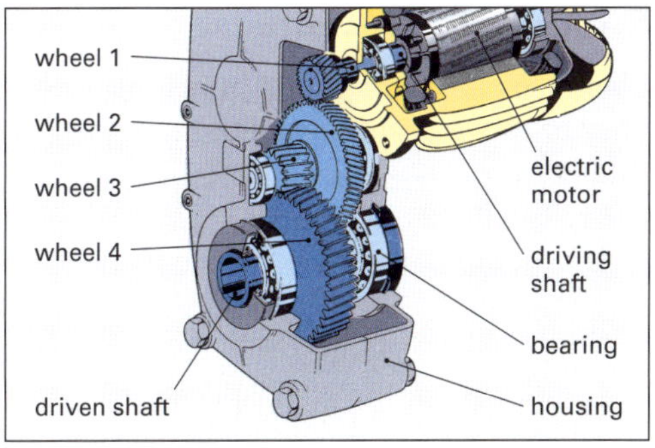

The teeth gear into each other positively locking. The rotary speed, torques and rotational directions can be changed.

Small torques can be transmitted as well as very large torques by gear wheel drives.

Exact transmission ratios are assured.

The gear consists of several gear pairs **(figure).**

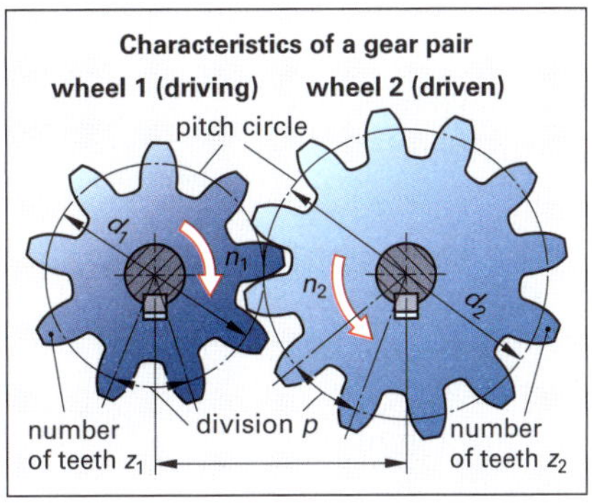

The division p determines the dimensions of a gear pair. p is the distance of two teeth and is indicated as radian measure in the pitch circle.

Another important dimension value of a gear pair is the module m.

It is calculated by p divided by the number π.

$$m = \frac{P}{\pi}$$

The values of the modules m are standardised according to a predefined progression *(see Metal Trade Handbook).*

The gear pairs in one gear always have the same module m. The pitch circle diameter d of a gear wheel is calculated as the product of the number of teeth z and the module m:

$$d_1 = z_1 \cdot m;\ d_2 = z_2 \cdot m$$

For gear wheel drives the longitudinal force F_u and the peripheral speed v of two gear wheels are of equal size. However, the diameters d_1 and d_2 of the wheels are different.

For this reason there are different speeds n_1 and n_2. The ratio of these speeds is called transmission ratio i.

$$i = \frac{n_1}{n_2};\ i = \frac{d_2}{d_1};\ i = \frac{z_2}{z_1}$$

The axial distance a between two wheels is determined by the two diameters of the pitch circles:

$$a = \frac{d_1 + d_2}{2}$$

If only one gear wheel pair is installed into a gear, it is called a one-stage gear. Series-connected gear wheel drives are called multistage gears. The total transmission ratio i_{ges} is the ratio of the initial speed n_a to the final speed n_e.

It is calculated as the product of the individual transmission ratios i_1, i_2, i_3 ...

$$i_{ges} = \frac{n_a}{n_e} = i_1 \cdot i_2 \cdot i_3 \ldots$$

Words

gear wheel drive	Zahnradtrieb
torque	Drehmoment
teeth	Zähne
to gear into each other	ineinandergreifen
positively locking	formschlüssig
rotary speed	Drehzahl
rotational direction	Drehrichtung
transmission ratio	Übersetzungs-verhältnis
to assure	gewährleisten
gear pair	Zahnradpaar
division	Teilung
radian measure	Bogenmaß
pitch circle	Teilkreis
module	Modul
divided by	dividiert durch
predefined	vorgegeben
progression	Reihe
number of teeth	Zähnezahl
longitudinal force	Umfangskraft
peripheral speed	Umfangsgeschwindig-keit
however	jedoch
diameter	Durchmesser
axial distance	Achsabstand
one-stage	einstufig
series-connected	hintereinander geschaltet
multi-stage	mehrstufig
total transmission ratio	Gesamtübersetzungs-verhältnis
initial speed	Anfangsdrehzahl
final speed	Enddrehzahl

Exercises

1. Answer the questions:
   a) Why has a gear wheel no slippage?
   b) Which formula is the module m calculated by?
   c) How do you calculate the transmission ratio of a gear pair by the number of teeth?

2. A one-stage gear has the pitch circle diameter d_1 = 24 mm for a gear wheel on the drive shaft. The axial distance between the drive shaft and the output shaft is 52.5 mm. The module is given by m = 1.5 mm. The drive motor has the speed n_1 = 1,620 min^{-1}.
   Calculate:
   a) the pitch circle diameter d_2 of the gear wheel on the output shaft.
   b) the numbers of teeth z_1 and z_2 of the two gear wheels.
   c) the transmission ratio i of the one-stage gear.
   d) the output speed n_2.

5.10 Electric motors

Electric motors are power machines. They provide the kinetic energy to move work machines, e.g. machine tools.

The essential components of an electric motor are **(figure)**:
- The stator, consisting of numerous electric windings with a laminated sheet stack on the inside of the housing.
- The rotor, consisting of a cylindric metal cage of two outside rings and rods, filled with a cylindric laminated sheet stack.
- The motor shaft, where the rotating motion is provided.
- The electric connection box.

Depending on the driving current, there are different types of electric motors: three-phase motors, DC motors, universal motors.

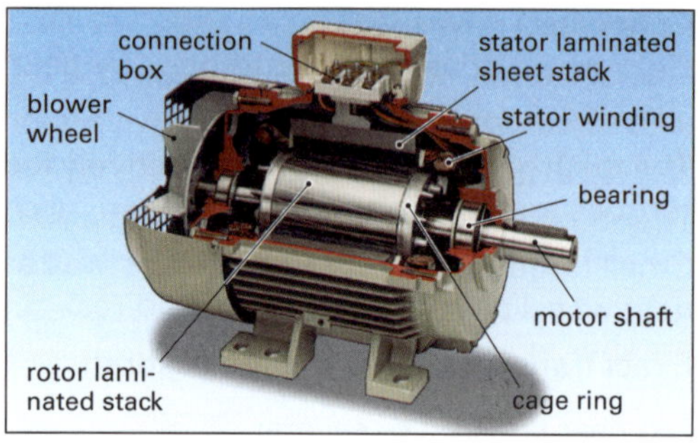

Three-phase motor

The most commonly used three-phase motor is the **three-phase asynchronous motor** (**figure** right hand above). This motor has a robust construction. It is low maintenance and suitable for continuous operation as well as for intermittent operation.

In the housing are three stator windings, which are distributed by 120°. When connected to a three-phase network, the three windings are sequentially flown with three alternating currents. A circulating magnetic field (rotating field) is formed and fortified by the stator sheets and stacks. By the magnetic field of the stator, an eddy current is induced in the aluminium rods of the rotor. A strong magnetic field is created in the rotor sheet stacks. The two magnetic fields of the stator and the rotor repel each other and set the rotor into rotation. The speed of the rotor is smaller by the slip than the speed of the rotating field. Thus the motor runs asynchronous to the rotating field.

The operating behaviour of an asynchronous electric motor is shown by the **torque-speed-diagram (figure)**.

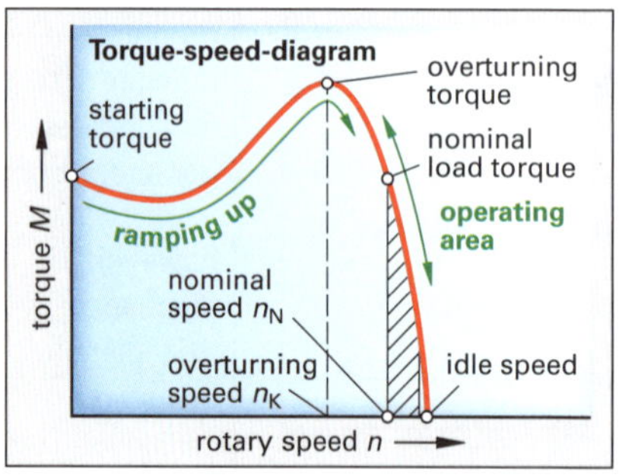

When starting, the starting torque is present. The motor ramps up until the nominal load torque at the nominal speed. If the load torque rises, the motor torque increases until the overturning torque is reached. Further increasing leads to the stop of the motor. If the load torque decreases, the motor torque decreases as well until the idle speed. The motor runs in an operating area around the nominal torque.

Exercises

1. Name the essential parts of an electric motor.
2. Answer the following questions:
   a) What are the uses of an electric motor?
   b) Which distinctive features do electric motors have?
   c) What are the advantages of the three-phase asynchronous motor?
   d) How does the value of the motor torque changes, if the load torque of the driven machine increases?
3. Complete the sentences:
   a) At a three phase asynchronous motor, the speed is ________________ than the rotating magnetic field.
   b) The speed at the nominal torque is called ___________.

Words (English)	Words (German)
electric motors	Elektromotoren
power machines	Kraftmaschinen
to provide	bereitstellen
essential	wesentlich
stator	Stator
to consist of	bestehen aus
windings	Wicklungen
laminated sheet stack	Blechpaket
rotor	Rotor
metal cage	Metallkäfig
connection box	Anschlusskasten
driving current	Antriebsstrom
three-phase motor	Drehstrommotor
DC motor	Gleichstrommotor
universal motor	Universalmotor
asynchronous	asynchron
robust construction	robuster Aufbau
low maintenance	wartungsarm
continuous operation	Dauerbetrieb
intermittent	unterbrochen
to distribute	verteilen
three-phase network	Drehstromnetz
sequential	nacheinander
alternating current	Wechselstrom
magnetic field	Drehfeld
to fortify	verstärken
eddy current	Wirbelstrom
to induce	induzieren
aluminium rods	Aluminiumstäbe
to repel each other	gegenseitig abstoßen
slip	Schlupf
operating behaviour	Betriebsverhalten
torque-speed-diagram	Drehmoment-Drehzahl-Diagramn
starting torque	Anfahrmoment
to ramp up	hochfahren
nominal load torque	Nennlastmoment
load torque	Lastmoment
to rise	ansteigen
to increase	sich erhöhen
overturning torque	Kippmoment
to decrease	sich verringern
idle speed	Leerlaufdrehzahl
distinctive feature	Unterscheidungsmerkmal

DC motor

The DC-motor (direct current motor) has a similar structure such as a three-phase motor: a stator with windings and sheet stacks as well as a rotor with windings and sheet stacks **(figure)**.

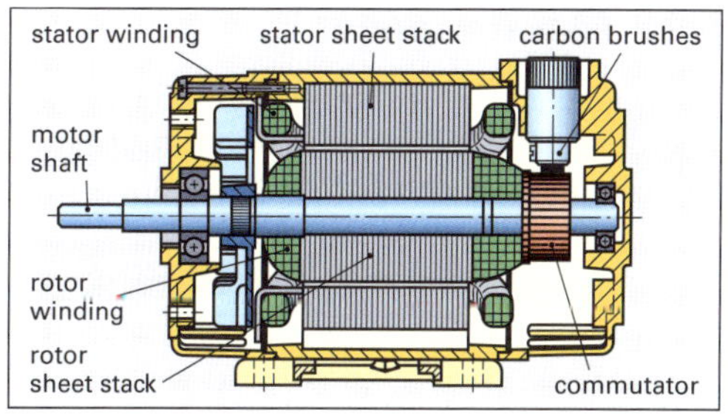

The characteristic of a DC motor is an assembly for pole-changing the DC current, the **commutator**. In order to get an alternating magnetic field in the motor, the direct current is fed by carbon brushes and pole-change in the commutator.

The mode of action of a DC motor is shown in the following **cross section figures** of one conductor loop.

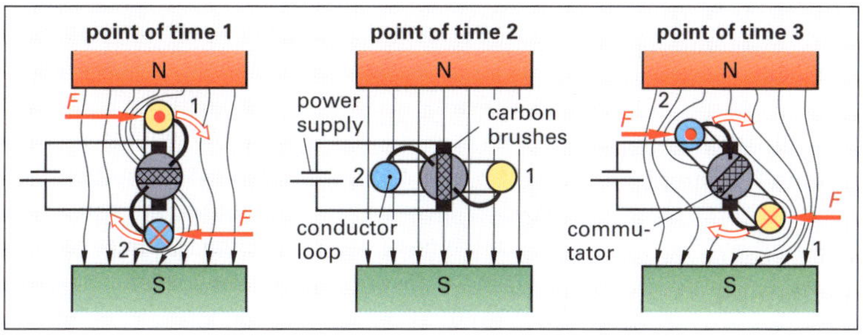

At point of time 1, the conductor loop is in a vertical position. Direct current flows through the conductor loop. The current flow causes, that the magnetic field is compressed on the one side of the conductor loop and weakened on the other side. The resulting forces produce a torque on the conductor loop and make it rotate. When the conductor loop reaches the horizontal position (point 2), the current flow will be commutated. Thereby the torque upholds its direction and the conductor loop continues to rotate (point 3).

There are permanently excited and separately excited motors. In a permanently excited motor a permanent magnet produces the magnetic field. In a separately excited motor the magnetic field builds up around the current-flown stator winding.

Permanently excited DC motors are used for low power ranges, e.g. in the wiper motors of cars. Separately excited DC motors are used for higher power ranges, e.g. in feed motors of machines.

Universal motors are a specific type of DC motors (**figure** below). It runs with alternating current (AC), which is everywhere available. Inside it has an upstream electric condenser, which converts the alternating current in direct current.

Universal motors have a high motor torque at low weight. If the load torque rises, the motor torque increases too and the speed decreases. This self-adjusting property makes it suitable for many applications, e.g. for handheld machine tools such as power drills.

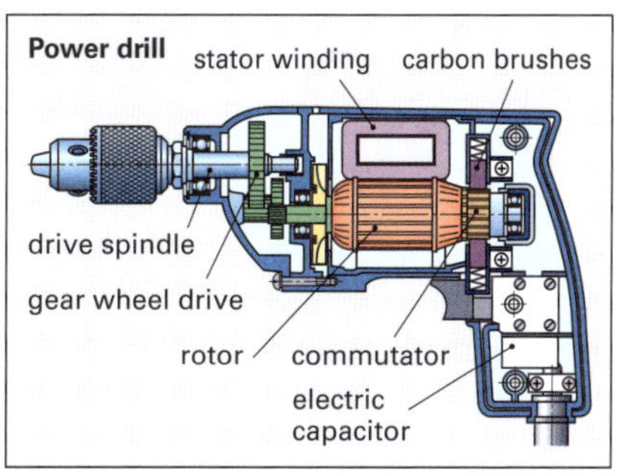

Words

direct current motor	Gleichstrommotor
similar structure	ähnlicher Aufbau
assembly	Baugruppe
pole-changing	Umpolen
commutator	Kommutator (Stromwender)
to feed (fed, fed)	zuführen
carbon brushes	Kohlebürsten
mode of action	Wirkungsweise
cross section figure	Querschnittsbild
conductor loop	Leiterschleife
point of time	Zeitpunkt
vertical	senkrecht
to compress	verdichten
to weaken	schwächen
torque	Drehmoment
to commutate	umpolen
horizontal	waagrecht
to uphold	beibehalten
permanently excited	permanent-erregt
separately excited	fremd-erregt
permanent magnet	Dauermagnet
stator winding	Statorwicklung
power range	Leistungsbereich
wiper motor	Wischermotor
feed motor	Vorschubmotor
available	verfügbar
upstream	vorgeschaltet
capacitor	Kondensator
to convert	umwandeln
motor torque	Motordrehmoment
self-adjusting property	selbstregelndes Verhalten
handheld machine tool	handgeführte Werkzeugmaschine
power drill	Handbohrmaschine

Exercises

1. What is the difference in the structure of a DC motor to a three-phase motor?
2. Match the following terms to the two types of DC motors: „permanently excited DC motor" and „separately excited DC motor" and add an explanation.
   a) Stator winding b) Permanent magnet c) Feed motor
   d) Wiper motor e) Low power range f) Elevator
3. Explain the principle of an universal motor by using the figure above of the illustrated power drill.

5.11 Maintenance

Maintenance comprises all activities which lead to a smooth production process in the long run: the service, the inspections, the repairs and the improvement of components, machines or complete production lines **(figure)**. Maintenance is the precondition for a long life time of machines and production lines.

maintenance

service	inspection	repair service	improvement
• cleaning	• observing	• repairing	• evaluating
• lubricating	• measuring	• substituting	• analysing
• refilling	• checking	• replacing	• deciding
• adjusting	• diagnosing	• checking	• implementing

Abrasion and reservoir of abrasion

The use of components, machines or production lines in a continuous production causes its abrasion. The reasons for the abrasion are e.g. wear, ageing and corrosion.

If you measure e.g. wear during the life time of a rotating component, you will detect different phases of wear **(figure)**.

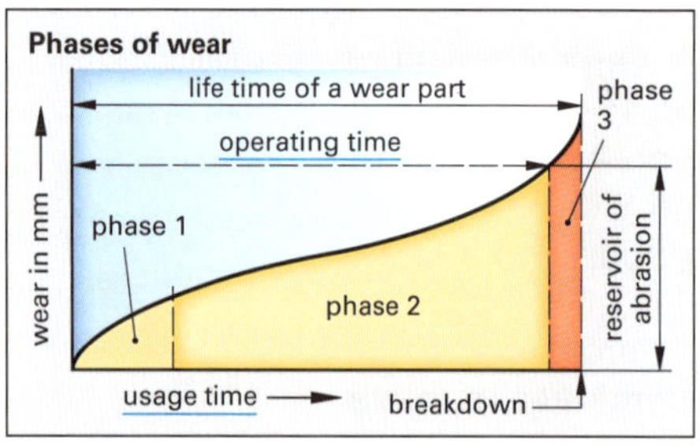

At the beginning (phase 1) the wear is high. In this phase the surface roughness of the component is removed. In phase 2 there is less wear. Here the surface is smoothed.

Towards the end of life time (phase 3) the wear increases rapidly until the breakdown.

The maximal abrasion (e.g. in mm), a component or a machine is allowed to be worn is the **reservoir of abrasion**.

The consumption of the abrasion reservoir of a component is shown in the following **figure**.

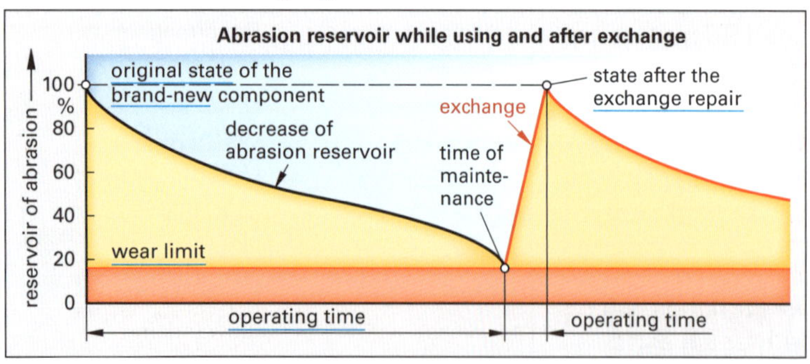

A brand-new component has a reservoir of abrasion of 100%. During the operating time it decreases by wear to the wear limit. Then maintenance has to be done; the worn-out component has to be changed. Then a new life time starts with the replaced component.

Words

English	German
maintenance	Instandhaltung
to comprise	umfassen
smooth production process	reibungsloser Fertigungsprozess
in the long run	auf Dauer
service	Wartung
inspection	Inspektion
repair	Instandsetzung
improvement	Verbesserung
production line	Fertigungsanlage
precondition	Voraussetzung
life time	Lebensdauer
to clean	reinigen
to lubricate	schmieren, ölen
to refill	auffüllen
to adjust	einstellen
to substitute	austauschen
to evaluate	auswerten
to decide	entscheiden
to implement	umsetzen
abrasion	Abnutzung
reservoir of abrasion	Abnutzungsvorrat
wear	Verschleiß
ageing	Alterung
corrosion	Korrosion
to measure	messen
to detect	erkennen
surface roughness	Oberflächenrauheit
to remove	abtragen
to smooth	glätten
operating time	Nutzungszeit
usage time	Nutzungsdauer
breakdown	Betriebsausfall
to wear (wore, worn)	abnutzen
consumption	Verbrauch
original state	Ausgangszustand
brand-new	fabrikneu
exchange repair	Auswechslung
wear limit	Abnutzungsgrenze
worn-out	verschlissen
to replace	ersetzen

Exercises

1. Explain the term *maintenance* in English.
2. Describe the diagram abrasion reservoir above.
3. Complete the following sentence: The abrasion of a component during the ______________________ is called ______________________.
4. Answer the following questions:
   a) Which actions have to be done for service and for inspections?
   b) Which measure has to be realised, if the reservoir of abrasion of a component is reached?
   c) Why does a component show different wear during its life time?
   d) How can the life time of a machine be prolonged?

Service

Service is a preventive activity of maintenance. It includes all workings to maintain a faultless production of a machine. Correct servicing delays the consumption of the reservoir of abrasion during the usage time of the machine.

Service works are executed in recommended intervals according to a service plan.

Example: Service workings of a machine tool.

cleaning

lubricating

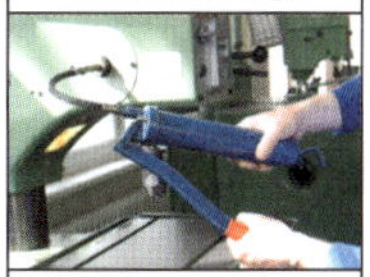

replacing

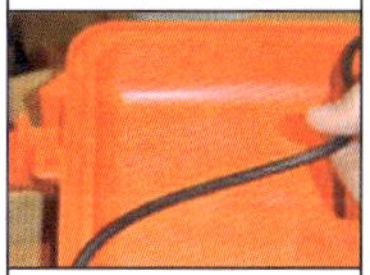

refilling

adjusting

conserving

Cleaning has to be done every day by brushing, vacuuming or sweeping. Swarf and foreign particles are removed from the machine room. Compressed air is not allowed to be used for cleaning; otherwise chips are pushed into the slideways and seals. One time per week the whole machine is cleaned thoroughly.

Lubricating by oiling, greasing or spraying at the lubrication points has to be done daily, weekly or monthly according to a service plan. Only specified lubricants have to be used.

Refilling of process material, e. g. lubrication oil, emulsions or hydraulic oil have to be filled up according to the plan or as required.

Adjusting is carried out as required, e. g. by tensioning the V-belts und toothed belts. Tools are measured and calibrated as needed.

Replacing of worn parts is done as needed or according to the service plan in quarterly intervals, e. g. carbon brushes of electric motors and filters.

Lines, cables, hoses and seals have to be observed any time and replaced if they are damaged.

Conserving e. g. is necessary, if the coating of a machine is damaged. The machine is sprayed with a corrosion protection coating.

If the service is done, the machine tool will be returned to operational readiness. The power supply is turned back and the staff members are informed about the end of the service.

When substantial maintenance workings are finished, a functional check must be operated. The maintenance workings, which have been done, must be documented in a maintenance list.

Exercises

1. What is the purpose to service a machine tool according to a service plan?

2. Arrange the following terms in the correct place of the service workings below:
   – to coat sth. with paint – oil change – to measure – to spray – to refill – to vacuum – carbon brushes – emulsion – to oil – to calibrate – to brush – damage line – protection

Cleaning	Lubricating	Refilling

Replacing	Adjusting	Conserving

Words

service	Wartungsarbeiten
preventive	vorbeugend
to include	einschließen
workings	Tätigkeiten
to maintain	aufrechterhalten
faultless	fehlerfrei
to delay	verzögern
consumption	Verbrauch
to execute	durchführen
recommended	empfohlen
interval	Zeitabschnitt
service plan	Wartungsplan
to clean	reinigen
to brush	bürsten
to vacuum	saugen
to sweep	fegen
swarf	Metallspäne
foreign particle	Fremdkörper
compressed air	Druckluft
slideway	Führungsbahn
thoroughly	ausführlich, gründlich
lubricating	Schmierung
to oil	einölen
to grease	fetten
to spray	einsprühen
lubrication point	Schmierstelle
specified	vorgeschrieben
to refill	auffüllen
process material	Hilfsstoffe
emulsion	Emulsion
hydraulic oil	Hydrauliköl
required	erforderlich
to adjust	einstellen
tensioning	spannen
V-belt	Keilriemen
toothed belt	Zahnriemen
to measure	vermessen
to calibrate	kalibrieren, nachstellen
to replace	auswechseln
worn part	verschlissenes Teil
carbon brush	Kohlebürste
filter	Filter
line	Leitung
cable	Kabel
hose	Schlauch
seal	Dichtung
to observe	beobachten
damaged	beschädigt
conserving	Erhalten, Konservieren
coating	Beschichtung
operational readiness	Betriebsbereitschaft
power supply	Energieversorgung
staff member	Mitarbeiter
substantial	ausführlich
functional check	Funktionsprüfung
maintenance list	Wartungsliste

6 Electrical engineering

6.1 Electrotechnical basics

Electric current is present in every workshop or factory. Almost all devices, machine tools and production lines work with electric current and contain electrical components.

In order to work safely and efficiently with machines and devices you have to know electrotechnical basics.

Electric circuit

Electric current only flows in a closed electrical circuit **(figure).** It consists of a voltage source, an electric load, e. g. a lamp, and electric lines of copper. For closing and opening the circuit there is a switch.

Voltage sources are e. g. a battery or a socket outlet of the current network.

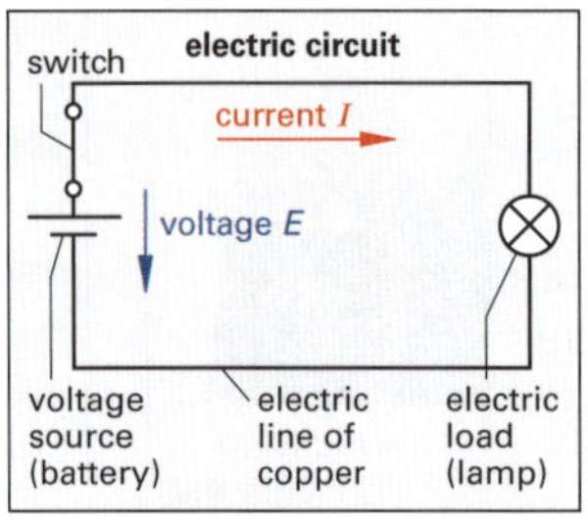

Electric voltage

Electric voltage is generated by the separation of electric charges.

The unit of the voltage is Volt (V). You distinguish direct current voltage (DC voltage) and alternating current voltage (AC voltage).

At DC voltage there is always an equal voltage value **(figure).** At AC voltage the voltage value and direction changes continuously. The AC voltage in Europe is 230 V.

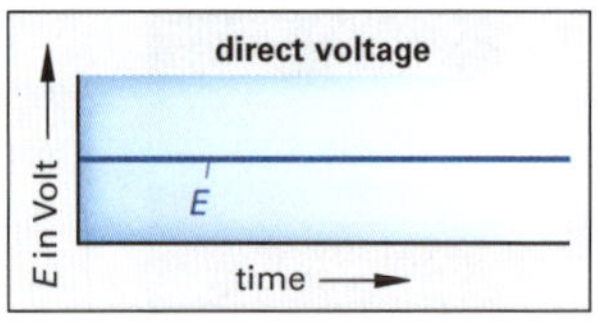

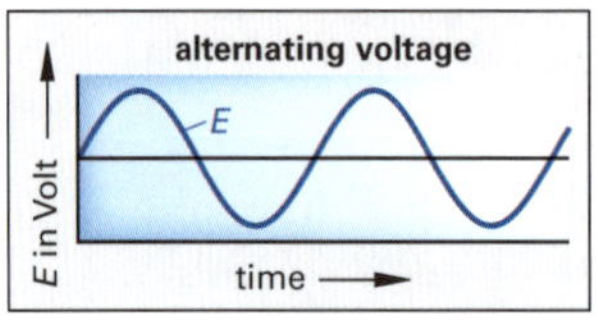

Current rating

The flow of electrons in an electric line is the electric current.

Its quantity is the current rating. Its unit is Ampere (A). Small values of the current rating are measured in mA.

In technical devices there are current ratings of very different height **(table).**

Electric device	Current
electronic chip	10 mA
LED-lamp	0.2 A
10 kW-motor	18 A
welding arc	200 A
arc furnace	150 000 A

Measuring voltage and current rating

The device for measuring current rating is the amperemeter Ⓐ.

For measuring the voltage you use a voltmeter Ⓥ.

For measuring these electric values, the measuring devices have to be installed at the right place in the circuit **(figure).** The amperemeter is connected in series in the electric circuit.

The voltmeter is switched in parallel to the load or the voltage source.

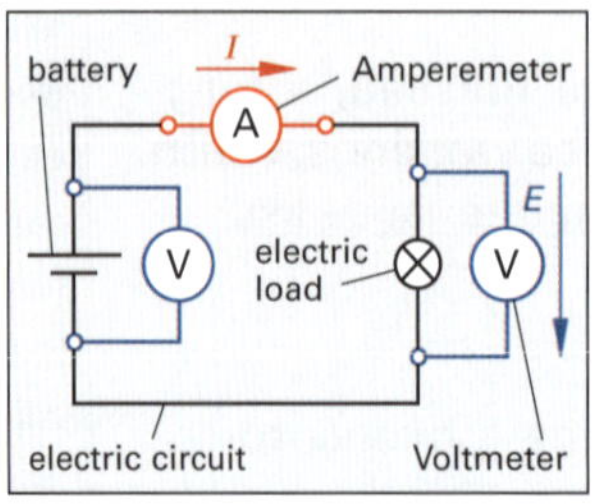

Words	
electrical engineering	Elektrotechnik
electrotechnical basics	elektrotechnische Grundlagen
electric current	elektrischer Strom
device	Gerät
machine tool	Werkzeugmaschine
electric circuit	Stromkreis
voltage source	Spannungsquelle
electric load	Verbraucher
electric line	elektrische Leitung
switch	Schalter
battery	Batterie
socket outlet	Steckdose
current network	Stromnetz
electric voltage	elektrische Spannung
to be generated	entstehen durch
separation	Trennung
electric charge	elektrische Ladung
to distinguish	unterteilen
direct current voltage	Gleichspannung
alternating current voltage	Wechselspannung
equal	gleich
direction	Richtung
continuous	fortlaufend
current rating	Stromstärke
flow	Strom
electron	Elektron
electronic chip	elektronischer Chip
welding arc	Schweißlichtbogen
arc furnace	Lichtbogenofen
amperemeter	Amperemeter
voltmeter	Voltmeter
to install	einbauen
connected in series	in Serie geschaltet
switched in parallel	parallel geschaltet
to draw	zeichnen, skizzieren
abbreviation	Abkürzung

Exercises

1. Draw an electric circuit and name its elements.
2. Give the English terms for: elektrische Leitung, Verbraucher, Spannungsquelle, Schalter.
3. What do the abbreviations mean: DC voltage, AC voltage?
4. What kind of current flows through: a) an electronic chip b) an LED-lamp c) a welding arc?
5. Complete the following sentences when connecting the measurement devices:
   a) An amperemeter is connected in an electric circuit ______________________.
   b) A voltmeter is switched ______________________ to measure the voltage of a load.

Electric resistance, Ohm's law

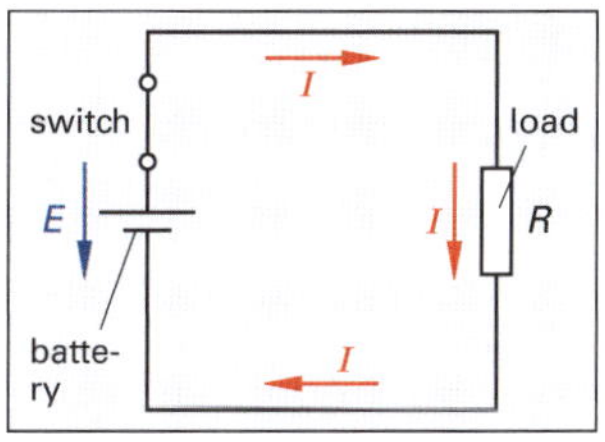

If you close the switch in an electric circuit, an electric current flows **(figure)**. The current rating I depends on the electric resistance R of the load and the voltage E of the battery.

At a constant voltage E of the battery, a load with a small resistance R leads to a great current rating I. If the load has a greater resistance R, a smaller current I flows.

The correlation between the voltage E, the electric resistance R and the current I in a circuit is described by a formula that is called Ohm's law. The unit of the electric resistance R is Ohm (Ω).
It is defined by the Ohm's law to $[R] = [E] / [I] = \text{V/A} = \Omega$.

Ohm's law
$I = \frac{E}{R}$ or $E = I \cdot R$

Specific electric resistance

The electric lines (usually copper wires) in a circuit have an electric resistance. It is called conductor resistance and depends on the material of the conductor. The characteristic of the resistance of a conductors material is the resistance of a wire with the length of 1 m and a cross sectional area of 1 mm². It is called specific electric resistance ϱ_{el}.

Material	Specific electric resistance ϱ_{el} in $\frac{\Omega \cdot mm^2}{m}$
copper	0.0179
silver	0.0149
aluminium	0.0265

Materials for conductors have low specific electric resistance: copper, aluminium and silver **(table)**.

The **resistance of a conductor R_c** is calculated by the formula aside.

Conductor resistance
$R_C = \frac{\varrho_{el} \cdot l}{A}$

l is the length of the conductor wire, A is the cross sectional area.

Resistors in electric circuits

In an electric circuit the resistors can be connected in different ways. Then the current I, the voltage U and the resistance R have different values.

In a **connection in series** all the resistors are connected in a row **(figure)**.

The current rating in every resistor is: $I = I_1 = I_2 = I_3 = \ldots$
The total voltage is: $E = E_1 + E_2 + E_3 + \ldots$
The total resistance is: $R = R_1 + R_2 + R_3 + \ldots$

In a **parallel circuit**, the electric flow is split into several parallel lines each with one resistor **(figure)**.

The total current rating is: $I = I_1 + I_2 + I_3 + \ldots$
The voltage in every line is: $E = E_1 = E_2 = E_3 = \ldots$
The total resistance is: $R = \frac{1}{\frac{1}{R_1} + \frac{1}{R_2} + \frac{1}{R_3}}$

Words	
electric resistance	elektrischer Widerstand (physikalische Größe)
to close	schließen
current rating	Stromstärke
correlation	Beziehung
to describe	beschreiben
formula	Gleichung
Ohm's law	Ohm'sches Gesetz
specific electric resistance	spezifischer elektrischer Widerstand
wire	Draht
conductor resistance	Leiterwiderstand
characteristic	Kennzahl
conductor material	Leiterwerkstoff
cross sectional area	Querschnittsfläche
aside	nebenstehend
resistor	Widerstand (elektrisches Bauteil)
to connect	verschalten
connection in series	Reihenschaltung
in a row	in einer Reihe
total	gesamt
parallel circuit	Parallelschaltung
to split, split, split	aufteilen
variable	Variable, Größe
to indicate	anzeigen

Example: Which resistance has a conductor wire of copper with 220 m length and a cross sectional area of 3 mm²?

Solution: $R_C = \frac{0.0179\ \Omega \cdot mm^2 \cdot 220\ m}{m \cdot 3\ mm^2} = \mathbf{1.31\ \Omega}$

Connection in series

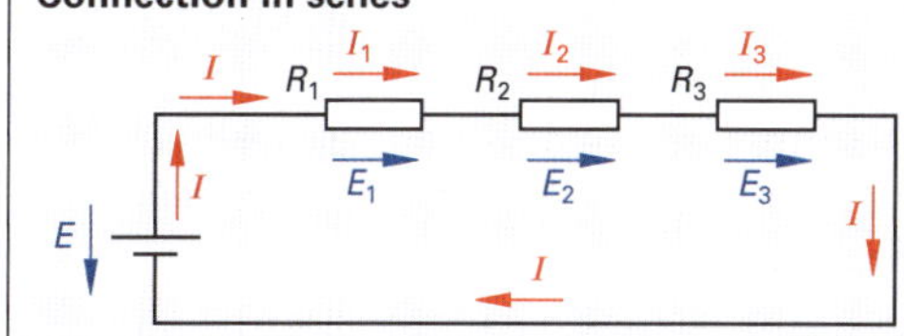

Parallel circuit

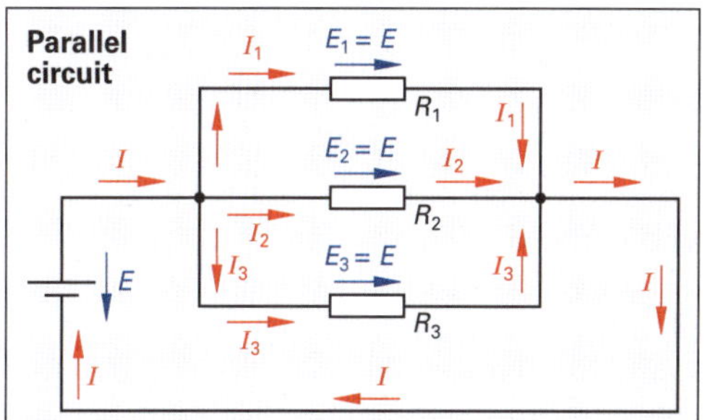

Exercises

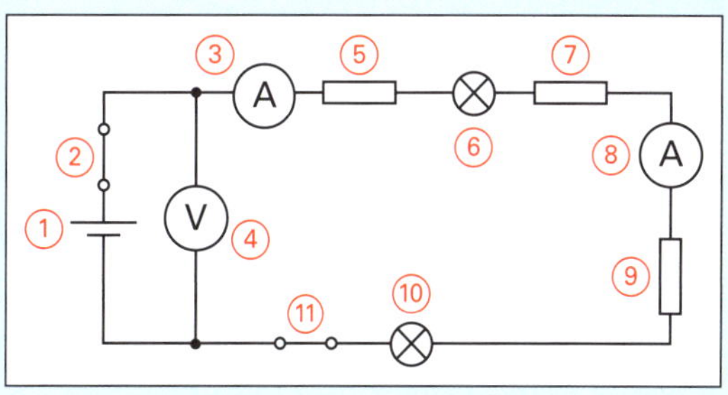

1. What does Ohm's law describe?
2. Write Ohm's law in form of an equation.
3. What does the specific electric resistance indicate?
4. In a circuit with a generator of 24 V flows a current of 0.25 A. Which electric resistance does the circuit have?
5. Name the components ① bis ⑩ in the electric circuit at right hand.

6.2 Types of current and electric networks

There are three types of current. They have different amplitudes and direction of the current.

Direct current (DC)

In direct current (shortly DC) the electron stream flows with constant amplitude in one direction. It has the same value over the time **(figure)**. DC with low voltage (e.g. 6V or 12V) and low current rate is provided by batteries. DC with high voltage and current rate is shaped by a rectifier from alternating current (AC). DC is applied in electronic devices, in DC motors, for galvanising and arc welding.

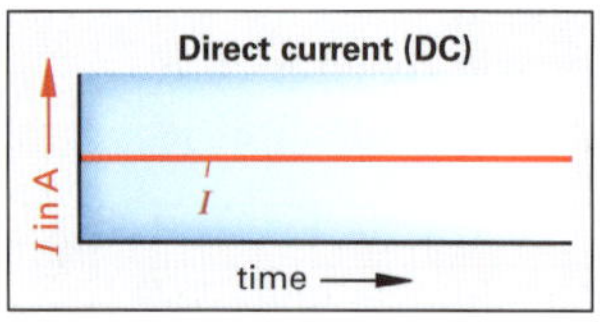

Alternating current (AC)

In AC the current rate I and direction continuously changes like a sinus curve **(figure)**. The number of oscillations in one second is called frequency f. Its unit is Hertz (Hz).

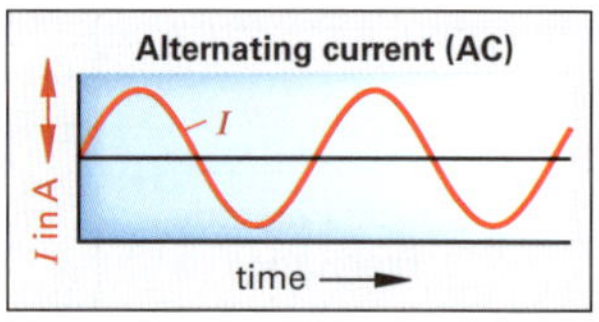

In the European electric network the frequency is 50 Hz. Almost all small devices and small motors work with AC of 230 V.

AC is provided by grounded socket outlets with three lines: L the voltage carrying line, N the returning line and PE the protection earth line **(figure)**. AC sockets are present in every house, workshop and factory.

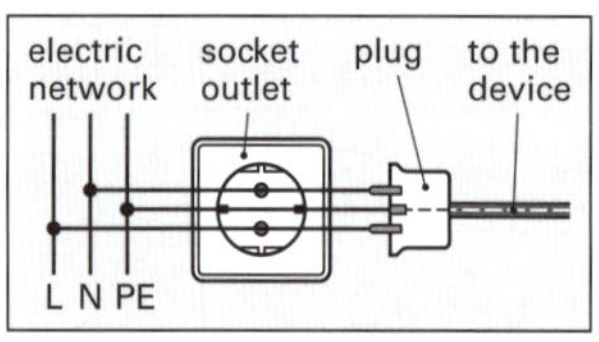

Three phase current

Three phase current has three current carrying lines: L1, L2, L3 **(figure)**. In every line there is an alternating current with 50 Hz. The three currents are phase-delayed.

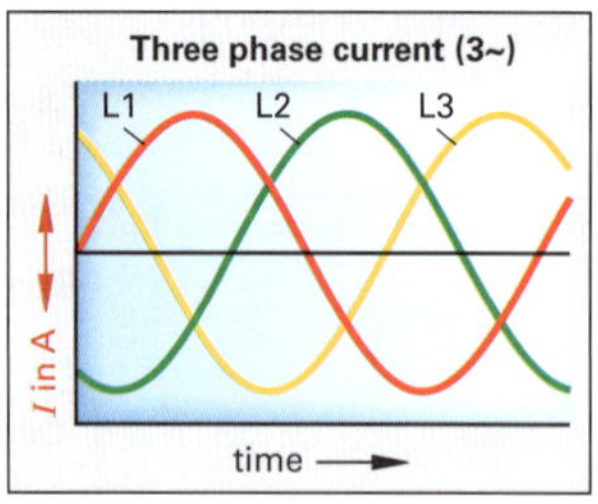

The three phase current is generated in a generator with three electric coils **(figure)**.

The three phase current network has five lines: three current carrying lines L1, L2, L3, the collective return line, which is called neutral line N and the protection earth line PE.

Between each of the lines L1, L2, L3 and N there is an alternating voltage of 230 V. You use it for the operation of lamps, devices and small motors.

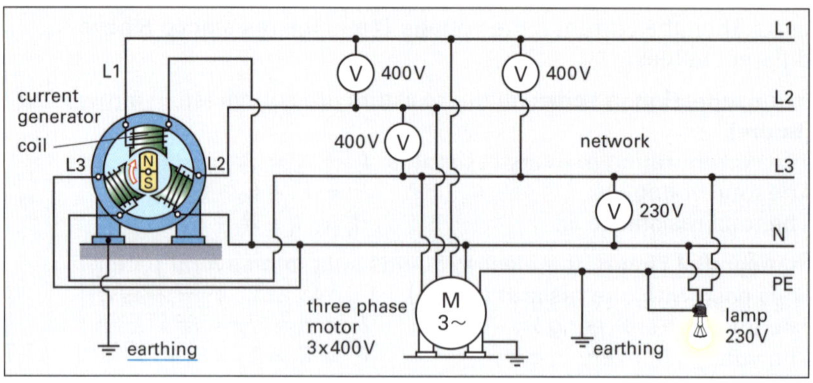

Between two voltage carrying lines, e. g. L1 and L2 or L2 and L3, there is an alternating voltage of 400 V (3~). With three phase current you drive e.g. high power motors and melting furnaces.

Words

English	German
type of current	Stromart
electric network	Stromnetz
amplitude	Amplitude, Größe
direct current (DC)	Gleichstrom
current rate	Stromstärke
to provide	bereitstellen
to shape	umformen
rectifier	Gleichrichter
alternating current (AC)	Wechselstrom
to apply	anwenden
galvanising	Galvanisieren
arc welding	Lichtbogenschweißen
sinus curve	Sinuskurve
oscillation	Schwingung
frequency	Frequenz
grounded socket outlet	Schutzkontakt-Steckdose
voltage carrying line	spannungsführende Leitung
protection earth line	geerdeter Schutzleiter
to be present	vorhanden sein
three phase current	Dreiphasen-Wechselstrom
current carrying line	stromführende Leitung
phase-delayed	phasenverschoben
to generate	erzeugen
electric coil	Wicklung
current network	Leitungsnetz
collective return line	gemeinsamer Rückleiter
neutral line	Neutralleiter
high power	leistungsstark
melting furnace	Schmelzofen
earthing	Erdung
abbreviation	Abkürzung

Exercises

1. What are the abbreviations for: Direct Current, Alternating Current?
2. What frequency does the European electric network have?
3. How many lines does a grounding socket outlet for AC have?
4. Name the lines of the AC grounding socket outlet and their function.
5. What are the functions of the lines? a) L1, L2, L3 b) N c) PE
6. Which lines of the three phase current network have to be connected with the 3~ motor **(figure)**?
7. What is the function of the earthing?

6.3 Electric work and electric power

The electric power companies provide electric energy for all electric consumers at the socket outlets and electric connection spots.
In electrical engineering, the electric energy is called **electric work *W***.
It is measured by an **electric counter (figure)** and called power consumption.
You calculate it by the formula $W = P \cdot t$.
The unit of the electrical energy or work *W* is kWh.

P is the **electrical power** taken from the network, ***t*** is the period of operation. The unit of the electric power is Watt (W) or Kilowatt kW.

The electric power, which is taken by a device, is specified e. g. on the power rating plate or at a lamp directly on it.

In contrary, the power rating plate at electric motors shows the power output of the motor **(figure)**. Besides, there are other important data listed.

Electric counter

Power rating plate of a motor

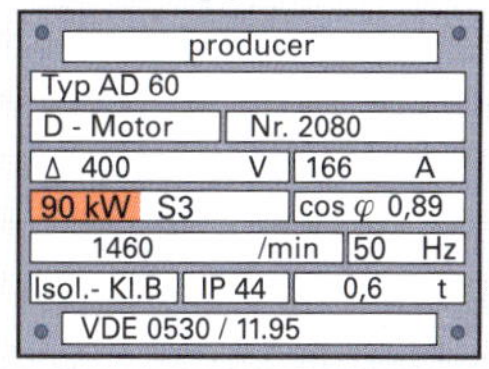

Electric power of loads

The electric power *P*, which is taken by a load, depends on the voltage *E* and the current *I* as well as on the electric characteristics of the load.

The electric power of a purely ohmic load **(figure)** at a direct or alternating current is calculated by: $P = E \cdot I$

If the purely ohmic loads are connected at a three phase current **(figure)**, the power is: $P = \sqrt{3} \cdot E \cdot I$

The factor $\sqrt{3}$ respects the three currents in the three lines of the load.

The electric power *P* of a load, which has an ohmic and an inductive resistance, is decreased by the **power factor** φ. The decreased electric power of this load is called **effective power**.

The effective power of a load with ohmic and inductive resistance **(figure)** connected at an alternating current (AC) is calculated by:
$P = E \cdot I \cdot \cos \varphi$

If the load has three lines and is connected at a three phase current **(figure)**, the effective power is:
$P = \sqrt{3} \cdot E \cdot I \cdot \cos \varphi$

The electric work *W* of such a load is:
$W = P \cdot t = \sqrt{3} \cdot E \cdot I \cdot \cos \varphi \cdot t$

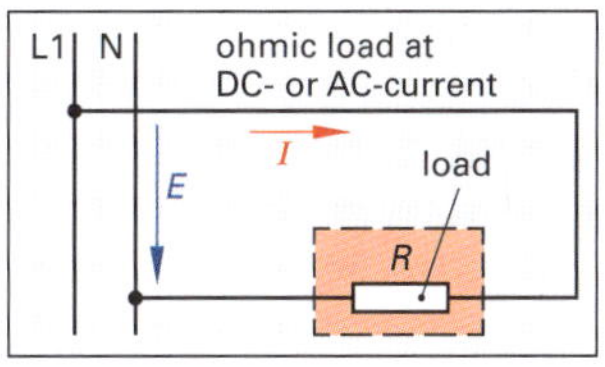

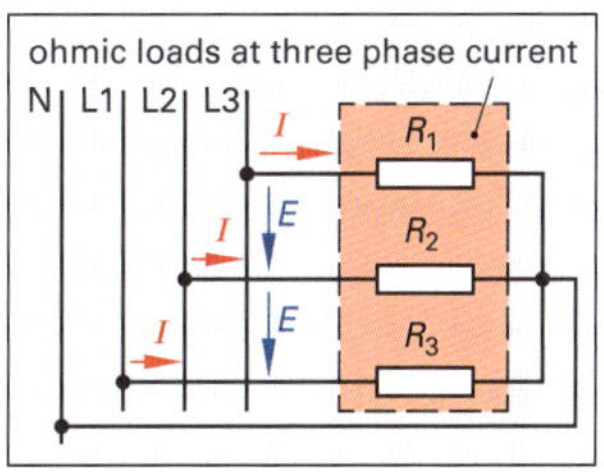

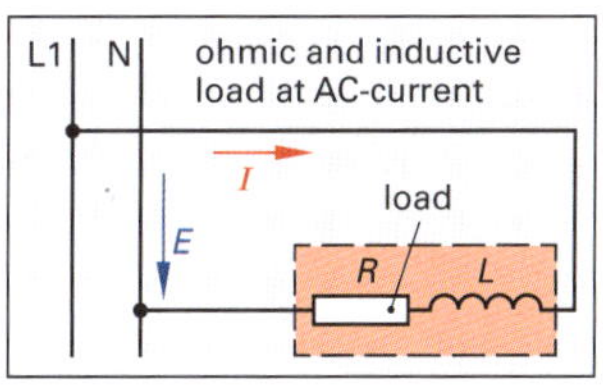

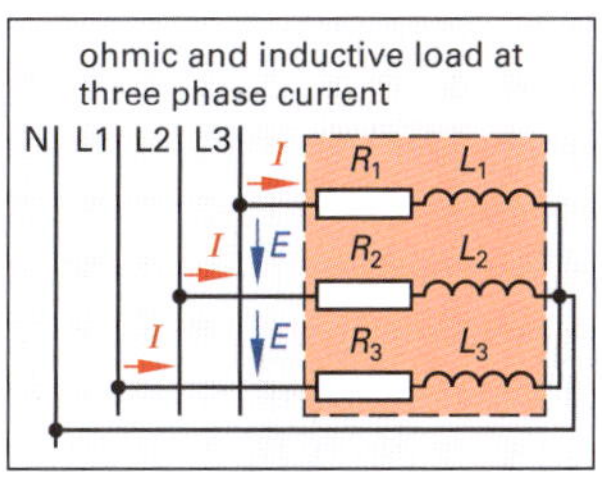

Words

English	German
electric work	elektrische Arbeit
electric power	elektrische Leistung
electric power company	Elektroversorgungs-unternehmen
consumer	Verbraucher
connection spot	Anschluss
electric counter	Zähler
power consumption	Stromverbrauch
to take	entnehmen
period of operation	Betriebsdauer
to specify	angeben, nennen
power rating plate	Leistungsschild
in contrary	im Gegensatz
power output	abgegebene Leistung
besides	außerdem
data	Daten
to list	aufzählen
load	Verbraucher (elektrisch)
characteristic	Eigenart
purely	rein, ausschließlich
ohmic load	Ohm'scher Verbraucher
to respect	berücksichtigen
inductive resistance	induktiver Widerstand
to decrease	vermindern
power factor φ	Leistungsfaktor φ
effective power	Wirkleistung
nominal current	Nennstrom
motor speed	Motordrehzahl
suitable	geeignet

Exercises

1. The electric counter right hand above indicates 417.3 kWh. One month later it indicates 722.6 kWh. Calculate the power consumption from the power network during the month.
2. The rating plate shown right hand above, shows the characteristic data of an electric motor. Name the data for:
   a) Voltage
   b) Nominal current
   c) Frequency of current
   d) Nominal power
   e) Power factor
   f) Nominal motor speed
3. A motor has the rating plate shown above. What kind of current is it suitable for?
4. Name the formula for the electric power of a three phase motor with an ohmic and inductive resistance.
5. Calculate the nominal electric power of the motor with the rating plate shown above.

6.4 Faults in electrical systems

If there is a defect in an electrical device and electric current flows through the body of a man, there is danger for health and life.

Electric currents with ratings over 50 mA and alternating voltages over 50 V are dangerous to life. To avoid these hazards, it is necessary to know the **type of defect** in an electric device e. g. in a motor (**figure** below).

A **short circuit** occurs if two voltage carrying lines with a defect insulation, come into contact **(figure).** As a result, a very high current flows. The upstream cutouts break the electric connection.

Line leakage happens e. g. at a damaged insulation in a switch and the following unintentional connection. The device cannot be switched off.

Housing leakage is existent, if there is a connection of a voltage carrying line and a conducting housing. By touching the housing, a fault current flows through the human body to earth (middle **figure**). Its rating depends on the resistance of the human body and the earth connection. When housing leakage exists, there is great danger for the staff.

Earth leakage happens when an electrical connection of a voltage carrying line with the earth or earthed components occurs. The resulting high current is broken by the cutout.

Overcurrent protection

These devices are the cutouts, also called circuit breakers. They are installed in the electric circuit and protect the machines, motors and devices against overload and men against fault currents.

Simple cutouts are **fuses (figure).** They contain a thin melting wire. In case of an overload current, the wire melts and cuts the circuit.

Automatic cutouts (figure) have two internal different circuit breakers: an electromagnetic quick-cut-out for breaking a short circuit and a bimetal overcurrent-breaker for breaking a continuous overload.

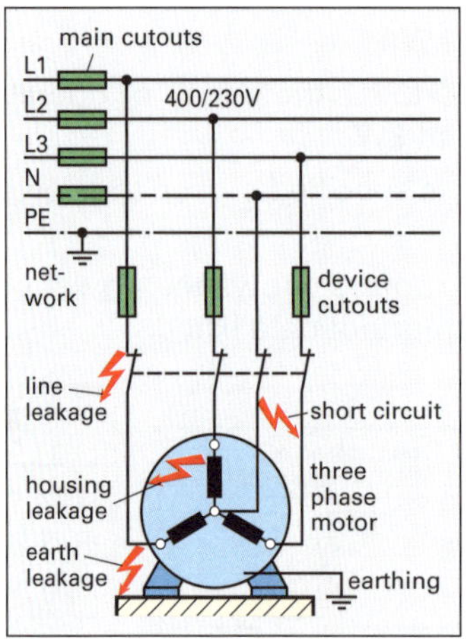

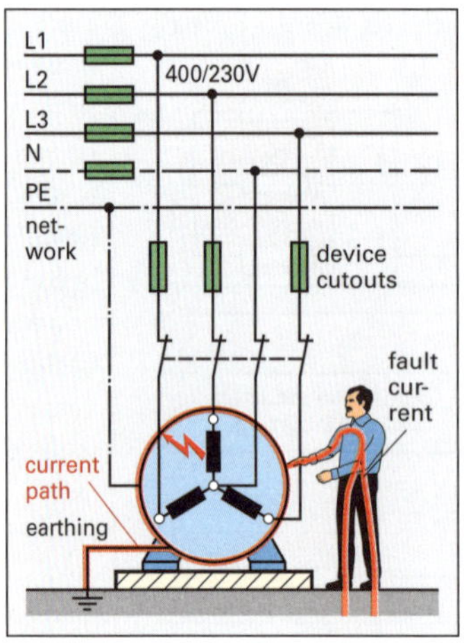

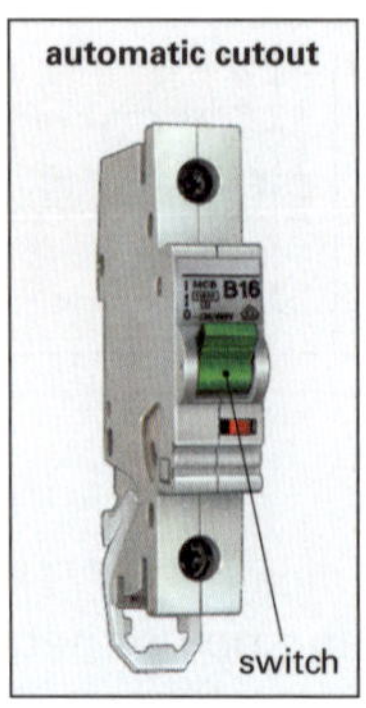

	Words	
fault, defect		Fehler, Störung
man, men		Mensch, Menschen
danger		Gefahr
health		Gesundheit
current rating		Stromstärke
dangerous to life		lebensgefährlich
to avoid		vermeiden
hazard		Gefahr
necessary		erforderlich
short circuit		Kurzschluss
to occur		eintreten, entstehen
insulation		Isolation
as a result		inofolgedessen
upstream		vorgeschaltet
cutout		elektrische Sicherung
to break		abschalten, unterbrechen
line leakage		Leiterschluss
to happen		entstehen, auftreten
damaged		beschädigt
switch		Schalter
unintentional		unbeabsichtigt
to switch off		abschalten
housing leakage		Körperschluss
is existent		liegt vor
conducting		leitend
touching		Berührung
fault current		Fehlerstrom
staff		Personal
earth leakage		Erdschluss
earthed		geerdet
overcurrent protection		Überstromschutz
circuit breaker		Stromkreisunterbrecher
fuse		Schmelzsicherung
melting wire		Schmelzdraht
overload current		Überlaststrom
automatic cutout		Sicherungsautomat
bimetal overcurrent breaker		Bimetall-Überlastschalter
maintenance worker		Wartungsarbeiter

Exercises

1. At which current and voltage rating is an electric current dangerous to life?
2. Describe the electric conditions a) of a short circuit b) of a housing leakage
3. What happens, if a maintenance worker touches a motor housing carrying a fault current?
4. Explain the reason, why in case of good earthing of the motor housing, the fault current, which flows through the body of someone touching the housing, is reduced? (figure above in the middle position)
5. Explain the function of a fuse.

6.5 Protection measures

Protective earth conductor (PE-conductor)

The power networks in all buildings and factories have a five-line cable which includes one protection earth conductor, called PE-conductor **(figure).** The housings of the devices and motors are connected by a yellow-green PE-line with the PE-conductor of the network. If there is a housing leakage, the fault current can flow through the PE-conductor to the earth.

If a person touches the voltage carrying housing, only a small current flows through the human body with its greater resistance. The bigger part of the current flows over the PE-conductor to the earth. At stationary machines, such as motors, the PE-conductor of the machine is permanently connected in the connection box with the earthed PE of the network. Movable devices e.g. a compressor, are connected by a grounding socket outlet with PE-conductor. High power devices have a five-line socket outlet and plug. Low power devices, e.g. a tempering oil bath, are connected by a three-line socket outlet and plug by a three-line cable with PE-conductor **(figure).** All these devices have the symbol aside.

Protective insulation

Protective insulation means that all conducting metal components in a device, that can be on voltage in case of a defect, are made of insulating materials. At a power drill e.g., the housing, the switch and the shaft between motor and gear are made of non-conducting plastic materials **(figure).** The symbol of the protective insulation is:

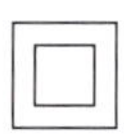

Protective housing

The housing protects the device against ingression of water and other dangerous substances, e.g. dust or gases. The types of housing protection are indicated by an IP-code number (IP = International Protection) and a symbol **(figure).**

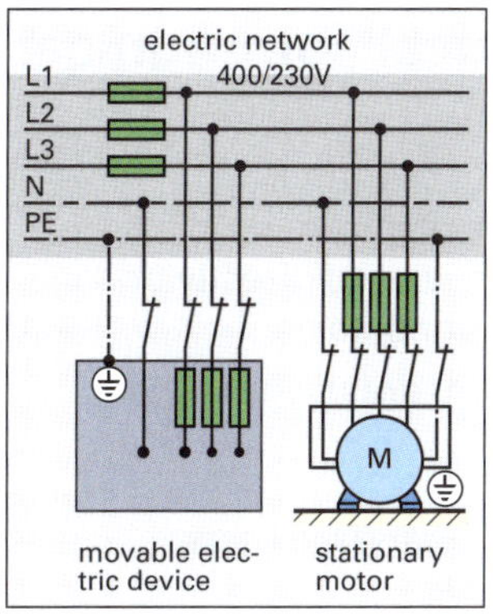

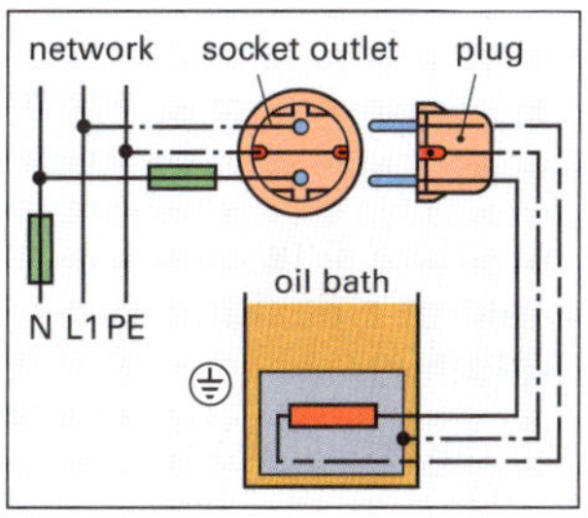

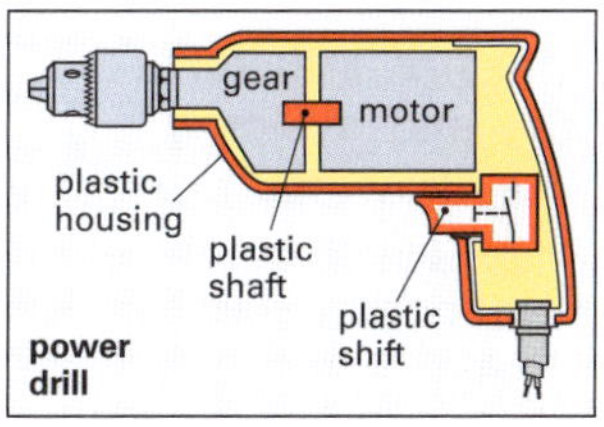

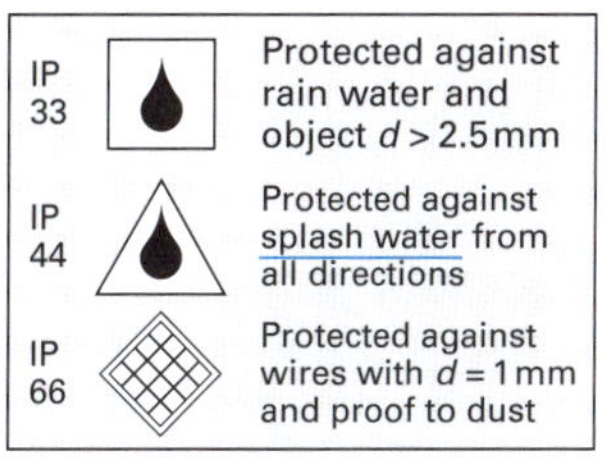

Words (English)	Words (German)
protection measure	Schutzmaßnahme
protective earth conductor (PE-conductor)	PE-Erdungsschutzleiter
five line cable	fünfadriges Kabel
to include	enthalten
housing leakage	Gehäuseschluss
to touch	berühren
voltage carrying	spannungsführend
bigger part	größere Teil
stationary	stationär
permanent	dauerhaft, fest
connection box	Anschlusskasten
movable	beweglich
grounding socket outlet	Schuko-Steckdose
plug	Stecker
tempering oil bath	Aufwärme-Ölbad
aside	nebenstehend
protection insulation	Schutzisolierung
to mean	bedeuten
in case of	im Fall
insulating material	isolierender Werkstoff
power drill	Handbohrmaschine
shaft	Welle
gear	Getriebe
plastic	Kunststoff
protective housing	Schutzgehäuse
ingression	Eindringen
dust	Staub
to indicate	kennzeichnen
IP-code number	IP-Kennziffer
splash water	Spritzwasser
fault circuit interruptor	Fehlerstrom-Schutzschalter
FI-switch	FI-Schalter
switching box	Schaltkasten
section	Bereich
forward and return line	Hin- und Rückleitung
to interrupt	unterbrechen
purpose	Zweck

Fault circuit interruptor (FI-switch)

The FI-switch **(figure)** is placed in the switching box of a section.

The FI-switch measures the current in the forward and return conductor of the room. If there is a difference, the FI-switch interrupts the connection immediately. The fault current then flows to the PE-conductor.

Exercises

1. What is the purpose of the protective earth conductor (PE-conductor)?
2. Complete the following sentences on protective measures:
   a) Electric power machines with a protection insulation have a housing of ______________.
   b) The FI-switch cuts the current connection when ______________.
3. A device has the following IP-code symbols: Name the protection measures of this device.

7 Technical communication

7.1 Technical drawings

Technical communication means the exchange of information for processing technical projects. This information is used directly or indirectly for the production of technical components.

Standards for the technical communication e.g. are used for the following applications:

- Production of technical drawings.
- Determination of shapes and dimensions of standard parts
- Designation codes and properties of materials.

There are several types of standards: National (e.g. German), European and International standards **(table)**.

Standards are published in *standard specification sheets*. In Germany you get it by the Beuth Verlag, Berlin; www.beuth.de.

The specific standard sheet is named by the standard type, the number, the title and the date of edition. **Example of a designation**: DIN EN 10025 Unalloyed structural steels (2005-04)

Additional technical organisations set up guidelines, e.g. the **VDI** (**V**erein **D**eutscher-**I**ngenieure) for the production of technical drawings. In Germany the **VDI-guidelines** are most commonly used.

Technical drawings are created to specify shape, size, structure and function of workpieces, assembly groups and systems. According to their content and purpose, these drawings are classified in freehand sketches, component drawings, assembly drawings, general arrangement drawings and exploded views.

The **figure** below shows the freehand sketch and the component drawing of two parts. In the figure right hand you see the general arrangement drawing of a roller bearing.

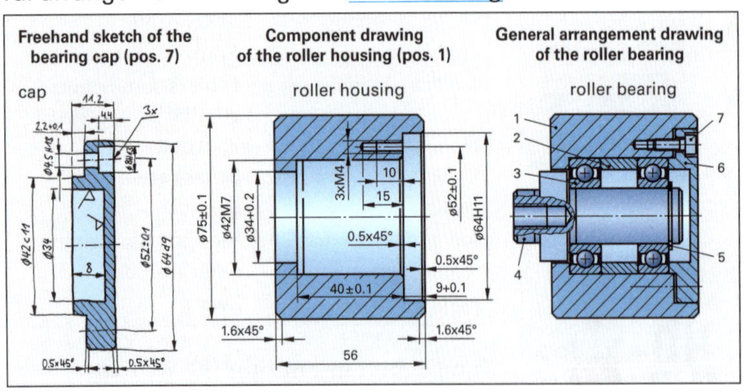

The freehand sketch of the bearing cap (pos. 7) is not true to scale. Sketches are used for single orders or repairs.

The component drawing of the roller housing (pos. 1) includes all the relevant information for the production of the workpiece, e.g. designation, form, measures, surface specifications, material and an instruction for the heat treatment. The general arrangement drawing shows the spatial arrangement and the interaction of the groups in the assembled state.

Table: Types of standards

Standard	Explanation
DIN	German standard (DIN = Deutsches Institut für Normung)
DIN EN	German standard, which correlates the European standard
DIN ISO	German standard, which correlates the International standard
DIN EN ISO	German standard, which correlates the European standard and the International standard

Words

communication	Kommunikation
technical drawing	technische Zeichnung
to process	ausführen
standard	Norm
to correlate	entsprechen
determination	Festlegung
shape	Form, Gestalt
standard part	Normteil
designation code	Kurzbezeichnung
standard specification sheet	Normblatt
date of edition	Ausgabedatum
organisation	Verband
to set up	aufstellen
guideline	Richtlinie
to create	anfertigen
to specify	festlegen
assembly group	Baugruppe
freehand sketch	Freihandskizze
component drawing	Teilzeichnung
assembly drawing	Gruppenzeichnung
general arrangement drawing	Gesamtzeichnung
exploded view	Explosionsdarstellung
freehand sketch	Freihandskizze
roller bearing	Laufrollenlager
bearing cap	Lagerdeckel
true to scale	maßstabsgetreu
single order	Einzelauftrag
repair	Reparatur
surface specification	Oberflächenangabe
heat treatment	Wärmebehandlung
spatial arrangement	räumliche Anordnung
interaction	Zusammenwirken

Exercises

1. Answer the following questions:
   a) What belongs to a technical drawing of a component?
   b) Which types of technical drawings do you know?
   c) Which information is given in the headline of a standard?

2. Describe the characteristics of
   a) a freehand sketch b) a component drawing c) an assembly drawing.

Computer Aided Design (CAD)

Nowadays the construction of products is mostly realised with the aid of a CAD-Software on a computer. The **figure** on the left shows the three dimensional volume model of a bending device, created by a CAD-Software.

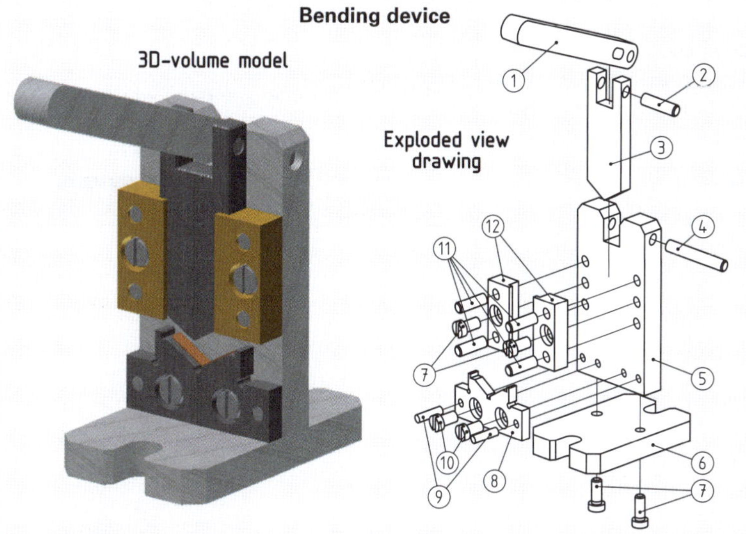

Parts list of the bending device

pos.	quantity	designation	material, standard
1	1	lever	E295
2	1	parallel pin	ISO 2338 – 5 h8 x 24
3	1	slider	C45+QT
4	1	parallel pin	ISO 2338 – 6 h8 x 45
5	1	vertical post	E295
6	1	base	E295
7	4	socket head screw	ISO 1207 – M5 x 12
8	1	part of a prism	C45+QT
9	2	parallel pin	ISO 2338 – 4 h8 x 18
10	2	socket head screw	ISO 1207 – M5 x 8
11	4	parallel pin	ISO 2338 – 5 h8 x 20
12	2	guide rail	E295

A CAD-Software creates a volume model by addition or subtraction of geometric base bodies.

With the stored data of the volume model in the software of the CAD-program, detail drawings, assembly drawings, general arrangement drawings, exploded view drawings and parts lists are created automatically by mouse click.

Exploded view drawings show the arrangement of the components of an assembly group (**figure** above, middle); the functional unit and structural organisation is visible. Complex assemblies can illustrate different views, groups and single parts.

The sequence of the assembly and the function of the single parts are shown clearly. Exploded view drawings are used as instruction for assembly or disassembly.

All components in group drawings and arrangement drawings are labelled with position numbers.

In the **parts list** the single parts are arranged in the sequence of the position numbers (**figure**, right hand above). It contains all components of the device.

The components are listed with their position number, the quantity, the designation and the standard designation code of the material or the standard type and number. Components, which are produced out of semi-finished products, are listed with the identification code and the dimensions.

Exercises

1. Give an answer to the following questions:
   a) What is the use of exploded view drawings?
   b) Which information is given in parts lists?
   c) How does the CAD-Software create a volume model of a component?
   d) What applications are possible by the stored volume model data?
2. Complete the following sentence:
   In general arrangement drawings and ____________ all components are provided with ________________.
3. Explain the difference between an assembly drawing and an exploded view drawing in English.

Words

computer aided design (CAD)	computergestütztes Konstruieren
nowadays	heutzutage
construction	Konstruktion
volume model	Volumenmodell
bending device	Biegevorrichtung
lever	Hebel
parallel pin	Zylinderstift
slider	Schieber
vertical post	senkrechter Ständer
base	Grundplatte
socket head screw	Zylinderschraube
part of a prism	Prismenstück
guide rail	Führungsleiste
to create	erzeugen
base body	Grundkörper
stored	gespeichert
parts list	Stückliste
arrangement	Anordnung
functional unit	Funktionseinheit
structural organisation	Ordnungsstruktur
view	Ansicht
sequence	Reihenfolge
assembly	Montage
instruction	Anleitung
disassembly	Demontage
to be labelled	versehen sein
position number	Positionsnummer
to arrange	ordnen
to contain	enthalten
standard designation code	Normbezeichnung
identification code	Kurzbezeichnung

7.2 Presentation of technical relationships

Technical relationships can be presented in form of tables or graphics. Thereby complex relationships can be identified quickly and precisely.

Tables have lines and columns. The table beside shows the different thread dimensions with increasing size of the threads: M4, M5 etc. By this table you can read the pitch P, the minor diameter of the bolt d_3 and the nut D_1 in dependence of the thread nominal diameter.

Table: Thread dimensions

designation / dimensions	M4	M5	M6	M8	M10
Pitch P	0.7	0.8	1	1.25	1.5
Minor diameter bolt d_3	3.14	4.02	4.77	6.47	8.16
Minor diameter nut D_1	3.24	4.13	4.92	6.65	8.38

Graphical display formats are: diagrams, nomograms, three dimensional figures, plans and circuit diagrams.

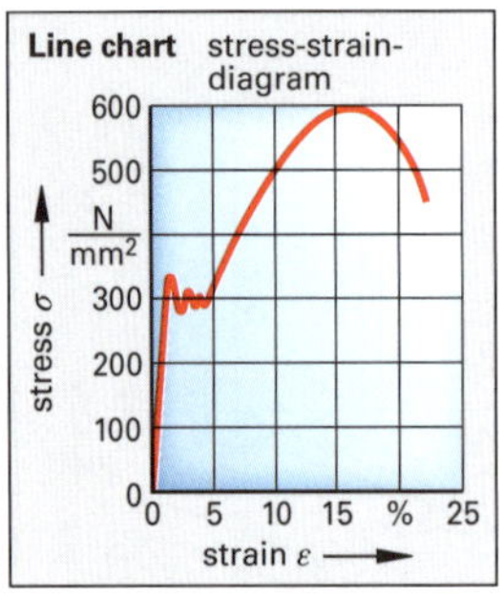

Diagrams

Diagrams are displayed within a coordinate system with mostly rectangular coordinates, rarely with polar coordinates.

They can be classified into different formats:

- **line charts**
- **bar charts (histogram)**
- **stacked bar charts**
- **pie charts**

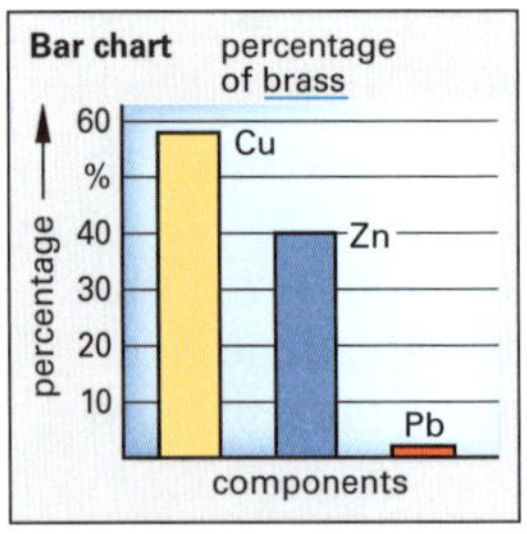

A **line chart**, e.g. the stress-strain-diagram **(figure)**, shows the dependence of one quantity by a variable, e.g. the increasing change of the stress σ in dependence of the increasing strain ε. The axes are named, they have a unit and are scaled.

Bar charts consist of vertically or horizontally arranged bars **(figure)**. They are used for comparison and contrast of different values. These values can be presented absolutely or in per cent. The bar chart of the figure shows the percentage of a brass material.

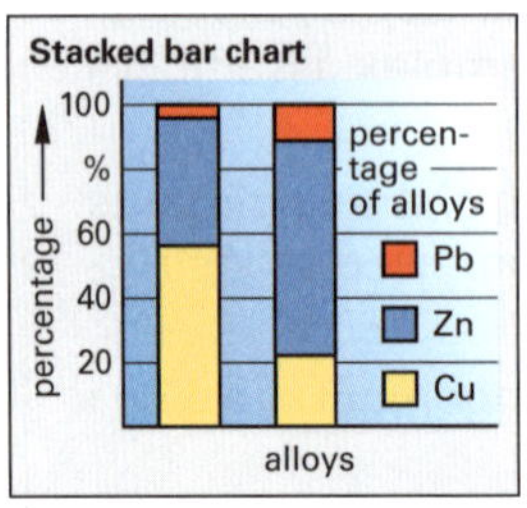

You get a **stacked bar chart** if several bars are arranged above each other **(figure)**. The stacked bars have together 100%. By the stacked bars you can compare the percentage distribution of the values of several bars directly.

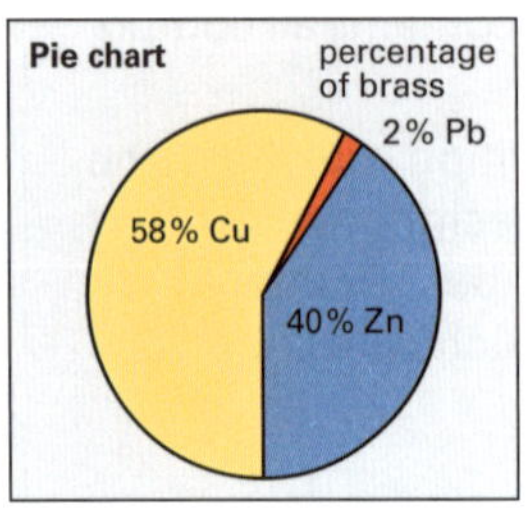

Pie charts are a common presentation of the percentage of a total amount **(figure)**. It is applied e.g. for the percentage of materials.

Words

presentation	Darstellung
relationship	Zusammenhang
table	Tabelle
line	Zeile
column	Spalte
thread dimension	Gewindemaß
pitch	Steigung
minor diameter	Kerndurchmesser
bolt	Schraube, Bolzen
nut	Mutter
display format	Darstellungsart
nomogram	Nomogramm
three dimensional	dreidimensional
circuit diagram	Schaltplan
to display	darstellen
coordinate system	Koordinatensystem
rectangular coordinates	rechtwinkelige Koordinaten
polar coordinates	Polarkoordinaten
line chart	Liniendiagramm
bar chart	Säulendiagramm
histogram	Histogramm
stacked bar chart	Stapelsäulendiagramm
pie chart	Kreisflächendiagramm
stress-strain diagram	Spannungs-Dehnungs-diagramm
unit	Einheit
scaled	skaliert, unterteilt
brass	Messing
arranged	angeordnet
percentage	Prozentgehalt
content	Gehalt
stacked bar	gestapelte Säule
distribution	Verteilung
common	häufig
total amount	Gesamtmenge
work accident	Arbeitsunfall
assembly	Montage
hardening shop	Härterei
foundry	Gießerei

Exercises

1. Name the different graphical display formats.
2. Answer the following questions:
   a) In which cases are presentations of line charts useful?
   b) How do you create a stacked bar chart?
   c) What are the advantages of a pie chart?
   d) What is the difference between a bar chart and a stacked bar chart?
3. In the **table** aside the numbers of work accidents for one year are documented in the different production areas.
   a) Calculate the percentage of accidents for each production area.
   b) Create a bar chart and a pie chart to show the accidents' percentage.

Table: Work accidents

production area	number
assembly	3
production	2
hardening shop	1
foundry	4

Nomograms

By a nomogram you can read approximately the result of a mathematic calculation or a complex technical relationship. The advantage of using a nomogram is a very fast determination of a required quantity without a calculator.

A special nomogram, the **rotary speed diagram (figure),** e.g. is used to read the required rotary speed *n* of a turning machine with staged speeds.

Example: You have to finish a shaft with 80 mm diameter and a cutting velocity of 30 m/min by a turning machine with the nomogram right hand. Which rotary speed has to be adjusted?
Solution: You follow the line vertically upwards from the diameter 80 mm and horizontally sideways from the cutting speed 30 m/min. At the intersection point you read at the red line: $\boldsymbol{n = 125\ \mathrm{min}^{-1}}$.

Rotary speed diagram for turning

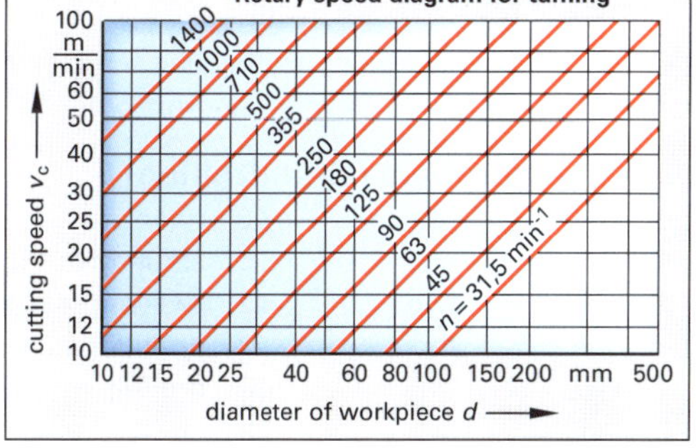

Three dimensional diagrams

Three dimensional diagrams illustrate the dependence of one quantity from two variables, e.g. the power consumption of a company in dependence on daytime and month **(figure).**
You can read, that the power consumption is high at daytime from 8 to 12 and 5 to 8 o'clock in the evening and in the course of one year in the months 1 to 2 and 9 to 12.

Three-dimensional diagram

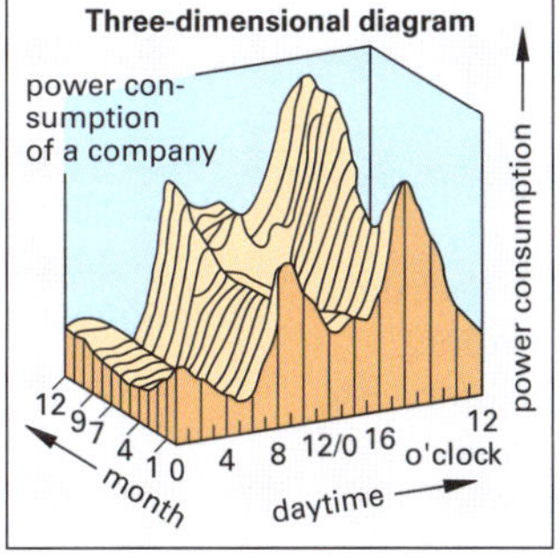

Special diagrams

Information about the interdependences in special sections is presented by special diagrams. They consider the special requirements of the section, e.g. block diagrams, pneumatic or circuit diagrams, work plans or assembly plans.

Block diagrams show the operations of a process in rectangles and the designations of the steps **(figure).** Lines and arrows give the sequence direction.

Block diagram

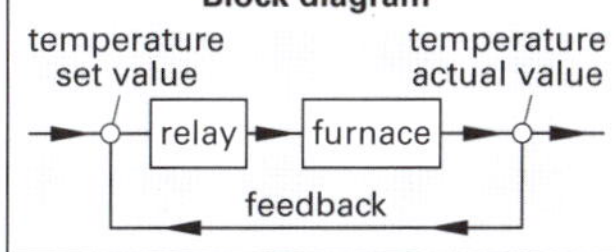

A **pneumatic circuit diagram (figure)** shows the interaction of components, e.g. of a cylinder with valves for the control of the cylinder. The connecting lines represent pneumatic lines. Magnets perform the movement of the directional valve.

Pneumatic circuit diagram

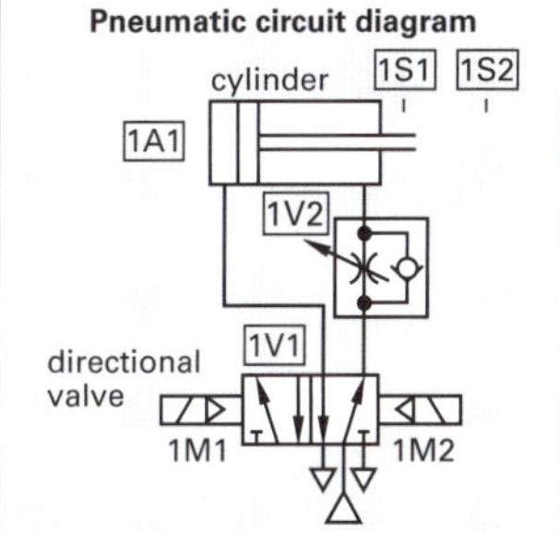

The **electric circuit diagram** illustrates the interaction between magnets and switches, which are connected by electric lines.

Electrical circuit diagram

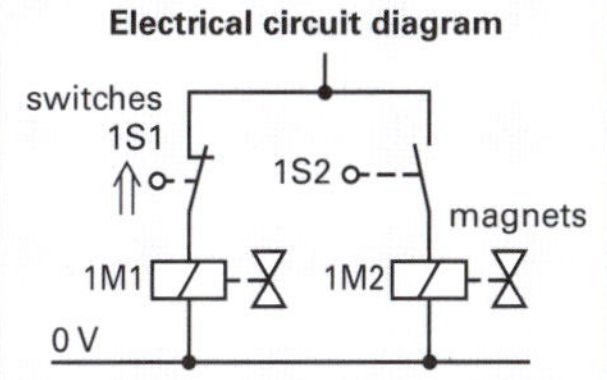

Words

nomogram	Nomogramm
approximately	näherungsweise
fast	schnell
determination	Ermittlung
quantity	Größe
rotary speed diagram	Drehzahldiagramm
turning machine	Drehmaschine
staged	gestuft
cutting velocity	Schnittgeschwindigkeit
to adjust	einstellen
intersection point	Schnittpunkt
three dimensional	dreidimensional
power consumption	Stromverbrauch
course	Verlauf
interdependence	Zusammenhang
section	Fachgebiet
to consider	berücksichtigen
requirement	Anforderung
circuit diagram	Schaltplan
work plan	Arbeitsplan
assembly plan	Montageplan
block diagram	Blockdiagramm
rectangle	Rechteck
arrow	Pfeil
sequence	Ablauf
cylinder	Zylinder
valve	Ventil
control	Steuerung
pneumatic line	Druckluftleitung
to perform	umsetzen
directional valve	Wegeventil
to illustrate	darstellen
switch	Schalter
drill hole	Bohrloch

Exercises

1. Answer the following questions:
   a) What is the difference between a nomogram and a chart line?
   b) What is shown in the pneumatic circuit diagram and in the electrical circuit diagram?
2. At a drilling machine, a drilled hole with a diameter of 20 mm has to be cut in a component. The maximum cutting speed for the drilling machine is 30 m/min.
   Determine the suitable rotary speed for the drilling machine by using the nomogram above.

Appendix

Anhang

English numerals

Englische Zahlwörter

Cardinal numbers (Grundzahlen)

0	null	zero, nil	20	zwanzig	twenty
1	eins	one	21	einundzwanzig	twenty-one
2	zwei	two	22	zweiundzwanzig	twenty-two
3	drei	three	23	dreiundzwanzig	twenty-three
4	vier	four	30	dreißig	thirty
5	fünf	five	31	einunddreißig	thirty-one
6	sechs	six	32	zweiunddreißig	thirty-two
7	sieben	seven	33	dreiunddreißig	thirty-three
8	acht	eight	40	vierzig	forty
9	neun	nine	41	einundvierzig	forty-one
10	zehn	ten	50	fünfzig	fifty
11	elf	eleven	51	einundfünfzig	fifty-one
12	zwölf	twelve	60	sechzig	sixty
13	dreizehn	thirteen	61	einundsechzig	sixty-one
14	vierzehn	fourteen	70	siebzig	seventy
15	fünfzehn	fifteen	71	einundsiebzig	seventy-one
16	sechzehn	sixteen	80	achtzig	eighty
17	siebzehn	seventeen	81	einundachtzig	eighty-one
18	achtzehn	eighteen	90	neunzig	ninety
19	neunzehn	nineteen	91	einundneunzig	ninety-one

100	hundert	one hundred
101	hunderteins	hundred and one
102	hundertzwei	hundred and two
110	hundertzehn	hundred and ten
200	zweihundert	two hundred
300	dreihundert	three hundred
451	vierhundert-einundfünfzig	four hundred and fifty-one
1000	(ein)tausend	a (oder) one thousand
2000	zweitausend	two thousand
10 000	zehntausend	ten thousand
1 000 000	eine Million	a (oder) one million
2 000 000	zwei Millionen	two million
1 000 000 000	eine Milliarde	Britisch: a (oder) one milliard Amerikanisch: a (oder) one billion

Ordinal numbers (Ordnungszahlen)

1.	erste	first	19.	neunzehnte	nineteenth
2.	zweite	second	20.	zwanzigste	twentieth
3.	dritte	third	21.	einundzwanzigste	twenty-first
4.	vierte	fourth	22.	zweiundzwanzigste	twenty-second
5.	fünfte	fifth	23.	dreiundzwanzigste	twenty-third
6.	sechste	sixth	30.	dreißigste	thirtieth
7.	siebente	seventh	31.	einunddreißigste	thirthy-first
8.	achte	eighth	40.	vierzigste	fortieth
9.	neunte	ninth	41.	einundvierzigste	forty-first
10.	zehnte	tenth	50.	fünfzigste	fiftieth
11.	elfte	eleventh	51.	einundfünfzigste	fifty-first
12.	zwölfte	twelfth	60.	sechzigste	sixtieth
13.	dreizehnte	thirteenth	61.	einundechzigste	sixty-first
14.	vierzehnte	fourteenth	70.	siebzigste	seventieth
15.	fünfzehnte	fifteenth	71.	einundsiebzigste	seventy-first
16.	sechzehnte	sixteenth	80.	achtzigste	eightieth
17.	siebzehnte	seventeenth	81.	einundachtzigste	eighty-first
18.	achtzehnte	eighteenth	90.	neunzigste	ninetieth

100.	hundertste	(one) hundredth
101.	hundertunderste	hundred and first
200.	zweihundertste	two hundredth
300.	dreihundertste	three hundredth
451.	vierhundert(und) einundfünfzigste	four hundred and fifty-first
1000.	tausendste	(one) thousandth
1100.	tausend(und) einhundertste	(one) thousand and (one) hundredth
2000.	zweitausendste	two thousandth
100 000.	einhundert-tausendste	(one) hundred thousandth
1 000 000.	millionste	millionth
10 000 000.	zehnmillionste	ten millionth

Decimal numbers (Dezimalzahlen)

4,217	4.217	four point two one seven
2700,8	2700.8	two thousand seven hundred point eight
−0,849	−0.849	minus zero point eight four nine
0,0072	0.0072	zero point zero zero seven two

Power to ten numbers (Zehnerpotenz-Zahlen)

$2,5 \cdot 10^3$	$2.5 \cdot 10^3$	two point five times ten to the third power
$3,18 \cdot 10^{-4}$	$3.18 \cdot 10^{-4}$	three point one eight times ten to minus fourth power

Fractional numbers

Bruchzahlen

½	ein halb	one half (oder) a half
⅓	ein Drittel	one third (oder) a third
¼	ein Viertel	one fourth (oder) a fourth (oder) a quarter
¾	drei Viertel	three fourths, three quarters
⅕	ein Fünftel	one fifth (oder) a fifth
⅒	ein Zehntel	one tenth (oder) a tenth
1/100	ein Hunderstel	one hundredth
1/1000	ein Tausendstel	one thousandth
1/1000000	ein Millionstel	one millionth
⅔	zwei Drittel	two thirds
¾	drei Viertel	three fourths (oder) three quarters
⅖	zwei Fünftel	two fifths
3/10	drei Zehntel	three tenths
1½	anderthalb	one and a half
2½	zwei(und)einhalb	two and a half
5⅜	fünf drei Achtel	five and three eights
1,1	eins Komma eins	one point one (1.1)

Muliples

Vervielfältigungszahlen

einfach	single
zweifach	double
dreifach	threefold, treble, triple
vierfach	fourfold, quadruple
fünffach	fivefold
hundertfach	(one) hundredfold

Mathematical operators

Mathematische Operatoren

Mathematisches Symbol	Deutsche Bezeichnung	Bedeutung	Englische Bezeichnung	Beispiel	Englisch ausgesprochen (English spoken)
+	plus	Addition	plus	$5 + 4 = 9$	Five plus four is nine
–	minus	Subtraktion	minus	$12 - 7 = 5$	Twelve minus seven is five
·	mal	Multiplikation	times	$3 \cdot 4 = 12$	Three times four is twelve
: oder —	geteilt durch	Division	over, divided by	$6 : 3 = 2$ $\frac{6}{3} = 2$	Six divided by three is two Six over three ist two
=	ist gleich		is, equal to	$v = s/t$	*v* is equal to *s* divided by *t*
%	Prozent		percent, of a hundred	11.3 %	Eleven point three percent
$\_^2$	hoch	Potenzieren	to the second power	4^2	Four to the second power
$\sqrt{\ }$	Wurzel	Wurzel ziehen	square root of	$\sqrt{25}$	Square root of twenty-five
> <	größer als kleiner als	Ungleichheit	greater than less than	a > b c < d	a is greater than b c is less than d

Exercises

1. Name and write the following numerals in English:
   a) 28 b) 85 c) 142 d) 25 000 000 e) 26. f) 104. g) ⅙ h) 2⅓
2. Write down how the formulas are spoken in English.
   a) $W = F \cdot s$ b) $s = \frac{1}{2} \cdot g \cdot t^2$ c) $1\ \text{N} = 1\ \frac{\text{kg} \cdot \text{m}}{\text{s}^2}$ d) $V = l \cdot b \cdot h$ e) $\eta = 86{,}3\,\%$

Dictionary English – German

Wörterbuch Englisch – Deutsch

A

abbreviated form	Kurzform
abbreviation	Abkürzung
abrasion	Abrieb, Abnutzung, Abtrag
abrasive particle	Schleifkorn
abrupt	schlagartig, stoßartig
abrupt load	stoßartige Belastung
absolut scale	Absolutmaßstab
absorption of vibrations	Dämpfung von Schwingungen
AC-current	Wechselstrom
accident	Unfall
accident prevention regulation	Unfallverhütungsvorschrift (UVV)
to accomplish	bewältigen, erzielen
according to	entsprechend, gemäß
to accumulate	sich häufen
accuracy	Genauigkeit
accurate	genau
accurate result	genaues Ergebnis
acetylene	Acetylen
to achieve	erreichen, erfüllen, erhalten, erzielen
acid	Säure
to act	wirken
active agent	Wirkstoff
to adapt	anpassen
to add	hinzufügen, addieren
addition	Zusatz
additional	zusätzlich
additive	zusammenfügend
additive	Zusatz
adhesive coating	Klebeschicht
adhesive joint	Klebeverbindung
adhesive	Klebstoff
adjacent	anschließend, nebenstehend
to adjust	einstellen
adjustment	Einstellung
admissible	zulässig
advantage	Vorteil
affection	Befall
to be afflicted with	mit etwas behaftet sein
ageing	Alterung
ageing resistance	Alterungsbeständigkeit
aid	Hilfsmittel
air	Luft
air cooling	Luftkühlung
air cylinder	Druckluftzylinder
aircraft	Flugzeug
Al-sheet	Al-Blech
to align	ausrichten, fluchten
alkyd resin	Alkydharz
to allow	erlauben
alloyed steel	legierter Stahl
alloying element	Legierungselement
along with	einher mit
alternately	abwechselnd
alternating current (AC)	Wechselstrom
alternating current voltage	Wechselspannung
aluminium	Aluminium
aluminium oxide	Aluminiumoxid
aluminium rods	Aluminiumstäbe
amorphous material	formloser Stoff
amount	Betrag, Höhe, Menge
amount of substance	Stoffmenge
amperemeter	Amperemeter
amplitude	Amplitude, Größe
angle	Winkel
angle steel	Winkelstahl
angular	winkelig
annealing	Glühen
angular ball bearing	Schrägkugellager
annealing furnace	Anlassofen
anodic oxidation	anodische Oxidation
to answer	beantworten
anti-corrosion	korrosionsverhindernd
anvil	Amboss
appealing	ansprechend
to appear	vorkommen, erscheinen
appearance	Aussehen
application	Anwendung
application hardness	Gebrauchshärte
application temperature	Anwendungstemperatur
to apply	anwenden, einsetzen
appropriate	angemessen
approximate	näherungsweise
arc	Lichtbogen
arc furnace	Lichtbogenofen
area for type of fits	Bereiche der Passungsarten
arithmetic average roughness R_a	Mittelrauwert R_a
arithmetic mean	arithmetisches Mittel
to arrange	ordnen, (an)ordnen, zuordnen
arranged	angeordnet
arrow	Pfeil
article of daily use	Gebrauchsgegenstand
as a result	infolgedessen
ascending	aufsteigend
aside	nebenstehend
aspect	Gesichtspunkt
to assemble	montieren, zusammenstellen
assembly	Zusammenbau, Montage, Baugruppe
assembly drawing	Montagezeichnung, Gruppenzeichnung
assembly group	Baugruppe
assembly plan	Montageplan
assembly process	Montagevorgang
assembly technique	Montagetechnik
to assess	beurteilen
to assure	gewährleisten
asynchronous	asynchron
at least	mindestens, wenigstens
at once	sofort
to attach	zuordnen
attachment	Befestigung
attack	Angriff
austenitic steel	austenitischer Stahl
autogenous	autogen
automatic cutout	Sicherungsautomat
automatic lathe	Drehautomat
automobile technology	Kraftfahrzeugtechnik
automotive industry	Automobilindustrie
auxiliary aid	Hilfsmittel
auxiliary scale	Hilfsskala
available	verfügbar
average peak to valley height R_z	Mittlere Rautiefe R_z
average process course	Durchschnittlicher Prozessverlauf
average value	Mittelwert
to avoid	vermeiden
avoidance of error	Fehlervermeidung
axial distance	Achsabstand
axial face seal, mechanical seal	Gleitringdichtung
axial force	Axialkraft
axial movable	axial verschiebbar
axle	Achse

B

back taper	Hinterschneidung
backward	rückwärts
to balance	ausgleichen
ball	Kugel
ball bearing	Kugellager
bar	Stab, Balken, Stange, Schiene
bar chart	Säulendiagramm

bare	blank
barred roller bearing	Tonnenrollenlager
barrel	Fass
bar stock	Stabstahl
base	Basis, Grundplatte, Lauge
base body	Grundkörper
base height	Steghöhe
to base on	basieren auf
base part	Ausgangsteil
base plate	Grundplatte
base quantity	Basiseinheit
base-resin	Basisharz
base shape	Grundform
base tube section	Ausgangs-Rohrabschnitt
basic	einfach
basic function	Grundfunktion
basic hole system	Einheitsbohrung
basic shaft system	Einheitswelle
basic size	Grundabmaß
basic structure	Grundaufbau
basic tolerance	Grundtoleranz
basics	Grundlagen
battery	Batterie
to bear	tragen
bearing balls	Lagerkugeln
bearing bush	Lagerbuchse
bearing cage	Lagerkäfig
bearing cap	Lagerdeckel
bearing centre	Lagermitte
bearing clearance	Lagerspiel
bearing cup	Lagerschale
bearing housing	Lagergehäuse
bearing race	Laufring
bearing shell	Lagerschale
bell-shaped curve	Glockenkurve
belt	Riemen
belt conveyor	Bandförderer
belt drive	Riementrieb
belt transmission	Riemengetriebe
bend allowance	Biege-Ausgleichswert
bend-reforming	Biegeumformen
bending	Biegen, Biegung
bending device	Biegevorrichtung
bending radius (radii)	Biegeradius
bent component	Biegeteil
besides	außerdem
bigger part	größerer Teil
bimetal overcurrent breaker	Bimetall-Überlastschalter
binder	Bindemittel
bit	Meißel
blank	Rohling
blank diameter	Ausgangsdurchmesser
blind hole	Grundloch
block diagram	Blockdiagramm
blowpipe	Schweißbrenner
body frame	Karosserierahmen
bolt	Bolzen, Schraube
bond	Bindung, Verbindung
bonding	Klebung, Bindung, Haftung
bonding metal	Bindemetall
bonding with adhesives	Kleben
bore	Bohrung
bottom	unteres Ende
to bounce	abprallen
bracket	Klammer, Bügel
brainstorming	Ideensammlung
branched assembly	verzweigte Montage
to be branded	versehen sein
brand-new	fabrikneu
brass	Messing
to break	abschalten
breakdown	Betriebsausfall
brittleness	Sprödigkeit
broaching	Räumen
bronze	Bronze
to brush	bürsten
building frame	Gebäudeskelett
bump	Erhebung
to burn	brennen
burner nozzle	Brennerdüse
burr	Grat
bush	Buchse
by the naked eye	mit bloßem Auge

C

cable	Kabel
cable drum	Seiltrommel
cage	Käfig
to calculate	berechnen
calculation	Berechnung
to calibrate	kalibrieren, nachstellen
calibration	Kalibrierung, Einstellung
calliper	Messschieber
cam	Nocke
camshaft	Nockenwelle
cap nut	Hutmutter
capable	fähig
capacitor	Kondensator (elektrisch)
car body frame	Karosserierahmen
car body nodal point	Karosserieknoten
car element	Autobauteil
car sheet metal	Autoblech
car tyre	Autoreifen
car wiper	Scheibenwischer
carbide	Hartmetall
carbide insert	Hartmetalleinsatz
carbide metal, hard metal, carbide	Hartmetall
carbon	Kohlenstoff
carbon brush	Kohlebürste
carbon code number	Kohlenstoffkennzahl
carbon content	Kohlenstoffgehalt
carbon dioxide	Kohlenstoffdioxid
carbon percentage	Kohlenstoffgehalt
carbon steel	unlegierter Baustahl
carburised layer	Kohlenstoff-angereicherte Randschicht
carelessness	Leichtsinn
carrier	Träger
to carry	tragen
to carry out	durchführen, ausführen
case hardened steel	Einsatzstahl
case hardening	Einsatzhärten
cast iron	Gusseisen
cast iron materials	Gusseisenwerkstoffe
cast steel	Stahlguss
casting	Gießen, Gussstück
casting alloy	Gusslegierung
casting mould	Gießform
castle nut	Kronenmutter
to catch	(sich) fangen
category (-ies)	Bereich, Kategorie, Gruppe (Gruppen)
cause	Ursache, Grund
to cause	verursachen
cause-and-effect diagram	Ursache-Wirkungs-Diagramm
to be caused by	verursacht werden von
cavity	Hohlraum
centralise	zentrieren
centre line	Mittellinie
centre punch	Körner
centre support	Werkzeugschlitten
centred	zentriert
centric	mittig
ceramic	Keramik
to certify	zertifizieren
chain drive	Kettentrieb
chain saw	Kettensäge
to change	ändern, verwandeln
character	Buchstabe
to characterise	bestimmen
characteristic	Kennwert, Eigenart, Kennzeichen, Kennzahl
characteristic	charakteristisch
chart	Schaubild
cheese head screw	Zylinderschraube
chemical	chemisch
chemical composition	chemische Zusammensetzung
chemical plant	Chemieanlage, Chemiefabrik
chemical symbol	chemisches Symbol

chip	Span
chip formation	Spanbildung
chip removal	spanabhebend
chip space	Spankammer
chisel	Meißel
chloride-containing	chloridhaltig
chlorinated	gechlort
choice	Auswahl
to choose, chose,chosen	auswählen
chromium	Chrom
chuck	Spannkopf
chucking flange	Spannflansch
circle	Kreis
circuit breaker	Stromkreisunterbrecher
circuit diagram	Schaltplan
circuit in series	Reihenschaltung
circular	rund, kreisförmig
circular saw	Kreissäge
circular spline connection	Kreiskeilverbindung
circumference	Umfang
to clamp	einspannen, spannen, klemmen
clamping device	Spannvorrichtung
clamping mark	Einspannkratzer
clamping table	Aufspanntisch
clamping unit	Spanneinheit
class of accuracy	Genauigkeitsklasse
classification	Einteilung
to classify	unterteilen, einteilen
claw coupling	Klauenkupplung
to clean	reinigen
cleaning slag	Reiningungsschlacke
clear varnish	Klarlack
clearance	Spiel
clearance angle	Freiwinkel
clearance fit	Spielpassung
clipping eyelets	Einhängeösen
close	eng
to close	schließen
close-tolerance bolt	Passschraube
cloth	Tuch
cloud	Wolke
coarse grain	Grobkorn
to coat	beschichten
coating	Beschichtung, Beschichten
cobalt	Cobalt
code	Kurzzeichen
code letter	Kennbuchstabe
code number factor	Kennzahlfaktor
coefficient of friction	Reibungszahl
coherence	Zusammenhalt
coil	Bandrolle, Wicklung
cold work steel	Kaltarbeitsstahl
to collect	sammeln
collective return line	gemeinsamer Rückleiter
column	Säule, Spalte
combined sliding and rolling friction	Wälzreibung
combustible	brennbar
combustion engine	Verbrennungskraftmaschine
common	üblich, häufig
communication	Kommunikation
to commutate	umpolen
commutator	Kommutator (Stromwender)
compact	kompakt, fest
comparable	vergleichbar
to compare	vergleichen
comparison	Vergleich
comparison measurement	Unterschiedsmessung
to compensate	ausgleichen
complete	ganz, vollständig
complex	kompliziert
component	Einzelteil, Bestandteil, Bauteil
component drawing	Teilzeichnung
to compose of	bestehen aus
to be composed of	bestehen aus
composed	zusammengesetzt, bestehend
composite material	Verbundwerkstoff
composition	Zusammensetzung
to compress	verdichten
compressed air	Druckluft
compression moulding	Formpressen unter Druck
compression strength	Druckfestigkeit
compressor	Verdichter
to comprise	umfassen
computer	Rechner, Datenverarbeitungsanlage
computer-aided	rechnergestützt
computer aided design (CAD)	computergestütztes Konstruieren
concentricity	Rundlaufgenauigkeit
concerning	betreffend
condition	Zustand
conditioning	Behandlung
to conduct	ausführen
conducting	leitend
conductor	Stromleiter
conductor material	Leiterwerkstoff
conductor resistance	Leiterwiderstand
conic	konisch
conical head	kegeliger Kopf
to connect (mechan.)	verbinden (mechan.)
to connect (electr.)	verschalten (elektrisch)
connected	nachgeschaltet
connected in series	in Serie geschaltet
connection	Verbindung
connection box	Anschlusskasten
connection spot	Anschluss
to conquer	erobern
conserving	Erhalten
to consider	berücksichtigen
considerably	beträchtlich
to consist of	bestehen aus
consistent	beherrscht
constriction	Einschnürung
to construct	konstruieren
construction	Aufbau
construction components	Konstruktionsbauteile
construction element	Konstruktionsbauteil
construction steel	Baustahl
construction units	Baueinheiten
consumer	Verbraucher
consumption	Verbrauch
contact	Berührung
contact pressure	Anpressdruck
contact surface	Berührungsfläche
to contain	enthalten
container	Behälter
content	Gehalt
continuous	fortlaufend
continuous operation	Dauerbetrieb
continuous variable	stufenlos einstellbar
contour	Kontur
contour turning	Formdrehen
contrary	entgegengesetzt
control	Steuerung
to control	steuern
control line	Eingriffsgrenze
control panel	Schalttafel, Bedienfeld
control unit	Steuereinheit
to convert	umrechnen, umwandeln
conveyor	Fördermittel
cooling	Abkühlen
cooling lubricant	Kühlschmiermittel
coordinate system	Koordinatensystem
cope box	Oberkasten
copper	Kupfer
copper alloy	Kupferlegierung
copper coin	Kupfermünze
core	Kern
core hole	Kernloch
corner angle	Eckenwinkel
corner milling	Eckfräsen
to correct	korrigieren
to correlate	entsprechen
correlation	Beziehung
corrosion	Korrosion
corrosion cell	Korrosionselement
corrosion protection	Korrosionsschutz
corrosion resistance	Korrosionsbeständigkeit

corrosion-resistant	korrosionsbeständig
corrosion-resistant steel	korrosionsbeständiger Stahl
corundum	Korund
cost-efficient	kostengünstig
to count	zählen
to count up	aufaddieren
to counteract	entgegenwirken
to counterbore	senken
countersink	Senker
to countersink, countersank, countersunk	ansenken
countersinking	Senkung
countersunk screw	Senkschraube
coupling	Kupplung
course	Verlauf
cover	Deckel, Deckschicht
to cover	bedecken
covered	umhüllt
covering	Umhüllung
crack	Riss
crane system	Krananlage
crankcase	Kurbelgehäuse
crankshaft	Kurbelwelle
crater corrosion	Muldenkorrosion
to create	erzeugen, herstellen, anfertigen
criteria	Kriterium
cross	Kreuz
cross feed	Quervorschub
cross section	Querschnitt
cross section figure conductor loop	Querschnittsbild-Leiterschleife
cross sectional area	Querschnittsfläche
cross slide	Querschlitten
to cross	überschreiten
cross-cut	Kreuzhieb
crossbar	Querbalken
crude oil	Erdöl
crumbling	ausbröckeln
cumulative total	kumulierte Gesamtzahl
current	laufend, Strom
current carrying line	stromführende Leitung
current conductivity	Stromleitung
current network	Leitungsnetz, Stromnetz
current rate	Stromstärke
current rating	Stromstärke
curve	Kurve
customer	Kunde
customer service	Kundendienst
customer specification	Kundenanforderung
to cut freely	freischneiden
cut	Hieb
cut number	Hiebzahl
to cut off	abtrennen
cut-off	Einzelmessstrecke
cutout	elektr. Sicherung
cutting	Trennen, Spanen
cutting angle	Spanwinkel
cutting ceramics	Schneidkeramik
cutting chisel	Drehmeißel
cutting data	Schnittdaten
cutting depth	Schnitttiefe, Zustelltiefe
cutting edge	Werkzeugschneide, Schneidkeil
cutting face	Spanfläche
cutting insert	Schneideplatte
cutting material	Schneidstoff
cutting motion	Schnittbewegung
cutting oil	Schneidöl
cutting punch	Schneidstempel
cutting tip	Schneidplättchen
cutting velocity	Schnittgeschwindigkeit
cutting wedge	Schneidkeil
cutting wedge angle	Einstellwinkel
cyclical	Periode, Zyklus
cylinder	Zylinder
cylinder bottom	Zylinderboden
cylinder cutter	Walzenfräser
cylinder flange	Zylinderflansch
cylinder head	Zylinderkopf
cylindrical	zylindrisch
cylindrical grinding	Rundschleifen
cylindrical head	zylindrischer Kopf
cylindrical roller	Zylinderrolle
cylindrical roller bearing	Zylinderrollenlager

D

to damage	beschädigen
damage	Zerstörung, Beschädigung
damaged	beschädigt
damaged spot	Schadstelle
to dampen	abschwächen
damping screw	Dämpfungsschraube
danger	Gefahr
dangerous to life	lebensgefährlich
dark	dunkel
data	Daten
data processing equipment	Datenverarbeitungsanlage
data quantity(ies)	Datenmenge(n)
data value	Datenwert
date of edition	Ausgabedatum
DC-current	Gleichstrom
DC motor	Gleichstrommotor
to deburr	entgraten
decarbonisation	Entkohlen
decarbonising	entkohlend
to decide	entscheiden
decimal multiples	dezimale Vielfache
to declare	angeben, nennen
decline	Minderung, Abnahme
to decrease	abnehmen, vermindern, verringern
decreasing trend	fallende Tendenz
deep drawing	Tiefziehen
deep groove ball bearing	Rillenkugellager
deep-drawing	Tiefziehen
deepening	Vertiefung
defect	Fehler, Störung
defect chart	Fehlersammelliste
to define	definieren
defined	festgelegt
definite size	bestimmte Größe
to deform	verformen
to deform permanently	bleibend verformen
to be deformed	verformt sein
degree	Grad
degree of accuracy	Genauigkeitsgrad
to delay	verzögern
delivered	angeliefert
dense networked	dicht vernetzt
density	Dichte
to depend on	abhängig sein von, abhängen von
depending on wire electrode	je nach Drahtelektrode
to deplace	abheben
depth	Zustellung, Tiefe
depth gauge	Tiefenmaß
derived quantity	abgeleitete Größe
to derust	entrosten
to describe	bezeichnen, beschreiben
to design	gestalten
to designate	beschriften, bezeichnen
designation	Bezeichnung
designation code	Kurzbezeichnung
designation system	Bezeichnungssystem
desired	gewünscht
to destroy	zerstören
destroyed	zerstört
detachable	lösbar
detachable connection	lösbare Verbindung
to detect	erkennen
determination	Ermittlung, Festlegung
to determine	bestimmen, festlegen
developed length	gestreckte Länge
to deviate	abweichen
deviation	Abweichung
device	Gerät
device housing	Gerätegehäuse
to devide	teilen
dial indicator	Messuhr

diameter	Durchmesser
die	Stempel
die casting	Druckgießen
die cutter	Gesenkfräser
die forging	Gesenkschmieden
to differ	sich unterscheiden
difference	Unterschied
different	verschieden, unterschiedlich
digital calliper	digitaler Messschieber
dimension	Größe
dimensional change	Größenänderung
dimensional relationship	Größenbeziehung
dimensional representative	Maßverkörperung
dimensional tolerance	Maßtoleranz
to dip	tauchen
direct current (DC)	Gleichstrom
direct current voltage	Gleichspannung
direction	Richtung
direction of rotation	Drehrichtung
direction of the centre	Zentrumsrichtung
directional valve	Wegeventil
dirt	Schmutz
disadvantage	Nachteil
disadvantageous	nachteilig
to disassemble	demontieren
disassembly	Demontage
disc milling cutter	Scheibenfräser
disc-shaped	scheibenförmig
discharge	Auslaufen, Austritt
disconnection point	Trennstelle
disc	Scheibe
displacement	Weg, Strecke, Versetzung
displacement force	Verschiebekraft
display	Anzeige, Display
to display	anzeigen, darstellen
display format	Darstellungsart
disposal	Beseitigung
to dissipate	ableiten, abführen
to dissolve	auflösen
distance	Entfernung, Weg
distinction	Unterscheidung
distinctive feature	Unterscheidungsmerkmal
to distinguish	unterteilen, unterscheiden
distribution	Verteilung
diverse	unterschiedlich, verschieden
to divide	unterscheiden, teilen
to be divided	aufgeteilt sein in
divided by	geteilt durch, dividiert durch
divider	Spitzzirkel
division	Teilung
double row	zweireihig
down-cut milling	Gleichlauffräsen
downsprue	Einguss
downtime	Stillstand
drag box	Unterkasten
drain	Abfluss
to draw	zeichnen, skizzieren
drawing	Zeichnung
drawing ratio	Ziehverhältnis
to be drawn	gezogen werden
drill	Bohrer
drill chuck	Bohrfutter
drill hole	Bohrloch
drill point	Bohrerspitze
drill spindle	Bohrspindel
drilling machine	Bohrmaschine
drilling process	Bohrvorgang
drilling table	Bohrtisch
drive shaft	Antriebswelle
drive spindle	Antriebsspindel
drive type connection	Mitnehmer-Verbindung
drive unit	Antriebseinheit
to drive	antreiben
driven	angetrieben
driving	(an-)treibend
driving component	Antriebsbauteil
driving current	Antriebsstrom
driving motor	Antriebsmotor
driving shaft	Antriebswelle
to drop	herunterfallen
ductile	zäh, dehnbar
ductile values	Zähigkeitswerte
ductility	Zähigkeit
to be due	bedingt werden durch
due to	aufgrund
due to this	daher
dungarees	Latzhose
dust	Staub
dust mask	Staubmaske
dynamic seal	Bewegungsdichtung
dynamic stressed	dynamisch belastet

E

ear muff	Gehörschutz
ear plug	Ohrstöpsel
earthing	Erdung
earth leakage	Erdschluss
earthed	geerdet
ease of motion	Leichtgängigkeit
economic	kostengünstig
eddy current	Wirbelstrom
edge	Schneidkante
to effect	bewirken
effective power	Wirkleistung
efficiency	Wirkungsgrad
efficient	effizient, kostengünstig
e.g. (for example)	z.B. (zum Beispiel)
elastic	elastisch
Elastomer plastic	Elastomer
electric charge	elektrische Ladung
electric circuit	Stromkreis
electric coil	elektrische Wicklung
electric conductivity	elektrische Leitfähigkeit
electric conductor	Stromleiter
electric counter	Zähler
electric current	elektrischer Strom
electric insulating	elektrisch isolierend
electric line	elektrische Leitung
electric load	Verbraucher
electric motor	Elektromotor
electric network	Stromnetz
electric power	elektrische Leistung
electric power company	Elektroversorgungsunternehmen
electric resistance	elektrischer Widerstand (physikalische Größe)
electric voltage	elektrische Spannung
electric work	elektrische Arbeit
electrical engineering	Elektrotechnik
electrically insulating	elektrisch isolierend
electrochemical reaction	elektrochemische Reaktion
electrode rod	Stabelektrode
electrolyte	Elektrolyt
electromagnetic inductor	elektromagnetische Spule
electronic chip	elektronischer Chip
electron	Elektron
electrotechnical	elektrotechnisch
to eliminate	beseitigen
elimination	Beseitigung
elongation	Verlängerung
elongation at fracture	Bruchdehnung
embrittlement	Versprödung
emergency	Notfall
emergency exit	Notausgang
emergency stop button	Not-Aus-Schalter
employee	Arbeitnehmer, Mitarbeiter
emulsion	Emulsion
emulsive	emulgierbar
to enable	ermöglichen
90°-end cutter	90°-Schaftfräser
end milling cutter	Schaftfräser
energy transforming	energieumsetzend
engine	Motor, Kraftmaschine
enginneering	Konstruktion
engineers square	Haarwinkel

to ensure	sicherstellen
to enter	eindringen, eintragen
entire	gesamt
entry	Eindringen
entry fit	Ansatz-Passung
environment	Umwelt, Umgebung
environmental	umgebungsbedingt
equal	gleich
to equal	ausgleichen, gleichen
equals	entspricht, ist gleich
equal surface corrosion	gleichmäßige Flächenkorrosion
equation	Formel, Gleichung
equipment	Vorrichtung, Einrichtung
error	Fehler
escape and rescue sign	Rettungszeichen
essential	wesentlich
to establish	herstellen
to evaluate	auswerten
evaluation length	Messstrecke
to evaporate	verdampfen
even	eben, noch, sogar
evenly	gleichmäßig
even number	gerade Anzahl
to examine	untersuchen
example	Beispiel
except	außer
exception	Ausnahme
excess	Überschuss
exchange repair	Auswechselung
to execute	ausführen, durchführen
to exhibit	darstellen
to be existent	vorliegen
expansion coefficient	Ausdehnungskoeffizient
to expect	erwarten
expendable casting	Gießen in verlorene Form
expensive	teuer
exploded view drawing	Explosionsdarstellung
expression	Ausdruck
expression at length	ausführlicher Begriff
external	Außen-
external hexagon	Außensechskant
external pump	externe Pumpe
external turning	Außendrehen
extract	Ausschnitt
extreme	Grenzwert
extruder screw	Extruderschnecke
extrusion die	Pressstempel
extrusion moulding	Strangpressen
extrusion profile	Strangpressprofil
eye	Auge

F

face milling cutter	Planfräser
face shield	Gesichtschutz
to facilitate	erleichtern
facing	Plandrehen
to fail	scheitern
fast	schnell
fastening thread	Befestigungsgewinde
fatigue strength	Dauerfestigkeit
fault	Fehler, Störung
fault circuit interruptor	Fehlerstrom-Schutzschalter
fault current	Fehlerstrom
fault detection	Fehlerentdeckung
faultless	fehlerfrei
faultless parts	fehlerfreie Teile
feather key	Passfeder
feather key connection	Passfederverbindung
feature	Größe, Merkmal
feed	Vorschub
feed direction	Vorschubrichtung
feed gear	Vorschubgetriebe
feed lever	Vorschubhebel
feed motion	Vorschubbewegung
feed motor	Vorschubmotor
feed of the drill	Bohrervorschub
feed of the table	Tischvorschub
feed power	Vorschubkraft
feed speed	Vorschubgeschwindigkeit
feed unit	Vorschubeinheit
feed velocity	Vorschubgeschwindigkeit
to feed, fed, fed	zuführen
fibre-reinforced	faserverstärkt
filamentary	fadenförmig
file	Feile
file shaft	Feilenschaft
file tooth, pl. teeth	Feilenzahn
filing	Feilen
filing marks	Riefen
filler metal	Zusatzstoff
filter	Filter
final check	Endkontrolle
final position	Endlage
final result	Endergebnis
final speed	Enddrehzahl
fine detail	Einzelheit
fine finishing	Feinbearbeitung
fingernail	Fingernagel
finish	Endbehandlung
to finish	endbearbeiten
finished	fertig bearbeitet
finished part	Fertigteil
finishing	Schlichten, Endbearbeitung
fire extinguisher	Feuerlöscher
firmly locking	stoffschlüssig
first aid box	Erste-Hilfe-Kasten
fishbone	Fischgräte
FI-switch	FI-Schalter
fit	Passung
to fit exactly	genau einpassen
fit system	Passungssystem
to fit tightly	fest einpassen
fitting surface	Passfläche
five line cable	fünfadriges Kabel
to fix	befestigen
fixed	fest, fixiert, feststehend
fixed bearing	Festlager
fixing screw	Befestigungsschraube, Halteschraube
flaky	plättchenförmig
flat	eben
flat	Flacherzeugnis
flat belt	Flachriemen
flat head screw	Senkschraube
flat rolled	flach gewalzt
flat seal	Flachdichtungen
flat steel	Flachstahl
flat-ground	plangeschliffen
flatness	Ebenheit
flexible	weich, dehnbar
flexible washer	federnde Scheibe
to float	schwimmen
floating bearing	Loslager
flow	Strom
flowing behaviour	Fließverhalten
fluid	Flüssigkeit
fluid flow energy	Strömungsenergie
fluid friction	Flüssigkeitsreibung
fluid power motor	Hydromotor
to flush away	fortspülen
flux	Flussmittel
to foam	schäumen
foil	Folie
folding meter (folding rule)	Gliedermaßstab
folding meter	Meterstab
following	folgende
foot	Fuß
forbidden	verboten
force	Kraft
force locking	kraftschlüssig
foreign body	Fremdkörper
forging	Schmiedestück, Schmieden
forging die	Schmiedegesenk
forging temperature	Schmiedetemperatur
to form	bilden
form, shape	Form
form-exact	formgenau
form-locking	formschlüssig
formability	Formbarkeit
formative	gestaltend
formed part	Formteil
formless	formlos
formula	Formel
to fortify	verstärken
forward	vorwärts

foundry	Gießerei
frame	Rahmen, Bügel, Halterung
free cutting alloy	Automatenlegierung
free cutting steel	Automatenstahl
freehand sketch	Freihandskizze
frequency	Häufigkeit, Frequenz
friction	Reibung
friction type	Reibungsart
front	Vorderseite
front side face milling	Stirn-Planfräsen
fuel gas	Brenngas
to fulfil	erfüllen
full mould casting	Vollformgießen
to function	wirken, dienen
functional assembly	Funktionsbaugruppe
functional check	Funktionsprüfung
functional product	Gebrauchserzeugnis
functional unit	Funktionseinheit
fundamental	grundlegend
fundamental deviation	Grundabmaß
fundamentals	Grundlagen
furnace	Glühofen
fuse	Schmelzsicherung

G

Galton board	Galton Brett
galvanic element	galvanisches Element
galvanising	Galvanisieren
to galvanize	galvanisieren
gap	Spalt, Lücke
gas	Gas
gas fusion welding	Gasschmelzschweißen
gas supply	Gasversorgung
gas-shielding arc welding	Schutzgas-Lichtbogenschweißen
gauge	Lehre
gauge block	Endmaß
gauge block stack	Endmaßstapel
Gaussian distribution	Gauß'sche Verteilung
gear	Getriebe
gear-box	Getriebe
gear housing	Getriebegehäuse
to gear into each other	ineinandergreifen
gear pair	Zahnradpaar
gear shaft	Getriebewelle
gear unit	Getriebeeinheit
gear-wheel	Zahnrad
gear wheel drive	Zahnradtrieb
general arrangement drawing	Gesamtzeichnung
to generate	erzeugen
to be generated	entstehen durch
geometrical determinated form	geometrisch bestimmte Form
geometry	geometrische Form
gland	Stopfbuchsbrille
glass pane	Glasscheibe
gliding area	Gleitfläche
Go side	Gutseite
go-and-return line	Hin- und Rückleitung
gradient of inclination	Neigung
grain	Korn, Gefügekorn
grain orientation	Faserverlauf
grain size	Korngröße
graphical aid	grafisches Hilfsmittel
gravity die casting	Kokillengießen
to grease	fetten, schmieren
greased	eingefettet
Great Britain	Großbritannien
great number	große Anzahl
grey cast iron	Grauguss
to grind, ground, ground	schleifen, schliff, geschliffen
grinding	Schleifen
grinding wheel	Schleifscheiben
gripper	Zange
groove	Nut, Rille, Fuge
groove distance	Rillenabstand
groove nut	Nutmutter
grooved ring	Nutringdichtung
ground	geschliffen
grounded socket outlet	Schutzkontakt-Steckdose
group assembly	Gruppenmontage
to be grouped in	in Gruppen unterteilt sein
to guarantee	garantieren
guard	Schutz
guide	Führung
guide bush	Führungsbuchse
guide carriage	Führungsschlitten
guide groove guiding	Führungsrille
guideline	Richtlinie
guide rail	Führungsleiste
guideway	Führungsbahn

H

H-beam	Breitflanschträger
hacksaw	Bügelsäge
hair net	Haarnetz
hammer	Hammer
to hammer	schlagen, einschlagen
hand casting	Handguss
hand chisel	Handmeißel
handheld	handgeführt
handheld machine tool	handgeführte Werkzeugmaschine
handle	Handgriff
handwheel	Handrad
to happen	entstehen, auftreten, stattfinden
hard material	Hartstoff
hard material grain	Hartstoffkorn
hard metal	Hartmetall
to harden	(aus-)härten
hardened	gehärtet
hardened skin	gehärtete Randschicht
hardened steel	gehärteter Stahl
hardening	Härten
hardening and tempering	vergüten
hardening shop	Härterei
hardness	Härte
hardness test	Härteprüfung
hazard	Gefahr
head stock	Spindelkasten, Spindelstock
heading	Überschrift
health	Gesundheit
heat	Hitze, Wärme
heat exchanger	Wärmetauscher
heating	Erwärmung
heat insulation	Wärmedämmung
heat treatment furnace	Wärmebehandlungsofen
heat treatment	Wärmebehandlung
to heat	erwärmen
heating flame	Heizflamme
heavy metal	Schwermetall
height	Höhe, Größe
height adjustment	Höhenverstellung
helical	wendelförmig
helical spring	Spiralfeder
helix angle	Drallwinkel
hewn file teeth	gehauene Feilenzähne
hexagon head cap screw	Sechskantschraube
hexagonal	sechseckig
hexagon nut	Sechskantmutter
high	groß, hoch
high grade	hochwertig
high mechanical	mechanisch hoch
high performance steel	Hochleistungsstahl
high power	leistungsstark
high speed steel	Schnellarbeitsstahl
to highlight	hervortreten
histogram	Histogramm
hole (bore)	Loch (Bohrung)
hole maximum dimension	Höchstmaß Bohrung
hole minimum dimension	Mindestmaß Bohrung
hollow body	Hohlkörper
hollow profile	Hohlprofil
homogenising screw	Knetschnecke
hook	Haken
Hooke's line	Hooke'sche Gerade

horizontal	waagrecht
hose	Schlauch
hot-air blower	Heißluftgebläse
hot-dip zinc coating	Feuerverzinken
hot hardness	Warmhärte
hot rolled bar	warm gewalzter Stabstahl
hot rolled sheet	warm gewalztes Blech
hot sintered	heiß gesintert
hot work steel	Warmarbeitsstahl
housing	Gehäuse
housing-cover	Gehäusedeckel
housing leakage	Körperschluss, Gehäuseschluss
however	jedoch
hub	Nabe
hub keyway	Nabennut
hub keyway base	Nabennut-Grund
human	Mensch
human body	menschlicher Körper
human failure	menschliches Versagen
humidity	Feuchtigkeit
hundredfold	hundertfach
hydraulic cylinder	Hydraulikzylinder
hydraulic fluid	Hydraulikflüssigkeit
hydraulic oil	Hydrauliköl
hydrodynamic	hydrodynamisch
hydrogen	Wasserstoff
hydrostatic	hydrostatisch

I

I-beam	I-Träger
i.e., von lat. id est	d.h. (das heißt)
idea	Vorstellung
identically	gleichlautend
identification code	Kennzeichnungscode, Kurzbezeichnung
to identify	kennzeichnen, erkennen
idle speed	Leerlaufdrehzahl
liquid	Flüssigkeit
to illustrate	darstellen
imperial unit	britisch-amerikanische Maßeinheit
to implement	umsetzen
importance	Wichtigkeit, Bedeutung
important	wichtig
impregnated	getränkt
impression specimen	Eindrückkörper
to improve	verbessern
improvement	Verbesserung
impulse scale	Impulsmaßstab
in a row	in einer Reihe
in accordance	gemäß
in case of	im Fall von
in contrary	im Gegensatz
in detail	ausführlich
in front of	vor
in the long run	auf Dauer
in the order	in der Reihenfolge
inaccurate	ungenau
inappropriate	ungünstig
to include	beinhalten, enthalten, einschließen
to increase	erhöhen, steigern
increase	Erhöhung
indentation	Eindrücken
to indicate	kennzeichnen, angeben, anzeigen
indicated value	angezeigter Wert
indication	Bezeichnung
indicative measuring devices	anzeigende Messgeräte
individual	einzelne
individual data	Einzelwert
induce	induzieren
to induce	erzeugen, induzieren
inductive resistance	induktiver Widerstand
industrial ceramic	Industriekeramik
industrial field	industrieller Bereich
inert	inert (nicht reagierend)
infeed	Zustellung
inflection point	Wendepunkt
influence	Wirkung, Einfluss
information	Information
ingression	Eindringen
initial	anfänglich
initial cross-section area	anfänglicher Bauteilquerschnitt
initial length	Anfangslänge, Anfangsmesslänge
initial speed	Anfangsdrehzahl
injection mould	Spritzgießform
injury	Verletzung
immediately	sofort
inner face	Innenseite
to insert	einsetzen
insert screw	Einziehschraube
insert tip	Wendeschneidplatte
inspection	Überprüfung, Inspektion
inspection aid	Messmittel
installation	Einbau
instruction	Anleitung
instructor	Ausbilder
insulating material	isolierender Werkstoff
insulation	Isolation
insulation plate	Isolierplatte
interaction	Zusammenwirken
interdependence	Zusammenhang
to interface	verbinden
to interfere	überlagern
interference fit	Übermaßpassung
intermediate layer	Mittellage
intermittent	unterbrochen
internal	Innen-
internal diameter	Innendurchmesser
internal hexagon	Innensechskant
internal pressure	Innendruck
internal pressure reforming	Innendruck-Umformen
internal shape	Innenform
internal thread	Innengewinde
internal turning	Innendrehen
to interrupt	unterbrechen
intersection point	Schnittpunkt
interval	Zeitabschnitt
to introduce	einführen
investment casting	Feingießen
invisible	unsichtbar
to be involved	miteinbezogen sein
IP-code number	IP-Kennziffer
iron	Eisen
iron-cast material	Gusswerkstoff
irregular	ungleichmäßig
irregularity	Unregelmäßigkeit
to issue	erlassen

J

jaw	Schenkel
jet engine	Strahltriebwerk
jewellery	Schmuckstück
jig	Vorrichtung
to join	fügen
joining technology	Fügeverfahren
joining	Fügen
to justify	begründen

K

to keep	behalten
to keep free	freihalten
keyboard	Tastatur
key fob	Schlüsselanhänger
kilogram	Kilogramm
kinetic energy	Bewegungsenergie
knurled nut	Rändelmutter

L

to label	beschriften, benennen
label	Etikett
labyrinth seal	Labyrinthdichtung
lamellar graphite	Lamellengrafit
laminated sheet stack	Blechpaket
to lap	läppen
lapped	geläppt
lateral forces	Querkräfte
lateral surface	Seitenfläche
lathe	Drehmaschine

lathe chuck	Drehmaschinenfutter
lathe slide	Bettschlitten
lathe tool	Drehwerkzeug
to lay out (laid, laid)	bereitlegen
layer	Schicht
lead	Blei
to lead back (led, led)	zuführen
to lead to	führen zu
leak-proof	dicht
leakage	Leckverlust
leakproofness	Dichtheit
least	wenigsten(s)
to leave	austreten, verlassen
left-hand twist	Linksdrall
length	Länge
less fluid	dickflüssig
letter	Buchstabe
levelled	ausgerichtet
levelling	Einebnen
lever	Hebel
to lie (lay, lain)	liegen
life time	Lebensdauer, Standzeit
lifting equipment	Hebezeug
lifting eye nut	Ringmutter
light	hell
light gap	Lichtspalt
light metal	Leichtmetall
light source angle	Lichteinfallwinkel
light weight construction	Leichtbaukonstruktion
to limit	begrenzen
limit line	Grenzlinie
line	Zeile, Leitung
linear	linienförmig, geradlinig
line chart	Liniendiagramm
line leakage	Leiterschluss
to line up	übereinstimmen
linear assembly	unverzweigte Montage
lip seal	Lippendichtung
liquid	flüssig, Flüssigkeit
liquid friction	Flüssigkeitsreibung
to list	aufführen, aufzählen
list of measured values	Messwertreihe
load	Belastung, Tragfähigkeit
load (electric)	Verbraucher (elektr.)
load torque	Lastmoment
loaded	belastet
loaded by tension	auf Zug belastet
loading	Belastung
loading capacity	Belastbarkeit
to locate	anordnen
lock	Feststellung, Sicherung, Sperre
to lock	klemmen
locking device	Losdrehsicherung
locking ring	Sicherungsring
locking screw	Feststellschraube, Stiftschraube
long chipping	langspanend
long rolled product	Langerzeugnis
long-term period	langfristiger Zeitraum
longitudinal force	Umfangskraft
longitudinal turning	Längsdrehen
loosely fixed	lose fixiert
loosened	gelöst
loss of material	Materialverlust
lost	verloren
low	niedrig
low cost	preiswert
low maintenance	wartungsarm
low melting	niedrig schmelzend
low-melting solder	niedrig schmelzendes Lot
lower	untere
to lower	senken
lower limit size	Mindestmaß
lower limit value	unterer Grenzwert
lubricant	Schmiermittel
to lubricate	schmieren, ölen
lubricating grease	Schmierfett
lubricating oil	Schmieröl
lubricating oil supply	Schmierölzufuhr
lubrication	Schmierung
lubrication equipment	Schmiereinrichtung
lubrication film	Schmierfilm
lubrication gap	Schmierspalt
lubrication point	Schmierstelle
lubrication system	Schmiersystem
luminous intensity	Lichtstärke

M

machine	Maschine
machine base	Maschinenfuß
machine bed	Maschinenbett
machine capability	Maschinenfähigkeit
machine capability index	Maschinenfähigkeitsindex
machine capability test (MCT)	Maschinenfähigkeitsuntersuchung (MFU)
machine casting	Maschinenguss
machine component	Maschinenbauteil
machine frame	Maschinengestell
machine knife (knives)	Maschinenmesser
machine operator	Maschinenbediener
machine setting	Maschinen-Einstellgröße
machine table	Maschinentisch
machine tap	Maschinengewindebohrer
machine tool	Werkzeugmaschine
machine vice	Maschinenschraubstock
machined	maschinell bearbeitet
machined surface	bearbeitete Oberfläche
machining center	Bearbeitungszentrum
machining chips	Späne
machining forces	Bearbeitungskräfte
machining process	spanender Bearbeitungsvorgang
machining variable	Zerspanungsgröße
machining variables	Spanungsgrößen
magnesium	Magnesium
magnetic field	Drehfeld
magnification	Vergrößerung
magnifying glass	Lupe
mail order	Bestellung
main	Haupt-
main branch	Hauptast, Hauptstelle
main dimension	Hauptabmessung
main function	Hauptfunktion
main scale	Hauptskale
main symbol	Hauptsymbol
main task	Hauptaufgabe
mainly	überwiegend
to maintain	aufrechterhalten
maintainability	Instandhaltungsfähigkeit
maintenance	Wartung, Instandhaltung
maintenance list	Wartungsliste
maintenance worker	Wartungsarbeiter
major	bedeutend, Haupt-
major edge	Hauptschneide
malfunction	Störung
malleable	schmiedbar
malleable cast iron	Temperguss
man, men	Mensch, Menschen
mandatory sign	Gebotszeichen
mandrel	Biegerolle, Dorn
manganese percentage	Mangangehalt
manifold	vielfältig
manipulated	geschönt
manpower	Arbeitskraft
manual	manuell
manual arc welding	Lichtbogenhandschweißen
manual gearbox	Schaltgetriebe
manual worker	Arbeiter
manufacturer	Hersteller
manufacturing cost	Herstellungskosten
manufacturing process	Fertigungsverfahren

mark	Markierung
to mark	hervorheben
marking	Markierung, Anreißen
marking gauge	Höhenreißer
marking paint	Anreißlack
marking table	Anreißtisch
martensitic steel	martensitischer Stahl
mass	Masse
mass component	Massenteil
mass product articles	massengefertigte Produkte
mass production component	Massenprodukt
to match	erfüllen, zuordnen
matching	zusammengehörend
material	Werkstoff
material behaviour	Werkstoffverhalten
material combination	Werkstoffpaarung
material engineering	Werkstofftechnik
material fatigue	Werkstoffermüdung
material removal	Materialabtrag
material transforming	stoffumsetzend
material-locking	stoffschlüssig
mating	passend
matrix	Grundgerüst, Matrix
matt (surface)	matt (Oberfläche)
maximum force	Höchstkraft
maximum limit size	Höchst-Grenzmaß
maximum peak to valley height R_{max}	Maximale Rautiefe R_{max}
mean	Mittelwert
to mean	bedeuten
mean chart	Mittelwertkarte
mean line	Mittellinie
mean value	Mittelwert
measure	Maßnahme, Maß
to measure	messen, vermessen
measuring	Messen
measuring capability	Messfähigkeit
measuring device	Messgerät
measuring error	Messfehler
measuring face	Messfläche
measuring force	Messkraft
measuring instrument	Prüfmittel
measuring task	Messaufgabe
measuring technique	Messtechnik
measuring tube	Messschenkel
mechanical	mechanisch
mechanical engineering	Maschinenbau, Maschinentechnik
mechanical load fracture	mechanische Bruchbelastung
median value	Medianwert
medium	mittlere
melt	Schmelze
melting furnace	Schmelzofen
melting point	Schmelzpunkt
melting temperature	Schmelzpunkt
melting wire	Schmelzdraht
to mention	nennen, erwähnen
mesh size	Maschenweite
metal	Metall
metal cage	Metallkäfig
metal coating	Metallbeschichtung
metal cutting machine tool	zerspanende Werkzeugmaschine
Metal Engineering Textbook	Fachkunde Metall
metal cutting manufacturing process	spanendes Fertigungsverfahren
metal powder	Metallpulver
metal rod	Metallstab
micrometer screw gauge	Bügelmessschraube
microscopic	mikroskopisch
microstructural change	Mikrogefügeänderung
microstructure	Mikrostruktur
milky-looking	milchartig
milling	Fräsen
milling cutter	Fräser
milling head	Fräskopf
milling tool	Fräswerkzeug
millionfold	Millionenfaches
mind map	Gedankenstütze
mineral oil	Mineralöl
minimal insertion	minimaler Ansatz, Anschnäbelung
minimal yield strength	Mindest-Streckgrenze
to minimize	minimieren
minor diameter	Kerndurchmesser
minor edge	Nebenschneide
mixed ceramics	Mischkeramik
mixed friction	Mischreibung
mixing ratio	Mischverhältnis
mode of action	Wirkungsweise
mode of function	Wirkungsweise
mode of operation	Betriebsweise, Wirkungsweise, Arbeitsweise
moderate load	mittlere Belastung
modification	Änderung
modification of material	Stoffeigenschaftsänderung
module	Modul
molten metal	Metallschmelze
molybdenum	Molybdän
most common	gebräuchlichste, häufigste
most effective	effektivste
motor block	Motorblock
motor coil	Motorwicklung
motor fuel	Kraftstoff
motor shaft	Motorwelle
motor speed	Motordrehzahl
motor torque	Motordrehmoment
mould	Form
to mould	formpressen
moulded	geformt
moulding	Formpressen
moulding procedure	Formverfahren
moulding tool	Formwerkzeug
to mount	zusammenbauen, befestigen, lagern
mounting diameter	Einbaudurchmesser
movable	beweglich
to move	bewegen
movement	Bewegung
multi-blade	mehrschneidig
multi-edged	vielschneidig
multi-stage	mehrstufig
multiform	vielgestaltig
to multiply by	multiplizieren mit
mutual guide	gegenseitige Führung

N

naked eye	mit bloßem Auge
to name	benennen
narrow	eng
to narrow	verengen
narrow gap	enger Spalt
necessary	notwendig, erforderlich
necking	Einschnürung
to need	benötigen
needle bearing	Nadellager
neutral flame	neutrale Flamme
neutral line	neutrale Faser
neutral line (elect.)	Neutralleiter (elektr.)
to neutralise	ausgleichen
newly-fabricated	neu gefertigt
next	als Nächstes
nickel	Nickel
nitrogen	Stickstoff
nitrogen gas	Stickstoffgas
No Go side	Ausschussseite
nodular	kugelig
noise	Geräusch, Lärm
noise development	Geräuschentwicklung
nominal current	Nennstrom
nominal diameter	Nenndurchmesser
nominal load torque	Nennlastmoment
nominal size	Nenngröße, Nennmaß
nominal value	Nennwert
nomogram	Nomogramm

non-cylindric	unrund
non-detachable	unlösbar
non-ferrous metal	Nichteisenmetall
non-positively locking	kraftschlüssig
non-standard	nicht genormt
non-switchable	nicht schaltbar
non-toxic	ungiftig
nonius	Nonius
normal distribution	Normalverteilung
normal force	Normalkraft
normalising	Normalglühen
notch impact energy	Kerbschlagarbeit
notch	Nut
nowadays	heutzutage
number	Wert, Anzahl
number of teeth	Zähnezahl
numerical interval	Ziffernschrittwert
numerical value	Zahlenwert
numerous	zahlreich
nut	Mutter

O

observation	Betrachtung
to observe	beobachten
obvious	offensichtlich
to occur	auftreten, vorkommen, entstehen
octagonal	achteckig
odd number	ungerade Zahl
off-centre	außermittig
Ohm's law	Ohm'sches Gesetz
ohmic load	Ohm'scher Verbraucher
oil pocket	Öltasche
oil return	Ölrücklauf
to oil	einölen
oil-quenching bath	Öl-Abschreckbad
on top of each other	übereinander
one disc clutch coupling	Einscheibenschaltkupplung
one-stage	einstufig
open flame	offene Flamme
open loop control	Steuerung
open on one side	einseitig offen
opening	Hohlraum
to operate	bedienen, arbeiten, verstellen, durchführen, betätigen
operating area	Arbeitsbereich
operating behaviour	Betriebsverhalten
operating force	wirkende Kraft
operating time	Nutzungszeit, Betriebszeit
operational readiness	Betriebsbereitschaft
operator fatigue	Bedienerermüdung
operator variation	Ableserabweichung
opposite	gegenüberliegend
opposite sliding ring	Gegengleitring
organisation	Verband, Organisation
original state	Ausgangszustand
O-ring seal	O-Ringdichtung
oscillating	hin und her gehend
oscillation	Schwingung
otherwise	andererseits
out of control	unkontrollierbar
outer diameter	Außendurchmesser
outer ring	Außenring
output	Ausgabe
oval head screw	Linsenschraube
over-bent	überbogen
overcurrent protection	Überstromschutz
overload current	Überlaststrom
oversize	Übermaß
overturning torque	Kippmoment
own weight	Eigengewicht
oxide ceramics	Oxidkeramik
oxygen	Sauerstoff

P

packing box	Stopfbuchsdichtung
parallax error	Parallaxefehler
parallel circuit	Parallelschaltung
parallel pin	Zylinderstift
Pareto analysis	Paretoanalyse
part of a prism	Prismenstück
partial function	Teilfunktion
partially	teilweise
particle	Teilchen
particle size	Teilchengröße
particular	bestimmt, eigen
parting off	Abstechen
partly	zum Teil
parts list	Stückliste
to pass	weitergeben an
pasty state	pastenartiger Zustand
path	Weg, Pfad
peak	Spitze, Höchstwert
pedestrian access	Fußgängerdurchgang
pencil	Bleistift
to penetrate	eindringen
penetration	Eindringen
per (over)	dividiert durch
percentage	Prozentanteil, Prozentgehalt
to perform	ausführen, durchführen, umsetzen
performance	Leistungsfähigkeit
period	Dauer
period of operation	Betriebsdauer
peripheral	Umfangsfräsen
peripheral face grinding	Umfangs-Stirnschleifen
peripheral speed	Umfangsgeschwindigkeit
Perlit-texture	Perlit-Gefüge
permanent	unlösbar, dauerhaft, unlösbar
permanent deformation	bleibende Verformung
permanent magnet	Dauermagnet
permanent mould casting	Gießen in Dauerformen
permanently excited	permanent-erregt
perpendicularity	Rechtwinkligkeit
person in duty	verantwortliche Person
phase-delayed	phasenverschoben
phenomenon	Phänomen
physical	physikalisch
pie chart	Kreisflächendiagramm
piece	Stückchen
pillar	Säule
pillar drilling machine	Säulenbohrmaschine, Ständerbohrmaschine
pillar guide	Säulenführung
pipe	Rohr, Rohrleitung
pipe coupling	Rohrverschraubung
piston	Kolben
piston pressure	Kolbendruck
piston rod	Kolbenstange
pitch	Steigung
pitch circle	Teilkreis
pitting corrosion	Lochfraß-Korrosion
pivot bolt	Gelenkbolzen
to place	einlegen, platzieren
plain bearing	Gleitlager
plane	Flugzeug
plastic	Kunststoff
plastic	plastisch
plastic deformation	plastische Verformung
plastic fibre	Kunststofffaser
plastic granulate	Kunststoffgranulat
plastic material	Kunststoff
plastic matrix	Kunststoffbindung
plastically deformed	plastisch verformt
pliers	Zange
to plot	ausgeben, zeichnen
plug	Stecker
plug gauge	Lehrdorn
plug limit gauge	Grenzlehrdorn
plunger	Kolben
pneumatic cylinder	Pneumatikzylinder
pneumatic line	Druckluftleitung
point angle	Spitzenwinkel
point of time	Zeitpunkt
polar coordinates	Polarkoordinaten

pole-changing	Umpolen
polystryrene	Polystyrol
polyurethane resin	Polyurethanharz
porous	porös
position measurement system	Wegmesssystem
position number	Positionsnummer
positively locking	formschlüssig
possible	möglich
to pour	gießen
pouring basin	Eingussstumpf
powder particles	Pulverteilchen
power consumption	Stromverbrauch
power drill	Elektrische Handbohrmaschine
power factor φ	Leistungsfaktor φ
power machine	Kraftmaschine
power output	abgegebene Leistung
power range	Leistungsbereich
power rating plate	Leistungsschild
power source	Spannungsquelle
power supply	Energieversorgung
power tool	Elektrowerkzeug
to power	antreiben
precaution	Vorsichtsmaßnahme
precipitation	Auslagern, Abscheiden
precise	präzise, genau
precondition	Voraussetzung
predefined	vorgegeben
preferably	bevorzugt
prefix	Vorsatz
preliminary run	Probelauf
preload force	Vorspannkraft
prescribed	vorgeschrieben
present	vorhanden
to be present	vorhanden sein
presentation	Darstellung
presetting	Voreinstellung
to press	drücken, betätigen
pressing	Eindrücken
pressure	Druck
pressure die casting	Druckguss
pressure distribution	Druckverteilung
pressure energy	Druckenergie
pressure reforming	Druckumformen
pressure regulator	Druckminderventil
pressure vessel	Druckbehälter
to prevent	verhindern
prevention	Vermeidung
preventive	vorbeugend
primary forming	Urformen
primary profile	Primärprofil
prism block	Prismablock, V-Block
procedure	Verfahren, Durchführung
to proceed	verlaufen
process	Prozess, Vorgang
to process	verarbeiten, ausführen
process capability	Prozessfähigkeit
process capability test	Prozessfähigkeitsuntersuchung
process material	Hilfsstoffe
process trend	Prozessentwicklung
processing property	Verarbeitungseigenschaft
producibility	Herstellbarkeit
product	Produkt
production	Herstellung
production hall	Produktionshalle
production line	Fertigungsanlage
production process	Fertigungsprozess
production short term study	Kurzzeituntersuchung
profile	Profil
profile seal	Profildichtung
program instruction	Programmanweisung
progression	Reihe, Ablauf
to prohibit	verbieten
prohibitive sign	Verbotszeichen
to project	projizieren
prolonged	verlängert
proper selection	richtige Auswahl
property (-ies)	Eigenschaft(en)
to propose	aufstellen
to protect	schützen
protection	Schutz
protective earth conductor (PE-conductor)	PE-Erdungsschutzleiter
protective insulation	Schutzisolierung
protection lip	Schutzlippe
protective measure	Schutzmaßnahme
protective coating	Schutzanstrich
protective gloves	Schutzhandschuhe
protective housing	Schutzgehäuse
protractor	Universalwinkelmesser
to provide	liefern, bereitstellen
to be provided	ausgestattet sein
to pull	ziehen
pulley	Riemenscheibe
pulley groove	Scheibenrille
pulling	Ziehen
pump	Pumpe
pump housing	Pumpengehäuse
punch	Stempel
purely	rein, ausschließlich
purpose	Zweck
to push	stoßen
push button	Taster, Druckknopf
push-pull reforming	Zug-Druck-Umformen
pushing direction	Stoßrichtung
Q	
quality assurance	Qualitätssicherung
quality characteristics	Qualitätsmerkmale
quality control chart	Qualitatsregelkarte
quality improvement	Qualitätsverbesserung
quality management	Qualitätsmanagement
quality tools	Qualitätswerkzeuge
quantitative	mengenmäßig
quantity, quantities	Menge, Größe
quantity of data	Datenmenge
quantity symbol	Formelzeichen
quench head	Brausenkopf
quenched and tempered steel	Vergütungsstahl
quenching	Abschrecken
quenching and tempering	Vergüten
question	Frage
R	
radial force	Radialkraft
radian measure	Bogenmaß
radiation	Strahlung
radius gauge	Radienlehre
rail	Schiene
to raise	anheben
to ramp up	hochfahren
ram	Druckstempel
random	zufällig, zufallsbedingt
random error	zufälliger Messfehler
random influence	zufälliger Einfluss
random sample	Zufallsstichprobe
range	Strecke, Spannweite, Messbereich
ratchet	Sperrrad, hier: Kupplung
ratchet screw	Sperrzahnschraube
raw data chart	Urwertkarte
raw material	Rohstoff
raw part	Rohteil
to react	reagieren
to read	lesen
to read off	ablesen
reading	Ablesen, Ablesewert
ready for use	gebrauchsfertig
to realise	durchführen
reaming	Räumen
to reassemble	zusammenbauen
to receive	aufnehmen
recess	Aussparung
to recognise	erkennen
recommended	empfohlen
to record	aufzeichnen, erfassen

recrystallisation	Rekristallisation
rectangle	Rechteck
rectangular	rechteckig, viereckig
rectangular coordinates	rechtwinkelige Koordinaten
rectifier	Gleichrichter
red hot	rotglühend
to reduce	vermindern
reference	Bezug
to refill	auffüllen
to reform	rückbilden
reforming	Umformen
to relate to	zusammenhängen
relationship	Beziehung, Zusammenhang
relatively	relativ
to release	entlasten, lösen
release of series	Serienfreigabe
reliability	Zuverlässigkeit
reliable	zuverlässig
to relocate	umlagern
to remain	verbleiben
remained	verbleibend
removal	Abbau
removal rate	Zerspanvolumen
to remove	abtragen, entfernen, demontieren
repair	Reparatur, Instandsetzung
repeating	wiederholen
to repel each other	gegenseitig abstoßen
repellent	abweisend
repetition accuracy	Wiederholgenauigkeit
to replace	ersetzen, auswechseln
to report	melden
to represent	darstellen
representation	Darstellung
representative	repräsentativ
to require	benötigen
required	gefordert, erforderlich
to be required	erforderlich sein
requirement	Anforderung
reservoir of abrasion	Abnutzungsvorrat
to reset	zurücksetzen
resistance	elektr. Widerstand (physikalische Größe)
resistance force	Widerstandskraft
resistor	Widerstand (elektrisches Bauteil)
respect	Hinsicht, Respekt
to respect	berücksichtigen
respective	jeweilig
respirator	Atemschutzgerät
result	Ergebnis
to result	(sich) ergeben
retension	Nachspannung
reused	wieder verwendet
revolution	Umdrehung
rhombic	rautenförmig
right before	kurz vor
rigid	starr
rim	Randzone, Kante
ring gauge	Ringlehre
rinsing	spülen
to rise	ansteigen
riser	Speiser
robust construction	robuster Aufbau
rod	Stab
rolling element	Wälzkörper
roller bearing	Wälzlager, Rollenlager
roller guide	Rollenbahn
rolling	Walzen
rolling friction	Rollreibung
rotary	drehbar
rotary cutting motion	rotierende Schnittbewegung
rotary frequency	Drehfrequenz
rotary motion	Drehbewegung
rotary shaft seal	Radial-Wellendichtung
rotary speed	Drehzahl
rotary speed diagram	Drehzahldiagramm
to rotate	rotieren
rotating	rotierend
rotation speed	Drehzahl, Drehfrequenz
rotational direction	Drehrichtung
rotational movement	Drehbewegung
rotational speed	Drehzahl, Drehfrequenz
rotor	Rotor
rotor blade	Rotorblatt
rough	uneben, rau
rough working	Grobbearbeitung
roughing	Schruppen
roughness	Rauheit
roughness comparator	Oberflächenvergleichsmuster
roughness depth	Rautiefe
roughness profile	Rauheitsprofil
round end cutter	Kugelschaftfräser
round O-ring	runder O-Ring
round-faced	rundstirnig
rounded	abgerundet
row of data	Datenreihe
row of pins	Nagelreihe
to rub	reiben
rubber body	Gummikörper
rubber buffer	Gummipuffer
rubber-elasticity	Gummielastizität
rule	Lineal
runner	Eingusskanal
running surface	Lauffläche
rust	Rost
rusty	rostig

S

safety	Sicherheit
safety device	Sicherheitseinrichtung
safety equipment	Sicherheitsausrüstung
safety measure	Sicherheitsmaßnahme
safety shoes	Sicherheitsschuhe
safety sign	Sicherheitszeichen
sample number	Stichprobennummer
sample size	Stichprobengröße
sampling test	Stichprobe
sandwich panel	Sandwichplatte
satisfaction	Zufriedenheit
to save	sparen
saw blade	Sägeblatt
sawing	Sägen
sawing gap	Sägespalt
sawing per hand	Sägen von Hand
scale	Maßstab, Skala
scale interval	Skalenteilungswert
scaled	skaliert
scaling	Größenstufung, Verzundern
to scan	abtasten
scanning principle	Abtast-Prinzip
scientist	Wissenschaftler
scoring distance	Riefenabstand
scrap	Ausschuss
to scrape	kratzen
scratch	Kratzer
screw	Schraube
screw connection	Schraubenverbindung
screw head	Schraubenkopf
screw joint	Schraubverbindung
screw locking device	Schraubensicherung
screw nut	Mutter
screw tap set	Gewindebohrersatz
screw tool	Schraubwerkzeug
scriber	Reißnadel
sea water	Meerwasser
seal	Dichtung
sealing effect	Dichtwirkung
sealing lip	Dichtlippe
sealing material	Dichtungswerkstoff
sealing ring	Dichtring
second	Sekunde
section	Bereich, Fachgebiet
to secure	fixieren, sichern
segregation	Ausscheidung
to seize	verklemmen
to select	auswählen
self-adjusting property	selbstregelndes Verhalten

self-aligning ball bearing	Pendelkugellager
self-lubricating	selbstschmierend
semi finished steel product	Stahl-Halbzeug
sensitive	empfindlich
sensitivity	Empfindlichkeit
to separate	trennen, entkuppeln
separately excited	fremd-erregt
separating cutter	Trennfräser
separation	Trennung
sequence	Reihenfolge, Ablauf
sequential	nacheinander
sequential value	aufeinanderfolgende Werte
serie	Serie
series production	Serienproduktion
series-connected	hintereinander geschaltet
serrated lock washer	Fächerscheibe
service	Wartung
service plan	Wartungsplan
service works	Wartungsarbeiten
to set (set, set)	einstellen
to set up	aufstellen
set-up	Einrichten
setting lock	Setzsicherung
shaft	Welle
shaft exit	Wellenaustritt
shaft groove	Wellennut
shaft journal	Wellenzapfen
shaft maximal dimension	Höchstmaß Welle
shaft minimal dimension	Mindestmaß Welle
shaft-hub connection	Welle-Nabe-Verbindung
shank dimension	Schaftabmessung
shank form	Schaftform
shape	Form, Gestalt, Bauform
to shape	formen, bilden, umformen
shape of a bell	Glockenform
shapeless substance	formloser Stoff
shaping	Stoßen
sharp-edged	scharfkantig
sharp	scharf
to sharpen	schärfen
shearing	Abscherung
sheet metal	Blech
sheet pre-cut	Blechzuschnitt
shell-type milling cutter	Aufsteckfräser
to shield	abschirmen, schützen
shift	Veränderung
to shift	verschieben
shine	Glanz
shock-absorbing	stoßdämpfend
shock	Stoß
short	kurz
short circuit	Kurzschluss
shoulder	Absatz
shrink joint	Schrumpfverbindung
side milling cutter	Scheibenfräser
sight comparison	Sichtvergleich
significant	bedeutend
silicium nitride	Siliciumnitrid
silicon carbide	Siliciumcarbid
similar	ähnlich
to be similar to	ähnlich sein zu ...
similar structure	ähnlicher Aufbau
simultaneous	gleichzeitig
single order	Einzelauftrag
single point	punktförmig
single row	einreihig
sink	Senker
sintered material	Sinterwerkstoff
sintering	sintern
sinus curve	Sinuskurve
size	Größe
size of the workpiece	Werkstückgröße
skeleton	Skelett
to sketch	einzeichnen
sketch	Skizze, Zeichnung
skilled	qualifiziert
skilled worker	Facharbeiter
skin disease	Hautkrankheit
slack side	Leertrum
slag	Schlacke
slaving	Mitnahme
sleeve	Skalenhülse
to slide	gleiten
slide bearing	Gleitlager
slide position	Schlittenposition
slide rail	Führungsschiene
slider	Schieber
slideway	Führungsbahn, Gleitbahn
sliding	gleitfähig, Gleiten
sliding bearing	Gleitlager
sliding friction	Gleitreibung
sliding property	Gleiteigenschaft
sliding ring	Gleitring
sliding skid	Gleitkufe
sliding speed	Gleitgeschwindigkeit
slightly	etwas
slightly angled	leicht angeschrägt
slip	Schlupf
slippage	Gleitfähigkeit, Schlupf
slot cutter	Nutenfräser
small parts	Kleinteile
small sized parts	Kleinteile
smooth	glatt, reibungslos
to smooth	glätten
to smooth out	einebnen
smooth running	weicher Lauf
snap gauge	Rachenlehre, Grenzrachenlehre
snap-connection	Schnappverbindung
soap	Seife
socket head screw	Zylinderschraube
socket outlet	Steckdose
socket screw	Inbusschraube
to soften	erweichen
soft face hammer	Schonhammer
soft rubber	Weichgummi
soft steel	weicher Stahl
soft-tempering	Weichglühen
to solder	löten
solder	Lot
soldering	Löten
soldering fit	Lötspalt
soldering point	Lötstelle
solid	fest
solid form	feste Form
solid friction	Festkörperreibung
solid lubricant	Festschmierstoff
solid material	Feststoff
solid substance	fester Stoff
solidification	Erstarren
to solidify	erstarren
solution	Lösung
solution annealing	Lösungsglühen
space	Spiel/Raum, Aussparung
spark	Funken
spatial arrangement	räumliche Anordnung
specific electric resistance	spezifischer elektrischer Widerstand
specification	Anforderungen
specified	vorgeschrieben, bestimmt
specified limit	Grenzmaße
to specify	angeben, festlegen
specimen	Prüfkörper
speed	Geschwindigkeit
speed adjustment	Drehzahlverstellung
sphere	Kugel
spherical	kugelförmig
spheroidal	kugelförmig
spindle	Spindel, Achse
spiral spring	Spiralfeder
splash water	Spritzwasser
spline hub	Keilnabe
spline shaft	Keilwelle
spline shaft profile	Keilwellenprofil
splint pin	Splint
to split, split, split	aufteilen
to spray	lackieren, einsprühen, aufspritzen
to spread	sich verteilen
spread of data	Streuung der Daten
spread out	weit verteilt
spreading	Streuung
spring	Feder

spring elasticity	Federelastizität
spring lock washer	Federring
springback	Rückfederung
square	quadratisch
square second	Quadrat Sekunde
stability	hier: Maßhaltigkeit
stable	stabil
stacked bar	gestapelte Säule
stacked bar chart	Stapelsäulendiagramm
staff	Personal
staff member	Mitarbeiter
stage	Phase
staged	gestuft
staggered order	versetzt angeordnet
stainless steel	rostfreier Stahl, nichtrostender Stahl
to stand	ertragen
standard	Norm
standard designation code	Normbezeichnung
standard deviation chart	Standardabweichungskarte
standard deviation	Standardabweichung
standard part	Normteil
standard size	Normgröße
standard specification sheet	Normblatt
standard value	Richtwert
standardisation	Normung
standardised	genormt
standardised dimension	festgelegtes Maß
star handle	Drehkreuz
starting material	Ausgangsstoff
starting torque	Anfahrmoment
state	Zustand
to state	aussagen, feststellen
state of aggregation	Aggregatzustand
state of friction	Reibungszustand
statement	Erklärung
static friction	Haftreibung
static seal	ruhende Dichtung
stationary	stationär
statistical	statistisch
statistical process control (SPC)	statistische Prozessregelung (SPC)
stator	Stator
stator winding	Statorwicklung
steel, steels	Stahl, Stähle
steel channel	U-Stahl
steel girder	Stahlträger
steel grade	Stahlgruppe
steel group	Stahlsorte
steel rule	Stahlmaßstab
steel type	Stahlsorte
step	Absatz
stereolithography 3 D-printing	stereolytischer 3 D-Drucker
stick slip	Ruckgleiten
stiff	steif
stiff construction parts	steife Formteile
stiffened	ausgesteift
storage tank	Vorratsbehälter
to store	speichern
stored	gespeichert
straight	gerade
straight edge	Haarlineal
straightness	Geradheit
strain	Dehnung
strain capacity	Belastungsfähigkeit
strain to rupture	Bruchdehnung
strength	Festigkeit
stress distribution	Spannungsverteilung
stress-relief tempering	Spannungarmglühen
stress-strain curve	Spannungs-Dehnungs-Kurve
stress-strain-diagram	Spannungs-Dehnungs-Diagramm
stressed	beansprucht
to strike off (struck, struck)	abschlagen
string	Schnur
structural order	Ordnungsstruktur
structural steel engineering	Stahlbau
structural steels	Baustähle
structure	Aufbau, Struktur
to be stuck	festbohren, festsetzen
stud	Zapfen, Stiftschraube
stylus	Tastnadel
stylus instrument	Tastnadelgerät
sub-group	Untergruppe
to subject	belasten
subsequent	anschließend
substantial	ausführlich
to substitute	austauschen
subtractive	abtragend
successful	erfolgreich
sufficient	ausreichend
sugarcoated	geschönt
suitable	geeignet, brauchbar
to summarise	zusammenfassen
sum	Summe
supervision	Überwachung
supplemental symbol	ergänzendes Symbol
support	Abstützen
to support	stützen, unterstützen
support and structural unit	Stütz- und Trageeinheit
supporting surface	Auflagefläche
surface	Oberfläche
surface finish	Oberflächengüte
surface hardening	Randschichthärten
surface quality	Oberflächengüte
surface roughness	Oberflächenrauheit
surface slip	Gleitfähigkeit
surface specification	Oberflächenangabe
surface texture	Oberflächenbeschaffenheit
surface texture parameter	Oberflächenkenngröße
surface wear	Oberflächenverschleiß
susceptible area	Schadstelle
to sustain	tragen
swarf	Metallspäne
to sweep	fegen
switch	Schalter
to switch	schalten
switchable	schaltbar
switched in parallel	parallel schalten
switching box	Schaltkasten
switching command	Schaltbefehl
to swivel	schwenken
synthetic	synthetisch
synthetic oil	synthetisches Öl
synthetic resin	Kunstharz
System of Units	Einheitensystem
systematic error	systematischer Messfehler

T

T-beam	T-Träger
table	Tabelle
tailstock	Reitstock
to take	entnehmen
to take care	Sorge tragen
to take inaccount	beachten
to take off	abtragen
to take out of service	außer Betrieb nehmen
taking up	aufnehmen
tally marks	Zählstriche
tally sheet	Strichliste
tape measure	Maßband
tape rule	Bandmaßstab
taper lead	Anschnitt
tapered roller bearing	Kegelrollenlager
tapping	Gewindeschneiden
tapping device	Gewindeschneidapparat
task	Aufgabe
technical classification	technische Einteilung
technical drawing	technische Zeichnung
technical failure	technisches Versagen
technical properties	technische Eigenschaften

English	German
technical qualification book	technisches Ausbildungsbuch
teeth	Zähne
teeth row	Zähnereihe
to temper	glühen
temperature run	Temperaturverlauf
tempering	Glühen
tempering diagram	Anlassschaubild
tempering oil bath	Aufwärme-Ölbad
to tend	neigen
tensile strength	Zugfestigkeit
tensile stress	Zugspannung
tensile test	Zugversuch
tension	Spannung, Zug
to tension	spannen, auf Zug spannen
tension roller	Spannrolle
tenth	Zehntel
term	Fachausdruck, Begriff
to test	prüfen
test blade	Messfläche
test pin	Prüfstift
test-impression	Prüfeindruck
texture	Struktur
thereby	dadurch
thermal conductivity	Wärmeleitfähigkeit
thermal destroyed	thermisch zerstört
thermal energy	Wärmeenergie
thermal expansion	thermische Ausdehnung
thermal resistance	Wärmebeständigkeit
thermal shock	Temperaturwechsel
thermodynamic	thermodynamisch
Thermoplastic	Thermoplast
Thermosetting plastic	Duroplast
thickness	Dicke
thimble	Skalentrommel
thin	dünn
thin fluid	dünnflüssig
thousandth	Tausendstel
thread	Gewinde
thread cutting	Gewindeschneiden
thread end	Gewindeende
thread pitch	Gewindesteigung
thread turning	Gewindedrehen
three-part	dreiteilig
three phase current	Dreiphasen-Wechselstrom
three-phase motor	Drehstrommotor
three-phase network	Drehstromnetz
through bolt	Durchsteckschraube
through hole	Durchgangsloch
thumb	Daumen
to tick	anhaken
tight	eng, fest
tight side	Lasttrum
to tighten	verspannen, festziehen
tightened	angezogen
time	Zeit
times	multipliziert mit (mal)
tin-lead	Zinn-Blei
tin	Zinn
tiny	winzig
titanium	Titan
toe dog	Spannfinger
tolerance	Toleranz
tolerance limit	Toleranzgrenze
tolerance range	Toleranzbereich
to tolerate	tolerieren
ton	Tonne
tool	Werkzeug
tool elements	Werkzeugteile
tool flank	Freifläche
tool grip	Werkzeuggriff
tool machine base	Werkzeugmaschinenbett
tool steel	Werkzeugstahl
tool wear	Werkzeugverschleiß
tooth	Zahn
tooth lock washer	Zahnscheibe
tooth pitch	Zahnteilung
tooth shaft connection	Zahnwelle-Verbindung
toothed belt	Zahnriemen
top	oberes Ende
top form	Kopfform
torque	Drehmoment
torque wrench	Drehmomentschlüssel
torque-speed-diagram	Drehmoment-Drehzahl-Diagramn
torsional speed	Drehzahl
total	gesamt
total amount	Gesamtmenge
total height	Gesamthöhe
total transmission ratio	Gesamtübersetzungsverhältnis
touch	Tast-, Berührung
to touch	berühren
touching	Berührung
tough core	zäher Kern
tough operation condition	raue Betriebsbedingung
tough-elastic	zähelastisch
toughness	Zähigkeit
toxic	giftig
tracking	Nachführung
traction	Zugkraft
trade association	Berufsgenossenschaft
to be traded	gehandelt werden
to transfer	umrechnen, übertragen
to transform	wandeln, umwandeln
transformation	Umsetzung, Umwandlung
transition fit	Übergangspassung
transmission	Übertragung, Getriebe
transmission ratio	Übersetzungsverhältnis
transmission unit	Übertragungseinheit
to transmit	übersetzen
tray	Wanne
triangular	dreieckig
true to scale	maßstabsgetreu
trunnion	Lagerzapfen
tube	Rohr
tungsten	Wolfram
tungsten carbide	Wolframkarbid, Hartmetall
turbine blade	Turbinenschaufel
turbo-charger	Turbolader
to turn back	zurückdrehen
turned part	Drehteil
to turn loose	losdrehen
turning	Drehen
turning lathe	Drehmaschine
turning machine	Drehmaschine
turning operation	Dreharbeit
turning step	Dreharbeitsgang
turning techniques	Drehverfahren
turning tool	Drehwerkzeug, Drehmeißel
twist drill	Spiralbohrer
two-piece	zweiteilig
two-track	zweispurig
type	Art, Sorte, Typ
type of corrosion	Korrosionsart
type of current	Stromart
type of manufacturing	Fertigungsverfahren
types of friction	Reibungsarten
tyre	Reifen

U

English	German
unalloyed steel	unlegierter Stahl
unalloyed structural steel	unlegierter Baustahl
unawareness	Unbewusstsein
unbalance	Unwucht
unbreakable	unzerbrechlich
uncertainty	Unsicherheit
to undergo	ertragen
unintended	unbeabsichtigt
unintentional	unbeabsichtigt
union nut	Überwurfmutter
unit	Einheit
universal joint shaft	Gelenkwelle
universal motor	Universalmotor
unknown	unbekannt
unloaded bearing side	unbelastete Lagerseite
unusable	unbrauchbar

up-cut milling	Gegenlauffräsen
to uphold	beibehalten
upper	obere
upper limit size	Höchstmaß
upper limit value	oberer Grenzwert
upstream	vorgeschaltet
uptight	verklemmt
usable	verwendbar
usage time	Nutzungsdauer
use	Einsatz
to use	verwenden
to be used	angewendet werden
usual	üblich

V

V-belt	Keilriemen
to vacuum	saugen, entgasen
valley	Tal
value	Wert
valve	Ventil
vanadium	Vanadium
variability	Schwankung
variable	Variable, Größe
variable transmission	stufenloses Getriebe
variation	Abweichung
variety of material	Vielfalt der Werkstoff
various	unterschiedlich, verschiedenartig
to vary	sich unterscheiden
vehicle	Fahrzeug
velocity	Geschwindigkeit
vernier calliper	Messschieber
vertical	senkrecht
vertical insertion	senkrechtes Einführen
vertical line	Senkrechte
vertical post	senkrechter Ständer
vessel	Reaktor, Tank
vibration	Schwingung
vice	Schraubstock
view	Ansicht
viscosity	Viskosität
viscous	dickflüssig
vocational training	Berufsausbildung
voltage	elektrische Spannung
voltage carrying line	spannungsführende Leitung
voltage carrying	spannungsführend
voltage source	Spannungsquelle
voltmeter	Voltmeter
volume	Volumen
volume flow	Volumenstrom
volume model	Volumenmodell
volume ratio	Volumenanteil
volume unit	Volumeneinheit

W

wagon construction	Waggonaufbau
wall thickness	Wandstärke
warehouse	Lagerhalle
warming	Erwärmung
warning line	Warngrenze
warning sign	Warnzeichen
wave distance	Wellenabstand
wave offset	Wellenschränkung
waviness	Welligkeit
waviness profile	Welligkeitsprofil
waxy	wachsartig
to weaken	schwächen
weakening	Schwächung
wear	Verschleiß, Abnutzung
to wear (wore, worn)	abnutzen
wear limit	Abnutzungsgrenze
wear parts	Verschleißteilchen
wear resistance	Verschleißfestigkeit
wear-resistant	verschleißfest
weathering	Bewitterung
weathering resistance	Wetterbeständigkeit
wedge angle	Keilwinkel
wedge connection	Keilverbindung
wedge profile	Keilform
wedge shaped	keilförmig
weight	Gewicht
to weld	schweißen
weldability	Schweißbarkeit
weldable	schweißbar
weldable fine-grained structural steel	Schweißgeeigneter Feinkornbaustahl
welded construction	Schweißkonstruktion
welding	Schweißen
welding arc	Schweißlichtbogen
welding capacity	Schweißleistung
welding filler	Schweißstab
welding gap	Schweißfuge
welding rod	Schweißstab
welding seam	Schweißnaht
welding torch	Schweißbrenner
well castable	gut vergießbar
wheel of adjustment	Verstellrad
wheel	Rad
wheel-rim	Radfelge
whiting	Schlämmkreide
wide	breit, umfangreich
wide flat steel	Breitflachstahl
wide I-beam	breiter I-Träger
wide-meshed	weitmaschig
widely	weitgehend
width	Breite
winding	Wicklung
wing nut	Flügelmutter
wiper motor	Wischermotor
wiper ring	Abstreifring
wire	Draht
wire grid	Drahtgitter
work	Arbeit
work accident	Arbeitsunfall
worker	Arbeiter
work plan	Arbeitsplan
work sequence	Arbeitsablauf
work steps	Arbeitsschritte
work unit	Arbeitseinheit
working environment	Arbeitsumfeld
work machine	Arbeitsmaschine
working material	Betriebsmittel
working spindle	Arbeitsspindel
workpiece	Werkstück
workpiece surface	Werkstückoberfläche
workshop	Werkstatt
workshop file	Werkstattfeile
worm gear	Schneckenrad
worn part	verschlissenes Teil
worn-out	verschlissen
wrought alloy	Knetlegierung

Y

yield point	Streckgrenze
yield strength	Streckgrenze

Z

zero line	Nulllinie
zinc	Zink
zinc coating	Zinkbeschichtung
zooming	Vergrößerung

Dictionary German – English

Wörterbuch Deutsch – Englisch

A

Abbau	removal
Abfluss	drain
Abfolge	sequence
abführen	to dissipate
abgegebene Leistung	power output
abgeleitete Größe	derived quantity
abgerundet	rounded
abhängig sein von	to depend on
abheben	to raise
Abkühlen	cooling
Abkürzung	abbreviation
Ablauf	sequence
ableiten	to dissipate
ablesen	to read, to read off
Ablesewert	reading
Ableserabweichung	operator variation
Ablesung	reading
abnehmen	to decrease
abnutzen	to wear (wore, worn)
Abnutzung, Verschleiß	wear, abrasion
Abnutzungsgrenze	wear limit
Abnutzungsvorrat	reservoir of abrasion
abprallen	to bounce
Abrieb	abrasion
Absatz	step, paragraph
Absatz (Welle)	shoulder (shaft)
abschalten	to break
Abscherung	shearing
abschirmen	to shield
abschlagen	to strike off (struck, struck)
Abschrecken	quenching
abschwächen	to dampen
Absolutmaßstab	absolut scale
Abstechen	parting off
Abstreifring	wiper ring
Abstützen	support
abtasten	to scan
Abtast-Prinzip	scanning principle
Abtrag	abrasion
abtragen	to remove, to take off
abtragend	subtractive
abtrennen	to cut off
abwechselnd	alternately
abweichen	to deviate
Abweichung	variation, deviation
abweisend	repellent
Acetylen	acetylene
Achsabstand	axial distance
Achse	axle, spindle
achteckig	octagonal
addieren	to add
Aggregatzustand	state of aggregation
ähnlich	similar
ähnlich sein zu ...	to be similar to
ähnlicher Aufbau	similar structure
Al-Blech	Al-sheet
Alkydharz	alkyd resin
als Nächstes	next
Alterung	ageing
Aluminium	aluminium
Aluminiumoxid	aluminium oxide
Aluminiumstäbe	aluminium rods
Amboss	anvil
Amperemeter	amperemeter
Amplitude, Größe	amplitude
andererseits	otherwise
ändern	to change
Änderung	modification
Anfahrmoment	starting torque
anfänglich	initial
anfänglicher Bauteilquerschnitt	initial cross-section area
Anfangsdrehzahl	initial speed
Anfangslänge	initial length
Anfangsmesslänge	initial length
Anforderung	requirement, specification
angeben	to specify, to indicate
angeben, nennen	to declare
angeliefert	delivered
angemessen	appropriate
angeordnet	arranged
angetrieben	driven
angewendet werden	to be used
angezeigter Wert	indicated value
angezogen, fest	tightened
Angriff	attack
anhaken	to tick
anheben	to raise
Anlassofen	annealing furnace
Anlassschaubild	tempering diagram
Anleitung	instruction
anodische Oxidation	anodic oxidation
anordnen	to arrange, to locate
anpassen	to adapt
Anpressdruck	contact pressure
Anreißen	marking
Anreißlack	marking paint
Anreißtisch	marking table
Ansatz-Passung	entry fit
anschließend	subsequent, adjacent
Anschluss	connection spot
Anschlusskasten	connection box
Anschnäbelung	minimal insertion
Anschnitt	taper lead
ansenken	to countersink, countersank, countersunk
Ansicht	view
ansprechend	appealing
ansteigen	to rise
antreiben	to power, to drive
Antriebsbauteil	driving component
Antriebseinheit	drive unit
Antriebsmotor	driving motor
Antriebsspindel	drive spindle
Antriebsstrom	driving current
Antriebswelle	drive shaft, driving shaft
anwenden	to apply
Anwendung	application
Anwendungstemperatur	application temperature
Anzahl	number
Anzeige, Display	display
anzeigen	to indicate, to display
anzeigende Messgeräte	indicative measuring devices
Arbeit	work
Arbeiter	worker
Arbeitnehmer	employee
Arbeitsablauf	work sequence
Arbeitsbereich	operating area
Arbeitseinheit	work unit
Arbeitskraft	manpower
Arbeitsmaschine	working machine
Arbeitsplan	work plan
Arbeitsschritte	work steps
Arbeitsspindel	working spindle
Arbeitsumfeld	working environment
Arbeitsunfall	work accident
Arbeitsweise	mode of operation
arithmetisches Mittel	arithmetic mean
asynchron	asynchronous
Atemschutzgerät	respirator
auf Dauer	in the long run
auf Zug belastet	loaded by tension
auf Zug spannen	to tension
aufaddieren	to count up
Aufbau	construction, structure
aufeinanderfolgende Werte	sequential value
aufführen	to list
auffüllen	to refill
Aufgabe	task
aufgeteilt sein in	to be divided
aufgrund	due to
Auflagefläche	supporting surface
auflösen	to dissolve
aufnehmen	to receive, to take up
aufrechterhalten	to maintain
Aufspanntisch	clamping table
aufspritzen	to spray
Aufsteckfräser	shell-type milling cutter
aufsteigend	ascending
aufstellen	to propose, to set up
aufteilen	to split, split, split
auftreten	to occur
Aufwärme-Ölbad	tempering oil bath

aufzählen	to list
aufzeichnen	to record
Auge	eye
Ausbilder	instructor
ausbröckeln	crumbling
Ausdehnungs-koeffizient	expansion coef-ficient
Ausdruck	expression
ausformen	to deform
ausführen	to process, to conduct, to carry out to execute, to perform
ausführlich	in detail, substan-tial
ausführlicher Begriff	expression at length
Ausgabe	output
Ausgabedatum	date of edition
Ausgangs-Rohr-abschnitt	base tube section
Ausgangsdurch-messer	blank diameter
Ausgangsstoff	starting material
Ausgangsteil	base part
Ausgangszustand	original state
ausgeben, zeichnen	to plot
ausgerichtet	levelled
ausgestattet sein	to be provided
ausgesteift	stiffened
ausgleichen	to neutralise, to balance, to compensate
aushärten	harden
Auslagern, Abscheiden	precipitation
Auslaufen	discharge
Ausnahme	exception
ausreichend	sufficient
ausrichten, fluchten	to align
aussagen	to state
Ausscheidung	segregation
Ausschnitt	extract
Ausschuss	scrap
Ausschussseite	No Go side
Aussehen	appearance
Außen-	external
Außendrehen	external turning
Außendurchmesser	outer diameter
Außenring	outer ring
Außensechskant	external hexagon
außer	except
außer Betrieb nehmen	to take out of service
außerdem	besides
außermittig	off-centre
Aussparung	space, recess
austauschen	to substitute
austenitischer Stahl	austenitic steel
austreten	to leave
Austritt	discharge
Auswahl	choice
Auswählen	choosing
auswählen	to select
auswählen	to choose, chose,chosen
auswechseln	to replace
Auswechselung	exchange repair
auswerten	to evaluate
Autobauteil	car element
Autoblech	car sheet metal
autogen	autogenous
Automatenlegie-rung	free cutting alloy
Automatenstahl	free cutting steel
Automobilindus-trie	automotive industry
Autoreifen	car tyre
axial verschiebbar	axial movable
Axialkraft	axial force

B

Balken	bar
Bandförderer	belt conveyor
Bandmaßstab	tape rule
Bandrolle	coil
basieren auf	to base on
Basis	base
Basiseinheit	base quantity
Basisharz	base-resin
Batterie	battery
Baueinheit	construction unit
Bauform	shape
Baugruppe	assembly, assembly group
Baustahl	construction steel
Baustähle	structural steels
Bauteil	component
beachten	to take into ac-count
beansprucht	stressed
beantworten	to answer
bearbeitet	machined
bearbeitete Oberfläche	machined surface
Bearbeitungskräfte	machining forces
Bearbeitungs-zentrum	machining center
bedecken	to cover
bedeuten	to mean
bedeutend	significant, major
Bedeutung	importance
bedienen, arbeiten	to operate
Bedienfeld	control panel
bedingt werden durch	to be due to
Befall	affection
befestigen	to fix
befestigen, lagern	to mount
Befestigung	attachment
Befestigungs-schraube	fixing screw
Befestigungs-gewinde	fastening thread
begrenzen	to limit
Begriff	term
begründen	to justify
behalten	to keep
Behälter	container
Behandlung	conditioning
beherrscht	consistent
beibehalten	to uphold
beinhalten, enthalten	to include
Beispiel	example
belastbar	resistant
Belastbarkeit	loading capacity
belasten	to subject
belastet	loaded
Belastung	loading, load
Belastungsfähigkeit	strain capacity
benennen	to label
benötigen	to need, to require
beobachten	to observe
berechnen	to calculate
Berechnung	calculation
Bereich	range, section
Bereich, Kategorie	category (-ies)
Bereiche der Passungsarten	range of type of fits
bereitlegen	to lay out (laid, laid)
bereitstellen	to provide
berücksichtigen	to consider, to respect
Berufsausbildung	vocational training
Berufsgenossen-schaft	trade association
berühren	to touch
Berührung	touching, contact
Berührungsfläche	contact surface
beschädigen	to damage
beschädigt	damaged
Beschädigung	damage
Beschichtung	coating
beschichten	to coat
beschreiben	to describe
beschriften	to label, to designate
beseitigen	to eliminate
Beseitigung	elimination, disposal
Bestandteil	component
bestehen aus	to consist of
bestehen aus	to compose of
bestehen aus	to be composed of
bestehend	composed
Bestellung	mail order
bestimmen	to determine, to characterise
bestimmt	specified, particular
bestimmte Größe	definite size
betätigen	to operate
beträchtlich	considerably
Betrachtung	observation
Betrag, Anzahl, Höhe	amount
betreffend	concerning
Betriebsausfall	breakdown
Betriebsbereit-schaft	operational readi-ness
Betriebsmittel	working material
Betriebsverhalten	operating beha-viour
Betriebsweise	mode of operation

Betriebszeit	operating time, period of operation
Bettschlitten	lathe slide
beurteilen	to assess
bevorzugt	preferably
bewältigen	to accomplish
bewegen	to move
beweglich	movable
Bewegung	movement
Bewegungsdichtung	dynamic seal
Bewegungsenergie	kinetic energy
bewirken	to effect
Bewitterung	weathering
bezeichnen	to describe, to designate
Bezeichnung	indication, designation
Bezeichnungs-Kurzzeichen	designation code
Bezeichnungssystem	designation system
Beziehung	correlation, relationship
Bezug	reference
Biege-Ausgleichswert	bend allowance
Biegen	bending
Biegeradius	bending radius
Biegerolle	mandrel
Biegeteil	bent component
Biegeumformen	bend-reforming
Biegevorrichtung	bending device
Biegung	bending
bilden	to form
Bimetall-Überlastschalter	bimetal overcurrent breaker
Bindemetall	bonding metal
Bindemittel	binder
Bindung	bond, bonding
blank	bare
Blech	sheet metal
Blechpaket	laminated sheet stack
Blechzuschnitt	sheet pre-cut
Blei	lead
bleibend verformen	to deform permanently
bleibende Verformung	permanent deformation
Bleistift	pencil
Blockdiagramm	block diagram
Bogenmaß	radian measure
Bohren	drilling
Bohrer	drill
Bohrerspitze	drill point
Bohrervorschub	feed of the drill
Bohrfutter	drill chuck
Bohrloch	drill hole
Bohrmaschine	drilling machine
Bohrspindel	drill spindle
Bohrtisch	drilling table
Bohrung	hole, bore
Bohrvorgang	drilling process
Bolzen	bolt
brauchbar	suitable
Brausenkopf	quench head
breit, umfangreich	wide
Breite	width
breiter I-Träger	wide I-beam
Breitflachstahl	wide flat steel
Breitflanschträger	H-beam
brennbar	combustible
brennen	to burn
Brennerdüse	burner nozzle
Brenngas	fuel gas
britisch-amerikanische Maßeinheit	imperial unit
Bronze	bronze
Bruchdehnung	strain to rupture, elongation at fracture
Buchse	bush
Buchstabe	character, letter
Bügel	bracket, frame
Bügelmessschraube	micrometer/screw gauge
Bügelsäge	hacksaw
bürsten	to brush

C

charakteristisch	characteristic
Chemieanlage	chemical plant
Chemiefabrik	chemical plant
chemisch	chemical
chemische Zusammensetzung	chemical composition
chemisches Symbol	chemical symbol
chloridhaltig	chloride-containing
Chrom	chromium
computergestütztes Konstruieren	computer aided design (CAD)

D

dadurch	thereby
d. h. (das heißt)	i. e. , von lat. id est
daher	due to this
Dämpfung von Schwingungen	absorption of vibrations
Dämpfungsschraube	damping screw
darstellen	to illustrate, to represent, to exhibit, to display
Darstellung	presentation, representation
Darstellungsart	display format
Daten	data
Datenmenge	quantity of data
Datenmenge(n)	data quantity(ies)
Datenreihe	row of data
Datenverarbeitungsanlage	data processing equipment, computer
Datenwert	data value
Dauer	period
Dauerbetrieb	continuous operation
Dauerfestigkeit	fatigue strength
dauerhaft, fest	permanent
dauerhaft, unlösbar	permanently
Dauermagnet	permanent magnet
Daumen	thumb
Deckel	cover
Deckschicht	cover
definieren	to define
Dehnung	strain
Demontage	disassembly
demontieren	to remove, to disassemble
dezimale Vielfache	decimal multiples
dicht	leak-proof
dicht vernetzt	dense networked
Dichte	density
Dichtheit	leakproofness
Dichtlippe	sealing lip
Dichtring	sealing ring
Dichtung	seal
Dichtungswerkstoff	sealing material
Dichtwirkung	sealing effect
Dicke	thickness
dickflüssig	viscous, less fluid
digitaler Messschieber	digital calliper
dividiert durch	per, over, divided by
Dorn	mandrel
Draht	wire
Drahtgitter	wire grid
Drallwinkel	helix angle
Dreharbeit	turning operation
Dreharbeitsgang	turning step
Drehautomat	automatic lathe
drehbar	rotatable
Drehbewegung	rotary motion, rotational movement
Drehen	turning
Drehfeld	magnetic field
Drehfrequenz	rotary frequency, rotational speed
Drehkreuz	star handle
Drehmaschine	lathe turning machine, turning lathe
Drehmaschinenfutter	lathe chuck
Drehmeißel	turning tool, lathe chisel, cutting chisel
Drehmoment	torque
Drehmoment-Drehzahl-Diagramm	torque-speed-diagram
Drehmomentschlüssel	torque wrench
Drehrichtung	direction of rotation, rotational direction
Drehstrommotor	three-phase motor
Drehstromnetz	three-phase network
Drehteil	turned part
Drehverfahren	turning techniques
Drehwerkzeug	turning tool, lathe tool

Drehzahl	rotational speed, rotation speed, rotary speed
Drehzahldiagramm	rotary speed diagram
Drehzahlverstellung	speed adjustment
dreidimensional	three dimensional
3 D-Drucker	stereolithography 3 D-printing
dreieckig	triangular
Dreiphasen-Wechselstrom	three phase current
dreiteilig	three-part
Druck	pressure
Druckbehälter	pressure vessel
Druckenergie	pressure energy
Druckfestigkeit	compression strength
Druckgießen	die casting
Druckguss	pressure die casting
Druckknopf	push button
Druckluft	compressed air
Druckluftleitung	pneumatic line
Druckluftzylinder	air cylinder
Druckminderventil	pressure regulator
Druckstempel	ram
Druckumformen	pressure reforming
Druckverteilung	pressure distribution
dunkel	dark
dünn	thin
dünnflüssig	thin fluid
durchführen	to perform, to realise, to operate, to conduct, to execute
Durchführung	procedure
Durchgangsloch	through hole
Durchmesser	diameter
Durchschnittswert Prozessverlauf	average value process course
Durchsteckschraube	through bolt
Duroplast	Thermosetting plastic
dynamisch belastet	dynamic stressed

E

eben	even
ebene Fläche	flat area
Ebenheit	flatness
Eckenwinkel	corner angle
Eckfräsen	corner milling
effektivste	most effective
effizient	efficient
Eigenart	characteristic
Eigengewicht	own weight
Eigenschaft(en)	property (-ies)
Einbau	installation
Einbaudurchmesser	mounting diameter
Eindringen	penetration, ingression, entry
eindringen	to penetrate, to enter
Eindrücken	pressing, indentation
Eindrückkörper	impression specimen
einebnen	levelling
einebnen	to smooth out
einfach	basic
Einfluss	influence
einführen	to introduce
eingefettet	greased
Eingriffsgrenze	control line
Einguss	downspure
Eingussstumpf	pouring basin
Einhängeösen	clipping eyelets
Einheit	unit
Einheitensystem	System of Units
Einheitsbohrung	basic hole system
Einheitswelle	basic shaft system
einher mit	along with
einlegen	to place
einölen	to oil
einreihig	single row
Einrichten	set-up
Einrichtung	equipment
Einsatz	use
Einsatzhärten	case hardening
Einsatzstahl	case hardened steel
Einscheibenschaltkupplung	one disc clutch coupling
einschlagen	to hammer
einschließen	to include
Einschnürung	necking, constriction
einseitig offen	open on one side
einsetzen	to insert
einsetzen, anwenden	to apply
einspannen	to clamp
Einspannkratzer	clamping mark
einsprühen	to spray
einstellen	to set (set, set)
einstellen	to adjust
Einstellung	adjustment
Einstellwinkel	cutting wedge angle
einstufig	one-stage
einteilen	to classify
Einteilung	classification
eintragen	to enter
eintreten, stattfinden	to occur
einzeichnen	to sketch
Einzelauftrag	single order
Einzelheit	fine detail
einzeln	individual
Einzelteil	component
Einzelwert	individual data
Einziehschraube	insert screw
Eisen	iron
elastisch	elastic
Elastomer	Elastomer plastic
elektr. Sicherung	cutout
elektrisch isolierend	electrically insulating
elektrische Arbeit	electric work
elektrische Ladung	electric charge
elektrische Leistung	electric power
elektrische Leitfähigkeit	electric conductivity
elektrische Leitung	electric line
elektrische Spannung	electric voltage
elektrische Wicklung	electric coil
elektrischer Strom	electric current
elektrischer Widerstand (physikalische Größe)	electric resistance
elektrochemische Reaktion	electrochemical reaction
Elektrolyt	electrolyte
elektromagnetische Spule	electromagnetic inductor
Elektromotor	electric motor
Elektron	electron
elektronischer Chip	electronic chip
Elektrotechnik	electrical engineering
elektrotechnisch	electrotechnical
Elektroversorgungsunternehmen	electric power company
Elektrowerkzeug	power tool
empfindlich	sensitive
Empfindlichkeit	sensitivity
empfohlen	recommended
emulgierbar	emulsive
Emulsion	emulsion
endbearbeiten	to finish
Endbearbeitung	finishing
Endbehandlung	finish
Enddrehzahl	final speed
Endergebnis	final result
Endkontrolle	final check
Endlage	final position
Endmaß	gauge block
Endmaßstapel	gauge block stack
energieumsetzend	energy transforming
Energieversorgung	power supply
eng	tight, narrow, close
enger Spalt	narrow gap
entfernen	to remove
Entfernung	distance
entgegengesetzt	contrary
entgegenwirken	to counteract
entgraten	to deburr
enthalten	to contain
Entkohlung	decarbonisation
entkohlend	decarbonising
entlasten	to release
entnehmen	to take
entrosten	to derust
entscheiden	to decide
entsprechen	to correlate
entsprechend	according to
entspricht, ist gleich	equals
entstehen, stattfinden	to occur
entstehen durch	to be generated

entstehen, auftreten	to happen
Erdöl	crude oil
Erdschluss	earth leakage
Erdung	earthing
Erdungsschutzleiter	protective earthing conductor
erfassen	to record
erfolgreich	successful
erforderlich	required, necessary
erforderlich sein	to be required
erfüllen	to fulfil, to achieve
ergänzendes Symbol	supplemental symbol
ergeben (sich)	to result
Ergebnis	result
Erhalten	conserving
erhalten	to achieve
Erhebung	bump
erhöhen	to increase
Erhöhung	increase
erkennen	to recognise, to detect
erklären	to explain
Erklärung	statement
erlassen	to issue
erlauben	to allow
erleichtern	to facilitate
Ermittlung	determination
ermöglichen	to enable
erobern	to conquer
erreichen	to achieve
erscheinen	to appear
ersetzen	to replace
Erstarren	solidification
erstarren	to solidify
Erste-Hilfe-Kasten	first aid box
ertragen	to stand, to undergo
erwärmen	to heat
Erwärmung	heating, warming
erwarten	to expect
erweichen	to soften
erzeugen	to create, to induce, to generate
erzielen	to accomplish, to achieve
Etikett	label
etwas, ein bisschen	slightly
Explosionsdarstellung	exploded view drawing
externe Pumpe	external pump
Extruderschnecke	extruder screw

F

fabrikneu	brand-new
Facharbeiter	skilled worker
Fachausdruck	term
Fächerscheibe	serrated lock washer
Fachgebiet	section
fadenförmig	filamentary
fähig	capable
Fahrzeug	vehicle
fallende Tendenz	decreasing trend
fangen (sich)	to catch
Faserverlauf	grain orientation
faserverstärkt	fibre-reinforced
Fass	barrel
Feder	spring
Federelastizität	spring elasticity
federnde Scheiben	flexible washers
Federring	spring lock washer
fegen	to sweep
Fehler	error, fault
Fehler, Störung	defect, fault
Fehlerentdeckung	fault detection
fehlerfrei	faultless
fehlerfreie Teile	faultless parts
Fehlersammelliste	defect chart
Fehlerstrom	fault current
Fehlerstrom-Schutzschalter	fault circuit interruptor
Fehlervermeidung	avoidance of error
Feile	file
Feilen	filing
Feilenschaft	file shaft
Feilenzahn, -zähne	file tooth, pl.-teeth
Feinbearbeitung	fine finishing
Feingießen	investment casting
fertig bearbeitet	finished
fertigen	to manufacture, to produce
Fertigteil	finished part
Fertigungsanlage	production line
Fertigungsprozess	production process
Fertigungsverfahren	manufacturing process
Fertigungsverfahren	type of manufacturing
fest	solid, tight
fest anliegen	to fit tightly
fest, fixiert	fixed
festbohren, festsetzen	to be stuck
feste Form	solid form
fester Stoff	solid substance
festgelegt	defined
festgelegtes Maß	standardised dimension
Festigkeit	strength
Festkörperreibung	solid friction
Festlager	fixed bearing
festlegen	to determine
Festlegung	determination
Festschmierstoff	solid lubricant
feststehend	fixed
feststellen	to state
Feststellschraube	locking screw
Feststoff	solid material
festziehen	to tighten
fetten	to grease
Feuchtigkeit	humidity
Feuerlöscher	fire extinguisher
Feuerverzinken	hot-dip zinc coating
Filter	filter
Fingernagel	fingernail
Fischgräte	fishbone
fixieren, sichern	to secure
FI-Schalter	FI-switch
flach gewalzt	flat rolled
Flachdichtung	flat seal
Fläche	surface
Flacherzeugnis	flat
Flachriemen	flat belt
Flachstahl	flat steel
Fließverhalten	flowing behaviour
Flugzeug	plane, aircraft
flüssig	liquid
Flüssigkeit	fluid, liquid
Flüssigkeitsreibung	fluid friction
Flussmittel	flux
folgende	following
Folie	foil
Fördermittel	conveyor
Form	shape, form
Form (Gussform)	mould
formativ	formative
Formbarkeit	formability
Formdrehen	contour turning
Formel	equation, formula
Formelzeichen	quantity symbol
formen, bilden	to shape
formgenau	form-exact
formlos	formless
formloser Stoff	shapeless substance, amorphous material
Formpressen	moulding
formpressen	to mould
Formpressen unter Druck	compression moulding
formschlüssig	positively, positively locking, form-locking
Formteil	formed part
Formverfahren	moulding procedure
Formwerkzeug	moulding tool
fortlaufend	continuous
fortspülen	to flush away
Frage	question
Fräsen	milling
Fräser	milling cutter
Fräskopf	milling head
Fräswerkzeug	milling tool
Freifläche	tool flank
freihalten	to keep free
Freihandskizze	freehand sketch
freischneiden	to cut freely
Freiwinkel	clearance angle
fremd-erregt	separately excited
Fremdkörper	foreign body
Frequenz	frequency
Fuge	groove
Fügen	joining
fügen	to join
Fügeverfahren	joining technology
führen zu	to lead to
Führung	guide, guiding
Führungsbahn	guideway, slideway
Führungsbuchse	guide bush
Führungsleiste	guide rail
Führungsrille	guide groove
Führungsschiene	slide rail
Führungsschlitten	guide carriage

fünfadriges Kabel	five line cable
Funke	spark
Funktionsbaugruppe	functional assembly
Funktionseinheit	functional unit
Funktionsprüfung	functional check
Fuß, Füße	foot, feet
Fußgängerdurchgang	pedestrian access

G

Galton Brett	Galton board
galvanisches Element	galvanic element
galvanisieren	to galvanize
ganz, vollständig	complete
garantieren	to guarantee
Gas	gas
Gasschmelzschweißen	gas fusion welding
Gasversorgung	gas supply
Gauß'sche Verteilung	Gaussian distribution
Gebäudeskelett	building frame
Gebotszeichen	mandatory sign
gebräuchlichst	most common
Gebrauchserzeugnis	functional product
gebrauchsfertig	ready for use
Gebrauchsgegenstand	article of daily use
Gebrauchshärte	application hardness
gechlort	chlorinated
Gedankenstütze	mind map
geeignet	suitable
geerdet	earthed
geerdeter Schutzleiter	protection earth line
Gefahr	danger, hazard
gefordert	required
geformt	moulded
Gefügeänderung	microstructural change
Gefügekorn	grain
Gegengleitring	opposite sliding ring
Gegenlauffräsen	up-cut milling
gegenseitig abstoßen	to repel each other
gegenseitige Führung	mutual guide
gegenüberliegend	opposite
Gehalt	content
Gehalt (Prozent)	percentage
gehandelt werden	to be traded
gehärtet	hardened
gehärtete Randschicht	hardened skin
gehärteter Stahl	hardened steel
gehauene Feilenzähne	hewn file teeth
Gehäuse	housing
Gehäusedeckel	housing-cover
Gehäuseschluss	housing leakage
Gehörschutz	ear muff
geläppt	lapped
Gelenkbolzen	pivot bolt
Gelenkwelle	universal joint shaft
gelöst	loosened
gemäß	according, in accordance
gemeinsamer Rückleiter	collective return line
genau	accurate, exact
genau einpassen	to fit exactly
genau festlegen	to specify
genaues Ergebnis	accurate result
Genauigkeit	accuracy
Genauigkeitsgrad	degree of accuracy
Genauigkeitsklasse	class of accuracy
genormt	standardised
geometrisch bestimmte Form	geometrically determinated form
geometrische Form	geometric form
gerade	straight
gerade Anzahl	even number
Geradheit	straightness
geradlinig	linear
Gerät	device
Gerätegehäuse	device housing
Geräusch	noise
Geräuschentwicklung	noise development
gesamt	total, entire
Gesamthöhe	total height
Gesamtmenge	total amount
Gesamtübersetzungsverhältnis	total transmission ratio
Gesamtzeichnung	general arrangement drawing
geschliffen	ground
geschönt	manipulated
Geschwindigkeit	speed, velocity
Gesenkfräser	die cutter
Gesenkschmieden	die forging
Gesichtschutz	face shield
Gesichtspunkt	aspect
gespeichert	stored
Gestalt	shape
gestalten	to design
gestapelte Säule	stacked bar
gestreckte Länge	developed length
gestuft	staged
Gesundheit	health
geteilt durch	divided by
getränkt	impregnated
Getriebe	gear, gear-box, transmission
Getriebeeinheit	gear unit
Getriebegehäuse	gear housing
Getriebewelle	gear shaft
gewährleisten	to assure
Gewicht	weight
Gewinde	thread
Gewindebohrersatz	screw tap set
Gewindedrehen	thread turning
Gewindeende	thread end
Gewindegang	thread turn
Gewindeschneidapparat	tapping device
Gewindeschneiden	tapping, thread cutting
Gewindesteigung	thread pitch
gewünscht	desired
gezogen werden	to be drawn
Gießen	casting
gießen	to cast, to pour
Gießen in Dauerformen	permanent mould casting
Gießen in verlorene Form	expendable casting
Gießerei	foundry
Gießform	casting mould
giftig	toxic
Glanz	shine
glasfaserverstärkt	fibre reinforced
Glasscheibe	glass pane
glatt	smooth
glätten	to smooth
gleich	equal
gleichen	to equal
Gleichlauffräsen	down-cut milling
gleichlautend	identically
gleichmäßig	evenly
gleichmäßige Flächenkorrosion	equal surface corrosion
Gleichrichter	rectifier
Gleichspannung	direct current voltage
Gleichstrom	direct current (DC), DC-current
Gleichstrommotor	DC motor
Gleichung	formular, equation
gleichzeitig	simultaneous
Gleitbahn	slideway
Gleiteigenschaft	sliding property
Gleiten	sliding
gleiten	to slide
gleitfähig	sliding
Gleitfähigkeit	surface slip, slippage
Gleitfläche	gliding area
Gleitgeschwindigkeit	sliding speed
Gleitreibung	sliding friction
Gleitkufe	sliding skid
Gleitlager	plain bearing, slide bearing, sliding bearing
Gleitreibung	sliding friction
Gleitring	sliding ring
Gleitringdichtung	axial face seal, mechanical seal
Gliedermaßstab	folding meter (folding rule)
Glockenform	shape of a bell
Glockenkurve	bell-shaped curve
Glühen	annealing, tempering
glühen	to temper
Glühofen	annealing, furnace
Grad	degree
grafisches Hilfsmittel	graphical aid
Grat	burr
Grauguss	grey cast iron

Grenzlehrdorn	plug gauge, plug limit gauge
Grenzlinie	limit line
Grenzmaße	specified limit
Grenzrachenlehre	snap gauge
Grenzwert	extreme, threshold
Grobbearbeitung	rough working
Grobkorn	coarse grain
groß, hoch	high
Großbritannien	Great Britain
Größe	size, dimension, feature, quantity, height
große Anzahl	great number
Größenänderung	dimensional change
Größenbezeichnung	dimensional relationship
Größenstufung	scaling
größerer Teil	bigger part
Grund	cause
Grundabmaß	basic size, fundamental deviation
Grundform	base shape
Grundfunktion	basic function
Grundgerüst	matrix
Grundkörper	base body
Grundlagen	basics, fundamentals
grundlegend	fundamental
Grundloch	blind hole
Grundplatte	base, base plate
grundsätzlicher Aufbau	basic structure
Grundtoleranz	basic tolerance
Gruppe (Gruppen)	category (-ies)
Gruppenmontage	group assembly
Gruppenzeichnung	assembly drawing
Gummielastizität	rubber-elasticity
Gummikörper	rubber body
Gummipuffer	rubber buffer
Gusseisen	cast iron
Gusseisenwerkstoff	cast iron material
Gusslegierung	casting alloy
Gussstück	casting
Gusswerkstoff	iron-cast material
gut vergießbar	well castable
Gutseite	Go side

H

Haarlineal	straight edge
Haarnetz	hair net
Haarwinkel	engineer's square
Haftreibung	static friction
Haftung (Klebung)	bonding
Haken	hook
Halbzeug	semi-finished product
Halterung	frame
Halteschraube	fixing screw
Hammer	hammer
elektrische Handbohrmaschine	power drill
handgeführt	handheld
handgeführte Werkzeugmaschine	handheld machine tool
Handgriff	handle
Handguss	hand casting
Handmeißel	hand chisel
Handrad	handwheel
Härte	hardness
Härten	hardening
härten	to harden
Härteprüfung	hardness test
Härterei	hardening shop
Hartmetall	carbide metal, hard metal, carbide
Hartmetalleinsatz	carbide insert
Hartstoff	hard material
Hartstoffkorn	hard material grain
Häufigkeit	frequency
häufigste	most common
Haupt-	main
Hauptabmessung	main dimension
Hauptast	main branch
Hauptaufgabe	main task
Hauptfunktion	main function
Hauptschneide	major edge
Hauptskale	main scale
Hauptsymbol	main symbol
Hautkrankheit	skin disease
Hebel	lever
Hebezeug	lifting equipment
heiß gesintert	hot sintered
Heißluftgebläse	hot-air blower
Heizflamme	heating flame
hell	light
Herstellbarkeit	producibility
herstellen	to produce, to establish, to create
Hersteller	manufacturer
Herstellung	production
Herstellungskosten	manufacturing cost
herunterfallen	to drop
hervorheben	to mark
hervortreten	to highlight
heutzutage	nowadays
Hieb (Feile)	cut
Hiebzahl	cut number
Hilfsmittel	aid, auxiliary aid
Hilfsskala	auxiliary scale
Hilfsstoffe	process material
hin und her gehend	oscillating
Hin- und Rückleitung	forward- and-return line
Hinsicht	respect
hintereinander geschaltet	in series connected
Hinterschneidung	back taper
hinzufügen	to add
Histogramm	histogram
Hitze	heat
hochfahren	to ramp up
Hochleistungsstahl	high performance steel
Höchst-Grenzmaß	maximum limit size
Höchstkraft	maximum force
Höchstmaß	upper limit size
Höchstmaß Welle	shaft maximum dimension
Höchstwert, Gipfel	peak
hochwertig	high grade
Höhe	height
Höhenreißer	marking gauge
Höhenverstellung	height adjustment
Hohlkörper	hollow body
Hohlprofil	hollow profile
Hohlraum	cavity, opening
Hooke'sche Gerade	Hooke's line
hundertfach	hundredfold
Hutmutter	cap nut
Hydraulikflüssigkeit	hydraulic fluid
Hydrauliköl	hydraulic oil
Hydraulikzylinder	hydraulic cylinder
hydrodynamisch	hydrodynamic
Hydromotor	fluid power motor
hydrostatisch	hydrostatic

I

I-Träger	I-beam
Ideensammlung	brainstorming
im Fall von	in case of
im Gegensatz	in contrary
Impulsmaßstab	impulse scale
Inbusschraube	socket screw
in der Reihenfolge	in the order
in einer Reihe	in a row
in Gruppen unterteilt sein	to be grouped in
Innensechskant	internal hexagon
induktiver Widerstand	inductive resistance
Industriekeramik	industrial ceramic
industrieller Bereich	industrial field
induzieren	to induce
ineinandergreifen	to gear into each other
inert (nicht reagierend)	inert
Information	information
Innen-	internal
Innendrehen	internal turning
Innendruck	internal pressure
Innendruck-Umformen	internal pressure reforming
Innendurchmesser	internal diameter
Innenform	internal shape
Innengewinde	internal thread
Innengewindebohren	tapping
Innenseite	inner face
infolgedessen	as a result
in Serie schalten	connected in series
Inspektion	inspection
Instandhaltung	maintenance
Instandhaltungsfähigkeit	maintainability
Instandsetzung	repair
IP-Kennziffer	IP-code number
Isolation	insulation
isolierender Werkstoff	insulating material
Isolierplatte	insulation plate

J	
je nach	depending on
jedoch	however
jeweilig	respective
K	
Kabel	cable
Käfig	cage
kalibrieren, nachstellen	to calibrate
Kalibrierung, Einstellung	calibration
Kaltarbeitsstahl	cold work steel
Karosserieknoten	car body nodal point
Karosserierahmen	body frame
kegeliger Kopf	conical head
Kegelrollenlager	tapered roller bearing
Keilform	wedge profile
keilförmig	wedge shaped
Keilnabe	spline hub
Keilriemen	V-belt
Keilverbindung	wedge connection
Keilwelle	spline shaft
Keilwellenprofil	spline shaft profile
Keilwinkel	wedge angle
Kennbuchstabe	code letter
Kennwert	characteristic
Kennzahlfaktor	code number factor
kennzeichnen	to indicate, to identify
Kennzeichnungscode	identification code
Keramik	ceramic
Kerbschlagarbeit	notch impact energy
Kern	core
Kerndurchmesser	minor diameter
Kernloch	core hole
Kettensäge	chain saw
Kettentrieb	chain drive
Kilogramm	kilogram
Kippmoment	overturning torque
Klammer	bracket
Klarlack	clear varnish
Klauenkupplung	claw coupling
Kleben	bonding with adhesives, to adhere
Klebeschicht	adhesive coating
Klebeverbindung	adhesive joint
Klebstoff	adhesive
Klebung	bonding
Kleinteile	small parts, small sized parts
klemmen	to lock
Knetlegierung	wrought alloy
Knetschnecke	homogenising screw
Kohlebürste	carbon brush
Kohlenstoff	carbon
kohlenstoffangereicherte Randschicht	carburised layer
Kohlenstoffdioxid	carbon dioxide
Kohlenstoffgehalt	carbon content
Kohlenstoffgehalt	carbon percentage
Kohlenstoffkennzahl	carbon code number
Kokillengießen	gravity die casting
Kolben	piston, plunger
Kolbendruck	piston pressure
Kolbenstange	piston rod
Kommunikation	communication
Kommutator (Stromwender)	commutator
kompakt, fest	compact
kompliziert	complex
Kondensator (elektrisch)	capacitor
konisch	conic
konstruieren	to construct
Konstruktion	enginneering
Konstruktionsbauteil	construction element, component
Kontur	contour
Koordinatensystem	coordinate system
Kopfform (Schraube)	top form
Korn	grain
Körner	centre punch
Korngröße	grain size
Körperschluss (elektrisch)	housing leakage
korrigieren	to correct
Korrosion	corrosion
Korrosionsart	type of corrosion
korrosionsbeständig	corrosion-resistant
korrosionsbeständiger Stahl	corrosion-resistant steel
Korrosionsbeständigkeit	corrosion resistance
Korrosionselement	corrosion cell
Korrosionsschutz	corrosion protection
korrosionsverhindernd	anti-corrosion
Korrosionswiderstand	corrosion resistance
Korund	corundum
kostengünstig	efficient, economic, cost-efficient
Kraft	force
Kraftfahrzeugtechnik	automobile technology
Kraftmaschine	engine, power machine
kraftschlüssig	non-positively locking, force locking
Kraftstoff	motor fuel
Krananlage	crane system
kratzen	to scrape
Kratzer	scratch
Kreis	circle
Kreisflächendiagramm	pie chart
kreisförmig	circular
Kreiskeilverbindung	circular spline connection
Kreissäge	circular saw
Kreuz	cross
Kreuzhieb	cross-cut
Kriterium	criteria
Kronenmutter	castle nut
Kugel	ball, sphere
kugelförmig	spherical, spheroidal
kugelig	nodular
Kugellager	ball bearing
Kugelschaftfräser	round end cutter
Kühlschmiermittel	cooling lubricant
kumulierte Gesamtzahl	cumulative total
Kunde	customer
Kundenanforderung	customer specification
Kundendienst	customer service
Kunstharz	synthetic resin
Kunststoff	plastic, plastic material
Kunststoffbindung	plastic matrix
Kunststofffaser	plastic fibre
Kunststoffgranulat	plastic granulate
Kupfer	copper
Kupferlegierung	copper alloy
Kupfermünze	copper coin
Kupplung	coupling
Kurbelgehäuse	crankcase
Kurbelwelle	crankshaft
Kurve	curve
kurz	shortly
kurz vor	right before
Kurzbezeichnung	designation code, identification code
Kurzform	abbreviated form
Kurzschluss	short circuit
Kurzzeichen	code
Kurzzeituntersuchung	production short term study
L	
Labyrinthdichtung	labyrinth seal
lackieren	to spray
Lagerbuchse	bearing bush
Lagerdeckel	bearing cap
Lagergehäuse	bearing housing
Lagerhalle	warehouse
Lagerkäfig	bearing cage
Lagerkugeln	bearing balls
Lagermitte	bearing centre
Lagerschale	bearing cup, bearing shell
Lagerspiel	bearing clearance
Lagerzapfen	trunnion
Lamellengrafit	lamellar graphite
Länge	length
Langerzeugnis	long rolled product
Längsdrehen	longitudinal turning
langspanend	long chipping

langfristiger Zeitraum	long-term period
läppen	to lap
Lärm	noise
Lastmoment	load torque
Lasttrum	tight side
Latzhose	dungarees
Lauf	run, operation
laufend	continuous current
Lauffläche	running surface
Laufring	bearing race
Laufrollenlager	roller bearing
Lauge	base
Lebensdauer	life time
lebensgefährlich	dangerous to life
Leckverlust	leakage
Leerlaufdrehzahl	idle speed
Leertrum	slack side
legierter Stahl	alloyed steel
Legierungselement	alloying element
Lehrdorn	plug gauge
Lehre	gauge
Lehrring	ring gauge
leicht angeschrägt	slightly angled
Leichtbaukonstruktion	light weight construction
Leichtgängigkeit	ease of motion
Leichtmetall	light metal
Leichtsinn	carelessness
Leistung	performance
Leistungsbereich	power range
Leistungsfähigkeit	performance
Leistungsfaktor φ	power factor φ
Leistungsschild	power rating plate
leistungsstark	high power
leitend	conducting
Leiterschleife	conductor loop
Leiterschluss (elektrisch)	line leakage
Leiterwerkstoff	conductor material
Leiterwiderstand	conductor resistance
Leitung	line
Leitungsnetz	current network
Lichtbogen	arc
Lichtbogenhandschweißen	manual arc welding
Lichtbogenofen	arc furnace
Lichteinfallwinkel	light source angle
Lichtspalt	light gap
Lichtstärke	luminous intensity
liefern	to provide
liegen	to lie (lay, lain)
liegt vor	to be existent
Lineal	rule
Liniendiagramm	line chart
linienförmig	linear
Linksdrall	left-hand twist
Linsenschraube	oval head screw
Lippendichtung	lip seal
Loch (Bohrung)	hole (bore)
Lochfraß-Korrosion	pitting corrosion
lösbar	detachable
lösbare Verbindung	detachable connection
losdrehen	to turn loose
Losdrehsicherung	locking device
lose fixiert	loosely fixed
lösen	release
Loslager	floating bearing
Lösung	solution
Lösungsglühen	solution annealing
Lot	solder
Löten	soldering
löten	to solder
Lötspalt	soldering fit
Lötstelle	soldering point
Luft	air
Luftabkühlung	air cooling
Lupe	magnifying glass

M

Magnesium	magnesium
mal	times
mal Tiefe	times depth
Mangangehalt	manganese percentage
manuell	manual
Markierung	mark, marking
martensitischer Stahl	martensitic steel
Maschenweite	mesh size
Maschine	machine
Maschinengewindebohrer	machine tap
Maschinen-Einstellgröße	machine setting
Maschinenbau	mechanical engineering
Maschinenbauteil	machine component
Maschinenbediener	machine operator
Maschinenbett	machine bed
Maschinenfähigkeit	machine capability
Maschinenfähigkeitsindex	machine capability index
Maschinenfähigkeitsuntersuchung (MFU)	machine process capability test (MCT)
Maschinenfuß	machine base
Maschinengestell	machine frame
Maschinenguss	machine casting
Maschinenmesser	machine knife (knives)
Maschinenschraubstock	machine vice
Maschinentechnik	mechanical engineering
Maschinentisch	machine table
Maß	measure
Maßband	tape measure
Masse	mass
Maße	dimensions
massengefertigte Produkte	mass product articles
Massenprodukt	mass production component
Massenteile	mass components
Maßnahme	measure
Maßstab	scale
maßstabsgetreu	true to scale
Maßtoleranz	dimensional tolerance
Maßverkörperung	dimensional representative
Materialabtrag	material removal
Materialverlust	loss of material
matt (Oberfläche)	matt (surface)
Maximale Rautiefe R_{max}	maximum peak to valley height R_{max}
mechanisch hoch	high mechanical
mechanische Belastung	mechanical load
Medianwert	median value
Meerwasser	sea water
mehrschneidig	multi-blade
mehrstufig	multi-stage
Meißel	bit, chisel
melden	to report
Menge	amount, quantity
mengenmäßig	quantitative
Mensch	human
Mensch, Menschen	man, men
menschlicher Körper	human body
menschliches Versagen	human failure
Messaufgabe	measuring task
Messbereich	range
Messen	measuring
messen	to measure
Messfähigkeit	measuring capability
Messfehler	measuring error
Messfläche	test blade, measuring face
Messgerät	measuring device
Messing	brass
Messkraft	measuring force
Messmittel	inspection aid
Messschenkel	measuring tube
Messschieber	vernier calliper
Messstrecke	evaluation length
Messtechnik	measuring technique
Messuhr	dial indicator
Messwertreihe	list of measured values
Metall	metal
Metallbeschichtung	metal coating
Metallkäfig	metal cage
Metallpulver	metal powder
Metallschmelze	molten metal
Metallspäne	swarf
Metallstab	metal rod
Meterstab	folding meter
mikroskopisch	microscopic
Mikrostruktur	microstructure
milchartig	milky-looking
Millionenfaches	millionfold
Minderung, Abnahme	decline
Mindest-Streckgrenze	minimal yield strength
mindestens	at least
Mindestmaß	lower limit size

Mindestmaß Bohrung	hole minimum dimension
Mindestmaß Welle	shaft minimum dimension
Mineralöl	mineral oil
minimieren	to minimize
Mischkeramik	mixed ceramics
Mischreibung	mixed friction
Mischverhältnis	mixing ratio
mit bloßem Auge	by the naked eye
mit etwas behaftet sein	to be afflicted with
Mitarbeiter	staff member, employee
miteinbezogen sein	to be involved
Mitnahme	slaving
Mitnehmer-Verbindung	drive type connection
Mittellage	intermediate layer
Mittellinie	centre line, mean line
Mittelrauwert R_a	arithmetic average roughness R_a
Mittelwert	mean, mean value, average value
Mittelwertkarte	mean chart
mittig	centric
mittlere	medium
mittlere Belastung	moderate load
Mittlere Rautiefe R_z	average peak to valley height R_z
Modul	module
möglich	possible
Molybdän	molybdenum
Montage	assembly
Montageplan	assembly plan
Montagetechnik	assembly technique
Montagevorgang	assembly process
Montagezeichnung	assembly drawing
montieren	to assemble
Motor	engine, motor
Motorblock	motor block
Motordrehmoment	motor torque
Motordrehzahl	motor speed
Motorwelle	motor shaft
Motorwicklung	motor coil
Muldenkorrosion	crater corrosion
multiplizieren mit	to multiply by
multipliziert mit (mal)	times
Mutter	nut, screw nut

N

Nabe	hub
Nabennut	hub keyway
Nabennut-Grund	hub keyway base
nacheinander	sequential
Nachführung	tracking
nachgeschaltet	connected
Nachspannung	retension
Nachteil	disadvantage
nachteilig	disadvantageous
Nadellager	needle bearing
Nagelreihe	row of pins
näherungsweise	approximately
Nebenschneide	minor edge
nebenstehend	adjacent, aside
neigen	to tend
Neigung	gradient of inclination
Nenndurchmesser	nominal diameter
nennen	to label, to name
Nenngröße	nominal size
Nennlastmoment	nominal load torque
Nennmaß	nominal size
Nennstrom	nominal current
Nennwert	nominal value
neu gefertigt	newly-fabricated
neutrale Faser	neutral line
neutrale Flamme	neutral flame
Neutralleiter	neutral line
nicht genormt	non-standard
nicht schaltbar	non-switchable
Nichteisenmetall	non-ferrous metal
nichtrostender Stahl	stainless steel
niedrig	low
niedrig schmelzend	low melting
niedrig schmelzendes Lot	low-melting solder
noch, sogar	even
Nocke	cam
Nockenwelle	camshaft
Nomogramm	nomogram
Nonius	nonius
Norm	standard
Normalglühen	normalising
Normalkraft	normal force
Normalverteilung	normal distribution
Normbezeichnung	standard designation code
Normblatt	standard specification sheet
Normgröße	standard size
Normteil	standard part
Normung	standardisation
Not-Aus-Schalter	emergency stop button
Notausgang	emergency exit
Notfall	case of need, emergency
notwendig	necessary
Nulllinie	zero line
Nut	groove, notch
Nutenfräser	slot cutter
Nutmutter	groove nut
Nutringdichtung	grooved ring
Nutzungsdauer	usage time
Nutzungszeit	operating time

O

O-Ringdichtung	O-ring seal
obere	upper
oberer Grenzwert	upper limit value
oberes Ende	top
Oberfläche	surface
Oberflächenangabe	surface specification
Oberflächenbeschaffenheit	surface texture
Oberflächengüte	surface quality, surface finish
Oberflächenkenngröße	surface texture parameter
Oberflächenrauheit	surface roughness
Oberflächenvergleichsmuster	roughness comparator
Oberflächenverschleiß	surface wear
Oberkasten (Gießen)	cope box
offene Flamme	open flames
offensichtlich	obvious
Ohm'sches Gesetz	Ohm's law
Ohm'scher Verbraucher	ohmic load
Ohrstöpsel	ear plug
Öl-Abschreckbad	oil-quenching bath
Ölrücklauf	oil return
Öltasche	oil pocket
ordnen	to arrange
Ordnungsstruktur	structural order
Oxidkeramik	oxide ceramics

P

Parallaxefehler	parallax error
parallel schalten	switched in parallel
Parallelschaltung	parallel circuit
Paretoanalyse	Pareto analysis
passend	mating
Passfeder	feather key
Passfederverbindung	feather key connection
Passfläche	fitting surface
Passschraube	close-tolerance bolt
Passung	fit
Passungssystem	fit system
pastenartiger Zustand	pasty state
PE-Erdungsschutzleiter	protective earthing conductor (PE-conductor)
Pendelkugellager	self-aligning ball bearing
Perlit-Gefüge	Perlit-texture
Periode	cycle period
permanent-erregt	permanently excited
Personal	staff
Personalermüdung	operator fatigue
Pfeil	arrow
Phänomen	phenomenon
Phase (Stufe)	stage
phasenverschoben	phase-delayed
physikalisch	physical
Plandrehen	facing
Planfräser	face milling cutter
plangeschliffen	flat-ground
plastisch	plastic
plastisch verformt	plastically deformed
plastische Verformung	plastic deformation
plättchenförmig	flaky
platzieren	to place

Pneumatikzylinder	pneumatic cylinder
Polarkoordinaten	polar coordinates
Polystyrol	polystryrene
Polyurethanharz	polyurethane resin
porös	porous
Positionsnummer	position number
präzise, genau	precise
preiswert	low cost
Pressstempel	extrusion die
Primärprofil	primary profile
Prisma, V-Block	prism block
Prismenstück	part of a prism
Probelauf	preliminary run
Produkt	product
Produktionshalle	production hall
Profil	profile
Profildichtungen	profile seal
Programmanweisung	program instruction
projizieren	to project
Prozentanteil	percentage
Prozentgehalt	percentage
Prozess	process
Prozessentwicklung	process trend
Prozessfähigkeit	process capability
prüfen	to test
Prüfkörper	specimen
Prüfmittel	measuring instrument
Prüfstift	test pin
Pulverteilchen	powder particles
Pumpe	pump
Pumpengehäuse	pump housing
punktförmig	single point

Q

Quadrat Sekunde	square second
quadratisch	square
qualifiziert	skilled
Qualitätsmanagement	quality management
Qualitätsmerkmale	quality characteristics
Qualitatsregelkarte	quality control chart
Qualitätssicherung	quality assurance
Qualitätsverbesserung	quality improvement
Qualitätswerkzeuge	quality tools
Querbalken	crossbar
Querkräfte	lateral forces
Querschlitten	cross slide
Querschnitt	cross section
Querschnittsbild	cross section figure
Querschnittsfläche	cross sectional area
Quervorschub	cross feed

R

Rachenlehre	snap gauge
Rad	wheel
Radfelge	wheel-rim
Radial-Wellendichtung	rotary shaft seal
Radialkraft	radial force
Radienlehre	radius gauge
Rahmen	frame
Rändelmutter	knurled nut
Randschichthärten	surface hardening
Randzone	surface zone
raue Betriebsbedingung	tough operation condition
Rauheit	roughness
Rauheitsprofil	roughness profile
Räumen	reaming, broaching
räumliche Anordnung	spatial arrangement
rautenförmig	rhombic
Rautiefe	roughness depth
reagieren	to react
Reaktor	vessel
Rechner	computer
rechnergestützt	computer-aided
Rechteck	rectangle
rechteckig	rectangular, square
rechtwinkelige Koordinaten	rectangular coordinates
Rechtwinkligkeit	perpendicularity
reiben	to rub
Reibung	friction
Reibungsart	type of friction
reibungslos	smooth
Reibungszahl	coefficient of friction
Reibungszustand	state of friction
Reifen	tyre
Reihe	raw, progression
Reihenfolge	sequence
Reihenschaltung	circuit in series
rein, ausschließlich	purely
reinigen	to clean
Reinigungsschlacke	cleaning slag
Reißnadel	scriber
Reitstock	tailstock
Rekristallisation	recrystallisation
relativ	relatively
Reparatur	repair
repräsentativ	representative
Rettungszeichen	escape and rescue sign
richtige Auswahl	proper selection
Richtlinie	guideline
Richtung	direction
Richtwert	standard value
Riefen	filing marks
Riefenabstand	scoring distance
Riemen	belt
Riemengetriebe	belt transmission
Riemenscheibe	pulley
Riementrieb	belt drive
Rille	groove
Rillenabstand	groove distance
Rillenkugellager	deep groove ball bearing
Ringmutter	lifting eye nut
Riss	crack
robuster Aufbau	robust construction
Rohling	blank
Rohr	pipe, tube
Rohrleitung	pipeline
Rohrverschraubung	pipe coupling
Rohstoff	raw material
Rohteil	raw part, blank
Rollbahn	running surface
Rollenbahn	roller guide
Rollenlager	roller bearing
Rollreibung	rolling friction
Rost	rust
rostfreier Stahl	stainless steel
rostig	rusty
rotglühend	red hot
rotieren	to rotate
rotierend	rotating
rotierende Schnittbewegung	rotary cutting motion
Rotor	rotor
Rotorblatt	rotor blade
rückbilden	to reform
Rückfederung	springback
Ruckgleiten	stick slip
rückwärts	backward
ruhende Dichtung	static seal
rund	circular
Runddichtung	O-ring
runder O-Ring	round O-ring
Rundlaufgenauigkeit	concentricity
Rundschleifen	cylindrical grinding
rundstirnig	round-faced

S

Sägeblatt	saw blade
Sägen	sawing
Sägen von Hand	sawing per hand
Sägespalt	sawing gap
sammeln	to collect
Sandwichplatte	sandwich panel
Sauerstoff	oxygen
saugen	to vacuum
Säule	pillar, column
Säulenbohrmaschine	pillar drilling machine
Säulendiagramm	bar chart
Säulenführung	pillar guide
Säure	acid
Schadstelle	damaged spot, susceptible area
Schaftabmessung	shank dimension
Schaftform	shank form
Schaftfräser	end milling cutter
Schaftfräser 90°	90°-end cutter
schaltbar	switchable
Schaltbefehl	switching command
schalten	to switch
Schalter	switch
Schaltgetriebe	manual gearbox
Schaltkasten	switching box
Schaltplan (elektr.)	circuit diagram
Schalttafel	control panel
scharf	sharp

schärfen	to sharpen
scharfkantig	sharp-edged
Schaubild	chart
schäumen	to foam
Scheibe	disc
scheibenförmig	disc-shaped
Scheibenfräser	side cutter, disc milling cutter
Scheibenrille	pulley groove
Scheibenwischer	car wiper
scheitern	to fail
Schenkel	jaw
Schicht	layer
Schieber	slider
Schiene	rail, bar
schlagartig	abrupt
schlagen	to hammer
Schlämmkreide	whiting
Schlauch	hose
Schleifen	grinding
schleifen, geschlif-fen	to grind, ground, ground
Schleifkorn	abrasive particle
Schleifscheibe	grinding wheel
Schlichten	finishing
schließen	to close
Schlittenposition	slide position
Schlupf	slip, slippage
Schlüsselanhänger	key fob
Schmelzdraht	melting wire
Schmelze	melt
Schmelzofen	melting furnace
Schmelzpunkt	melting point
Schmelztemperatur	melting tempera-ture
Schmelzsicherung	fuse
schmiedbar	malleable
Schmiedegesenk	forging die
Schmieden	forging
Schmiedestück	forging
Schmiede-temperatur	forging tempera-ture
Schmiereinrich-tung	lubrication equip-ment
schmieren	to grease
schmieren, ölen	to lubricate
Schmierfett	lubricant grease
Schmierfilm	lubrication film
Schmiermittel	lubricant
Schmieröl	lubricating oil
Schmierölzufuhr	lubricating oil supply
Schmierspalt	lubrication gap
Schmierstelle	lubrication point
Schmierstoff	lubricant
Schmiersystem	lubrication system
Schmierung	lubrication
Schmuckstück	jewellery
Schmutz	dirt
Schnappverbin-dung	snap-connection
Schneckenrad	worm gear
Schneidplatte	cutting inserts
Schneidkante	edge
Schneidkeil	cutting wedge
Schneidkeil	cutting edge
Schneidkeramik	cutting ceramics
Schneidöl	cutting oil
Schneidplättchen	cutting tip
Schneidstempel	cutting punch
Schneidstoff	cutting material
schnell	fast
Schnellarbeitsstahl	high speed steel
Schnittbewegung	cutting motion
Schnittdaten	cutting data
Schnittgeschwin-digkeit	cutting velocity
Schnittpunkt	intersection point
Schnitttiefe	cutting depth
Schnur	string
Schonhammer	soft-head hammer
Schrägkugellager	angular ball bear-ing
Schraube	screw, bolt
Schraubenkopf	screw head
Schrauben-sicherung	screw locking device
Schraubenverbin-dung	screw connection
Schraubstock	vice
Schraubverbin-dung	screw joint, screw connections
Schraubwerkzeug	screw tool
Schrumpfverbin-dung	shrink joint
Schruppen	roughing
Schuko-Steckdose	grounding socket outlet
Schutz	protection, guard
Schutzanstrich	protection paint
schützen	to shield, to protect
Schutzgas-Licht-bogenschweißen	gas-shielding arc welding
Schutzgehäuse	protective housing
Schutzhandschuhe	protective gloves
Schutzisolierung	protection insula-tion
Schutzkontakt-Steckdose	grounded socket outlet
Schutzlippe	protection lip
Schutzmaßnahme	protection meas-ure
schwächen	to weaken
Schwächung	weakening
Schwankung	variability
schweißbar	weldable
Schweißbarkeit	weldability
Schweißbrenner	welding torch, blowpipe
Schweißen	welding
schweißen	to weld
Schweißfuge	welding gap
schweißgeeigneter Feinkornbaustahl	weldable fine-grained structural steel
Schweißleistung	welding capacity
Schweißkonstruk-tion	welded construc-tion
Schweißlichtbogen	welding arc
Schweißnaht	welding seam
Schweißstab	welding rod, weld-ing filler
schwenken	to swivel
Schwermetall	heavy metal
schwimmen	to float
schwingend	oscillating, vibrat-ing
Schwingung	oscillation, vibra-tion
sechseckig	hexagonal
Sechskantmutter	hexagon nut
Sechskantschraube	hexagon head cap screw
Seife	soap
Seiltrommel	cable drum
Seitenfläche	lateral surface
Sekunde	second
selbstregelndes Verhalten	self-adjusting property
selbstschmierend	self-lubricating
senken	to counterbore, to countersink
absenken	to lower
Senker	sink, countersink
senkrecht	vertical
Senkrechte	vertical line
senkrechter Ständer	vertical post
senkrechtes Einführen	vertical insertion
Senkschraube	flat head screw
Senkschraube	countersunk screw
Senkung	countersinking
Serie	series
Serienfreigabe	release of series
Serienproduktion	series production
Setzsicherung	setting lock
sich erhöhen	to increase
sich häufen	to accumulate
sich unterscheiden	to differ, to vary
sich verteilen	to spread
Sicherheit	safety
Sicherheitsaus-rüstung	safety equipment
Sicherheitseinrich-tung	safety device
Sicherheitsmaß-nahme	safety measure
Sicherheitsschuhe	safety shoes
Sicherheitszeichen	safety sign
sichern	to secure
sicherstellen	to ensure
Sicherung (mechan.)	lock
Sicherung (elektr.)	fuse
Sicherungsautomat	automatic cutout
Sicherungsring	locking ring
Sichtvergleich	sight comparison
Siliciumcarbid	silicon carbide
Siliciumnitrid	silicium nitride
sintern	sintering
Sinterwerkstoff	sintered material
Sinuskurve	sinus curve
Skala	scale
Skalenhülse	sleeve
Skalenteilungswert	scale interval
Skalentrommel	thimble
skaliert	scaled
Skelett	skeleton
Skizze, Zeichnung	sketch

sofort	at once, immediately
Sorge tragen	to take care
Spalt, Lücke	gap
Spalte (Tabelle)	column
Span	chip, machining chips
spanabhebend	chip removal
Spanbildung	chip formation
Spanen	cutting
spanender Bearbeitungsvorgang	machining process
spanendes Fertigungsverfahren	metal cutting manufacturing process
Spanfläche	cutting face
Spankammer	chip space
Spanneinheit	clamping unit
spannen	to clamp, to tension
Spannfinger	toe dog
Spannflansch	chucking flange
Spannkopf	chuck
Spannrolle	tension roller
Spannung (mechanisch)	tension
Spannung (elektrisch)	voltage
Spannungarmglühen	stress-relief tempering
Spannungs-Dehnungs-Diagramm	stress-strain-diagram
Spannungs-Dehnungs-Kurve	stress-strain curve
spannungsführend	voltage carrying
spannungsführende Leitung	voltage carrying line
Spannungsquelle	voltage source, power source
Spannungsverteilung	stress distribution
Spannvorrichtung	clamping device
Spannweite	range
Spanungsgrößen	machining variables
Spanwinkel	cutting angle
sparen	to save
speichern	to store
Speiser	riser
Sperre	lock
Sperrzahnschraube	ratchet screw
spezifischer elektrischer Widerstand	specific electric resistance
Spiel	clearance
Spiel/Raum	space
Spielpassung	clearance fit
Spindel	spindle
Spindelkasten	head stock
Spindelstock	head stock
Spiralbohrer	spiral drill, twist drill
Spiralfeder	spiral spring, helical spring
Spitze (Gipfel)	peak
Spitzenwinkel	point angle
Spitzzirkel	divider

Splint	splint pin
Spritzgießform	injection mould
Spritzwasser	splash water
Sprödigkeit	brittleness
spülen	rinsing
Stab	bar, rod
Stabstahl	bar stock
Stabelektrode	electrode rod
stabil	stable
Stahl-Halbzeug	semi finished steel product
Stahl, Stähle	steel, steels
Stahlbau	structural steel engineering
Stahlgruppe	steel grade
Stahlguss	cast steel
Stahlmaß	steel rule
Stahlsorte	steel group, steel type
Stahlträger	steel girder
Standardabweichung	standard deviation
Standardabweichungskarte	standard deviation chart
Ständerbohrmaschine	pillar drill
Standzeit	life time
Stange	bar
Stapelsäulendiagramm	stacked bar chart
starr	rigid
stationär	stationary
statistisch	statistical
Statistische Prozessregelung (SPC)	statistical process control (SPC)
Stator	stator
Statorwicklung	stator winding
stattfinden	to happen
Staub	dust
Staubmaske	dust mask
Steckdose	socket outlet
Stecker	plug
Steghöhe	base height
steif	stiff
steife Formteile	stiff construction parts
steigern	to increase
Steigung (Gewinde)	pitch
Stempel	punch, die
stereolytografischer 3 D-Drucker	stereolithography 3 D-printing
Steuereinheit	control unit
steuern	to control
Steuerung	control, open loop control
Stichprobe	sampling test
Stichprobengröße	sample size
Stichprobennummer	sample number
Stickstoff	nitrogen
Stickstoffgas	nitrogen gas
Stiftschraube	locking screw
Stillstand	downtime
Stirn-Planfräsen	front side face milling

Stoffeigenschaft	modification of material
Stoffmenge	amount of substance
stoffschlüssig	material-locking, firmly locking
stoffumsetzend	material transforming
Stopfbuchsbrille	gland
Stopfbuchsdichtung	packing box
Störung	malfunction
Stoß	shock
stoßartig	abrupt
stoßartige Belastung	abrupt load
stoßdämpfend	shock-absorbing
Stoßen	shaping
stoßen	to push
Stoßrichtung	pushing direction
Strahltriebwerk	jet engine
Strahlung	radiation
Strangpressen	extrusion moulding
Strangpressprofil	extrusion profile
Strecke	range
Streckgrenze	yield strength, yield point
Streuung	spreading
Streuung der Daten	spread of data
Strichliste	tally sheet
Strom	flow, current
Stromart	type of current
stromführende Leitung	current carrying line
Stromkreis	electric circuit
Stromkreisunterbrecher	circuit breaker
Stromleiter	conductor
Stromleitung	current conductivity
Stromnetz	current network, electric network
Stromstärke	current rate, current rating
Strömungsenergie	fluid flow energy
Stromverbrauch	power consumption
Struktur	structure, texture
Stückchen	piece
Stückliste	parts list
stufenlos einstellbar	continuous variable
stufenloses Getriebe	variable transmission
Stütz- und Trageeinheit	support and structural unit
stützen	to support
suchen	to look for, to search
Summe	sum
synthetisch	synthetic
synthetisches Öl	synthetic oil
systematischer Messfehler	systematic error

T

I-Träger	I-beam
Tabelle	table, chart
Tal	valley
Tast-	touch
Tastatur	keyboard
Taster	push button
Tastnadel	stylus
Tastnadelgerät	stylus instrument
tauchen	to dip
Tausendstel	thousandth
technische Eigenschaften	technical properties
technische Einteilung	technical classification
technische Zeichnung	technical drawing
technisches Ausbildungsbuch	technical qualification book
technisches Versagen	technical failure
Teilchen	particle
Teilchengröße	particle size
teilen	to devide
Teilfunktion	partial function
Teilkreis	pitch circle
Teilung	division
teilweise	partially
Teilzeichnung	component drawing
Temperaturverlauf	temperature sequence
Temperaturwechsel	thermal shock
Temperguss	malleable cast iron
teuer	expensive
thermisch zerstört	thermal destroyed
thermische Ausdehnung	thermal expansion
thermodynamisch	thermodynamic
Thermoplast	Thermoplastic
Tiefe	depth
Tiefenmaß	depth gauge
Tiefziehen	deep drawing
Tischvorschub	feed of the table
Titan	titanium
Toleranz	tolerance
Toleranzbereich	tolerance range
Toleranzgrenze	tolerance limit
tolerieren	to tolerate
Tonne	ton
Tonnenrollenlager	barred roller bearing
tragen	to carry, to sustain, to bear
Träger	carrier, beam
Tragfähigkeit	load capacity
treibend	driving
Trennen	cutting
trennen, entkuppeln	to separate
Trennfräser	separating cutter
Trennstelle	disconnection point
Trennung	separation
Tuch	cloth
Turbinenschaufel	turbine blade
Turbolader	turbo-charger

U

U-Stahl	steel channel
überbogen	over-bent
übereinander	on top of each other
übereinstimmen	to line up
Übergangspassung	transition fit
überlagern	to interfere
Überlaststrom	overload current
Übermaß	oversize
Übermaßpassung	interference fit
Überprüfung	inspection
überschreiten	to cross
Überschrift	heading
Überschuss	excess
übersetzen	to transmit
Übersetzungsverhältnis	transmission ratio
Überstromschutz	overcurrent protection
übertragen	to transfer
Übertragung	transmission
Übertragungseinheit	transmission unit
Überwachung	supervision
überwiegend	mainly
Überwurfmutter	union nut
üblich	usual, common
Umdrehung	revolution
Umfang	circumference
Umfangs-Stirnschleifen	peripheral face grinding
Umfangsfräsen	peripheral grinding
Umfangsgeschwindigkeit	peripheral speed
Umfangskraft	longitudinal force
umfassen	to comprise
Umformen	reforming
umformen	to shape, to reform
Umgebung	environment
umgebungsbedingt	environmental
Umhüllung, umhüllt	covering, covered
umlagern	to relocate
Umpolung	pole-changing
umpolen	to commutate
umrechnen	to transfer, to convert
umsetzen	to implement, to perform
Umsetzung	transformation
umwandeln	to transform, to convert
Umwandlung	transformation
Umwelt	environment
unbeabsichtigt	unintended, unintentional
unbekannt	unknown
unbelastete Lagerseite	unloaded bearing side
Unbewusstsein	unawareness
unbrauchbar	unusable
uneben, rau	rough
Unfall	accident
Unfallverhütungsvorschrift (UVV)	accident prevention regulation
ungenau	inaccurate
ungerade Zahl	odd number
ungiftig	non-toxic
ungleichmäßig	irregular
ungünstig	inappropriate
Universalmotor	universal motor
Universalwinkelmesser	protractor
unkontrollierbar	out of control
unlegierter Baustahl	unalloyed structural steel, carbon steel
unlegierter Stahl	unalloyed steel
unlösbar	non-detachable, permanent
Unregelmäßigkeit	irregularity
unrund	non-cylindric
Unsicherheit	uncertainty
unsichtbar	invisible
unterbrechen	to interrupt
unterbrochen	intermittent
untere	lower
unterer Grenzwert	lower limit value
unteres Ende	bottom
Untergruppe	sub-group
Unterkasten (Gießen)	drag box
unterscheiden	to divide, to distinguish
Unterscheidung	distinction
Unterscheidungsmerkmal	distinctive feature
Unterschied	difference
unterschiedlich	diverse, various, different
Unterschiedsmessung	comparison measurement
unterstützen	to support
untersuchen	to examine
unterteilen	to classify, to distinguish
unterteilen	to divide, to classify
unverzweigter Monategeablauf	linear assembly
Unwucht	unbalance
unzerbrechlich	unbreakable
Urformen	primary forming
Ursache	cause
Ursache-Wirkungs-Diagramm	cause-and-effect diagram
Urwertkarte	raw data chart

V

Vanadium	vanadium
Variable, Größe	variable
Ventil	valve
Veränderung	shift
verantwortliche Person	person in duty
verarbeiten	to process
Verarbeitungseigenschaft	processing property
Verband	organisation
verbessern	to improve

German	English
Verbesserung	improvement
verbieten	to prohibit
verbinden	to connect, to interface
Verbindung	connection
verbleiben	to remain
verbleibend	remained
verboten	forbidden
Verbotszeichen	prohibitive sign
Verbrauch	consumption
Verbraucher	consumer
Verbraucher (elektr.)	load, electric load
Verbrennungs-kraftmaschine	combustion engine
Verbundwerkstoff	composite material
verdampfen	to evaporate
verdichten	to compress
Verdichter	compressor
verengen	to narrow
Verfahren	procedure
verformt sein	to be deformed
verfügbar	available
Vergleich	comparison
vergleichbar	comparable
vergleichen	to compare
Vergrößerung	magnification
vergüten	quenching and tempering, hardening and tempering
Vergütungsstahl	quenched and tempered steel
verhindern	to prevent
verklemmen	to seize
verklemmt	uptight
verlängert	prolonged
Verlängerung	elongation
Verlauf	course
verlaufen (fort-schreiten)	to proceed
Verletzung(en)	injury, injuries
verloren	lost
vermeiden	to avoid
Vermeidung	prevention
vermessen	to measure
vermindern	to reduce, to decrease
verringern	to decrease
verschalten	to connect
Verschiebekraft	displacement force
verschieben	to shift
verschieden	different, diverse
verschiedenartig	various
Verschleiß	wear
verschleißfest	wear-resistant
Verschleißfestigkeit	wear resistance
Verschleißteilchen	wear parts
verschlissen	worn-out
verschlissenes Teil	worn part
versehen sein	to be branded, to be labelled
versetzt angeordnet	staggered order
Versetzung	displacement
verspannen	to tighten
Versprödung	embrittlement
verstärken	to fortify
verstellen	to operate
Verstellrad	wheel of adjust-ment
verteilen	to distribute
Verteilung	distribution
Vertiefung	deepening
verursachen	to cause
verursacht werden von	to be caused by
verwandeln	to change
verwendbar	usable
verwenden	to use
Verwendungs-zweck	purpose
verzögern	to delay
Verzundern	scaling
verzweigte Montage	branched assem-bly
Vielfalt der Werk-stoffe	variety of materials
vielfältig	manifold
vielgestaltig	multiform
vielschneidig	multi-edged
viereckig	rectangular
Viskosität	viscosity
Vollformgießen	full mould casting
Voltmeter	voltmeter
Volumen	volume
Volumenanteil	volume ratio
Volumeneinheit	volume unit
Volumenmodell	volume model
Volumenstrom	volume flow
vor	in front of
Voraussetzung	precondition
vorbereiten	to prepare
vorbeugend	preventive
Vorderseite	front
Voreinstellung	presetting
Vorgang	process
vorgegeben	predefined
vorgeschaltet	upstream
vorgeschrieben	prescribed, spe-cified
vorhanden	present
vorhanden sein	to be present
vorkommen	to occur, to appear
Vorratsbehälter	storage tank
Vorrichtung	equipment, jig
Vorsatz	prefix
Vorschub	feed
Vorschubbewe-gung	feed motion
Vorschubeinheit	feed unit
Vorschubge-schwindigkeit	feed velocity, feed speed
Vorschubgetriebe	feed gear
Vorschubhebel	feed lever
Vorschubkraft	feed power
Vorschubmotor	feed motor
Vorsichtsmaß-nahme	precaution
Vorspannkraft	preload force
Vorstellung (Idee)	idea
Vorteil	advantage
vorwärts	forward

W

German	English
waagrecht	horizontal
wachsartig	waxy
Waggonaufbau	wagon construc-tion
wählen	to choose
Wälzkörper	rolling element
Walzen	rolling
Walzenfräser	cylinder cutter
Wälzlager	roller bearing
Wälzreibung	combined sliding and rolling fric-tion
wandeln	to transform
Wandstärke	wall thickness
Wanne	tray
warm gewalzter Stabstahl	hot rolled bar
warm gewalztes Blech	hot rolled sheet
Warmarbeitsstahl	hot work steel
Wärme	heat
Wärmebehandlung	heat treatment
Wärmebehand-lungsofen	heat treatment furnace
Wärmebeständig-keit	thermal resistance
Wärmedämmung	heat insulation
Wärmeenergie	thermal energy
Wärmeleitfähigkeit	thermal conduc-tivity
Wärmetauscher	heat exchanger
Warmhärte	hot hardness
Warngrenze	warning line
Warnzeichen	warning sign
Wartung	service, mainten-ance
Wartungsarbeiten	service works, jobs, tasks
Wartungsarbeiter	maintenance worker
wartungsarm	low maintenance
Wartungsliste	maintenance list
Wartungsplan	service plan
Wasserstoff	hydrogen
Wechselspannung	alternating current voltage
Wechselstrom	alternating current, AC-current
Weg	distance
Weg, Pfad	path
Weg, Strecke	displacement
Wegeventil	directional valve
Wegmesssystem	position measur-ing system
weich	flexible
weicher Lauf	smooth running
weicher Stahl	soft steel
Weichglühen	soft-tempering
Weichgummi	soft rubber
weit verteilt	spread out
weitergeben an	to pass
weitgehend	widely
weitmaschig	wide-meshed
Welle	shaft
Welle-Nabe-Verbindung	shaft-hub connec-tion

Wellenabstand	wave distance
Wellenaustritt	shaft exit
Wellennut	shaft groove
Wellenschränkung	wave offset
Wellenzapfen	shaft journal
Welligkeit	waviness
Welligkeitsprofil	waviness profile
wendelförmig	helical
Wendepunkt	inflection point
Wendeschneidplatte	insert tip
wenig	a little
wenigsten(s)	least
wenigstens	at least
Werkstatt	workshop
Werkstattfeile	workshop file
Werkstoff	material
Werkstoffermüdung	material fatigue
Werkstoffpaarung	material combination
Werkstofftechnik	material engineering
Werkstoffverhalten	material behaviour
Werkstück	workpiece
Werkstückgröße	size of the workpiece
Werkstückoberfläche	workpiece surface
Werkzeug	tool
Werkzeuggriff	tool grip
Werkzeugmaschine	machine tool
Werkzeugmaschinenbett	tool machine base
Werkzeugschlitten	centre support
Werkzeugschneide	cutting edge
Werkzeugstahl	tool steel
Werkzeugteile	tool elements
Werkzeugverschleiß	tool wear
Wert	value, number
wesentlich	essential
Wetterbeständigkeit	weathering resistance
wichtig	important
Wichtigkeit	importance
Wicklung	coil
Wicklungen (elektr.)	windings
Widerstand (elektrisches Bauteil)	resistor
Widerstandskraft	resistance force
wieder verwendet	reused
wiederholen	repeating
Wiederholgenauigkeit	repetition accuracy
Winkel	angle
winkelig	angular
Winkelstahl	angle steel
winzig	tiny
Wirbelstrom	eddy current
wirken	to act,
wirken, dienen	to function, to act, to operate
wirkende Kraft	operating force
Wirkleistung	effective power
Wirkstoff	active agent
Wirkung	influence
Wirkungsgrad	efficiency
Wirkungsweise	mode of operation, mode of function, mode of action
Wischermotor	wiper motor
Wissenschaftler	scientist
Wolfram	tungsten
Wolframkarbid (Hartmetall)	tungsten carbide
Wolke	cloud

Z

z. B. (zum Beispiel)	e. g. (for example)
zäh, dehnbar	ductile
zähelastisch	tough-elastic
zäher Kern	tough core
Zähigkeit	ductility, toughness
Zähigkeitswerte	ductile values
zählen	to count
Zahlenwert	numerical value
Zähler	electric counter
zahlreich	numerous
Zählstriche	tally marks
Zähne	teeth
Zähnereihe	teeth row
Zähnezahl	number of teeth
Zahnrad	gear-wheel
Zahnradpaar	gear pair
Zahnradtrieb	gear wheel drives
Zahnriemen	toothed belt
Zahnscheibe	tooth lock washer
Zahnteilung	tooth pitch
Zahnwelle-Verbindung	tooth shaft connection
Zange	pliers, gripper
Zapfen	stud
Zehntel	tenth
zeichnen, skizzieren	to draw
zeichnerische Hilfsmittel	graphical aids
Zeichnung	drawing
Zeile	line
Zeit	time
Zeitabschnitt	interval
Zeitpunkt	point of time
zentrieren	centralise
zentriert	centred
Zentrumsrichtung	direction of the centre
zerspanende Werkzeugmaschine	metal cutting machine tool
Zerspanungsgröße	machining variable
Zerspanvolumen	removal rate
zerstören	to destroy
Zerstörung	damage
zertifizieren	to certify
Ziehen	pulling
ziehen	to pull
Ziehverhältnis	drawing ratio
Ziffernschrittwert	numerical interval
Zinkbeschichtung	zinc coating
Zinn	tin
zufällig	random
zufällige Einflüsse	random influences
zufälliger Messfehler	random error
zufallsbedingt	randomly
Zufallsstichprobe	random sample
Zufriedenheit	satisfaction
zuführen	to feed (fed, fed)
zuführen	to lead back (led, led)
Zug	tension
Zug-Druck-Umformen	push-pull reforming
Zugfestigkeit	tensile strength
Zugkraft	traction
Zugspannung	tensile stress
Zugversuch	tensile test
zulässig	admissible
zum Teil	partly
zuordnen	to match, to arrange, to attach
zurückdrehen	to turn back
zurücksetzen	to reset
Zusammenbau	assembly
zusammenbauen	to mount
zusammenfassen	to summarise
zusammenfügend	additive
zusammenbauen	to reassemble
zusammengehörend	matching
zusammengesetzt	composed
Zusammenhalt	coherence
Zusammenhang	relationship, interdependence
zusammenhängen	to relate to
Zusammensetzung	composition
zusammenstellen	to assemble
Zusammenwirken	interaction
Zusatz	addition, additive
zusätzlich	additional, further, more
Zusatzstoff	filler metal
Zustand	condition, state
Zustelltiefe	cutting depth
Zustellung	infeed, depth
zuverlässig	reliable
Zuverlässigkeit	reliability
Zweck	purpose
zweireihig	double row
zweispurig	two-track
zweiteilig	two-piece
Zylinder	cylinder
Zylinderboden	cylinder bottom
Zylinderflansch	cylinder flange
Zylinderkopf	cylinder head
Zylinderrolle	cylinderical roller
Zylinderrollenlager	cylindrical roller bearing
Zylinderschraube	socket head screw, cheese head screw
Zylinderstift	parallel pin
zylindrisch	cylindrical
zylindrischer Kopf	cylindrical head
Zyklus	cycle, run